HMH | into Math™

Grade 6

Dear Students and Families,

Welcome to *Into Math,* Grade 6! In this program, you will develop skills and make sense of mathematics by solving real-world problems, using hands-on tools and strategies, and collaborating with your classmates.

With the support of your teacher and by engaging with meaningful practice you will learn to persevere when solving problems. *Into Math* will not only help you deepen your understanding of mathematics, but also build your confidence as a learner of mathematics.

Even more exciting, you will write all your ideas and solutions right in your book. In your *Into Math* book, writing and drawing on the pages will help you think deeply about what you are learning, help you truly understand math, and most important, you will become a confident user of mathematics!

Sincerely,
The Authors

Authors

Edward B. Burger, PhD
President, Southwestern University
Georgetown, Texas

Matthew R. Larson, PhD
Past-President, National Council
of Teachers of Mathematics
Lincoln Public Schools
Lincoln, Nebraska

Juli K. Dixon, PhD
Professor, Mathematics Education
University of Central Florida
Orlando, Florida

Steven J. Leinwand
Principal Research Analyst
American Institutes for Research
Washington, DC

Timothy D. Kanold, PhD
Mathematics Educator
Chicago, Illinois

Consultants

English Language Development Consultant

Harold Asturias
Director, Center for Mathematics
Excellence and Equity
Lawrence Hall of Science, University of California
Berkeley, California

Program Consultant

David Dockterman, EdD
Lecturer, Harvard Graduate School of Education
Cambridge, Massachusetts

Blended Learning Consultant

Weston Kiercshneck
Senior Fellow
International Center for Leadership in Education
Littleton, Colorado

STEM Consultants

Michael A. DiSpezio
Global Educator
North Falmouth, Massachusetts

Marjorie Frank
Science Writer and
Content-Area Reading Specialist
Brooklyn, New York

Bernadine Okoro
Access and Equity and
STEM Learning Advocate and Consultant
Washington, DC

Cary I. Sneider, PhD
Associate Research Professor
Portland State University
Portland, Oregon

© Houghton Mifflin Harcourt Publishing Company

Unit 1

Number Systems and Operations

Build Conceptual Understanding   Connect Concepts and Skills   Apply and Practice

© Houghton Mifflin Harcourt Publishing Company • Image Credit: ©Brownstock Inc./Alamy

Unit 2 Ratio and Rate Reasoning

MODULE 5 Ratios and Rates

© Houghton Mifflin Harcourt Publishing Company • **Image Credits:** (t) ©A²ïc/age fotostock; (b) ©kali9/E+/Getty Images

Build Conceptual Understanding   Connect Concepts and Skills   Apply and Practice

© Houghton Mifflin Harcourt Publishing Company • **Image Credit:** ©Eric Isselee/Shutterstock

Unit 3
Expressions, Equations, and Inequalities

MODULE 8 Numerical and Algebraic Expressions

○ Build Conceptual Understanding   ○ Connect Concepts and Skills   ○ Apply and Practice

© Houghton Mifflin Harcourt Publishing Company

Unit 4
Relationships in Geometry

© Houghton Mifflin Harcourt Publishing Company • Image Credit: Max Earey/Alamy

Build Conceptual Understanding   Connect Concepts and Skills   Apply and Practice

Unit 5 Data Collection and Analysis

Build Conceptual Understanding   Connect Concepts and Skills   Apply and Practice

MODULE 16 Variability and Data Distribution

Build Conceptual Understanding   Connect Concepts and Skills   Apply and Practice

My Progress on Mathematics Standards

The lessons in your *Into Math* book provide instruction for Mathematics Standards for Grade 6. You can use the following pages to reflect on your learning and record your progress through the standards.

As you learn new concepts, reflect on this learning. Consider inserting a checkmark if you understand the concepts or inserting a question mark if you have questions or need help.

	Student Edition Lessons	My Progress
Domain: RATIOS & PROPORTIONAL RELATIONSHIPS		
Cluster: Understand ratio concepts and use ratio reasoning to solve problems.		
Understand the concept of a ratio and use ratio language to describe a ratio relationship between two quantities.	5.1	
Understand the concept of a unit rate $\frac{a}{b}$ associated with a ratio $a:b$ with $b \neq 0$, and use rate language in the context of a ratio relationship.	5.2, 5.4	
Use ratio and rate reasoning to solve real-world and mathematical problems, e.g., by reasoning about tables of equivalent ratios, tape diagrams, double number line diagrams, or equations.	5.5, 6.1 *See also below.*	
• Make tables of equivalent ratios relating quantities with whole-number measurements, find missing values in the tables, and plot the pairs of values on the coordinate plane. Use tables to compare ratios.	5.2, 5.3	
• Solve unit rate problems including those involving unit pricing and constant speed.	5.4, 5.5	
• Find a percent of a quantity as a rate per 100 (e.g., 30% of a quantity means $\frac{30}{100}$ times the quantity); solve problems involving finding the whole, given a part and the percent.	7.1, 7.2, 7.3	
• Use ratio reasoning to convert measurement units; manipulate and transform units appropriately when multiplying or dividing quantities.	6.2, 6.3	

Domain: THE NUMBER SYSTEM		
Cluster: Apply and extend previous understandings of multiplication and division to divide fractions by fractions.		
Interpret and compute quotients of fractions, and solve word problems involving division of fractions by fractions, e.g., by using visual fraction models and equations to represent the problem.	3.1, 3.2, 3.3, 3.4, 3.5	
Cluster: Compute fluently with multi-digit numbers and find common factors and multiples.		
Fluently divide multi-digit numbers using the standard algorithm.	4.3	
Fluently add, subtract, multiply, and divide multi-digit decimals using the standard algorithm for each operation.	4.1, 4.2, 4.4, 4.5	
Find the greatest common factor of two whole numbers less than or equal to 100 and the least common multiple of two whole numbers less than or equal to 12. Use the distributive property to express a sum of two whole numbers 1–100 with a common factor as a multiple of a sum of two whole numbers with no common factor.	2.3, 2.4, 3.5	
Cluster: Apply and extend previous understandings of numbers to the system of rational numbers.		
Understand that positive and negative numbers are used together to describe quantities having opposite directions or values (e.g., temperature above/below zero, elevation above/below sea level, credits/debits, positive/negative electric charge); use positive and negative numbers to represent quantities in real-world contexts, explaining the meaning of 0 in each situation.	1.1	
Understand a rational number as a point on the number line. Extend number line diagrams and coordinate axes familiar from previous grades to represent points on the line and in the plane with negative number coordinates.	2.1 *See also below.*	
• Recognize opposite signs of numbers as indicating locations on opposite sides of 0 on the number line; recognize that the opposite of the opposite of a number is the number itself, e.g., $-(-3) = 3$, and that 0 is its own opposite.	1.1	
• Understand signs of numbers in ordered pairs as indicating locations in quadrants of the coordinate plane; recognize that when two ordered pairs differ only by signs, the locations of the points are related by reflections across one or both axes.	11.1, 11.3	

• Find and position integers and other rational numbers on a horiz ontal or vertical number line diagram; find and position pairs of integers and other rational numbers on a coordinate plane.	2.1, 2.2, 11.1, 11.2, 11.3	
Understand ordering and absolute value of rational numbers.	*See below.*	
• Interpret statements of inequality as statements about the relative position of two numbers on a number line diagram.	2.2	
• Write, interpret, and explain statements of order for rational numbers in real-world contexts.	1.2, 2.3, 2.4	
• Understand the absolute value of a rational number as its distance from 0 on the number line; interpret absolute value as magnitude for a positive or negative quantity in a real-world situation.	1.3, 2.1	
• Distinguish comparisons of absolute value from statements about order.	1.3, 2.1	
Solve real-world and mathematical problems by graphing points in all four quadrants of the coordinate plane. Include use of coordinates and absolute value to find distances between points with the same first coordinate or the same second coordinate.	11.3, 11.4	

Domain: EXPRESSIONS & EQUATIONS

Cluster: Apply and extend previous understandings of arithmetic to algebraic expressions.

Write and evaluate numerical expressions involving whole-number exponents.	8.1, 8.2	
Write, read, and evaluate expressions in which letters stand for numbers.	*See below.*	
• Write expressions that record operations with numbers and with letters standing for numbers.	8.3	
• Identify parts of an expression using mathematical terms (sum, term, product, factor, quotient, coefficient); view one or more parts of an expression as a single entity.	8.2, 8.3	
• Evaluate expressions at specific values of their variables. Include expressions that arise from formulas used in real-world problems. Perform arithmetic operations, including those involving whole-number exponents, in the conventional order when there are no parentheses to specify a particular order (Order of Operations).	8.4, 12.1, 12.2, 12.3, 13.2, 13.3	

© Houghton Mifflin Harcourt Publishing Company

Interactive Standards

Apply the properties of operations to generate equivalent expressions.	8.5	
Identify when two expressions are equivalent (i.e., when the two expressions name the same number regardless of which value is substituted into them).	8.5	
Cluster: Reason about and solve one-variable equations and inequalities.		
Understand solving an equation or inequality as *a* process of answering a question: which values from a specified set, if any, make the equation or inequality true? Use substitution to determine whether a given number in a specified set makes an equation or inequality true.	9.1, 9.5	
Use variables to represent numbers and write expressions when solving a real-world or mathematical problem; understand that a variable can represent an unknown number, or, depending on the purpose at hand, any number in a specified set.	8.3	
Solve real-world and mathematical problems by writing and solving equations of the form $x + p = q$ and $px = q$ for cases in which p, q and x are all non-negative rational numbers.	9.1, 9.2, 9.3, 9.4	
Write an inequality of the form $x > c$ or $x < c$ to represent a constraint or condition in a real-world or mathematical problem. Recognize that inequalities of the form $x > c$ or $x < c$ have infinitely many solutions; represent solutions of such inequalities on number line diagrams.	9.5	
Cluster: Represent and analyze quantitative relationships between dependent and independent variables.		
Use variables to represent two quantities in a real-world problem that change in relationship to one another; write an equation to express one quantity, thought of as the dependent variable, in terms of the other quantity, thought of as the independent variable. Analyze the relationship between the dependent and independent variables using graphs and tables, and relate these to the equation.	10.1, 10.2, 10.3	
Domain: GEOMETRY		
Cluster: Solve real-world and mathematical problems involving area, surface area, and volume.		
Find the area of right triangles, other triangles, special quadrilaterals, and polygons by composing into rectangles or decomposing into triangles and other shapes; apply these techniques in the context of solving real-world and mathematical problems.	12.1, 12.2, 12.3, 12.4	

Find the volume of a right rectangular prism with fractional edge lengths by packing it with unit cubes of the appropriate unit fraction edge lengths, and show that the volume is the same as would be found by multiplying the edge lengths of the prism. Apply the formulas $V = lwh$ and $V = bh$ to find volumes of right rectangular prisms with fractional edge lengths in the context of solving real-world and mathematical problems.	13.2, 13.3	
Draw polygons in the coordinate plane given coordinates for the vertices; use coordinates to find the length of a side joining points with the same first coordinate or the same second coordinate. Apply these techniques in the context of solving real-world and mathematical problems.	11.2, 11.4	
Represent three-dimensional figures using nets made up of rectangles and triangles, and use the nets to find the surface area of these figures. Apply these techniques in the context of solving real-world and mathematical problems.	13.1	

Domain: STATISTICS & PROBABILITY

Cluster: Develop understanding of statistical variability.

Recognize a statistical question as one that anticipates variability in the data related to the question and accounts for it in the answers.	14.1	
Understand that a set of data collected to answer a statistical question has a distribution which can be described by its center, spread, and overall shape.	16.5	
Recognize that a measure of center for a numerical data set summarizes all of its values with a single number, while a measure of variation describes how its values vary with a single number.	15.1, 15.2, 16.4	

Cluster: Summarize and describe distributions.

Display numerical data in plots on a number line, including dot plots, histograms, and box plots.	14.2, 14.3, 16.2	
Summarize numerical data sets in relation to their context, such as by:	*See below.*	
• Reporting the number of observations.	14.1, 15.2	
• Describing the nature of the attribute under investigation, including how it was measured and its units of measurement.	14.1	

• Giving quantitative measures of center (median and/or mean) and variability (interquartile range and/or mean absolute deviation), as well as describing any overall pattern and any striking deviations from the overall pattern with reference to the context in which the data were gathered.	16.1, 16.3, 16.4, 16.5	
• Relating the choice of measures of center and variability to the shape of the data distribution and the context in which the data were gathered.	15.3, 16.4, 16.5	

Event Organizer

STEM
POWERING INGENUITY

Have you ever been to a wedding or other formal party? If so, there is a good chance that an event organizer helped make it happen. Event organizers plan all the details of big events like parties, banquets, concerts, conventions, and fundraisers. Event organizers face math problems every day, from calculating how to seat hundreds of guests to using geometry and measurement to plan decorations.

STEM Task:

Combinatorics is a branch of math focused on arrangements of objects. Jorge is an event organizer who must seat 102 guests. He has circular tables that seat 10 people each and square tables that seat 4 people each. He wants to use as many circular tables as possible but have no empty seats. Explain how he could arrange the tables he will need.

Learning is a process by which you constantly build new skills and knowledge through experience and study. Anything that you have already learned can help you learn new things now, and what you learn now will help you learn more in the future. When you first encounter a new topic, reflect upon past work and apply what you learned to new learning tasks.

- What knowledge do you already have that can help you understand the new topic?

- What strategies have you used to learn new topics in the past, and which ones might work now?

Reflect

Q What real-world knowledge did you use to understand the STEM Task?

Q What strategies or methods from your previous learning did you use to complete the STEM Task?

© Houghton Mifflin Harcourt Publishing Company • Image Credit: ©Steve Debenport/E+/Getty Images

Identify and Interpret Integers

(I Can) graph positive and negative integers and find their
opposites.

Spark Your Learning

Fergal is recording the number of yards his school's football team
gained or lost on successive plays. How can you model or represent
the opposite of each loss or gain shown in the table?

Quantity	Opposite
gain of 2 yards	
loss of 4 yards	
loss of 8 yards	
gain of 13 yards	
loss of 2 yards	

 Turn and Talk Write several pairs of your own opposite quantities. Explain
how you know they are opposites.

Build Understanding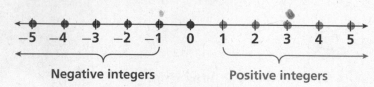

Positive numbers can be written with or without a positive sign (+), but they are usually written without it. *Negative numbers* are always written with a negative sign (−).

Connect to Vocabulary

A **positive number** is a number greater than zero.

A **negative number** is a number less than zero.

Negative integers · Positive integers

1 ▶ The results of three football plays are shown in the table.

Result	Net Yards
4 yard gain	4
1 yard loss	−1
4 yard loss	−4

A. What does 0 represent in this situation?

1 yard loss

B. What do negative numbers represent in this situation?

C. What do positive numbers represent in this situation?

D. Complete the number line. Then graph each result from the table on the number line.

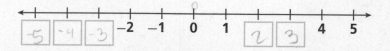

-5 -4 -3 −2 −1 0 1 2 3 4 5

 Turn and Talk How can you describe a pattern in the positive numbers as you move left to right on a number line? Does the same pattern apply for the negative numbers as well? Explain.

Name _____

2 ▸ Complete the number line. Then graph the number −2.

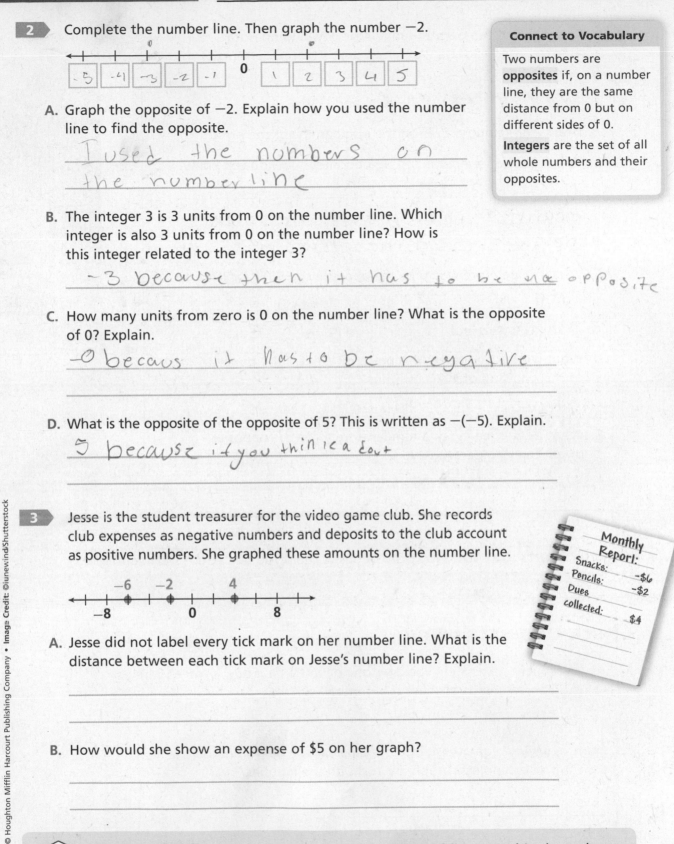

A. Graph the opposite of −2. Explain how you used the number line to find the opposite.

I used the numbers on the number line

B. The integer 3 is 3 units from 0 on the number line. Which integer is also 3 units from 0 on the number line? How is this integer related to the integer 3?

−3 because then it has to be the opposite

C. How many units from zero is 0 on the number line? What is the opposite of 0? Explain.

−0 becaus it has to be negative

D. What is the opposite of the opposite of 5? This is written as −(−5). Explain.

5 because if you think about

3 ▸ Jesse is the student treasurer for the video game club. She records club expenses as negative numbers and deposits to the club account as positive numbers. She graphed these amounts on the number line.

Monthly Report:
Snacks: −$6
Pencils: −$2
Dues collected: $4

A. Jesse did not label every tick mark on her number line. What is the distance between each tick mark on Jesse's number line? Explain.

_____

_____

B. How would she show an expense of $5 on her graph?

_____

_____

Turn and Talk Jesse's number line has 0 in the middle. Does this always have to be the case? Explain.

© Houghton Mifflin Harcourt Publishing Company • Image Credit: ©iunewind/Shutterstock

Module 1 • Lesson 1

4 The morning temperature in a large city in Minnesota was recorded each day for seven days. The temperatures recorded were:

−7 °F, 4 °F, 0 °F, 2 °F, −4 °F, 7 °F, and −10 °F

A. Graph the temperatures on the number line at the right.

B. Which pairs of temperatures are opposites? How do you know?

negtive 2   negtive 3
negtive 2 is on the oppostie side
negtive 3 is on the otherside

C. What temperature would be the opposite of −7 °F? Explain.

7°F ⅅ90°   7°F is a opposite of
othernomdors 90° is a anglen

D. What would a point at 10 represent? What is the opposite of the opposite of 10?

it could be " the opposite of
opposite" better is the other way)

E. What does it mean for a temperature to be the opposite of another temperature?

ⅅ 90° is haft a angle

Number line at right marked from 10 down to −10, with 5, 0, −5 labeled. A "4" is marked near the 4 position.

Turn and Talk How can opposites help you talk about real-world values?

Check Understanding

1. An investment gains $5 in value on one day. The next day, it loses $3 in value. Represent each of these using integers.

_____

2. Iman is playing a game. On one turn she earns 2 points and on the next turn she loses 5 points. Graph her turns on the number line.

<-------|---|---|---|---|---|---|---|---|---|---|---|---->
        −6   0   6

Find the opposite of the integer.

3. 4   4. −8   5. −25   6. 121

_____   _____   _____   _____

On Your Own

For Problems 7–9, use the following information.

(MP) **Use Structure** Every week, Tiana runs 3 miles and records how long it takes to complete the run. She also records the change in time from the previous week.

7. Last week, her time spent running decreased by 2 minutes. What integer could represent this change? _~~take~~ -2_

8. This week, her time spent running increased by 1 minute. What integer could represent this change? _~~8~~ 1_

9. In words, what is the opposite of "increased by 1 minute"? What integer represents this opposite?

   ~~the is the opposite of ~~ decreased by
   _-1 L_

For Problems 10–11, use the following information.

The transactions on a bank account are listed as −$15, $10, −$4, and $15.

10. What does a transaction of −$4 represent?

   (−1) _~~these the opposite changes~~_

11. Which pairs of transactions are opposites? Explain.

   For example 90° & 40° and ⊕ 7°F
   is the opposites 90° is the opposites of 7°F

12. The number line shown includes 5 graphed integers. Fill in the labels for the integers. Which graphed integers are opposites?

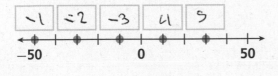

| ~1 | ~2 | −3 | 4 | 5 |

   −50   0   50

   _____

13. (MP) **Reason** Two integers are opposites of each other. One integer is 3 units to the right of 1 on a number line. What are the two integers?

   _____

14. Rona starts at the base of a hill that has an elevation of 25 feet below sea level. Then Rona climbs to the top of the hill which has an elevation of 25 feet above sea level. Represent these elevations as integers. How are they related?

   _____

On Your Own

15. (MP) **Use Structure** The low temperatures on three days are shown at the right. What are the opposites of the three temperatures? Graph the temperatures and their opposites on the number line.

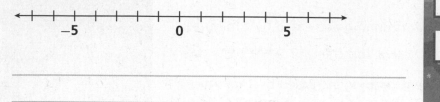

Monday: −2 °F

Tuesday: 4 °F

Wednesday: −7 °F

_____

_____

16. (MP) **Reason** Explain how to use a number line to find the opposites of the integers that are 4 units away from −6.

_____

_____

_____

_____

17. Atoms are made of tiny particles called protons, neutrons, and electrons. Protons and neutrons are in the center of the atom, making up the nucleus. The electrical charges on the proton and electron are exactly the same size but opposite. If a proton has a positive charge of 1, what is the charge of the corresponding electron? _____

For Problems 18–20, write the opposite of the integer.

18. −6   **19.** −2   **20.** 17

_____   _____   _____

21. Graph the integers on a number line: −2, 4, −5, 10.

− ×
+ ÷   **I'm in a Learning Mindset!**

What can I apply from previous work to better understand how to find opposites of negative numbers?

_____

_____

Name _____

Compare and Order Integers on a Number Line

(I Can) order integers from least to greatest and use inequalities to compare integers.

Spark Your Learning

PAIRS

The thermometer shows temperatures that are above zero and temperatures that are below zero. Find a temperature to complete each statement. Then describe a thermometer to someone who may not have seen one.

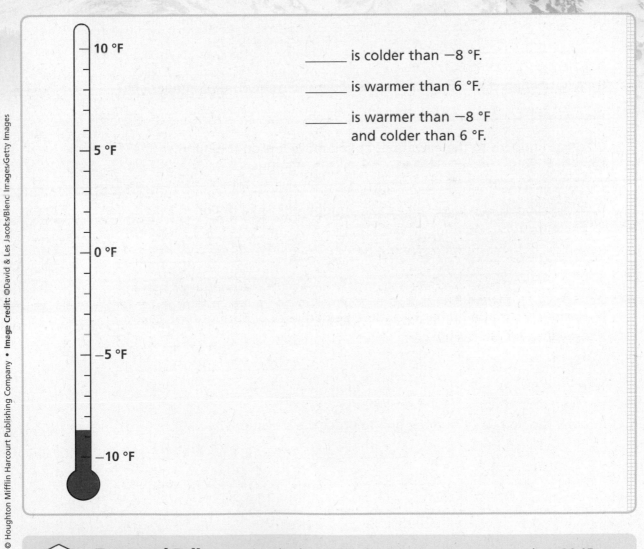

_____ is colder than −8 °F.

_____ is warmer than 6 °F.

_____ is warmer than −8 °F
and colder than 6 °F.

Turn and Talk Describe the location of a temperature warmer than 20 °F on a thermometer. Can you extend the drawing of the thermometer to show warmer and colder temperatures? Describe how.

© Houghton Mifflin Harcourt Publishing Company • Image Credit: ©David & Les Jacobs/Blend Images/Getty Images

Build Understanding

1 The table below shows the elevations above or below sea level of several lakes. Sea level is considered to be an elevation of zero feet.

Lakes	Elevation (feet)
Beldon Lake	−18.5
Forest Lake	90
Springbrook Lake	−75.2
Western Lake	44.5
Pleasant Lake	4.5

A. How could you use a horizontal number line to compare the elevations?

_____

_____

B. What happens to the elevations as you move right on the number line?

_____

C. What happens to the elevations as you move left on the number line?

_____

D. Which lake is at a lower elevation, Springbrook Lake or Forest Lake? Explain your reasoning.

_____

_____

E. Which lake is at a higher elevation, Beldon Lake or Springbrook Lake? Explain your reasoning.

_____

_____

F. How can you use a number line to order the elevations?

_____

_____

_____

 Turn and Talk Describe another situation that uses elevations to describe locations. Give an example.

2 ▶ Deshaun, Chris, Tonya, and Austin play a game. Each turn, a player can lose a point or win a point. At the end of the game the scores are as shown.

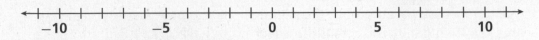

	Final Score
Deshaun:	2
Chris:	−4
Tonya:	−5
Austin:	3

A. Graph the scores on the number line.

```
←+—+—+—+—+—+—+—+—+—+—+—+—+—+—+—+—+—+—+—+—+→
   −10        −5         0          5         10
```

B. Is Deshaun's or Tonya's score greater? Explain how you know.

_____

_____

_____

C. Is Chris's score greater than Tonya's? Explain how you used the number line to compare the numbers.

_____

_____

_____

D. From left to right, do the values on the number line increase or decrease? Explain.

_____

_____

_____

E. Use the number line to write the scores from least to greatest. How did you find the correct order?

_____

_____

_____

_____

The mathematical sentences −3 < 5 and 2 > −4 are examples of *inequalities*.

The symbol "<" is read "is less than." So, −3 < 5 means "−3 is less than 5."

The symbol ">" is read "is greater than." So, 2 > −4 means "2 is greater than −4."

3 In golf, scores are based on par. If someone scores less than par, their score is recorded as a negative integer. If someone scores more than par, their score is recorded as a positive integer. After two holes, Jaylen's score was −3, Kyro's score was 1, and Keyana's score was 3.

A. Use a number line to order the scores. Write the scores in order from least to greatest. Explain your reasoning.

_____

_____

B. What two inequalities could you write to compare Jaylen's and Kyro's scores? If a lower score is better, explain who did better, Jaylen or Kyro.

_____

_____

C. Two new golfers, Jon and Tiana, are in a competition. Tiana scores a −3 and Jon scores a −1. Write an inequality to compare their scores. Since in golf the lowest score wins, who won the match? Explain.

_____

_____

Check Understanding

Two research submarines are exploring a coral reef. Submarine 1 is at an elevation of −58 feet. Submarine 2 is at an elevation of −65 feet. Which elevation is farther from sea level? Explain.

_____

_____

Write an inequality to compare −24 and −14.

_____

On Your Own

3. The temperatures on four mornings are −8 °F, −2 °F, −11 °F, and 0 °F.

   A. Graph the temperatures on the number line.

   B. What was the temperature on the coldest morning?

   _____

   C. What was the temperature on the warmest morning?

   _____

   D. Use the number line to write the temperatures from least to greatest.

   _____

4. **(MP) Reason** Bank accounts can have a positive or negative balance. When a person takes out more money than is in the account, the account's balance will be negative. A bank account's balance is −$26. Graph −26 on the number line. If a second bank account has a balance that is less than −$26, identify a possible second balance. Write an inequality to compare the balances.

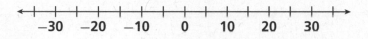

_____

5. The depth of a deep-sea diver can be represented by a negative integer. If the diver is 5 feet below the surface of the water, then the diver's elevation is −5 feet.

   A. One diver's elevation is −30 feet and another's is −25 feet. Which number is less? Graph the elevations on the number line to answer the question.

   _____

   B. Write an inequality to compare the two elevations. Use the number line to answer the question.

   _____

   C. What does 0 feet mean?

   _____

For Problems 6–8, graph the numbers on the number line. Then write an inequality to compare the numbers.

6. −14 and −6

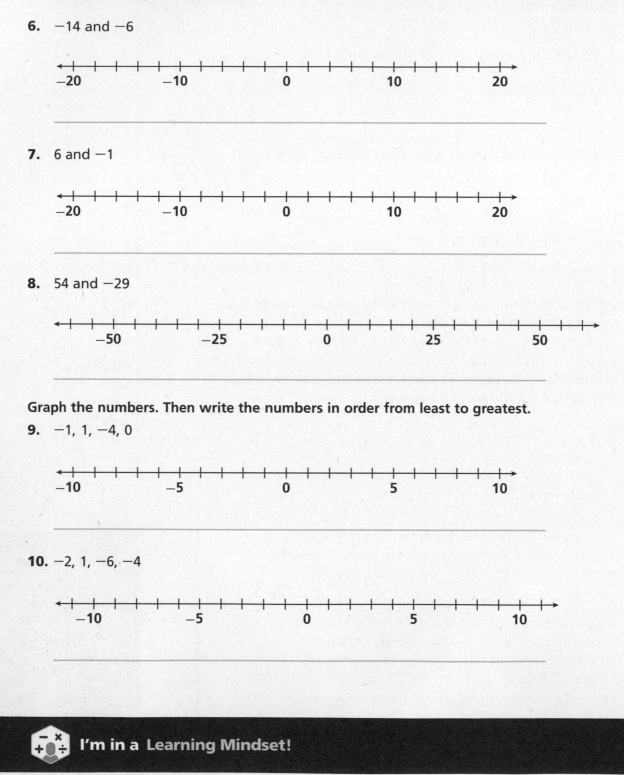

7. 6 and −1

8. 54 and −29

Graph the numbers. Then write the numbers in order from least to greatest.

9. −1, 1, −4, 0

10. −2, 1, −6, −4

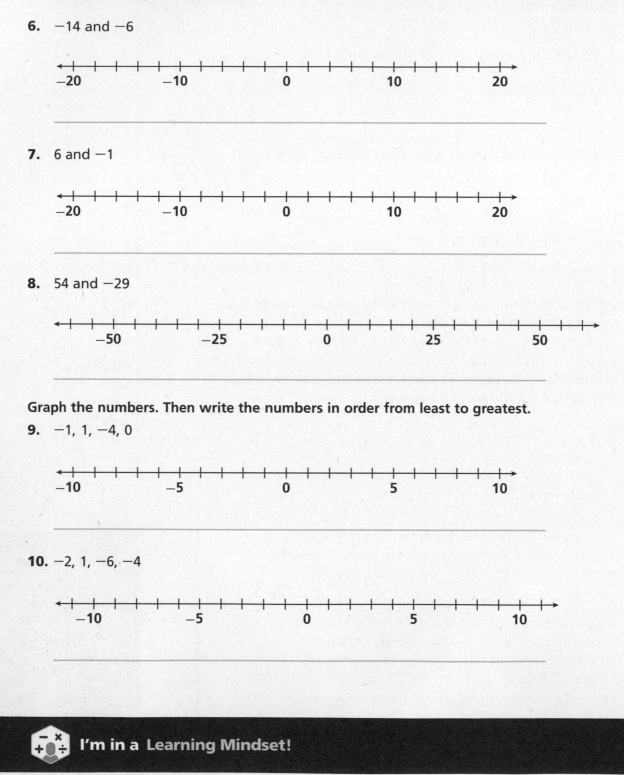

![I'm in a] **I'm in a Learning Mindset!**

What did I learn from Task 2 that I can use in my future learning?

LESSON 1.2
**More Practice/
Homework**

ONLINE

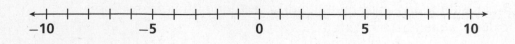

Video Tutorials and
Interactive Examples

Compare and Order Integers on a Number Line

1. Tracy and Maria each choose a card from a deck of cards with positive and negative numbers. Tracy picked −12 and Maria picked −6. Who picked the greater number?

   _____

2. **STEM** The average temperature on the planet Neptune is −214 °C. The temperature on the south pole of Neptune is thought to be 10 °C. Is this colder or warmer than the average temperature? Write an inequality to support your answer.

   _____

   _____

3. An office building uses positive numbers and negative numbers for floors as shown. Nathan is going to floor 1, and Eva is going to floor −1. Who is going to the higher floor?

   _____

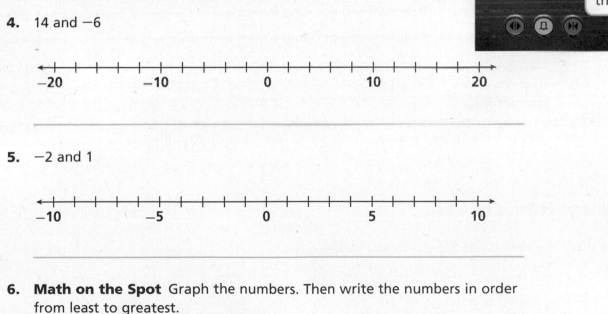

Negative numbers represent floors below the lobby

For Problems 4–5, graph the numbers on the number line. Then write an inequality to compare the numbers.

4. 14 and −6

```
<----+--+--+--+--+--+--+--+--+--+--+--+--+--+--+--+--+--+--+--+--+---->
   -20          -10           0          10          20
```

   _____

5. −2 and 1

```
<----+--+--+--+--+--+--+--+--+--+--+--+--+--+--+--+--+--+--+--+--+---->
   -10          -5           0           5          10
```

   _____

6. **Math on the Spot** Graph the numbers. Then write the numbers in order from least to greatest.

   5, −3, 2

```
<----+--+--+--+--+--+--+--+--+--+--+--+--+--+--+--+--+--+--+--+--+---->
   -10          -5           0           5          10
```

   _____

Test Prep

7. Tanner, Caleb, Lamar, and Tammy play a game of disc golf, which is similar to golf and played with a flying disc. They record their scores relative to par. Their total scores, after two holes, are shown in the table.

Tanner	−1
Caleb	2
Lamar	−2
Tammy	1

Which choice shows the scores in order from least to greatest?

Ⓐ −1, 2, −2, 1   Ⓒ 2, 1, −1, −2

Ⓑ −1, −2, 1, 2   Ⓓ −2, −1, 1, 2

8. The temperature in the morning was −2 °F. In the afternoon, a cold front passed and the temperature was −6 °F. Which statements are true? Choose all that apply.

Ⓐ It was colder in the morning than in the afternoon.

Ⓑ It was colder in the afternoon than in the morning.

Ⓒ It was warmer in the morning than in the afternoon.

Ⓓ It was warmer in the afternoon than in the morning.

Ⓔ The temperature in the morning was greater than the temperature in the afternoon.

Ⓕ The temperature in the afternoon was greater than the temperature in the morning.

9. Choose the correct symbol from $<$, $>$, and $=$ to compare the numbers.

−6 ＿＿＿＿＿ −8

Spiral Review

10. What number is ten times as great as 450?

＿＿＿＿＿＿＿＿＿＿＿＿＿＿＿＿＿＿＿＿＿＿＿＿＿

11. Cynthia gave $\frac{1}{5}$ of her toys to her little sister. If she originally had 25 toys, how many did she give away?

＿＿＿＿＿＿＿＿＿＿＿＿＿＿＿＿＿＿＿＿＿＿＿＿＿

12. Laquan has 2 pieces of fabric, each measuring $3\frac{1}{4}$ feet long. How many feet of fabric does Laquan have in total?

＿＿＿＿＿＿＿＿＿＿＿＿＿＿＿＿＿＿＿＿＿＿＿＿＿

© Houghton Mifflin Harcourt Publishing Company

Name

Find and Apply Absolute Value

I Can find and use absolute value and magnitude to describe real-world situations.

Spark Your Learning PAIRS

The table shows the low temperatures in Nome, Alaska, for five days in December. Find the distance from zero to each number.

Date	Dec. 18	Dec. 19	Dec. 20	Dec. 21	Dec. 22
Low temperature	−10 °F	−15 °F	−16 °F	8 °F	3 °F

Turn and Talk Name a real-world situation where finding the distance between two points can be useful.

Build Understanding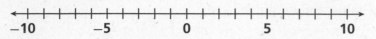

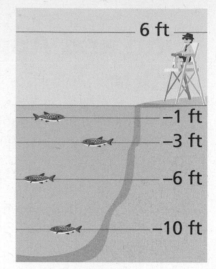

6 ft

−1 ft

−3 ft

−6 ft

−10 ft

1 The elevations of four fish in a lake are shown. The elevation of the top of a lifeguard stand is 6 feet. Graph the integers on the number line.

$$\overset{\displaystyle\longleftrightarrow}{\underset{\begin{matrix}-10 \quad\quad -5 \quad\quad 0 \quad\quad 5 \quad\quad 10\end{matrix}}{}}$$

A. What is the distance from zero to each elevation on the number line?

_____

_____

_____

_____

B. The distance from a number to zero on the number line is called the *absolute value* of the number. Complete each of the following sentences using the number line above.

The absolute value of −1 is _____.

The absolute value of 6 is _____.

The absolute value of −3 is _____.

The absolute value of −10 is _____.

The absolute value of −6 is _____.

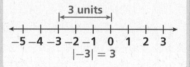
C. The absolute value of a number is written using the symbols | |. For example, the absolute value of −8 is written |−8|. Find the absolute values using the values from Part B.

|−1| = ☐ |6| = ☐ |−3| = ☐ |−10| = ☐ |−6| = ☐

D. Negative numbers are less than positive numbers. Does this mean that the absolute value of a negative number must be less than the absolute value of a positive number? Explain.

_____

_____

_____

 Turn and Talk Can the absolute value of a number ever be negative? Explain.

Step It Out

The *magnitude* of a number is its size or amount, without considering its sign. The magnitude of a number is the same as its absolute value.

2 ▶ Some insects produce a chemical that prevents the water in their bodies from freezing and helps them survive extreme cold. An insect's supercooling point is the lowest temperature at which it can survive. The table shows the supercooling points of several insects.

Insect	Supercooling Point (°C)
Pythid beetle	−54
Common banded hoverfly	−35
New Zealand alpine weta	−9
Pink rice borer	−6.8
Woolly bear caterpillar	−70

Woolly bear caterpillar

A. Graph the supercooling points on the number line.

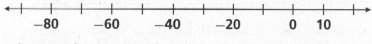

B. What are the magnitudes of −70, −54, and −35?

_____

_____

C. Complete these number sentences, which use absolute-value symbols to show the magnitude of each number from Part B.

$|-70| = \boxed{}$ $|-54| = \boxed{}$ $|-35| = \boxed{}$

D. Write an inequality to show the relationship between −70 and −35.

_____

E. Which supercooling point is closest to 0 on the number line? Explain.

_____

_____

F. Which insect has the lowest supercooling point?

_____

Check Understanding

1. A withdrawal, or money removed from a bank account, is listed on a bank statement as a negative number. Which represents a greater withdrawal, −$45 or −$50? _____

2. What does the absolute value of −2 represent?

_____

On Your Own

3. (MP) **Reason** A model for the distance traveled from a cabin in a state park represents distances south of the cabin as negative numbers and distances north of the cabin as positive numbers. The number line shows the locations of two hikers.

   A. Who walked farther from the cabin? Explain.

   _____

   B. How many miles is Maurice from the cabin?

   _____

4. **Geography** The equator is an imaginary circle around Earth halfway between the North Pole and the South Pole. Lines of latitude are imaginary circles around Earth parallel to the equator, used to determine position north and south of the equator. The equator is the line of 0° latitude.

   A. What latitude is opposite of 30° north latitude?

   _____

   B. How do these latitudes compare?

   _____

   _____

5. The average low surface temperature for Mars is −80 °F. The average low surface temperature for Jupiter is −234 °F. Which temperature has the greater absolute value? Explain.

   _____

   _____

For Problems 6–9, find the absolute value.

6. $|9|$ 7. $|-1|$ 8. $|-56|$ 9. $|0|$

   _____   _____   _____   _____

I'm in a Learning Mindset!

What strategies do I use to stay on task when working on my own?

_____

_____

Rational Number Concepts

Which Fraction Does **Not** Belong?

Pizza slices are left over from a party. Each whole pizza was the same size, but was cut into a different number of equal slices.

For each pizza, write a fraction that represents the part of the pizza that is left over.

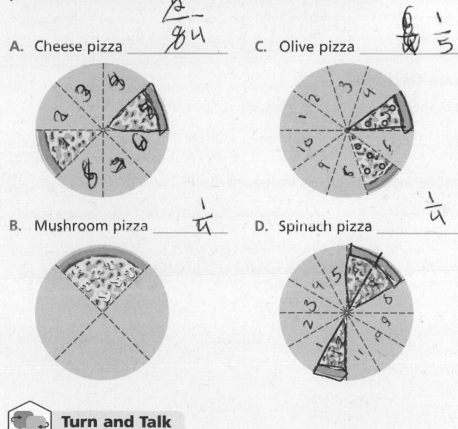

A. Cheese pizza ___ $\frac{2}{84}$ ___

C. Olive pizza ___ $\frac{6}{5}$ ___

B. Mushroom pizza ___ $\frac{1}{4}$ ___

D. Spinach pizza ___ $\frac{1}{4}$ ___

Turn and Talk

- Which fraction does not belong? Explain why.

- Which type of pizza has the least amount left over? Tell how you know.

- Can you make a whole pizza with the leftover pieces? Explain.

Stephanie H

 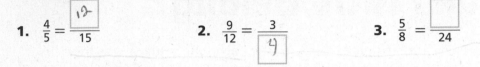

Are You Ready?

Complete these problems to review prior concepts and skills you will need for this module.

Multiply or Divide to Find Equivalent Fractions

Multiply or divide to find the equivalent fraction.

1. $\frac{4}{5} = \frac{12}{15}$

2. $\frac{9}{12} = \frac{3}{4}$

3. $\frac{5}{8} = \frac{\square}{24}$

Compare Fractions

Complete the statement using the symbol $<$, $>$, or $=$.

4. $\frac{7}{8}$ ___ $\frac{9}{8}$

5. $\frac{5}{8}$ ___ $\frac{5}{9}$

6. $\frac{3}{4}$ ___ $\frac{5}{6}$

Compare Decimals

Complete the statement using the symbol $<$, $>$, or $=$.

7. 0.51 ___ 0.46

8. 1.073 ___ 1.703

9. 3.60 ___ 3.6

Opposites and Absolute Value

10. Use the number line to complete the table. The first row is completed as shown.

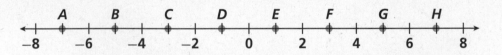

Point	Opposite	Absolute Value
A	H	7
C		
D		
G		

Name _____

Interpret Rational Numbers

(I Can) find and use absolute values and the opposite of a number to solve real-world problems.

Spark Your Learning

The magnitude of a star is a number that is a measure of its brightness as seen on Earth. The brighter the star, the lower its magnitude. The data below show the magnitudes of five stars in our galaxy. Between what two consecutive integers is the magnitude of each star located? In most applications, the magnitude of a number is its size or amount. However, when talking about the magnitude of a star, magnitude includes negative numbers.

Polaris (The North Star): 1.97

Sirius (The Dog Star): −1.45

Hadar (Beta Centauri): 0.61

Arcturus: −0.04

Canopus: −0.72

 Turn and Talk How many decimals are between the numbers 0 and −1? Explain your thinking.

Build Understanding

1 ▶ The average low temperature in Nome, Alaska, in January, is the rational number −2.8 °F.

A **rational number** is a number that can be written in the form $\frac{a}{b}$, where a and b are integers and $b \neq 0$.

Connect to Vocabulary

A. Consecutive marks on a number line increase and decrease by the same amount. What marks would you need to graph −2.8 on a number line?

_____

_____

B. Between what two consecutive integers is −2.8 located on a number line?

−2.8 is between the integers ☐ and ☐ .

C. How would you graph −2.8 on a number line?

I would plot a point ☐ tenths to the _____ of −2.

D. Complete the statement to describe the position of −2.8 compared to 0.

−2.8 is ☐ units to the _____ of 0.

E. What is the opposite of −2.8?

The opposite of −2.8 will be ☐ units to the _____ of 0.

So, the opposite of −2.8 is ☐ .

F. Graph −2.8 and its opposite on the number line.

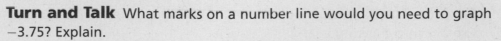

−3   −2   −1   0   1   2   3

2 ▶ The legs of a display swing set are buried in the ground as shown.

A. What marks on a number line would you need to graph $\frac{1}{2}$?

_____

B. Describe the position of $\frac{1}{2}$ on a number line.

$\frac{1}{2}$ is between the integers ☐ and ☐ .

$\frac{1}{2}$ is ☐ unit to the _____ of 0.

C. The opposite of $\frac{1}{2}$ will be ☐ unit to the _____ of 0.

So, the opposite of $\frac{1}{2}$ is ☐ .

D. Graph $\frac{1}{2}$ and its opposite on the number line.

−1   0   1

Legs are buried $\frac{1}{2}$ foot in the ground.

Turn and Talk What marks on a number line would you need to graph −3.75? Explain.

Name _____

Step It Out

In a previous lesson, you found the absolute values of integers. You can find the absolute values of rational numbers in the same way.

3 The lowest elevation at Death Valley National Park is approximately −0.05 mile.

A. What distance is this from sea level?

_____

B. Between what two consecutive integers is −0.05 located on a number line?

_____

C. Complete the number sentence.

$|-0.05| = \boxed{}$

4 Mrs. Sutter withdraws money from the bank. The withdrawal transactions are recorded on her bank statement.

A. Find the absolute value of each withdrawal amount.

$|-5.25| = $ _____ $\qquad$ $|-7.10| = $ _____

$|-3.50| = $ _____ $\qquad$ $|-4.75| = $ _____

B. Which is greater, −7.10 or −3.50? Which is a greater withdrawal, −$7.10 or −$3.50? Explain.

_____

_____

_____

_____

```
          Receipt
*************************
Withdrawal       −$5.25
Withdrawal       −$7.10
Withdrawal       −$3.50
Withdrawal       −$4.75
- - - - - - - - - - - - - - - -
Bank Card
************0000
Date/Time    21.03.2018
*********************
```

Check Understanding

1. The average weight of a newborn panda is 0.2, or $\frac{2}{10}$, pound. Between what two integers is the weight of a newborn panda?

_____

For Problems 2–4, graph each number on the number line and then find the absolute value.

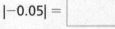

```
←|||||||||||||||||||||||||||||||||||||||||||→
 −2        −1        0        1        2
```

2. $|-0.2| = $ _____ $\qquad$ 3. $|-1.5| = $ _____ $\qquad$ 4. $|0.8| = $ _____

On Your Own

5. A bank statement shows transactions of −$10.40 and $8.50.

    A. Do these transactions represent deposits or withdrawals?

        _____

    B. How can you use absolute value to decide which transaction represented the greater change?

        _____

        _____

        _____

6. Two deep-sea divers are exploring shipwrecks in Lake Erie, one of the Great Lakes. Write the depth of the shipwreck as an integer. What is the absolute value of the depth of the shipwreck?

    _____

    _____

sea level

−200 feet

For Problems 7–9, use the number line to graph the opposite of each number. Label each point.

```
<-+++++++++++++++++++++++++++++++++++++++++++++->
  -4   -3   -2   -1   0   1   2   3   4
```

7. −3.25   **8.** 0.25   **9.** −1.5

10. (MP) **Use Structure** Graph each number and its opposite on the number line.

$-1\frac{2}{10}, -\frac{5}{10}, \frac{3}{10}, \frac{9}{10}$

```
<-+++++++++++++++++++++++++++++++++++++++++++++->
     -2        -1        0        1        2
```

For Problems 11–13, find the absolute value of each number.

11. $\left|\frac{6}{5}\right|$ _____   **12.** $\left|-5.10\right|$ _____   **13.** $\left|-2\frac{3}{4}\right|$ _____

I'm in a Learning Mindset!

How can I use marks on the number line to effectively compare rational numbers?

_____

_____

Name _____

LESSON 2.1
More Practice/ Homework

ONLINE

Video Tutorials and
Interactive Examples

Interpret Rational Numbers

1. Graph 1.7, −0.3, and 0.5 and their opposites on the number line.

```
<---+-+-+-+-+-+-+-+-+-+-+-+-+-+-+-+-+-+-+-+--->
   −2        −1        0         1         2
```

2. (MP) **Use Tools** A marine biologist collects coral species from the bottom of a coral reef. The biologist swims to depths of $3\frac{1}{4}$ meters, $2\frac{5}{8}$ meters, and $4\frac{1}{2}$ meters below sea level.

A. Represent these depths as rational numbers.

_____

B. Graph and label these depths and their opposites on the number line.

3. **STEM** Liquids freeze at different temperatures as shown in the table. Complete the table by finding the absolute value of each temperature.

Liquid	Freezing Point	Absolute Value
Water	0 °C	
Benzene	5.5 °C	
Salt Water	−1.85 °C	
Vinegar	−2.2 °C	

4. (MP) **Construct Arguments** Hector says that −3.8 °C and 3.8 °C are not the same in terms of their relationship with 0 °C. Is Hector correct? Explain.

_____

_____

5. (MP) **Reason** On Friday, the value of one stock changed by −$2.75, and the value of a second stock changed by $2.75. How can you use a number line to show that these values are opposites?

_____

_____

_____

Find the opposite and absolute value of each number.

6. $\frac{3}{10}$ _____ **7.** −4.06 _____ **8.** $-1\frac{1}{5}$ _____

9. 2.19 _____ **10.** $2\frac{1}{2}$ _____ **11.** 0.75 _____

Test Prep

12. A stock market index drops by 1.38 points. What rational number represents the change in the index?

_____

13. An ampere is a unit used to measure electric current. The electrical current is −2.5 amperes in one part of a circuit and 0.6 ampere in another part. Graph the values on the number line.

14. Amos says that the opposite and the absolute value of a number are always the same. Which rational number can be used to show that this statement is incorrect?

Ⓐ −0.9

Ⓑ 0

Ⓒ −1.1

Ⓓ $\frac{1}{10}$

15. Use the number line to match each point with its opposite.

Point A ●   ● 1.5

Point B ●   ● −1.5

Point C ●   ● −3.25

Point D ●   ● 3.25

Spiral Review

16. A pond loses water from evaporation each week. Week 1 had a change in water level of −6 inches. Week 2 had a change in water level of −7 inches. Week 3 had a change in water level of −3 inches. Write the numbers from least to greatest.

_____

17. Write an inequality to compare the numbers 11 and −9.

_____

18. The low temperature in St. Paul, Minnesota, was −9 °F while the low temperature in Minot, North Dakota, was −1 °F on the same day. Which has a smaller magnitude?

_____

Name _____

Compare Rational Numbers on a Number Line

(I Can) compare positive and negative rational numbers using a number line.

Step It Out

You can compare fractions by graphing them on a number line.

1 ▶ Mrs. Smith and Mr. Jones each have 30 students in their class. If Mrs. Smith corrected $\frac{3}{4}$ of last week's math assignments and Mr. Jones corrected $\frac{5}{8}$ of last week's science assignments, which teacher corrected the greater portion of the assignments?

A. What marks on a number line would you need to graph $\frac{3}{4}$ and $\frac{5}{8}$?

_____

_____

B. Graph the fractions on the number line.

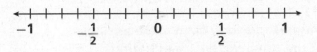

C. Note the locations of the numbers.

$\frac{3}{4}$ is to the _____ of $\frac{5}{8}$ on the number line, so $\frac{3}{4}$ is _____ $\frac{5}{8}$.

D. Write an inequality statement.

$\frac{3}{4}$ ☐ $\frac{5}{8}$

So, Mrs. Smith corrected | less than / more than | Mr. Jones.

E. Use the number line to help you write an inequality comparing $-\frac{5}{8}$ and $-\frac{3}{4}$.

_____

_____

Turn and Talk How do the numbers in Parts D and E compare? How can a number line help you to determine the relationship between the numbers in Parts D and E? Explain.

© Houghton Mifflin Harcourt Publishing Company

You also can compare decimals using a number line.

2 ▶ The record low temperatures for five cities are Ashton −0.6 °F, Barres −1.7 °F, Carl 0.7 °F, Davison 0.4 °F, and Edgeville −1.5 °F. Graph the temperatures on the number line and label each with the first letter of the city's name.

<---++--->
     −2   −1   0   1   2

A. Note the locations of the numbers for Barres and Edgeville.

−1.7 is to the [left / right] of −1.5, so Barres's low temperature is

[colder / warmer] than the low temperature for Edgeville.

B. Complete the inequality in two different ways.

−1.7 ☐ −1.5   −1.5 ☐ −1.7

Turn and Talk What do you notice about the rational numbers as you move from left to right on a number line? Use examples to support your answer.

Check Understanding

1. Researchers measure the thickness of the ice at several locations in the Antarctic and compare the measures to a long-term average thickness. A set of ice-level data from the Antarctic Weather Station is shown measured in meters.

−1.2, 2.6, −1.3, 1.8, 2.1, −0.9, 1.5

A. Graph the numbers on the number line to compare the data.

<---++--->
    −2   −1   0   1   2   3

B. Use the number line to complete the inequalities.

2.6 ☐ −0.9   1.8 ☐ 2.1   −1.2 ☐ −1.3

C. Is 1.5 to the left or right of −0.9?

_____

D. Is −1.2 to the left or right of −2.1?

_____

On Your Own

Diego measuring ingredients

2. **(MP) Use Tools** Diego is participating in a cooking competition in which the judges rate performance for various criteria using fractions between −1 and 2. The scores for four competitors are shown.

$\frac{1}{8}$, $-\frac{1}{4}$, $1\frac{1}{2}$, $-\frac{3}{4}$

A. Complete the number line to compare the four scores.

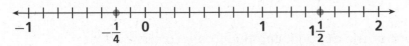

B. How do the locations of $-\frac{3}{4}$ and $-\frac{1}{4}$ compare? Which number is less? Explain.

_____

3. A sprint triathlon consists of a 750-meter swim, a 20-kilometer bicycle ride, and a 5-kilometer run. The race organizers recorded the difference between 5 athletes' times and the average time to complete the triathlon. Each value is the amount of time above or below the average in minutes.

2.5, −1.25, 0.8, 1.5, −1.2

A. Graph the athletes' differences from the average time on the number line.

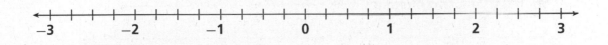

B. Compete the inequality statements.

-1.2 ☐ -1.25 0.8 ☐ 1.5 2.5 ☐ -1.25

C. Which inequality in Part B is comparing the differences from the average time for the slowest and fastest athletes in the group? Explain.

_____

_____

4. **Open Ended** A cave system inside a mountain has caves at different elevations above and below sea level. One cave has an elevation of $-4\frac{1}{4}$ meters. How can you use a vertical number line to determine whether the elevation of a second cave is greater than or less than $-4\frac{1}{4}$ meters?

_____

_____

5. On this map of Main Street, distances are in miles. The plotted points indicate the locations of landmarks. The library is located at point 0.

A. Find the the locations of the other landmarks and record them in the table in decimal form.

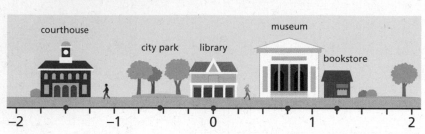

Points of Interest	
Name	**Location**
city park	
courthouse	
bookstore	
museum	

B. How do the locations of the city park and the library compare? Write an absolute value inequality to compare the distances from point 0 to the two buildings.

_____

C. How do the locations of the bookstore and the courthouse compare? Write an absolute value inequality to compare the distances from point 0 to the two buildings.

_____

_____

D. How do the locations of the museum and the bookstore compare? Write an absolute value inequality to compare the distances from point 0 to the two buildings.

_____

_____

Use the number line to compare the rational numbers.

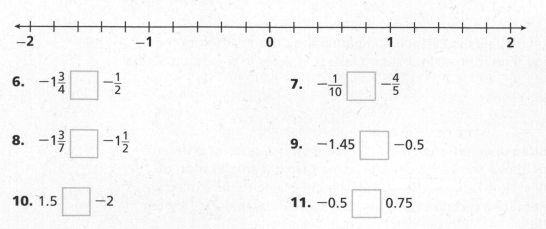

6. $-1\frac{3}{4}$ ☐ $-\frac{1}{2}$

7. $-\frac{1}{10}$ ☐ $-\frac{4}{5}$

8. $-1\frac{3}{7}$ ☐ $-1\frac{1}{2}$

9. -1.45 ☐ -0.5

10. 1.5 ☐ -2

11. -0.5 ☐ 0.75

Compare Rational Numbers on a Number Line

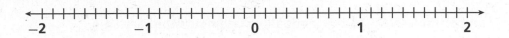
1. The high temperature of four different towns in Norway were measured on the same day. The temperatures are 0.9 °C, −0.5 °C, −1.3 °C, and 1.2 °C.

   A. Graph the temperatures on the number line.

   ```
   ←++++++++++++++++++++++++++++++++++++++++→
     −2        −1        0        1        2
   ```

   B. Complete each statement.

   −0.5 °C is _____ than −1.3 °C, because −0.5 is to the _____ of −1.3.

   0.9 °C is _____ than 1.2 °C, because 0.9 is to the _____ of 1.2.

2. **STEM** A circuit board manufacturer rejects a 100-ohm resistor if its measured resistance is 0.15 ohm or more away from 100 ohms. Resistors A and B are rejected. Resistor A's resistance differs from 100 ohms by +0.15 ohm. Resistor B's resistance differs from 100 ohms by −0.78 ohm. Which resistor has a resistance closer to 100 ohms?

   _____

   _____

   _____

   _____

   Resistors on a circuit board

3. Graph the numbers on the number line and complete the inequalities.

   $\frac{1}{20}, -\frac{1}{20}, \frac{6}{20}, -\frac{6}{20}$

   ```
   ←++++++++++++++++++++++++++++++→
    −1              0              1
   ```

   $-\frac{6}{20}$ ☐ $-\frac{1}{20}$

   $\frac{6}{20}$ ☐ $\frac{1}{20}$

For Problems 4–5, use the number line to write two different inequalities to compare the numbers.

```
←++++++++++++++++++++++++++++++→
  −2      −1      0      1      2
```

4. −1.25 and $-1\frac{1}{8}$

   _____

5. $-\frac{2}{5}$ and −0.5

   _____

Test Prep

6. Use the number line to locate 1.6 and $-1\frac{1}{5}$. Then complete the inequality.

1.6 ☐ $-1\frac{1}{5}$

7. Using the number line, select all the inequality statements that are true.

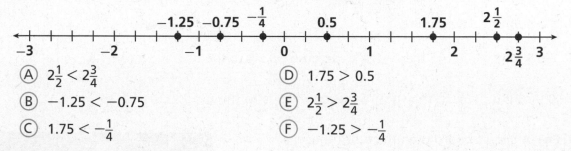

Ⓐ $2\frac{1}{2} < 2\frac{3}{4}$ Ⓓ $1.75 > 0.5$

Ⓑ $-1.25 < -0.75$ Ⓔ $2\frac{1}{2} > 2\frac{3}{4}$

Ⓒ $1.75 < -\frac{1}{4}$ Ⓕ $-1.25 > -\frac{1}{4}$

8. Which inequality is correct?

Ⓐ $0.6 < -0.3$

Ⓑ $0.5 > 0.6$

Ⓒ $-0.8 > 0.4$

Ⓓ $-0.3 > -0.8$

Spiral Review

9. The average elevation of New Orleans, Louisiana, is 8 feet below sea level. What integer is used to represent this elevation?

_____

10. During a football game, a team lost 10 yards on its first play and 20 yards on its third play. Write two integers to represent these losses. Which play had the greater loss? Explain.

_____

11. Write an inequality to compare $|-5|$ and $|4|$.

_____

Name Stephanie Hernandez

Find and Apply <u>LCM</u> and <u>GCF</u>

(I Can) find and use the <u>GCF</u> or <u>LCM</u> to solve problems.

Step It Out

1 ▶ Three runners leave the starting line at the same time. Lena runs each lap in 3 minutes, Aria runs each lap in 5 minutes, and Tran runs each lap in 6 minutes. When is the first time, in minutes, that all three runners will cross the starting line together?

A. How many minutes does it take Lena to run 12 laps?

$$\boxed{12} \text{ laps} \times \frac{\boxed{3} \text{ minutes}}{1 \text{ lap}} = \boxed{36} \text{ minutes}$$

> **Connect to Vocabulary**
>
> You have seen that a multiple of a number is the product of the number and any whole number except 0. A **least common multiple** (LCM) is the least number that is a multiple of two or more given numbers.

B. Complete the table.

Lap	1	2	3	4	5	6	7	8	9	10		
Lena's time (min)	3	6	9	12	15	18	21	24	27	30		3-minute lap
Aria's time (min)	5	10	15	20	25	30	35	40	45	50		5-minute lap
Tran's time (min)	6	12	18	24	30	36	42	48	54	60		6-minute lap

C. Look at the results in the table. What do you notice about the times in each row? <u>they are all common multiple</u>

D. Look at the rows for the three runners. Do they have any time in common? If so, what is it? <u>Yes, by the number 30</u>

The first time in minutes that all three runners finish a lap at the same time is the least common multiple of their times.

<u>30</u> is the least common multiple of <u>6</u>, <u>5</u>, and <u>10</u>.

> **Turn and Talk** If you extended the table, what would the next common multiple be? What pattern do you notice in the common multiples?

☰ = Albreto

2 ▶ Taylor and Jake are in charge of bringing snacks for their chess club. They have 24 granola bars and 16 water bottles. They want to set out the snacks so that the snacks are distributed evenly in snack packs with no granola bars or water bottles left over. What is the greatest number of snack packs that Taylor and Jake can make?

Connect to Vocabulary

You know that a **factor** is a number that is multiplied by another number to get a product. A **greatest common factor** (GCF) is the largest common factor of two or more given numbers.

A. Complete the tables to find the possible numbers of snack packs and numbers of granola bars and water bottles in each snack pack.

Snack Packs	Granola Bars per Pack
1	24
2	12
3	8
4	6
6	4
8	3
12	2
24	1

Snack Packs	Water Bottles per Pack
1	16
2	8
4	4
8	2
16	1

24 granola bars

16 water bottles

B. In the first table, the numbers of snack packs and the numbers of granola bars per pack are factors of _____.

In the second table, the numbers of snack packs and the numbers of water bottles per pack are **factors** of _____. Using the tables, list all the possible numbers of snack packs for each item.

Granola Bars: _____

Water Bottles: _____

C. What numbers occur in both lists? _____

D. What is the greatest number of snack packs a volunteer can make?

_____

E. The greatest common factor of 24 and 16 is _____.

F. You can use the greatest common factor to write the total number of bottles of water and granola bars, 24 + 16, as a sum of products.

Number of snack items = Number of granola bars + Number of water

bottles = ☐ (☐) + ☐ (☐)

You can use the **Distributive Property** to write the total number of snack items as the product of the GCF and another sum.

☐ (☐) + ☐ (☐) = ☐ (☐ + ☐) = ☐ (☐) snack items

3 ▶ Which is greater, $\frac{5}{6}$ or $\frac{7}{10}$?

A. Complete the lists of multiples of the denominators.

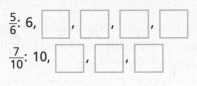

$\frac{5}{6}$: 6, ☐, ☐, ☐, ☐

$\frac{7}{10}$: 10, ☐, ☐, ☐

B. The least common multiple (LCM) of the numbers in the lists is _____.

C. Rewrite the fractions using the LCM as the **common denominator**.

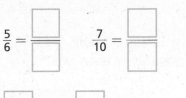

$\frac{5}{6} = \dfrac{☐}{☐}$ $\frac{7}{10} = \dfrac{☐}{☐}$

D. Use the new fractions to write an inequality to compare the original fractions.

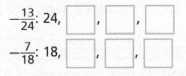

$\dfrac{☐}{☐} ☐ \dfrac{☐}{☐}$, so $\frac{5}{6} ☐ \frac{7}{10}$

4 ▶ Which is greater: $-\frac{13}{24}$ or $-\frac{7}{18}$?

A. Complete the lists of multiples for the denominators.

$-\frac{13}{24}$: 24, ☐, ☐, ☐

$-\frac{7}{18}$: 18, ☐, ☐, ☐

B. The least common multiple (LCM) of the numbers in the lists is _____.

C. Rewrite the fractions using the LCM of the **denominators** and complete the inequality to compare the original fractions.

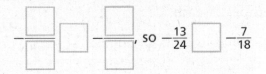

$-\dfrac{☐}{☐} ☐ -\dfrac{☐}{☐}$, so $-\frac{13}{24} ☐ -\frac{7}{18}$

D. How would you compare the numbers using $-\frac{1}{2}$ as a benchmark?

_____

_____

Check Understanding

1. Paper cups are sold in packages of 6, and napkins are sold in packages of 8. Ted wants to buy the same number of each. What is the least number of cups and napkins he needs to buy? _____

2. A florist has 60 tulips and 72 daffodils. The florist will make bouquets with the same number of tulips and the same number of daffodils in each using all the flowers. What is the greatest number of bouquets the florist can make?

_____

3. Which is greater, $\frac{11}{16}$ or $\frac{24}{32}$? _____

On Your Own

4. Jamie makes plates and bowls. She needs to ship 48 plates and 54 bowls to a store. She wants to ship the same number of items in each box. Plates and bowls are shipped separately.

   A. What is the greatest number of items she can ship in each box?

   _____

   B. How many boxes of items will Jamie ship if she ships the greatest number possible in each box?

   Boxes of plates: ☐   Boxes of bowls: ☐

   C. ⓂⓅ **Use Structure** What is the greatest common factor of 48 and 54? Use the greatest common factor to write the total number of plates and bowls as a sum of products. Then use the distributive property to write the total number of items as a product.

   _____

5. Grant is making muffins for a reunion. The recipe for blueberry muffins makes 12 muffins. The recipe for bran muffins makes 18 muffins. He wants to make the same number of each kind of muffin using only full recipes of each.

   A. What is the least number of each type of muffin Grant can make?

   _____

   B. How many batches of each recipe will Grant make if he makes the least number of each type of muffin possible?

   Blueberry: _____ batches   Bran: _____ batches

6. A year is $\frac{1}{3}$ of the lifespan of a fire ant queen. A year is $\frac{1}{30}$ of a termite queen's lifespan. Write an inequality to compare the fractions of the insects' lifespans that a year represents.

Fire ant queen   Termite queen

_____

7. ⓂⓅ **Reason** Cameron and Tatiana volunteer at the public library. Cameron shelves one book every $\frac{1}{4}$ minute. Tatiana shelves one book every $\frac{3}{10}$ minute. Who is quicker at shelving books? Explain how you found your answer.

_____

_____

_____

© Houghton Mifflin Harcourt Publishing Company • **Image Credits:** (l) ©Scott Camazine/Science Source ;(r) ©Dante Fenolio/Science Source

8. Darnell helps to make lunches at a picnic. Each picnic basket will have the amounts of ham salad and potato salad shown in the illustration. Which is greater, the amount of ham salad or the amount of potato salad? Show your work.

9. **(MP) Critique Reasoning** Ryan is making biscuits. The recipe calls for 0.25 quart of milk and 2.5 cups of flour. He has $\frac{1}{5}$ quart of milk and $\frac{9}{4}$ cups of flour. Ryan makes the recipe with the milk and flour that he has. Explain his error.

10. Use the LCM to find a common denominator for the fractions $\frac{3}{8}$ and $\frac{1}{10}$. Write the fractions with the new denominator. Then write an inequality involving the rewritten fractions to show which is greater.

11. Groups of sixth graders and seventh graders compete in a race. The contestants include $\frac{3}{4}$ of the sixth graders and $\frac{4}{5}$ of the seventh graders. Which group has a greater fraction of their grade represented?

12. **Open Ended** How can you determine which of the numbers below is greatest?

$$\frac{13}{20}, \frac{5}{8}, \frac{3}{5}, \frac{3}{10}$$

13. The table shows the rainfall in four towns on the same day. Which town had more rain, Brighton or Springfield? Morristown or Pine Grove?

Town	Morristown	Brighton	Springfield	Pine Grove
Rainfall (inches)	$3\frac{9}{16}$	$3\frac{5}{16}$	$3\frac{8}{12}$	$3\frac{13}{24}$

14. (MP) **Use Structure** The table shows the distance below ground of items found at an archaeological site. Researchers also found a mouse fossil at the same site. Which, if any, of the items in the table were a greater distance below ground than the mouse fossil?

$5\frac{3}{4}$ feet deep

Item	Distance below ground (feet)
spoon	$5\frac{3}{8}$
key	$6\frac{3}{4}$
cup	$4\frac{3}{12}$
bowl	$5\frac{5}{6}$

Find the LCM of the number pair.

15. 8 and 4

16. 5 and 12

17. 4 and 9

18. 6 and 21

19. 15 and 9

20. 20 and 8

Find the GCF of the number pair.

21. 16 and 30

22. 24 and 32

23. 26 and 39

24. 28 and 14

25. 32 and 40

26. 54 and 36

Complete the inequality using the symbol > or <.

27. $\frac{4}{10}$ ☐ $\frac{5}{6}$

28. $\frac{3}{33}$ ☐ $\frac{40}{100}$

29. $\frac{5}{12}$ ☐ $\frac{3}{20}$

Write an inequality to compare the fractions.

30. $\frac{24}{18}$ and $\frac{25}{15}$

31. $-\frac{3}{8}$ and $-\frac{5}{7}$

32. $-\frac{18}{42}$ and $-\frac{15}{21}$

33. $\frac{12}{16}$ and $\frac{16}{24}$

34. $\frac{5}{12}$ and $\frac{11}{28}$

35. $-\frac{7}{10}$ and $-\frac{5}{9}$

Find and Apply LCM and GCF

1. (MP) **Model with Mathematics** Martha ran $\frac{5}{8}$ of a mile and Terry ran $\frac{6}{15}$ of a mile on the weekend. Who ran a larger portion of a mile? Write an inequality to compare the portions of a mile.

_____

2. (MP) **Reason** A radio station is giving away concert tickets to every 60th caller and a concert T-shirt to every 45th caller. What will be the number of the first caller to get both items? Explain.

_____

3. A cuckoo clock has birds that pop out of their nests every 6 minutes and dancers that pop out every 15 minutes. The birds and dancers have just popped out at the same time. When will this happen again in the next 60 minutes?

_____

4. String-cheese sticks are sold in packs of 10 and celery sticks in packs of 15. Mr. Deluca wants to give each of 30 students one string-cheese stick and one celery stick. What is the least number of packs he should buy so there are none left over?

_____

Math on the Spot Find the GCF of each set of numbers.

5. 8 and 12

6. 10, 15, and 30

7. 18, 36, and 60

_____

8. Use the GCF of 48 and 30 to write the sum of the two numbers as the product of their GCF and another sum.

$$\square(\square) + \square(\square) = \square(\square + \square) = \square(\square)$$

For Problems 9–11, compare the fractions using the LCM.

9. $\frac{1}{7}, \frac{2}{3}$

10. $\frac{3}{5}, \frac{1}{4}$

11. $\frac{4}{6}, \frac{4}{8}$

For Problems 12–14, compare the fractions.

12. $\frac{10}{14}, \frac{3}{7}$

13. $-\frac{14}{21}, -\frac{3}{9}$

14. $\frac{30}{20}, \frac{8}{2}$

Test Prep

15. Which expression shows the sum of 72 and 96 as the product of the GCF and a sum of two numbers with no common factor?

(A) $12(6 + 8)$

(B) $24(3 + 4)$

(C) $24(6 + 8)$

(D) $48(3 + 4)$

16. Write an inequality to compare the numbers 12.7 and $12\frac{3}{4}$.

_____

17. Ambrose and Kaitlin are volunteering at a food bank. They both start at the same time. Kaitlin takes 13 minutes to pack a box with donated food. Ambrose takes 7 minutes to pack a box. After how many minutes will they finish packing boxes at the same time?

_____

18. Jewel has 20 apples and 16 bananas that she wants to arrange in baskets. There needs to be the same number of apples and the same number of bananas in each basket. What is the greatest number of baskets she can make? How many apples and bananas will be in each basket?

_____

Spiral Review

19. Write an inequality to compare the numbers.

−13 and −10

_____

20. Write the list of numbers in order from least to greatest.

5, −6, 4, −3, 8, 7, −5

_____

21. Which number, −12 or −18, has the greater absolute value?

_____

Name _____

Order Rational Numbers

(I Can) order positive and negative rational numbers of different forms.

Step It Out

1 ▷ The average weight of an adult African pygmy mouse is 0.27 ounce. Weights of the mice vary depending on age, diet, and whether the mouse is male or female. The differences from average weight in ounces for a set of African pygmy mice at a zoo are shown.

0.09, −0.14, 0.12, 0.06, −0.1

A. How can you use a number line to order the numbers?

_____

_____

_____

B. Graph the numbers on the number line.

```
<--+++++++++++++++++++++++++++++++++++++++-->
  −0.2       −0.1        0        0.1       0.2
```

C. Complete the statements using the graph in Part B.

A number to the left of a second number on a number line is

| less / greater | than the second number.

D. Write an inequality to compare 0.09 and −0.1.

_____

E. Write an inequality to compare −0.14 and −0.1.

_____

F. Write the numbers in order from least to greatest.

_____

 Turn and Talk How are 0.5 and 0.29 related? Explain.

One way to compare rational numbers is to rewrite them in the same form.

2 ▶ Look at the list of numbers.

$-1\frac{2}{5}, -0.62, -1.18, -\frac{3}{5}$

A. Rewrite each decimal as a fraction.

$-0.62 = -\dfrac{\boxed{}}{100} = -\dfrac{\boxed{}}{50}$ $-1.18 = -1\dfrac{\boxed{}}{100} = -1\dfrac{\boxed{}}{50}$

B. What is the least common multiple, or LCM, of the denominators of all the fractions?

_____

C. What are the numbers written with the LCM as the common denominator?

$-1\frac{2}{5} = -1\dfrac{\boxed{}}{50}$ $-0.62 = -\dfrac{\boxed{}}{50}$ $-1.18 = -1\dfrac{\boxed{}}{50}$ $-\frac{3}{5} = -\dfrac{\boxed{}}{50}$

D. Write the numbers in order in their new forms and then in their original forms from least to greatest.

_____

Turn and Talk Is there another method you can use to order the numbers $2\frac{1}{2}$, -0.25, 1.5, and $-\frac{7}{8}$?

3 ▶ Look at the list of numbers below.

$-0.4, \frac{3}{5}, -1.8, -\frac{6}{5}, 0.2$

A. Rewrite each decimal as a fraction.

$-0.4 = -\dfrac{4}{\boxed{}} = -\dfrac{\boxed{}}{5}$ $-1.8 = -1\dfrac{8}{\boxed{}} = -1\dfrac{\boxed{}}{5}$ $0.2 = \dfrac{\boxed{}}{10} = \dfrac{1}{\boxed{}}$

B. Use the number line to graph all the numbers.

C. Write the numbers from least to greatest in their original form.

_____

4 A fun run was held to raise money. The differences between the average finishing time and the actual times for five runners are shown below. Order the differences in time from least to greatest.

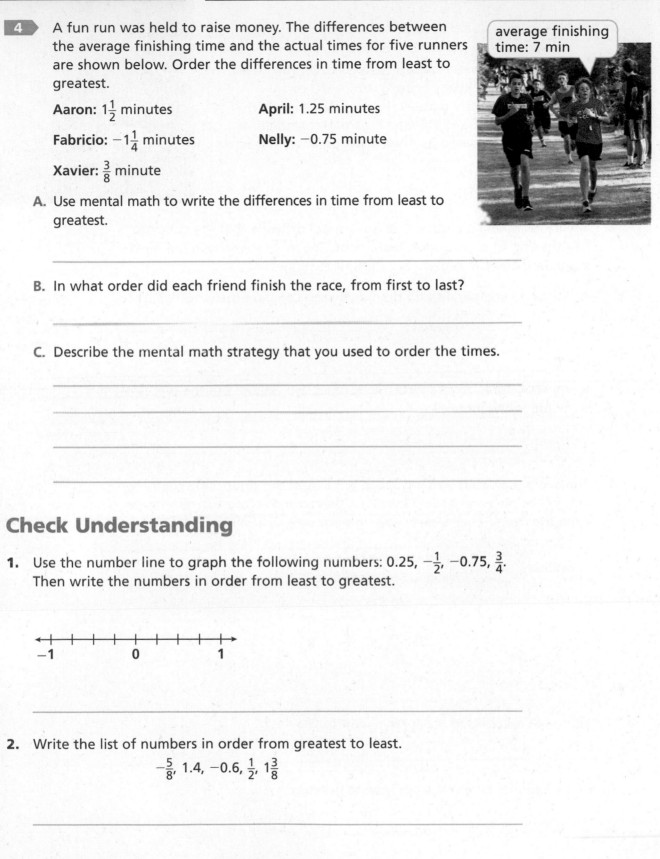

average finishing time: 7 min

Aaron: $1\frac{1}{2}$ minutes **April:** 1.25 minutes

Fabricio: $-1\frac{1}{4}$ minutes **Nelly:** -0.75 minute

Xavier: $\frac{3}{8}$ minute

A. Use mental math to write the differences in time from least to greatest.

_____

B. In what order did each friend finish the race, from first to last?

_____

C. Describe the mental math strategy that you used to order the times.

_____

_____

_____

_____

Check Understanding

1. Use the number line to graph the following numbers: 0.25, $-\frac{1}{2}$, -0.75, $\frac{3}{4}$. Then write the numbers in order from least to greatest.

$$\overset{\textstyle -1 \qquad\qquad 0 \qquad\qquad 1}{\longleftarrow|\;|\;|\;|\;|\;|\;|\;|\;|\;|\;|\longrightarrow}$$

_____

2. Write the list of numbers in order from greatest to least.

$$-\frac{5}{8},\ 1.4,\ -0.6,\ \frac{1}{2},\ 1\frac{3}{8}$$

_____

On Your Own

3. A musician uses water glasses to play music. The glasses contain 0.5 cup, $\frac{4}{6}$ cup, $\frac{1}{3}$ cup, and $\frac{4}{5}$ cup of water. To play the glasses, the musician lines them up from least amount of water to greatest amount of water. Write the amounts of water in order from least to greatest.

_____

4. Sakura is making a mobile. She has a spool of twine that she cuts into lengths of $\frac{5}{6}$ foot, 0.75 foot, and $\frac{4}{5}$ foot. The mobile will have pieces of twine in lengths in order from shortest to longest.

A. What do you need to do before you can compare the lengths?

_____

_____

B. In what order, from shortest to longest, will Sakura use the pieces of twine in the mobile?

_____

5. The average human walking speed is 3.1 miles per hour. Shoe company employees measure people's walking speeds and record the difference from the average walking speed for each person. The results are shown.

Walker	Differences from Average Walking Speed (mph)
A	−0.5
B	$\frac{3}{10}$
C	0.7
D	$-\frac{4}{5}$

Write the numbers in order from least to greatest.

_____

Order the rational numbers from least to greatest.

6. $\frac{7}{8}$, −0.25, $-\frac{1}{16}$, 0.75 _____

7. −2.1, $1\frac{2}{5}$, $-\frac{9}{10}$, 0.7 _____

Fraction Division

A Perplexing Pet Puzzle

30 pets

Ms. Tran wrote a set of clues about her pets.

Use the clues to complete the table with the number of each type of pet she owns.

I have 30 pets in all.

I have $\frac{1}{2}$ as many cats as mice.

I have $\frac{1}{3}$ as many dogs as cats.

Exactly $\frac{1}{5}$ of my pets are mice.

The rest of my pets are fish.

Type of Pet	Number
Cat	
Dog	
Mouse	
Fish	

Turn and Talk

- Which type of pet did you start with when completing the table? Why did you start with this pet?

- How could you tell that the number of dogs would be less than the number of mice without performing any calculations?

Are You Ready?

Complete these problems to review prior concepts and skills you will need for this module.

Factors

Find all factor pairs for each number.

1. 18

2. 21

3. 48

4. 65

Add Fractions and Decimals

Find each sum or difference.

5. $7.2 + 2.6$

6. $8.5 - 7$

7. $7.55 - 3.25$

8. $\frac{1}{3} + \frac{1}{5}$

9. $\frac{9}{10} - \frac{7}{8}$

10. $\frac{1}{6} + \frac{5}{12}$

Multiply Fractions

Find each product.

11. $\frac{3}{4} \times \frac{5}{8}$

12. $\frac{5}{6} \times \frac{9}{10}$

13. $\frac{1}{2} \times \frac{1}{4}$

Divide with Unit Fractions and Whole Numbers

Find each quotient.

14. $6 \div \frac{1}{3}$

15. $1 \div \frac{1}{10}$

16. $\frac{1}{4} \div 6$

Name _____

Understand Fraction Division

(I Can) divide fractions with like denominators with and without models.

Spark Your Learning

Jayson is making sushi rolls. He has $\frac{5}{6}$ cup of rice and will use $\frac{2}{6}$ cup for each sushi roll. How many whole sushi rolls can he make?

 Turn and Talk How many sushi rolls can Jayson make if he uses up all the rice? Explain.

Build Understanding

1   Malik is making eggrolls to share with Jayson. Malik has $\frac{4}{5}$ pound of chicken and will use the amount shown per batch. How many batches of eggrolls can Malik make?

A. Write an **expression** to show how you would divide a fraction by a fraction to solve this problem.

_____ ÷ _____

$\frac{2}{5}$ pound of chicken per batch

B. Explain how you can use a model to find how many groups of $\frac{2}{5}$ are in $\frac{4}{5}$. Then make a model.

C. How many groups of $\frac{2}{5}$ are there in $\frac{4}{5}$? How many batches of eggrolls can Malik make?

_____

2   Suppose Malik had $\frac{3}{4}$ pound of chicken and uses $\frac{3}{8}$ pound to make one batch of eggrolls. How many batches of eggrolls could he make?

A. Draw the fraction strip you could use to begin to find the solution.

B. Will the fraction strip you drew in Part A help you to make groups of $\frac{3}{8}$? If not, what other fraction strip could help? Explain why.

_____

_____

C. Draw the fraction strip you chose in Part B in the answer box in Part A. How many groups of $\frac{3}{8}$ are in $\frac{3}{4}$? Explain.

D. How many batches of eggrolls can Malik make?

_____

© Houghton Mifflin Harcourt Publishing Company • **Image Credit:** ©Andrea Skjold Mink/Shutterstock

3 ▸ Suyin is making a dog house. She needs to cut a board that is $\frac{5}{9}$ yard long into smaller pieces. How many pieces can she cut if each piece needs to be $\frac{2}{9}$ yard long?

A. Complete the following to express the problem in words. Suyin needs to find how many groups of

_____ are in _____.

B. What division expression can you use to answer this question?

_____

C. Complete the bar model to show the division problem in Part B.

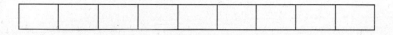

D. Write an explanation of how the bar model represents the quotient in Part B.

E. What is the number of pieces of board, each $\frac{2}{9}$ yard long, that Suyin can cut? Did Suyin use up all the wood? If not, how long is the leftover piece of board?

_____

 Turn and Talk What fraction of another piece can Suyin make with what is left over?

4 The diagram shows part of a road that is $\frac{9}{10}$ mile long. Consider the expression $\frac{9}{10} \div \frac{2}{10}$.

A. Write a problem that can be modeled with the given expression and that uses the information in the diagram.

$\frac{2}{10}$ mile

_____

_____

_____

_____

_____

B. Show or describe how to find the **quotient**.

C. Recall that the **dividend** is the number to be divided in a division problem. The **divisor** is the number you are dividing by. In your problem, what do the dividend and divisor represent?

_____

_____

D. How does the answer to the question in Part A compare to the quotient in Part B? Explain.

_____

_____

Check Understanding

1. Hana is organizing a $\frac{3}{4}$-mile fun run. There will be a water station every $\frac{1}{4}$ mile after the start.

   A. How many groups of $\frac{1}{4}$ are in $\frac{3}{4}$? _____

   B. How many water stations will there be? _____

2. Janice is cutting ribbon to decorate a present. She has $\frac{7}{8}$ foot of ribbon. She needs to make pieces that are $\frac{3}{8}$ foot each. How many $\frac{3}{8}$-foot pieces will she get from the $\frac{7}{8}$-foot ribbon? _____

On Your Own

3. Jasmine has $\frac{4}{5}$ pound of fertilizer. She wants to store the fertilizer in separate containers, each with $\frac{1}{5}$ pound of fertilizer. How many containers will she need? _____

4. (MP) **Reason** A city places street lights at equal intervals along a city street beginning $\frac{3}{8}$ mile from one end of the street. If the street is $\frac{7}{8}$ mile long, how many street lights will the city use? Explain.

$\frac{3}{8}$ mile

_____

_____

_____

5. Eric has $\frac{9}{16}$ pound of bird feed left. If he feeds his bird $\frac{1}{8}$ pound each day, how many days can he feed the bird before he needs to buy more food?

_____

6. Daryl has $\frac{2}{3}$ of a bag of dog food. His dog eats $\frac{4}{9}$ of a bag per week.

A. How many weeks will the dog food last? _____

B. What fraction strip could you use to solve this problem? Explain why.

_____

_____

7. How long will it take Sarah to paint $\frac{11}{12}$ of a fence if she paints $\frac{2}{12}$ of the fence each day?

_____

8. How many $\frac{1}{3}$-cup servings are there in $\frac{10}{3}$ cups of dried beans?

_____

9. Tressa's home is $\frac{4}{5}$ mile from school. Anton's home is $\frac{3}{5}$ mile from school. How many times the distance from Anton's home to school is the distance from Tressa's home to school?

_____

10. (MP) **Model with Mathematics** Tom is pouring $\frac{3}{32}$-gallon servings from a bottle that contains $\frac{15}{32}$ gallon of tomato juice. Write and evaluate a division expression to find the number of servings in the bottle.

_____

11. (MP) **Model with Mathematics** It takes $\frac{1}{3}$ pint of paint to cover a birdhouse. There are $12\frac{1}{3}$ pints of paint in a can. Write and evaluate a division expression to find the number of birdhouses that can be painted.

_____

12. Juan has $\frac{5}{8}$ pound of beef. He wants to make burgers using the meat. If the meat in each burger weighs $\frac{1}{8}$ pound, how many burgers can he make?

_____

13. Felice lives $\frac{9}{10}$ mile from a park. She needs to stop several times while walking her new puppy to the park, including her final stop when she reaches the park. How many times will she stop when walking to the park?

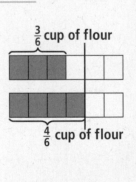

Must rest every $\frac{3}{10}$ mile.

_____

14. (MP) **Critique Reasoning** Darius says that $\frac{1}{3} \div \frac{2}{3}$ is 2, because you can't make groups of $\frac{2}{3}$ from $\frac{1}{3}$ so you need to make groups of $\frac{1}{3}$ from $\frac{2}{3}$. Darius' answer is not correct. What mistake did he make? What is the correct answer?

_____

_____

_____

15. Write and solve a real-world problem that can be modeled by the diagram shown and the division expression $\frac{3}{6} \div \frac{4}{6}$.

$\frac{3}{6}$ cup of flour

$\frac{4}{6}$ cup of flour

_____

_____

_____

_____

© Houghton Mifflin Harcourt Publishing Company • **Image Credit:** ©Dorottya Mathe/Shutterstock

 **I'm in a Learning Mindset!**

Is using a model to divide fractions an effective strategy? Why or why not?

_____

_____

Understand Fraction Division

$\frac{3}{4}$ hour workout

1. Yu has a part of an hour for his workout. He would like to do a different exercise each $\frac{1}{4}$ hour. How many different exercises does he have time for?

   _____

2. A phone has $\frac{5}{8}$ of its battery charge left. If the battery loses $\frac{3}{8}$ of its full charge every hour, how many hours will the battery last?

   _____

3. Sonia takes a $\frac{4}{5}$-mile walk every day. What part of her walk has she completed once she has walked $\frac{3}{5}$ mile?

   _____

4. **(MP) Reason** A bread recipe requires that $\frac{5}{8}$ teaspoon of yeast be added to flour and water. Alejandro only has a $\frac{1}{8}$-teaspoon measuring spoon. How many measuring spoons of yeast will he need to add to the flour and water? Explain your reasoning.

   _____

   _____

   _____

   _____

5. **Open Ended** Write and solve a real-world problem that can be modeled by the division expression $\frac{8}{12} \div \frac{9}{12}$. Identify what the dividend, divisor, and quotient represent in your problem. Show your work.

Test Prep

6. Jolene is cutting a strip of yarn that is $\frac{11}{12}$ inch long into pieces that are $\frac{2}{12}$ inch long for a collage. How many complete pieces can she make?

_____

7. Sinh has $\frac{14}{16}$ pound of nuts. He separates them into $\frac{2}{16}$-pound servings. How many servings can he make?

Which expression models the situation?

Ⓐ $\frac{2}{16} \div \frac{14}{16}$

Ⓑ $\frac{2}{16} \times \frac{14}{16}$

Ⓒ $\frac{14}{16} \div \frac{2}{16}$

Ⓓ $\frac{14}{16} - \frac{2}{16}$

8. Which question can be answered using the expression $\frac{3}{8} \div \frac{5}{8}$?

Ⓐ How many $\frac{5}{8}$-cup servings of apple cider are in $\frac{3}{8}$ cup of cider?

Ⓑ How many $\frac{3}{8}$-cup servings of apple cider are in $\frac{5}{8}$ cup of cider?

Ⓒ Dan drank $\frac{3}{8}$ of a $\frac{5}{8}$-cup serving of apple cider. How much did he drink?

Ⓓ Dan drank $\frac{5}{8}$ of a $\frac{3}{8}$-cup serving of apple cider. How much did he drink?

9. Terell is cutting a piece of trimming that is $\frac{15}{18}$ foot long into pieces that are $\frac{3}{18}$ foot long. How many pieces will Terell have?

Ⓐ 3 pieces

Ⓑ 5 pieces

Ⓒ 6 pieces

Ⓓ 8 pieces

Spiral Review

10. What is the absolute value of −8?

_____

11. Write an inequality to compare the integers −5 and −6.

_____

12. Find the product: $\frac{2}{3} \times \frac{3}{8}$.

_____

Name _____

Explore Division of Fractions with Unlike Denominators

(I Can) divide two fractions with unlike denominators using several methods.

Spark Your Learning

Roselyn is making a stir fry. The recipe calls for 4 cups of broccoli, but Roselyn has only a $\frac{2}{3}$-cup measure. How many measuring cups of broccoli should she add?

Turn and Talk What if the recipe says to add 3 cups of summer squash? How many measuring cups of squash should she add? Explain.

Build Understanding

1 ▶ Roselyn also needs to add $\frac{5}{8}$ cup of orange juice to make a sauce for her stir fry. If she uses a $\frac{1}{4}$-cup measuring cup, how many measuring cups will she need to add?

A. How can you divide $\frac{5}{8}$ into groups of $\frac{1}{4}$? Complete the following statement.

Since $\frac{1}{4} = \frac{\square}{8}$, you can divide $\frac{5}{8}$ into groups of _____.

B. Use the number line to show the number of groups of $\frac{1}{4}$ in $\frac{5}{8}$.

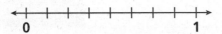

0   1

C. How many measuring cups of orange juice will Roselyn need to add?

_____

D. How many measuring cups of juice will Roselyn need to add if she uses a $\frac{1}{8}$-cup measuring cup or a $\frac{3}{8}$-cup measuring cup? Use your results to complete the first column of the table.

_____

_____

_____

_____

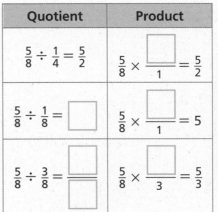

$\frac{1}{4}$ cup

Quotient	Product
$\frac{5}{8} \div \frac{1}{4} = \frac{5}{2}$	$\frac{5}{8} \times \dfrac{\square}{1} = \frac{5}{2}$
$\frac{5}{8} \div \frac{1}{8} = \square$	$\frac{5}{8} \times \dfrac{\square}{1} = 5$
$\frac{5}{8} \div \frac{3}{8} = \dfrac{\square}{\square}$	$\frac{5}{8} \times \dfrac{\square}{3} = \frac{5}{3}$

E. *Reciprocals* can help you find quotients. You find the reciprocal of a fraction by switching the **numerator** and **denominator**. Complete the following equations with the correct reciprocals.

$\frac{1}{4} \times \dfrac{\square}{\square} = 1$ $\dfrac{\square}{\square} \times \frac{1}{8} = 1$ $\frac{3}{8} \times \dfrac{\square}{\square} = 1$

F. Now complete the second column of the table. Look for a pattern in the table to complete the following statements.

To find the quotient of two fractions, multiply

the _____ fraction by the reciprocal of

the _____ fraction. In each row of the

table, the quotient _____ the _____.

$\dfrac{a}{b} \div \dfrac{c}{d} = \dfrac{a}{b} \times \dfrac{\square}{\square} = \dfrac{\square}{\square}$

© Houghton Mifflin Harcourt Publishing Company • Image Credit: ©annapospyelova/Shutterstock

Step It Out

2 Eric and Tom are making small bows for presents. They will need pieces of ribbon like the one shown, which will be cut from a ribbon that is $\frac{3}{4}$-yard long. They used two different methods to find the number of $\frac{2}{9}$-yard pieces they could cut from a $\frac{3}{4}$-yard ribbon.

$\frac{2}{9}$ yard

Eric's Method:	Tom's Method:
$\frac{3}{4} \div \frac{2}{9} = \frac{3}{4} \times \frac{9}{2}$	$\frac{3}{4} \div \frac{2}{9} = \frac{27}{36} \div \frac{8}{36}$
$= \frac{27}{8}$	$= 27 \div 8$
$= 3\frac{3}{8}$ pieces	$= \frac{27}{8}$
	$= 3\frac{3}{8}$ pieces

A. Explain Eric's solution method.

_____

_____

_____

B. Explain Tom's solution method.

_____

_____

_____

_____

_____

C. How many whole pieces can they cut from the long ribbon?

_____

D. What does the $\frac{3}{8}$ in the quotient $3\frac{3}{8}$ mean in this situation?

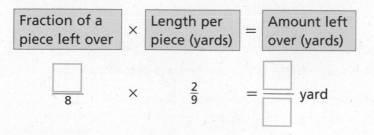

$\frac{\boxed{}}{8}$ × $\frac{2}{9}$ = $\frac{\boxed{}}{\boxed{}}$ yard

$\frac{3}{8}$ is the amount of ribbon left over, or _____ yard of ribbon.

Turn and Talk Whose method do you prefer and why do you prefer it?

3   Tina feeds her dog $\frac{4}{7}$ pound of dog food per day. If she buys a bag containing 9 pounds of dog food, how many days will it last?

9 pounds

A. What expression could you use to solve the problem?

_____

B. What do you need to do first to find the quotient?

_____

C. What do you need to do next?

_____

_____

D. Complete the number sentence to find the number of days the bag of dog food will last.

$$9 \div \frac{\square}{\square} = \frac{9}{1} \times \frac{\square}{\square} = \frac{\square}{4} = \underline{\hspace{1cm}} \text{ days}$$

The dog food will last _____ days.

 Turn and Talk About how many 9-pound bags of dog food will Tina need to feed her dog for an entire year?

Check Understanding

1. Marcus needs to measure out $\frac{2}{3}$ liter of a solution. He is using a container that holds $\frac{1}{6}$ liter. How many groups of $\frac{1}{6}$ are in $\frac{2}{3}$? How many times will Marcus need to fill the container?

_____

2. Roberta bought $\frac{9}{10}$ pound of raisins. She put $\frac{2}{5}$ pound in bags for her lunch. How many $\frac{2}{5}$-pound bags can Roberta fill? Does she have any left over?

_____

For Problems 3–6, divide the fractions.

3. $\frac{6}{10} \div \frac{2}{5}$ _____

4. $\frac{3}{8} \div \frac{1}{3}$ _____

5. $\frac{5}{9} \div \frac{2}{3}$ _____

6. $10 \div \frac{2}{5}$ _____

Name _____

On Your Own

$\frac{8}{10}$ acre of land

(MP) **Model with Mathematics** For Problems 7–11, write an expression to model each situation. Then answer the question.

7. Mr. Duale would like to plant a vegetable garden. He has a part of an acre of land, which he plans to divide into $\frac{2}{5}$-acre sections. How many sections will he have?

_____

8. **STEM** The width of a single atom of aluminum is $\frac{7}{25}$ nanometer, which is more than 100,000 times smaller than a millimeter. Scientists sometimes use Ångströms to measure distances on an atomic scale. One Ångström is $\frac{1}{10}$ nanometer. How many Ångströms wide is a single atom of aluminum?

_____

9. At a school, each class period is $\frac{3}{4}$ hour long. If there are 6 hours of class time in a school day, how many class periods are there?

_____

10. A pitcher contains $\frac{8}{10}$ liter of juice and is used to fill cups that hold $\frac{1}{5}$ liter. How many cups can be filled?

_____

11. (MP) **Reason** Patrick has $\frac{7}{10}$ pound of flour. A batch of biscuits requires $\frac{1}{8}$ pound of flour. How many whole batches of biscuits can Patrick make? Explain your reasoning.

_____

_____

_____

12. (MP) **Critique Reasoning** Hannah is asked to divide $\frac{1}{6}$ by $\frac{1}{2}$. She says that the answer is 3, because the product of $\frac{1}{2}$ and 6 is equal to 3. Is she correct? Why or why not?

_____

_____

13. **(MP)** **Model with Mathematics** Diane had $\frac{15}{16}$ cup of butter. A recipe for a cake calls for $\frac{1}{4}$ cup of butter. Diane was able to make 3 whole cakes. How much butter did she use? How much butter does she have left over? Show how to model and solve this problem.

14. Sandy is a jeweler. She has 2 grams of gold. If each earring she makes must contain $\frac{3}{16}$ gram of gold, how many earrings can Sandy make? How many earrings could she make from a gold bar of 1,000 grams of gold? Show your work.

For Problems 15–18, find the reciprocal.

15. $\frac{5}{16}$ _____   **16.** $\frac{1}{5}$ _____   **17.** 4 _____   **18.** $\frac{4}{9}$ _____

For Problems 19–27, divide the fractions.

19. $\frac{5}{12} \div \frac{1}{3}$ _____   **20.** $\frac{2}{3} \div \frac{1}{6}$ _____   **21.** $\frac{1}{2} \div \frac{7}{8}$ _____

22. $\frac{11}{15} \div \frac{3}{5}$ _____   **23.** $\frac{1}{6} \div \frac{2}{3}$ _____   **24.** $\frac{5}{14} \div \frac{5}{7}$ _____

25. $\frac{4}{5} \div \frac{24}{25}$ _____   **26.** $\frac{5}{6} \div \frac{5}{9}$ _____   **27.** $\frac{7}{8} \div \frac{3}{16}$ _____

I'm in a Learning Mindset!

What strategies do I use to ensure I can complete my work on dividing fractions with different denominators?

_____

Explore Division of Fractions with Unlike Denominators

1. A small bookshelf is $\frac{8}{12}$ yard long. How many books can fit on the shelf if the width of each book is $\frac{1}{24}$ yard? Explain.

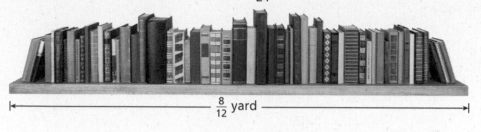

|← ———————————— $\frac{8}{12}$ yard ———————————— →|

2. (MP) **Reason** Isabella owns a rectangular lot with an area of $\frac{9}{32}$ square mile. If the length of the western side of her lot is $\frac{3}{4}$ mile, what is the length of the northern side? How can you find the length?

_____

_____

_____

_____

3. **Math on the Spot** Show two methods for finding the quotient $\frac{3}{8} \div \frac{3}{4}$.

_____

_____

4. (MP) **Construct Arguments** When $\frac{9}{10}$ is divided by $\frac{2}{5}$, will the quotient be greater than 1 or less than 1? How do you know?

_____

_____

For Problems 5–8, find the reciprocal.

5. $\frac{7}{8}$ _____

6. $\frac{1}{10}$ _____

7. 12 _____

8. $\frac{14}{16}$ _____

For Problems 9–17, divide the fractions.

9. $\frac{3}{8} \div \frac{2}{3}$ _____

10. $\frac{9}{2} \div \frac{4}{10}$ _____

11. $\frac{3}{14} \div \frac{2}{6}$ _____

12. $\frac{5}{8} \div \frac{1}{24}$ _____

13. $\frac{5}{6} \div \frac{5}{24}$ _____

14. $\frac{3}{4} \div \frac{1}{24}$ _____

15. $12 \div \frac{18}{25}$ _____

16. $20 \div \frac{15}{16}$ _____

17. $16 \div \frac{10}{11}$ _____

Test Prep

18. How many $\frac{1}{2}$ cups are in $\frac{7}{8}$ cup?

_____

19. An expression is shown.

$\frac{2}{10} \div \frac{5}{4}$

What is the value of the expression?

(A) $\frac{1}{50}$ (C) $\frac{8}{50}$

(B) $\frac{4}{10}$ (D) $\frac{1}{2}$

20. A large toy weighs $\frac{5}{8}$ pound. How many small toys that each weigh $\frac{5}{16}$ pound have a combined weight equal to the weight of the large toy?

_____

21. Select all the expressions that have the same value as $\frac{3}{5} \div \frac{6}{8}$.

(A) $\frac{3}{5} \div \frac{8}{6}$

(B) $\frac{3}{5} \times \frac{8}{6}$

(C) $\frac{5}{3} \times \frac{6}{8}$

(D) $\frac{24}{40} \div \frac{30}{40}$

(E) $\frac{24}{40} \times \frac{40}{30}$

Spiral Review

22. On Monday, the temperature was $-5\ °F$. On Tuesday, the temperature was $-8\ °F$. Which temperature has a greater absolute value? Which temperature is colder?

_____

23. What is the product of $2\frac{1}{2}$ and $1\frac{1}{4}$?

_____

24. Order the numbers from least to greatest.

$-\frac{9}{4}$, -2.5, $2\frac{1}{2}$, 0, $-2\frac{1}{3}$

_____

Name _____

Explore Division of Mixed Numbers

 I Can find the quotient of a mixed number or fraction and a mixed number, fraction, or whole number.

Spark Your Learning

PAIRS

Four friends go hiking. They bring snacks, a compass, and $3\frac{1}{3}$ quarts of water. If they share the water equally, how many quarts will each person get?

$\frac{1}{2}$

Turn and Talk How could you use a model to solve this problem? Explain.

Build Understanding

1 Three friends go on a hike that is $4\frac{1}{2}$ miles long. If they take breaks as shown at the right, then how many breaks will they take?

> taking a break every $\frac{3}{4}$ mile

A. Draw a bar model to represent the mixed number $4\frac{1}{2}$. How many equal-sized rectangles did you need? How many of them did you shade?

B. How can you find how many times the hikers must take a break?

C. Use your bar model to find how many breaks the three friends will take. How did you do it?

D. How many groups of $\frac{3}{4}$ are in $4\frac{1}{2}$? Use your model to count.

E. Write an expression to show what operation you would use to represent this situation.

Turn and Talk How could you use another method to solve this problem?

© Houghton Mifflin Harcourt Publishing Company • **Image Credits:** ©Jordan Siemens/Getty Images

Step It Out

2 Jamarion has $4\frac{2}{5}$ pounds of peanuts that he needs to divide evenly into 6 bins. How many pounds of peanuts will be in each bin?

A. What expression could you use to solve the problem?

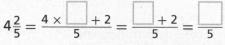

B. Will the quotient be greater than or less than 1? How do you know?

_____

C. Write the mixed number as a fraction greater than 1.

$$4\frac{2}{5} = \frac{4 \times \square + 2}{5} = \frac{\square + 2}{5} = \frac{\square}{5}$$

D. Complete the steps to divide $4\frac{2}{5}$ by 6.

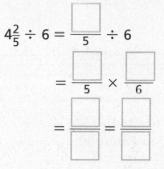

$$4\frac{2}{5} \div 6 = \frac{\square}{5} \div 6$$

$$= \frac{\square}{5} \times \frac{\square}{6}$$

$$= \frac{\square}{\square} = \frac{\square}{\square}$$

E. Complete the sentences to describe how to solve the division problem.

Write the _____ as a fraction greater than 1.

Change the operation to _____ and replace the _____ with its reciprocal.

Multiply. There will be _____ pound of peanuts in each bin.

3 Consider the division problem $2\frac{1}{4} \div \frac{3}{8}$. Complete the steps to show how to divide the mixed number by the fraction.

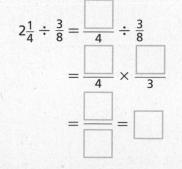

$$2\frac{1}{4} \div \frac{3}{8} = \frac{\square}{4} \div \frac{3}{8}$$

$$= \frac{\square}{4} \times \frac{\square}{3}$$

$$= \frac{\square}{\square} = \square$$

Turn and Talk When will the quotient be greater than the dividend in a division problem?

Module 3 • Lesson 3

79

© Houghton Mifflin Harcourt Publishing Company • Image Credits: ©Houghton Mifflin Harcourt

4 ▶ Phil works at a pet store where fish are sold. He has $5\frac{1}{4}$ liters of water to add to several aquariums. If each aquarium needs $\frac{7}{8}$ liter of water, how many aquariums can he fill?

A. What expression do you need to use to solve the problem?

_____

B. Will the quotient be greater than or less than 1? How do you know?

_____

C. Complete the steps to show how to divide the mixed number by the fraction. Then complete the solution.

$$5\frac{1}{4} \div \frac{7}{8} = \frac{\boxed{}}{\boxed{}} \div \frac{7}{8} = \frac{\boxed{}}{\boxed{}} \times \frac{\boxed{}}{\boxed{}} = \frac{\boxed{}}{\boxed{}} = \boxed{}$$

Phil can fill _____ aquariums with $5\frac{1}{4}$ liters of water.

D. In Part C, you multiplied the fractions and then divided to get the answer. However, you can **simplify** the solution before you multiply. Complete the steps to see how to do this.

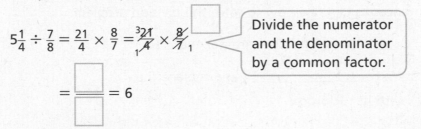

$$5\frac{1}{4} \div \frac{7}{8} = \frac{21}{4} \times \frac{8}{7} = \frac{^3\cancel{21}}{_1\cancel{4}} \times \frac{\cancel{8}^{\boxed{}}}{\cancel{7}_1}$$

Divide the numerator and the denominator by a common factor.

$$= \frac{\boxed{}}{\boxed{}} = 6$$

Check Understanding

1. Dion has a pitcher of lemonade holding $3\frac{1}{2}$ pints, and he wants to make $\frac{1}{2}$-pint servings.

   A. How many groups of $\frac{1}{2}$ are in $3\frac{1}{2}$? _____

   B. Write an expression to show what operation you would use to represent this situation.

   _____

2. Jessica runs $2\frac{1}{2}$ miles in $16\frac{1}{4}$ minutes. What is Jessica's average time per mile in minutes?

   _____

Javier's exercise: cardio and weightlifting

Name _____

On Your Own

3. Javier exercises for $2\frac{1}{2}$ hours every Saturday. His exercise includes two parts. If he spends the same amount of time on both parts, how many hours does he spend weightlifting?

_____

_____

4. (MP) **Reason** A baker would like to store $12\frac{3}{4}$ pounds of flour in containers that each hold $3\frac{1}{2}$ pounds of flour. How many containers will the baker need? Explain.

5. A rectangular garden has an area of $46\frac{1}{2}$ square feet. If the garden is $7\frac{1}{2}$ feet long, how many feet wide is it?

_____

6. Kim is building a fence that is $32\frac{1}{2}$ feet long. She has already put the first post in place. There will be additional posts every $2\frac{1}{2}$ feet. How many additional posts will Kim need?

_____

7. Dana has a piece of lumber that is $22\frac{3}{4}$ feet long. She needs pieces that are $3\frac{1}{4}$ feet long. How many pieces can she cut from the $22\frac{3}{4}$-foot piece of lumber?

_____

For Problems 8–11, divide.

8. $2\frac{5}{6} \div \frac{1}{2}$ _____

9. $5\frac{1}{5} \div 3$ _____

10. $1\frac{1}{5} \div 2\frac{3}{10}$ _____

11. $\frac{3}{4} \div 2\frac{3}{8}$ _____

12. At a zoo, a tiger eats $8\frac{3}{4}$ pounds of a specially-prepared ground beef every day. If the zookeeper buys $87\frac{1}{2}$ pounds of the ground beef, how many days will it last?

_____

13. At her bakery, Sherry has $6\frac{1}{2}$ pounds of cherries to make tarts. If she uses $\frac{1}{4}$ pound of cherries for each tart, how many tarts can she make?

_____

14. (MP) **Critique Reasoning** Dan says that $24\frac{1}{2} \div 12\frac{1}{2} = 2$, because $24 \div 12 = 2$. Sam disagrees and thinks there will be fewer than 2 groups of $12\frac{1}{2}$ in $24\frac{1}{2}$. Who is correct and why? What is $24\frac{1}{2} \div 12\frac{1}{2}$?

15. (MP) **Reason** Mason is laying tiles on an entryway. The tiles are each $\frac{2}{9}$ foot long, and the entryway is $7\frac{1}{2}$ feet long. How many tiles will Mason need to cover the length of the entryway? Explain.

_____

_____

For Problems 16–19, write the equivalent multiplication expression.

16. $2\frac{1}{6} \div \frac{3}{4}$ _____

17. $4\frac{5}{8} \div 2\frac{1}{2}$ _____

18. $3\frac{1}{3} \div \frac{9}{10}$ _____

19. $5\frac{2}{5} \div 1\frac{7}{8}$ _____

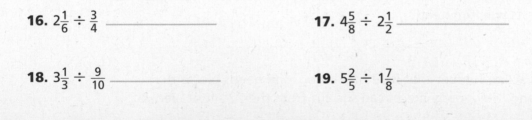

I'm in a Learning Mindset!

What can I apply from my previous work with LCMs and GCFs to better understand division with mixed numbers?

_____

_____

LESSON 3.3
**More Practice/
Homework**

ONLINE
😊Ed Video Tutorials and
Interactive Examples

Explore Division of Mixed Numbers

1. Darlene cuts a $9\frac{1}{2}$-foot-long pipe into pieces that are $2\frac{3}{8}$ feet long. How many pieces of pipe does she have? Explain.

_____

_____

$9\frac{1}{2}$ feet

2. (MP) **Attend to Precision** Jonathan will run a $6\frac{1}{4}$-mile relay with 4 other team members, where each team member runs an equal distance. How many miles will Jonathan run?

_____

_____

3. Every 14 days, Debbie's dog eats $4\frac{1}{5}$ pounds of dog food. If Debbie's dog eats the same amount of food each day, how many pounds does her dog eat per day?

_____

_____

4. **Math on the Spot** One serving of Roberto's favorite yogurt is $6\frac{1}{2}$ ounces. How many servings are in a $16\frac{1}{4}$-ounce container?

_____

_____

5. Brad reads his favorite book for $1\frac{1}{4}$ hours each day. If he has read the book for $22\frac{1}{2}$ hours so far, how many days has he read it? Show how you know.

For Problems 6–11, find the quotient.

6. $\frac{3}{4} \div 1\frac{1}{10}$ _____

7. $5\frac{1}{2} \div 6$ _____

8. $1\frac{2}{15} \div \frac{1}{5}$ _____

9. $2\frac{1}{2} \div 2\frac{5}{8}$ _____

10. $4\frac{2}{3} \div 2\frac{1}{3}$ _____

11. $2\frac{1}{5} \div 3\frac{1}{7}$ _____

Test Prep

12. Harley rides her bicycle the same distance every day for 4 days. The total distance she rides is $8\frac{1}{4}$ miles. How many miles does she ride each day?

_____

13. An equation is shown.

$$1\frac{2}{3} \times \boxed{} = \frac{1}{4}$$

What factor is missing from the equation?

Ⓐ $\frac{3}{20}$

Ⓑ $\frac{5}{12}$

Ⓒ $2\frac{2}{5}$

Ⓓ $6\frac{2}{3}$

14. An expression is shown.

$$1\frac{3}{7} \div 1\frac{1}{3}$$

What is the value of the expression as a mixed number? _____

15. What multiplication expression would you use to find the quotient of

$3\frac{1}{2} \div 2\frac{1}{5}$?

Ⓐ $\frac{2}{7} \times \frac{5}{11}$

Ⓑ $\frac{2}{7} \times \frac{11}{5}$

Ⓒ $\frac{7}{2} \times \frac{5}{11}$

Ⓓ $\frac{7}{2} \times \frac{11}{5}$

Spiral Review

16. Which number is greater, -18 or -16?

_____

17. An expression is shown.

$$\frac{4}{3} \times \frac{4}{5}$$

What is the value of the expression? _____

18. An expression is shown.

$$\frac{4}{5} \div \frac{3}{5}$$

What is the value of the expression? _____

84

Name _____

Practice and Apply Division of Fractions and Mixed Numbers

(**I Can**) divide mixed numbers and fractions to solve problems.

Step It Out

1 Kevin is making hamburgers for a cookout. He bought $10\frac{1}{4}$ pounds of ground meat. How many $\frac{1}{4}$-pound hamburger patties can he make?

A. Complete the division problem that answers this question.

$$10\frac{1}{4} \div \frac{1}{4} = \frac{\boxed{}}{4} \div \frac{1}{4}$$

$$= \frac{\boxed{}}{\overset{1}{\cancel{4}}} \times \frac{\overset{1}{\cancel{4}}}{1}$$

$$= \frac{\boxed{}}{1} = \boxed{}$$

B. He can make _____ $\frac{1}{4}$-pound patties.

2 Kevin's friend Justin is bringing juice to the cookout. If he brings $43\frac{3}{4}$ pints of juice, then how many $2\frac{1}{2}$-pint bottles can be filled?

A. Complete the division problem that answers this question.

$$43\frac{3}{4} \div 2\frac{1}{2} = \frac{\boxed{}}{4} \div \frac{\boxed{}}{2}$$

$$= \frac{\boxed{}}{4} \times \frac{\boxed{}}{\boxed{}} = \frac{\boxed{}}{\boxed{}}$$

$$= \boxed{}\frac{\boxed{}}{\boxed{}} = \boxed{}\frac{\boxed{}}{\boxed{}}$$

B. How many $2\frac{1}{2}$-pint bottles can be filled completely? Explain.

_____

 Turn and Talk If Kevin made $\frac{1}{2}$-pound patties, how many could he make? How does this compare to the number of $\frac{1}{4}$-pound patties? Explain.

© Houghton Mifflin Harcourt Publishing Company • Image Credit: ©avebreakmedia/Shutterstock

Step It Out

© Houghton Mifflin Harcourt Publishing Company • **Image Credit:** ©m-imagephotography/iStock/Getty Images Plus/Getty Images

> 4 miles in $38\frac{1}{2}$ minutes

3 ▶ Cedric finished a 4-mile race. If he ran each mile at the same pace, how many minutes did he average for each mile?

A. Write an expression to represent this situation.

_____

B. Evaluate the division expression using the reciprocal of the divisor. Show your work.

C. How many minutes did Cedric take to run each mile?

_____

 Turn and Talk How could you use a model to find how many minutes Cedric used to run each mile?

Check Understanding

1. Yousef is cutting pieces of construction paper so he can make cards for his family. Each piece of paper is $11\frac{1}{2}$ inches wide. If he cuts that width so he would have two equal-sized smaller pieces, how wide will each smaller piece be?

_____

2. Marisol has $4\frac{1}{2}$ cups of flour. A biscuit recipe she wants to try requires $\frac{3}{4}$ cup of flour for a single batch of biscuits. How many batches of biscuits can Marisol make?

_____

For Problems 3–8, divide the mixed numbers or fractions.

3. $3\frac{1}{8} \div \frac{1}{8}$ _____

4. $6\frac{2}{5} \div 4\frac{1}{10}$ _____

5. $4\frac{1}{2} \div 3\frac{2}{3}$ _____

6. $2\frac{5}{8} \div 1\frac{3}{4}$ _____

7. $5\frac{3}{4} \div \frac{1}{2}$ _____

8. $7\frac{5}{6} \div 2\frac{1}{3}$ _____

On Your Own

9. To paint a bedroom, Jade estimates she will need to buy $3\frac{1}{4}$ gallons of paint. How many $\frac{1}{2}$-gallon cans of paint should she buy? Explain.

10. (MP) **Critique Reasoning** Jefferson shows the following work for a division problem. What mistake did Jefferson make? What is the correct answer to his original division problem?

$$5\frac{2}{5} \div 2\frac{1}{3} = \frac{27}{5} \div \frac{6}{3}$$
$$= \frac{27}{5} \times \frac{3}{6}$$
$$= \frac{81}{30} = 2\frac{21}{30} = 2\frac{7}{10}$$

11. A cube has a surface area of $253\frac{1}{2}$ square inches. What is the area of one face of the cube in square inches? How do you know?

12. Darlene has $6\frac{3}{4}$ gallons of gasoline. Every time she mows a lawn, she uses $\frac{3}{8}$ gallon. How many times can she mow a lawn before she needs more gas?

13. A rectangle has an area of $24\frac{1}{2}$ square feet. If the length of the rectangle is $4\frac{3}{8}$ feet, what is the width in feet?

On Your Own

14. **Open Ended** Write a story problem that is modeled by the expression $10\frac{1}{2} \div 5\frac{1}{2}$. What is the answer to your problem?

_____

_____

_____

15. Jack mails 10 packages that each weigh the same amount. If the combined weight of all 10 packages is $67\frac{1}{2}$ pounds, how much does one package weigh? Show your work.

_____

_____

16. Peter is building a fence. If each section is $4\frac{1}{2}$ feet long, how many sections will there be in the finished fence shown?

_____

_____

←—— finished fence: $38\frac{1}{4}$ feet long ——→

17. Jill has a pail of water that holds $6\frac{1}{2}$ quarts. She needs to give some plants $\frac{1}{8}$ quart each. How many plants can she water?

_____

_____

For Problems 18–23, divide.

18. $1\frac{1}{2} \div \frac{1}{2}$ _____

19. $6\frac{1}{5} \div 2$ _____

20. $3\frac{2}{5} \div \frac{1}{4}$ _____

21. $\frac{6}{5} \div \frac{1}{5}$ _____

22. $1\frac{4}{8} \div \frac{2}{3}$ _____

23. $10\frac{1}{5} \div 3\frac{3}{10}$ _____

LESSON 3.4
**More Practice/
Homework**

ONLINE

Video Tutorials and
Interactive Examples

Practice and Apply Division of Fractions and Mixed Numbers

1. Andy works at a grocery store. The manager of the store would like Andy to set up a display of apples. Part of the display will include bags of apples. Each bag of apples has the same weight as shown. If there are 39 pounds of apples in the back of the store, how many bags of apples can Andy make for the display?

APPLES
$1\frac{1}{2}$-pound bags

_____

_____

2. (MP) **Attend to Precision** Gilbert needs to move $20\frac{3}{4}$ pounds of soil from a truck to a garden. His wheelbarrow can move 6 pounds at one time. How many loads of soil will he have to move? Explain.

_____

_____

_____

3. **Math on the Spot** The area of a rectangular garden is $53\frac{5}{6}$ square feet. The length of the garden is $9\frac{1}{2}$ feet. What is the width?

_____

4. Ramon is making book shelves. He bought a board that is $\frac{4}{5}$ meter long. He needs 5 shelves. If he cuts 5 equal-sized pieces from the board, how long is each piece?

_____

For Problems 5–10, divide.

5. $\frac{5}{4} \div \frac{1}{10}$ _____

6. $1\frac{1}{2} \div 8$ _____

7. $4\frac{1}{10} \div \frac{2}{5}$ _____

8. $5\frac{1}{2} \div 6\frac{1}{3}$ _____

9. $10 \div 3\frac{3}{4}$ _____

10. $9\frac{1}{5} \div \frac{1}{10}$ _____

Test Prep

11. Which two expressions are equivalent to $4\frac{1}{2} \div 2\frac{1}{4}$?

Ⓐ $4\frac{1}{2} \times 2\frac{4}{1}$

Ⓑ $\frac{9}{2} \div \frac{9}{4}$

Ⓒ $\frac{8}{2} \times \frac{8}{4}$

Ⓓ $\frac{9}{2} \times \frac{4}{9}$

Ⓔ $\frac{8}{2} \times \frac{4}{9}$

12. An expression is shown.

$3\frac{1}{8} \div 2\frac{3}{4}$

What is the value of the expression?

_____

13. Tara made $2\frac{3}{4}$ cups of white rice for a dinner party. She has 3 friends coming to the party and will give each person, including herself, the same amount of rice. How many cups of rice will she serve each friend and herself?

Ⓐ $\frac{7}{20}$ cup

Ⓑ $\frac{11}{16}$ cup

Ⓒ $1\frac{7}{20}$ cups

Ⓓ $1\frac{11}{16}$ cups

14. Foster needs to divide a plot of land covering $5\frac{3}{8}$ acres into plots covering $\frac{3}{4}$ acre each. How many whole plots can he make?

_____

15. An alligator is $11\frac{3}{4}$ feet long. Its tail is $5\frac{7}{8}$ feet long. What fraction of the alligator's total length is its tail?

_____

Spiral Review

16. Write the numbers in order from least to greatest: -5, 0, -10, 1, -18.

_____

17. Add the fractions: $\frac{1}{5} + \frac{1}{10}$.

_____

Practice Fraction Operations

(**I Can**) use the LCM and GCF to write fractions with like denominators and solve fraction problems using the four operations.

Step It Out

1 ▶ Tom is running an obstacle course. Monkey bars make up $\frac{1}{4}$ of the course, and hurdles make up $\frac{1}{3}$ of the course. A wall climb and sprint make up the rest. What fraction of the course do the monkey bars and the hurdles make up?

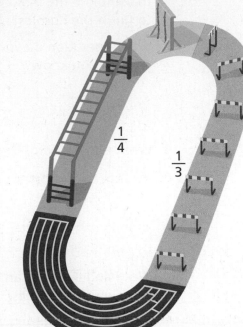

A. What operation do you need to use to solve this problem? How do you know?

_____

_____

B. How is the least common multiple used when adding fractions with unlike denominators?

_____

_____

C. What is the LCM of the two denominators? How do you know?

_____

D. Rewrite $\frac{1}{4}$ using the LCM of 3 and 4.

$$\frac{1}{4} \times \frac{3}{\boxed{}} = \frac{\boxed{}}{12}$$

E. Rewrite $\frac{1}{3}$ using the LCM of 3 and 4.

$$\frac{\boxed{}}{\boxed{}} \times \frac{\boxed{}}{\boxed{}} = \frac{\boxed{}}{\boxed{}}$$

F. Write and evaluate an expression to find the fraction of the course the monkey bars and hurdles make up together.

$$\frac{\boxed{}}{\boxed{}} + \frac{\boxed{}}{\boxed{}} = \frac{\boxed{}}{\boxed{}}$$

Turn and Talk Is there another way to solve this problem? Explain.

2 ➤ Tina takes $2\frac{1}{4}$ fewer seconds to finish the hurdles than to complete the monkey bars. How long does Tina take to finish the hurdles?

$7\frac{1}{2}$ seconds to complete monkey bars

A. What operation do you need to use to solve this problem? How do you know?

_____

_____

B. What is the LCM of the denominators in this problem? _____

C. Rewrite the fractions using the LCM.

D. Write and evaluate an expression to find how long it takes Tina to complete the hurdles.

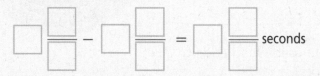 seconds

3 ➤ Davon spent $\frac{2}{15}$ of his savings on a video game. He then spent $6\frac{1}{4}$ times as much on a bike. What fraction of his original savings did he spend on the bike?

A. What operation do you need to use to solve this problem? Explain.

_____

_____

B. To multiply a fraction and a mixed number, convert _____ from a

_____ to a _____.

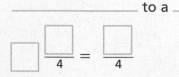

C. Write and evaluate an expression to find the fraction of his savings Davon spent on his bike. Use the GCF to write your answer in **simplest form**.

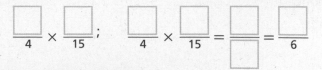

Turn and Talk Explain how you used the GCF to write your answer in Part C of Task 3 in simplest form.

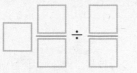 On Saturday, Pedro has $3\frac{1}{2}$ hours to practice on an obstacle course. If it takes him $\frac{1}{4}$ hour to complete the course, how many times can he go through the course in $3\frac{1}{2}$ hours?

A. Write a division expression to represent this situation.

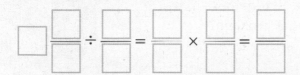

$$\boxed{\ }\ \frac{\boxed{\ }}{\boxed{\ }} \div \frac{\boxed{\ }}{\boxed{\ }}$$

B. Evaluate the division expression using the reciprocal of the divisor. Show your work.

$$\boxed{\ }\ \frac{\boxed{\ }}{\boxed{\ }} \div \frac{\boxed{\ }}{\boxed{\ }} = \frac{\boxed{\ }}{\boxed{\ }} \times \frac{\boxed{\ }}{\boxed{\ }} = \frac{\boxed{\ }}{\boxed{\ }}$$

C. Explain how you can use the GCF to write your answer from Part B in simplest form.

_____

D. How many times can Pedro complete the obstacle course?

_____

Check Understanding

1. At college, Tyrell has science for $5\frac{1}{2}$ hours per week. If his lab work takes up $\frac{2}{5}$ of his science class time, how many hours does Tyrell spend in the lab?

   _____

2. Lena played two piano pieces at a recital. One piece was $5\frac{1}{2}$ minutes long. The other lasted $4\frac{2}{3}$ minutes. How long did Lena play during the recital? What operation did you use to solve the problem?

   _____

3. Sean is making fruit punch. He has $1\frac{5}{8}$ quarts of orange juice and $1\frac{2}{3}$ quarts of pineapple juice.

   A. Write each amount using the LCM. _____

   B. If Sean uses all of the juice he has, how much punch can he make?

   _____

For Problems 4–6, perform the operation shown.

4. $2\frac{2}{5} \div 3\frac{1}{5}$ _____

5. $3\frac{3}{5} \times 2\frac{1}{2}$ _____

6. $3\frac{1}{6} + 2\frac{5}{9}$ _____

On Your Own

7. There are 12 miles of hiking trails in a state park. Each trail is rated for difficulty: $\frac{3}{8}$ of the trails are rated easy, $\frac{1}{6}$ are rated moderate, $\frac{1}{4}$ are rated hard, and $\frac{5}{24}$ are rated difficult. What fraction of the trails are rated easy or moderate?

_____

8. Terri peeled $2\frac{1}{6}$ pounds of potatoes for a stew. How many more pounds of potatoes does she need to peel so she peels $3\frac{3}{4}$ pounds of potatoes all together? What operation could you use to solve this problem?

_____

9. (MP) **Attend to Precision** Agatha drives $73\frac{1}{2}$ miles through two towns in $2\frac{1}{3}$ hours. What is her average speed in miles per hour? Show how you know.

10. Roy, Joseph, and Caitlyn have $3\frac{3}{4}$ pints of chicken soup.

    A. If they each eat the same amount of soup, how many pints will each person eat?

    _____

    B. If they decide to include one more of their friends, how many pints will each person eat?

    _____

For Problems 11–14, perform the given operation on $4\frac{4}{5}$ and $2\frac{1}{2}$.

11. $4\frac{4}{5} - 2\frac{1}{2}$ _____

12. $4\frac{4}{5} \times 2\frac{1}{2}$ _____

13. $4\frac{4}{5} \div 2\frac{1}{2}$ _____

14. $4\frac{4}{5} + 2\frac{1}{2}$ _____

15. A wall is $56\frac{1}{2}$ feet long. The art club will paint different murals that are each $14\frac{1}{8}$ feet long along the wall. How many murals will fit on the wall?

_____

16. (MP) **Attend to Precision** Patty rides her bike $2\frac{3}{4}$ miles to school. She rides $3\frac{5}{6}$ miles to get back home, because she needs to meet her brother at his school first. How many miles does Patty ride her bike? Explain how you know that your answer is reasonable.

17. William runs $6\frac{1}{5}$ miles daily. One day he runs $2\frac{1}{2}$ times as far as that. How many miles does he run that day?

_____

18. Music A note represents the pitch and duration of a musical sound. In a four/four measure, a whole note is equal to two half notes, four quarter notes, or eight eighth notes. In a given measure, a composer wants to divide a half note into sixteenth notes. How many sixteenth notes should be used? Write and evaluate an expression to answer the question.

_____

19. (MP) **Reason** Alex is setting up an inline skating course 21 feet long to practice weaving around cones. He wants a cone every $3\frac{1}{2}$ feet, but not at the start or end of the course. How many cones will he need? Explain your reasoning.

_____

_____

_____

For Problems 20–23, perform the indicated operation.

20. $7\frac{1}{2} - \frac{3}{4}$ _____

21. $2\frac{2}{5} + 2\frac{1}{8}$ _____

22. $\frac{1}{4} \times 1\frac{3}{5}$ _____

23. $4\frac{1}{3} \div 1\frac{2}{3}$ _____

24. Beth participated in a triathlon that consisted of swimming, bicycling, and running. Her finishing time is shown below. If she completed the swimming portion in $1\frac{1}{4}$ hours and the bicycling portion in $6\frac{1}{3}$ hours, how long did it take her to complete the running portion of the triathlon?

_____ $12\frac{2}{3}$ hours to complete triathlon

25. (MP) **Construct Arguments** Raja claims that to add two fractions with unlike denominators, first you need to determine the smallest number that is a multiple of both denominators. Then change the denominators in both fractions and keep the numerators the same. What is incorrect about his claim?

_____

_____

_____

_____

26. A recipe for bread calls for $3\frac{1}{2}$ cups of flour, $\frac{1}{8}$ cup of salt, and $1\frac{1}{4}$ cups of milk. What is the total amount of the three ingredients? Explain the process you used to answer the question and how you used the LCM.

_____

_____

_____

27. A gasoline tank holds $12\frac{1}{2}$ gallons of gasoline. If there are $5\frac{1}{5}$ gallons of gasoline in the tank, how many more gallons can it hold?

_____

For Problems 28–30, perform the indicated operation.

28. $5\frac{1}{3} - \frac{2}{9}$ _____

29. $11\frac{2}{7} + 6\frac{1}{2}$ _____

30. $2\frac{1}{2} \div \frac{3}{4}$ _____

© Houghton Mifflin Harcourt Publishing Company • Image Credits (from left to right): ©Paul Bradbury/Caiaimage/Getty Images; ©SAYAM TRIRATTANAPAIBOON/Shutterstock; ©ygalic/E+/Getty Images

Name _____

Add and Subtract Multi-Digit Decimals

(I Can) add and subtract multi-digit decimals to the thousandths with or without a model.

Step It Out

The 10 × 10 grid represents 1 whole. There are 100 squares, so each square represents 0.01 or $\frac{1}{100}$ of the whole.

1 ▸ Find the sum of 0.13 + 0.58 using a 10 × 10 grid.

   A. How can you represent 0.13 on the grid?

   _____

   B. Shade the grid to represent 0.13.

   C. How can you represent 0.58 on the grid?

   _____

   D. Shade the grid to represent 0.58.

   E. How many total squares are shaded? _____

   So, 0.13 + 0.58 = _____.

Adding decimals is similar to adding whole numbers. You must first write the numbers so that like places are aligned. Then add from right to left and regroup when necessary.

2 ▸ While at a grocery store, Robert bought 0.26 pound of red grapes and 0.34 pound of green grapes. How many total pounds of grapes did Robert buy?

   A. You can use a table to align the places of decimals to make it easier to add. Write 0.34 in the table at the right. Add from right to left, regrouping when necessary.

   B. Did you need to regroup? Explain.

   _____

   _____

	0	.	2	6
+				

   C. Robert bought ☐ pound of grapes.

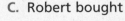 **Turn and Talk** How is adding decimals different from adding whole numbers? Explain.

3 Find the difference of 0.42 − 0.19 using a 10 × 10 grid.

A. How can you represent 0.42 on the grid? How can you represent subtracting 0.19?

_____

_____

B. How many shaded squares remain?

_____

C. So, 0.42 − 0.19 = _____.

4 A cardinal weighs 1.5 ounces. Find the difference in ounces between the weights of a cardinal and a bluebird. The weight of a bluebird is shown.

A. What subtraction problem can you write to represent this situation?

_____

B. Write 1.5 in the table. Add a zero as a placeholder.

C. Write 1.09 in the table. Subtract from right to left, regrouping when necessary.

D. So, the weight of the cardinal is _____ ounce more than the weight of the bluebird.

Bluebird
1.09 ounces

Turn and Talk How can you subtract a decimal from a whole number?

Check Understanding

1. Julia has $1 for a snack. She buys an apple for $0.49. How much does she have left after buying the apple?

_____

2. A group of friends spent $31.95 on movie tickets and $12.54 on refreshments. How much did they spend in all?

_____

On Your Own

3. Chu rides his bike 1.39 miles from his home to baseball practice. On the way home he takes a shorter route than the route he took to baseball practice. How far does he ride his bicycle from baseball practice to home?

_1.21_

The route home is 0.18 mile shorter.

4. Matias is working on a science project in school. He needs 0.33 kilogram of dry ice and 0.55 kilogram of regular ice for his project. How many total kilograms of ice does Matias need for his project?

_0.22_

5. When two decimals are added or subtracted, in what order should you add or subtract the digits in the decimals?

6. Use the table to subtract 378.5 − 26.19.

2	7	8	.	0	5
2	8	.	1	9	0
1	7	8	.	0	9

7. **(MP) Use Structure** Add 2.31 + 0.89 using the 10 × 10 grids.

   A. Shade the grids to model the problem 2.31 + 0.89.

   B. How many total squares are shaded?

   _3.20_

   C. What is the sum?

   _3.00_

For Problems 8–11, find the sum or difference.

8.
$$\begin{array}{r} 0.105 \\ +0.213 \\ \hline 0.318 \end{array}$$

9.
$$\begin{array}{r} 2.651 \\ +1.580 \\ \hline 4.231 \end{array}$$

10.
$$\begin{array}{r} 0.92 \\ -0.56 \\ \hline 0.56 \end{array}$$

11.
$$\begin{array}{r} 0.837 \\ -0.408 \\ \hline 0.429 \end{array}$$

12. **STEM** In the periodic table each element is shown with its atomic mass. The atomic mass of silicon is approximately 28.09. The atomic mass of potassium is approximately 39.10. About how much greater is the atomic mass of potassium than that of silicon?

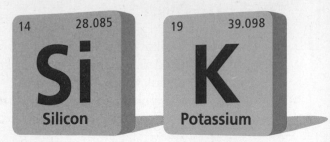

14   28.085

Si

Silicon

19   39.098

K

Potassium

_____

13. **Open Ended** Describe a general method for adding a decimal with two decimal places to a decimal with three decimal places. Give an example.

_____

_____

_____

14. Look at the subtraction problem shown. Explain how to regroup so you can subtract in the hundredths place.

$$\begin{array}{r} 4.05 \\ -2.76 \\ \hline \end{array}$$

_____

_____

_____

_____

15. **MP Critique Reasoning** Look at the addition problem shown. Is the sum correct? Why or why not?

$$\begin{array}{r} 13.805 \\ +12.738 \\ \hline 25.533 \end{array}$$

_____

_____

For Problems 16–19, find the sum or difference.

16. $0.35 + 0.26 =$ _____

17. $1.60 + 1.98 =$ _____

18. $0.88 - 0.49 =$ _____

19. $2.212 - 1.304 =$ _____

Name _Stewart C_

LESSON 4.1
**More Practice/
Homework**

ONLINE
Video Tutorials and
Interactive Examples

Add and Subtract Multi-Digit Decimals

1. Deangelo babysits for his neighbor. Over a two-week period, he babysat 3.8 hours the first week and 5.25 hours the second week. How many total hours did Deangelo babysit over the two weeks?

   _9.05_

2. Babe Ruth, a professional baseball player known for hitting home runs, had a batting average of 0.342. Hank Aaron, another record home run hitter, had a batting average of 0.305. How much greater was Babe Ruth's batting average than Hank Aaron's?

   _0.647_

3. **STEM** The pH level of a substance is a measure of how acidic or alkaline it is. The pH of lemonade is 2.6, while orange juice has a pH of 4.09. What is the difference in the pH levels of orange juice and lemonade?

   _2.09_

4. A recipe for blintzes, a very thin type of pancake, calls for 0.06 liter of melted butter and 0.236 liter of milk. What is the total amount of butter and milk needed for the recipe?

   _.296_

5. **Math on the Spot** Jared ran two sprints in track practice. His time for the first sprint was 4.64 seconds. His time for the second sprint was 4.3 seconds. What was Jared's total time for the two sprints?

   8.94 seconds.

For Problems 6–11, find the sum or difference.

6.   4.105
   +3.685
   ‾‾‾‾‾‾
     7.790

7.   0.089
   −0.075
   ‾‾‾‾‾‾
     0.014

8.   12.15
   +6.832
   ‾‾‾‾‾‾
    18.982

9. 1.25 + 2.39
   _3.64_

10. 4.08 − 3.975
    _1.910_

11. 0.91 − 0.487
    _0.570_

Test Prep

For Problems 12–13, use the following information.

Several teams, each consisting of 4 athletes, ran a relay race. The top two teams won ribbons. Team Rocket finished in 3.48 minutes and Team Jaguar finished in 3.471 minutes.

12. How much faster was Team Jaguar's finish compared to Team Rocket's finish?

 minute

13. Team Tortoise took twice as long to finish the race as Team Jaguar. How long did it take Team Tortoise to finish the race?

 minutes

14. In 2018, the state sales tax in Maine was 5.5%, or 0.055. The state sales tax in Florida was 6%, or 0.06. How much greater was the sales tax in Florida than in Maine?

_____

15. The Nürburgring in Germany is a racetrack that hosts racing events all year. Two of the fastest laps ever driven on the track are 6 minutes 47.30 seconds and 6 minutes 52.01 seconds. How much faster is the 6 minutes 47.30 seconds time than the 6 minutes 52.01 seconds time?

_____

16. A hectare is a measure of area. There are 2.471 acres in 1 hectare. What is the area of 3 hectares?

Ⓐ 0.529 acre   Ⓑ 5.471 acres   Ⓒ 4.942 acres   Ⓓ 7.413 acres

Spiral Review

17. What is the quotient of $\frac{1}{5} \div \frac{2}{3}$?

_____

18. A garden bed has 4 sections of vegetables. The garden is $8\frac{1}{2}$ yards long. If each section is equal in length, what is the length of each section?

_____

19. The elevation of a coral reef is 12 feet below sea level. The elevation of a snorkeler is 2 feet below sea level. Write an inequality to compare the elevations using integers.

_____

Name _____

Multiply Multi-Digit Decimals

(I Can) multiply multi-digit decimals, up to thousandths.

Step It Out

One way to multiply decimals is by using a decimal grid. The grid represents 1 whole, where each square unit is 0.01.

1 ▶ Find the product of 0.5 × 0.4.

A. To represent 0.5, I can shade ☐ columns, which is ☐ squares.

B. To represent 0.4, I can shade ☐ rows, which is ☐ squares.

C. Shade the grid to represent 0.5 and 0.4. How many squares have been shaded twice?

_____

D. The double-shaded squares represent the decimal ☐ .

So, 0.5 × 0.4 = ☐ .

Another way to multiply decimals is to use an area model.

$3.50 PER POUND

2 ▶ Cara buys 11.2 pounds of pork chops for $3.50 per pound.

A. How can you find the total cost of the pork chops?

_____

B. An area model shows partial products using place values. Complete the area model by multiplying to find the partial products. List the partial products.

_____

C. What is the sum of the partial products?

_____

_____

D. How much does Cara pay for the pork chops?

_____

_____

	1	1	2
3	3 × 10 = 30	3 × 1 = 3	3 × 0.2 = ☐
5	0.5 × 10 = ☐	0.5 × 1 = 0.5	0.5 × 0.2 = ☐

Turn and Talk What do the labels given on the area model represent?

3 Jared mows the grass every weekend in the summer. The amount of gas he uses per hour is shown. How much gas does he use in 5.8 hours?

A. Write an expression to represent this situation.

_____

B. Find an estimate of this product by rounding each factor to the nearest whole number and then multiplying. _____

1.2 liters of gasoline each hour

C. Another way to multiply decimals is to multiply as you would with whole numbers. Then count the number of decimal places after the decimal point in the factors. What is the product 58×12? How many decimal places are in the factors 5.8 and 1.2?

_____

_____

D. The product must have the same number of decimal places as the total number of decimal places in the factors. How many decimals places should there be in the product 5.8×1.2? _____

E. What is the product of 5.8×1.2? Explain how you knew where to place the decimal point.

_____

_____

_____

F. Check your answer for reasonableness.

My estimate of _____ is close to the product _____, so my answer is reasonable.

> **Turn and Talk** How close should an estimate be to the product of two decimals for the answer to be reasonable? Explain your reasoning.

Check Understanding

1. Last summer Rachel worked 38.5 hours per week at a grocery store. She earned $9.70 per hour. How much did she earn in a week? Complete the area model to help find the answer.

_____

	3	8	5
9	$9 \times 30 =$	$9 \times 8 =$	$9 \times 0.5 =$
7	$0.7 \times 30 =$	$0.7 \times 8 =$	$0.7 \times 0.5 =$
0	$0 \times 30 =$	$0 \times 8 =$	$0 \times 0.5 =$

2. Find the product of 2.3×0.6.

_____

Name _____

On Your Own

> Denise runs 1 mile in 8.5 minutes.

3. Denise runs a 10-kilometer race (6.2 miles). Her time per mile is shown. What is her total time for the race? Explain.

   _____

   _____

4. (MP) **Critique Reasoning** Antwon says that he can multiply 14 and 12 to find the product of 0.14 × 0.12. Is Antwon correct? Explain your reasoning.

   _____

   _____

   _____

5. (MP) **Attend to Precision** A city park is 0.85 mile long and 0.7 mile wide. The city wants to put in new plants and grass that need less watering.

   A. Write an expression that can be used to find the area of the park. Then find the area of the park in square miles.

   .595 _____

   B. The city calculates that only $\frac{6}{10}$ of the park will need plants and grass. What decimal can be used to calculate the area of the park that will have plants and grass?

   _____

   C. What is the total area of the park in square miles that will have plants and grass? Explain how you found your answer.

   _____

For Problems 6–7, use the grid to find the product.

6. 0.2 × 0.7 = __.14__

7. 0.4 × 0.8 = __.32__

For Problems 8–9, find the product.

8. 10.05 × 5.6 = __56.280__

9. 7.9 × 5.1 = __40.29__

Module 4 • Lesson 2

© Houghton Mifflin Harcourt Publishing Company • Image Credit: ©Michael Turner/Alamy

111

10. Nita will bake 3.2 batches of muffins for the school bake sale. Each batch uses 1.75 cups of whole-wheat flour. How much whole-wheat flour does Nita need to make the muffins?

    A. Estimate the product by rounding each factor to the nearest whole number and multiplying.

    _____

    B. What is the actual product of 3.2 × 1.75?

    _____

    C. Using your estimate, is your answer reasonable? Explain.

    _____

11. (MP) **Reason** How does estimating help you know whether you have placed the decimal point correctly in a product?

_____

_____

_____

12. Colin needs 14.5 yards of fabric to cover a sofa. The fabric he likes costs $7.95 per yard. Write an expression that represents the cost of the fabric. Then simplify the expression to find the cost. Round to the nearest hundredth.

_____

13. Open Ended Describe a general method to multiply two numbers written in tenths. Show an example.

_____

_____

_____

_____

14. Use the area model to find the product 7.34 × 2.6.

	7	3	4
2	2 × 7 = 14	2 × 0.3 = ☐	2 × 0.04 = ☐
6	0.6 × 7 = ☐	0.6 × 0.3 = ☐	0.6 × 0.04 = 0.024

The product is _____.

For problems 15–17, find the product.

15. 23.2 × 4.1 = _____   **16.** 0.05 × 0.07 = _____   **17.** 7.89 × 8.7 = _____

© Houghton Mifflin Harcourt Publishing Company • Image Credits: (l) ©D. Hurst/Alamy Images; (r) ©Thomas M Perkins/Shutterstock

Name _____

Divide Multi-Digit Whole Numbers

(I Can) divide multi-digit whole numbers by multi-digit numbers with or without remainders.

Step It Out

1 ▶ Mr. Soto buys a new phone for $432 on a payment plan. He pays $18 each month. How many months will it take him to pay for his phone?

A. Write an expression that could be used to find the number of months Mr. Soto will pay for the phone.

$$432 \div 18 =$$

B. Estimate the quotient. Explain how you found your estimate.

20

C. Complete the division problem shown to find the number of months Mr. Soto will be paying for his new phone.

D. How many months will Mr. Soto be paying for his new phone?

~~$20 000$~~ 24 months

E. How can you use your estimate to check if your answer is reasonable?

_____

$$\begin{array}{r} 2\,4 \\ 18\overline{)432} \\ -36\downarrow \\ \hline 7\,2 \\ -7\,2 \\ \hline 0 \end{array}$$

2 ▶ An experimental airplane is flying at an altitude of 8,000 feet when it begins descending to land. If the plane descends at a constant rate of 125 feet per minute, how long will it take to land the plane?

A. Estimate the quotient. Explain how you found your estimate.

_____

B. How do you decide where to place the first number in the quotient?

_____

_____

$$\begin{array}{r} \square \\ 125\overline{)8000} \\ -\square\downarrow \\ \hline 500 \\ -\square \\ \hline 0 \end{array}$$

C. How long will it take the plane to land? How can you use your estimate to check if your answer is reasonable?

_____

_____

 Turn and Talk Why is it important to estimate before finding the exact answer?

3 An art class is making mosaics with glass squares. Each of the 121 students will get the same number of glass squares to use. The total number of glass squares for the students to use is shown. How many glass squares will each student get?

1,240 glass squares

A. Write an expression that can be used to find the number of glass squares each student will receive.

_____

B. Complete the given division problem to find the number of squares each student will receive.

C. How many whole glass squares will each student receive?

_____

D. A remainder is the amount left over when an amount cannot be divided equally. What does the remainder mean in this context?

_____

_____

$$121\overline{)1240}$$

30

R ☐

 Turn and Talk What is another way you could find the total number of squares each student would get?

Check Understanding

1. It took the Pioneer 11 spacecraft 2,372 days to reach Saturn.

    A. How many whole years did it take Pioneer 11 to reach Saturn?
    Note: 1 year = 365 days.

    _____

    B. Is there a remainder? Explain what it means.

    _____

    _____

    _____

2. A college student has $4,032 he earned from working during the summer. If he earned $288 per week, how many weeks did he work? Complete the division problem to find the quotient.

    _____

$$288\overline{)4032}$$

1152

LESSON 4.3
**More Practice/
Homework**

ONLINE
😊Ed

Video Tutorials and
Interactive Examples

Divide Multi-Digit Whole Numbers

1. At a paper mill, paper is placed into reams, or stacks of
500 sheets. A robot separates big stacks of sheets into reams.
How many reams can the robot make with 9,500 sheets of paper?

_____

2. **STEM** Osmium is the densest chemical element. A cubic centimeter of
osmium has a mass of about 23 grams. If a chemist has 2,530 grams of
osmium, about how many cubic centimeters does the chemist have?

_____

3. The Burj Khalifa building in Dubai, United Arab Emirates, is one of
the tallest buildings in the world at 2,717 feet tall. An American
football field is 360 feet in length. Approximately how many football
fields tall is the Buri Khalifa building? Round to the nearest tenth.

_____

4. (MP) **Construct Arguments** The longest road in the United States
is U.S. Route 20, measuring 3,365 miles long from coast to coast. A
transport truck driver drives about 520 miles per day. How many days
would it take the driver to drive from one end of U.S. Route 20 to
the other end? Explain.

_____

_____

_____

2,717 ft

The Burj Khalifa is
one of the tallest
buildings in the
world.

5. **Math on the Spot** A total of 1,043 players signed up for a citywide
soccer league. Each team in the league can have up to 18 members.
How many teams will be needed?

_____

6. (MP) **Attend to Precision** There are 365 days in a year and 24 hours
in a day. An airport video camera records for 18 hours and then
automatically resets itself to start recording again.

A. How many times does the video camera reset itself in a year?

_____

B. If the camera is started at the beginning of a year, how many hours
will it record in the following year before resetting again?

For Problems 7–10, find the whole-number quotient and remainder, if there is one.

7. 3,760 ÷ 145   8. 500 ÷ 25   9. 646 ÷ 38   10. 9,311 ÷ 400

_____   _____   _____   _____

Test Prep

11. A cattle ranch has 1,400 acres of grazing land. The ranch has 140 cows. How many acres of grazing land does the ranch have per cow?

_____

12. A new amusement-park ride that lasts 1 minute can have up to 1,200 riders per hour of operation. How many riders can ride per minute?

_____

13. A small concert venue earned $6,804 in ticket sales. All tickets were the same price. If the venue sold 252 tickets, how much did each ticket cost?

_____

14. What is the whole-number quotient and remainder?

7,810 ÷ 215

Ⓐ 36 R33   Ⓑ 36 R70   Ⓒ 36 R79   Ⓓ 36 R170

15. Which is a reasonable estimate for 89,877 ÷ 31?

Ⓐ 30   Ⓑ 300   Ⓒ 3,000   Ⓓ 30,000

Spiral Review

16. Bea withdraws $25 from her bank account. What integer represents the withdrawal?

_____

17. Which two points on the number line represent a number and its absolute value?

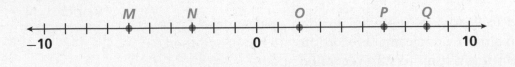

_____

18. Naruto practices his harmonica $\frac{1}{4}$ hour, spends $\frac{2}{3}$ hour working on homework, and takes another $\frac{1}{2}$ hour to do chores every day. How much longer does Naruto spend practicing his harmonica and doing his chores than working on homework?

_____

Name _____

Divide Multi-Digit Decimals

(I Can) divide a multi-digit decimal by a decimal to the hundredths place.

Step It Out

1 ▶ Six toy blocks of the same length are lined up next to each other. What is the length of one toy block?

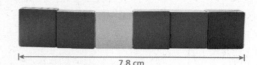

|←——————————— 7.8 cm ———————————→|

   A. What division problem models this situation?

   _____

   B. Divide to find the length of one toy block. _____

2 ▶ Mr. Leon drives his car 443.75 miles and uses 12.5 gallons of gasoline. How many miles does Mr. Leon get per gallon?

   A. Write a division problem to model this situation.

   _____

   B. In a previous grade, you wrote a fraction and then an **equivalent fraction** with a whole-number denominator to solve a division problem. Write a fraction and an equivalent fraction with a whole-number denominator to represent this situation.

   _____

   C. You can do the same process as Part B by multiplying both the divisor and the dividend by the same power of ten. What power of 10 do you need to multiply by to make the divisor a whole number? Why is it helpful to make the divisor a whole number?

   _____

   _____

   _____

$$125\overline{)4437.5}$$

   D. How do you show this change in long division?

   $443.75 \times 10 = 4437.5$ $12.5\overline{)443.75} \rightarrow 125\overline{)4437.5}$
   $12.5 \times 10 = 125$

   E. Complete the given division problem to find the quotient.

   F. How many miles does Mr. Leon get per gallon?

Turn and Talk Is it possible to make both the divisor and the dividend a whole number when finding Mr. Leon's gas mileage? Explain.

3 A teacher drove a rental car 276.3 miles and used a total of 10.230 gallons of gas. Two students, Kierra and Shawna, both calculate how many miles the car got per gallon. Whose solution is correct? Explain the error(s) in the incorrect solution. How could you check the result?

Kierra's Solution	Shawna's Solution
2.7008 1023)2763.0000 2046 7170 −7161 90 − 0 9000 −8184 816	27.008 1023) 27630.000 −2046 7170 −7161 90 − 0 900 − 0 9000 −8184 816
about 2.70 miles to the gallon	about 27.01 miles to the gallon

_____

_____

_____

_____

_____

 Turn and Talk Why are both the dividend and divisor multiplied by the same number? Explain.

Check Understanding

1. A taxi driver fills the gas tank and calculates that the car traveled 356.25 miles using 9.5 gallons of gas. How many miles per gallon did the car get?

_____

2. Gr███████ full of Lincoln pennies. She knows that a Lincoln penny has a ███████ ams. The total mass of the pennies in her bag is 1,320 gram███ many pennies does Greta have?

_____

On Your Own

3. Members of a soccer team who participated in a fundraiser sold a total of $109.80 in tickets. Each player sold $12.20 worth of tickets. How many members of the soccer team participated in the fundraiser?

_____

4. Christy is painting pinwheels to sell at a fair. It takes her 1.5 hours to paint each pinwheel. How many pinwheels will she be able to paint in 13.5 hours?

_____

5. (MP) **Attend to Precision** A large box is to be filled with smaller boxes. The bottom of the large box is a square whose sides measure 18.3 inches. The smaller boxes also have a square bottom. The sides of the smaller boxes are 6.1 inches long. How many of the smaller boxes will completely fill the bottom of the larger box? Explain.

_____

_____

6. (MP) **Critique Reasoning** Sean and Kyle have the amount of ribbon shown. They need lengths of 0.6 meter to make bows. Sean says that they can make 2 bows since 12.6 ÷ 0.6 = 2.1. Kyle says they can make 21 bows since 12.6 ÷ 0.6 = 21. Who is right?

A. What were Sean and Kyle trying to figure out?

_____

_____

12.6 meters

B. Who made a mistake, Sean or Kyle? Explain the error.

_____

_____

C. How can you check Sean and Kyle's answers without doing the division yourself?

_____

For Problems 7–12, find the quotient.

7. 92.8 ÷ 16

8. 0.56 ÷ 0.025

9. 40.32 ÷ 4.8

10. 24.186 ÷ 6

11. 198.86 ÷ 6.1

12. 5.44 ÷ 3.4

13. A rectangle has the area shown. If the length of the rectangle is 6.7 meters, what is the width in meters?

$A = 59.63\ m^2$

_____

14. A class of 25 students collects $175.75 for a charity. Each student collects the same amount. How much money is collected by each student?

_____

15. A bus travels 358.5 miles in 6.2 hours at a constant speed. What is the bus's speed in miles per hour to the nearest tenth?

_____

16. Roberto cycled 66.5 miles in 3.5 hours. If he cycled at a constant speed, how far did he cycle in 1 hour?

_____

17. Financial Literacy Jamilla paid $8.40 for sliced turkey. The amount she bought is shown. How much did Jamila pay per pound for the sliced turkey?

_____

18. Eight friends purchase groceries for a camping trip and agree to share the total cost equally. They spend $345.20 at the grocery store. How much should each friend pay?

_____

19. Pedro's family drove 495.88 miles. Pedro calculated that the car traveled 32.2 miles per gallon of gas. How many gallons of gas did the car use? Show your work.

_____

For Problems 20–23, find the quotient.

20. 5.44 ÷ 3.4

21. 0.14 ÷ 0.025

22. 40.32 ÷ 4.8

23. 198.86 ÷ 6.1

© Houghton Mifflin Harcourt Publishing Company • Image Credits: top, ©Steve Debenport/E+/Getty Images; middle, ©O. Bellini/Shutterstock; bottom, ©PeopleImages/iStock/Getty Images Plus/Getty Image

Name _____

Divide Multi-Digit Decimals

1. Fiona can assemble a bookcase in 0.8 hour. She works for 4 hours. How many bookcases can she assemble in this time?

_____

2. **STEM** 1 kg ≈ 2.2 lb. About how many kilograms are there in 34.76 pounds?

_____

3. (MP) **Reason** Stanley can purchase a 15.4-ounce bottle of olive oil for $5.39 or a 23.6-ounce bottle of olive oil for $7.08. Which bottle is the better buy? Explain.

_____

_____

_____

$7.08

$5.39

4. (MP) **Use Structure** Susan divided 38.08 by 23.80.

A. Write an expression with a whole-number divisor to solve the problem. Will both the divisor and the dividend be whole numbers? Why or why not?

_____

_____

_____

B. Find the quotient. $38.08 \div 23.80 =$ _____

5. Donna is a pacer in a marathon. She finishes 26.2 miles in 3 hours 45 minutes (3.75 hours) while running at a constant speed. What is Donna's speed in miles per hour to the nearest whole number?

_____

6. **Math on the Spot** Sadie spent $12.46 to download songs that were on sale for $0.89 each. How many songs did she download?

_____

For Problems 7–10, find the quotient.

7. $3.78 \div 12.6$

8. $5.535 \div 1.23$

9. $322.56 \div 25.6$

10. $270.72 \div 6$

Test Prep

11. Tabitha collects quarters from different states. The value of her collection is $17.75. How many quarters does she have in her collection?

_____

12. Roast beef at a deli sells for $6.40 per pound. A package of the roast beef costs $16.64. How many pounds of roast beef are in the package?

_____

13. A grass fertilizer is sold in 5-pound bags. Stuart calculates that he needs enough fertilizer to cover 4,350 square feet. If each pound of fertilizer covers 362.5 square feet, how many 5-pound bags does Stuart need to buy?

_____

14. The perimeter of a square is 23.28 inches. What is the length of each side of the square?

(A) 5.28 inches   (C) 5.82 inches

(B) 5.43 inches   (D) 6.04 inches

15. Which expressions have a value of 21.06? Select all that apply.

(A) $63.18 \div 3$ (D) $6318 \div 0.3$

(B) $6.318 \div 3.0$ (E) $631.8 \div 0.03$

(C) $6.318 \div 0.3$ (F) $631.8 \div 30$

Spiral Review

16. A rectangular driveway is 23.5 feet long and 9.25 feet wide. What is the area of the driveway in square feet?

_____

17. A stationery store ships 5,712 pounds of paper in boxes that each hold 24 pounds of paper. How many boxes are needed?

_____

18. Write the following numbers in order from least to greatest:

$-5.6, 7.95, 2.06, 0, -6.89$

_____

19. Shameka buys a blue garden hose that is 16.5 feet long and a green garden hose that is 14.75 feet long. How many feet of garden hose does she buy?

_____

Name _____

Apply Operations with Multi-Digit Decimals

(I Can) determine which operation is needed and use all four operations to solve problems with multi-digit decimals.

Step It Out

1▶ Harold bought 3.5 pounds of red apples that cost $1.79 per pound. How much did Harold spend on the red apples?

A. Estimate the product by rounding each number to the nearest whole number and multiplying.

_____   ×   _____   =   _____

pounds of red apples   cost per pound   total cost of apples
(estimated)   (estimated)   (estimated)

B. _____ to find out exactly how much Harold spent. Round your answer to the nearest cent.

_____   ×   _____   =   _____

pounds of red apples   cost per pound   total cost of apples

C. Since the estimate _____ is close to the exact product of _____, the answer is reasonable.

D. So, Harold spent _____ on the red apples.

2▶ Tavon hikes 6.1 miles in 2.5 hours. Tavon says that he can find out how fast he hiked by subtracting 6.1 − 2.5.

A. Explain Tavon's error. _____

_____

B. Write an expression Tavon could use to find out how fast he hiked.

_____

C. Tavon hiked _____ miles per hour.

 Turn and Talk How can you determine the correct operation to use when solving a word problem?

© Houghton Mifflin Harcourt Publishing Company • Image Credit: ©Lı.k Lau/EyeEm/Getty Images

3 A "mole" is a standard unit used in chemistry for measuring large quantities of very small objects, such as atoms. One mole of hydrogen atoms has a mass of 1.0079 grams. One mole of oxygen atoms has a mass of 15.9994 grams. A mole of hydroxide is made up of 1 mole of hydrogen and 1 mole of oxygen. What is the mass of a mole of hydroxide?

A. Use _____ to find the mass of a mole of hydroxide atoms.

B. Add the mass of 1 mole of oxygen atoms and 1 mole of hydrogen atoms.

_____ + _____ = _____
  mass of 1 mole of   mass of 1 mole of   mass of 1 mole of
   hydrogen atom   oxygen atom   hydroxide

C. So, the mass of a mole of hydroxide atoms is _____ grams.

> **Turn and Talk** Can you check your answer? Explain.

Check Understanding

1. The area of a rectangle is 69.75 square inches. The rectangle has a length of 9.3 inches. What is the width of the rectangle?

_____

2. Three friends are going camping. They buy a pound of raisins costing $2.93 and a half of a pound of nuts costing $3.75.

A. What operation should you use to find the total cost of the raisins and nuts?

_____

B. What is the total cost of the nuts and raisins?

_____

3. The price of a gallon of gasoline is shown. How much does it cost to fill an empty 12.5-gallon gas tank?

A. Write an expression you could use to find the cost.

_____

$2.389
PER GALLON

B. Calculate the cost of filling the gas tank. Round your answer to the nearest cent.

_____

On Your Own

4. A sprinkler sprays 0.7 gallon of water per minute. If it takes 45 minutes to water a lawn, how many gallons of water does the sprinkler spray?

   _____

5. Petra buys a pair of jeans for $28.39 and a T-shirt that costs $6.40. How much does Petra spend?

   _____

6. A tailor spends $63.75 to buy 7.5 yards of satin. What is the cost of the satin fabric per yard?

   _____

7. **(MP) Critique Reasoning** Gael harvested 3 bags of potatoes that weigh 25.5 pounds, 32.25 pounds, and 27 pounds. He says that he harvested a total of 350.7 pounds. Explain and correct Gael's error.

   _____

   _____

   Gael's work:

   25.5
   32.25
   + 27
   ─────
   350.7

8. Cassie volunteers at an animal shelter. She needs a total of 40 hours of volunteer time for a class. So far, she has volunteered for 18.5 hours. How many more hours does she need to volunteer?

   _____

9. An adult African elephant eats about 0.25 ton of food per day. If the zoo orders 2.3 tons of food for the elephant, how many full days will the food last?

   _____

African elephants

10. A collector purchased a rare book for $97.56 and then sold the book in an online auction for $141.82. The auction charged the collector $8.25 in fees for the use of its service. How much did the collector earn by selling the book?

    _____

11. A carpenter installing cabinets uses thin pieces of material called shims to fill gaps. The carpenter uses four shims to fill a gap that is 1.5 centimeters wide. The widths of three of the shims are 0.75 centimeter, 0.125 centimeter, and 0.1 centimeter. What is the width of the fourth shim?

    _____

12. How much fence is needed to surround a garden with side lengths of 2.1 meters, 3.5 meters, 1.9 meters, and 2.25 meters?

_____

13. Simone Manuel, an American competitive swimmer, won a gold medal in the women's 100-meter freestyle event at the 2016 Rio Olympics. Her winning time was 52.70 seconds. Assuming she swam at a constant speed, how long did it take her to swim one meter?

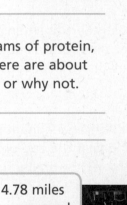

_____

14. When a puppy was adopted, it weighed 4.5 pounds. Now it weighs 12.25 pounds. How much weight did the puppy gain?

_____

15. A recipe for chicken soup calls for 3 boxes of chicken broth measuring 15.8 ounces each. How many ounces of broth are used in the recipe?

_____

16. (MP) **Critique Reasoning** A box of cereal contains 98.7 grams of protein, and 1 serving contains 7.05 grams of protein. Kevin says there are about 1.4 servings in the box of cereal. Is he correct? Explain why or why not.

_____

_____

17. The speed at which the Hubble Telescope orbited Earth is given. How far did the telescope travel in 3 seconds?

4.78 miles per second

_____

18. Selma has to hike 11 miles to reach the top of Electric Peak in Yellowstone Park. After hiking 2.4 miles, she takes a break. How much farther does she have to hike?

_____

For Problems 19–24, add, subtract, multiply, or divide.

19. 10.26 + 7.55 = _____

20. 1.2 − 0.51 = _____

21. 5.5 × 1.3 = _____

22. 158.18 ÷ 5.5 = _____

23. 23.26 − 17.1 = _____

24. 231.65 + 0.45 = _____

Ratio and Rate Reasoning

Music Producer

Music producers play key roles in all aspects of music recording. They may help choose songs for an album, coach singers and other musicians, manage recording sessions, and more. Music producers often work for record companies and may help to find new musical acts and sign them to contracts. One purpose of a contract is to specify the amount of money a musician receives when songs are streamed or downloaded.

STEM Task:

Thomas Edison invented the phonograph with records shaped like cylinders in 1877. Soon after, Emile Berliner introduced the gramophone and the disc-shaped phonograph record. Early records were designed to spin 78 times per minute. Later records spun either 45 or $33\frac{1}{3}$ times per minute. For each of these three speeds, find the number of full revolutions a record completes in 3 minutes. Explain your reasoning.

Learning Mindset
Challenge-Seeking Defines Own Challenges

Finding the appropriate level of challenge can be tricky. On the one hand, a task that is familiar and easy can lead to boredom and carelessness. On the other hand, a task that is too difficult may cause you to feel frustrated and discouraged. Here are some suggestions for keeping an appropriate level of challenge in your work. Can you think of others?

- If you are bored or uninterested, try to determine why. Is it because the task is too easy or too difficult?

- If a task is too difficult, can you break it down into easier pieces that are more manageable?

- If a task is too easy, can you find a new and creative way to complete it? How many ways can you find to finish the task? Can you find ways to extend or expand upon the task?

Reflect

Q How do you know whether a task is an appropriate challenge for you? Did the STEM Task have the right level of challenge?

Q How could you modify the STEM Task to make it more challenging? Less challenging?

Ratios and Rates

USE *PAINT* PATTERNS

The cafeteria at Frost Middle School is being painted sky blue. The table shows the amounts of bright blue paint that must be mixed with different amounts of white paint to make sky-blue paint.

Use number patterns to complete the table and answer the questions.

Mixing Sky-Blue Paint					
Bright blue paint (gallons)	2	4	6	8	10
White paint (gallons)	3	6	9	12	15

The painting crew needs 40 gallons of sky-blue paint for the cafeteria. What amounts of bright blue paint and white paint should they mix?

_____ gallons of bright blue paint and _____ gallons of white paint

Turn and Talk

- Describe the patterns you used to complete the table.

- How did you use patterns in the table to find the amounts of bright blue paint and white paint needed for the cafeteria?

Are You Ready?

Complete these problems to review prior concepts and skills you will need for this module.

Multiply or Divide to Find Equivalent Fractions

Multiply or divide to find the equivalent fraction.

1. $\frac{5}{8} = \frac{20}{32}$

2. $\frac{45}{55} = \frac{9}{11}$

3. $\frac{4}{7} = \frac{16}{28}$

Find two equivalent fractions, one by multiplying and one by dividing.

4. $\frac{12}{16}$

5. $\frac{8}{10}$

6. $\frac{9}{15}$

_____   _____   _____

Analyze Patterns and Relationships

Complete each pattern.

7. 10, 15, 20, _____, _____, _____, _____, _____

8. 17, 22, 27, _____, _____, _____, _____, _____

9. How are the patterns related?

_____

_____

_____

_____

_____

Division Involving Decimals

Find the quotient.

10. $11.6 \div 4$ _____

11. $48 \div 0.6$ _____

12. $1.18 \div 0.2$ _____

13. $4.96 \div 1.6$ _____

14. $5.4 \div 3.6$ _____

15. $7.67 \div 1.3$ _____

A ratio can be written in several different ways.

5 to 4   5:4 $\frac{5}{4}$

A ratio can compare a part to a part, a part to the whole, or the whole to a part. The quantities in a ratio are sometimes called *terms*.

Connect to Vocabulary

A **ratio** is a comparison of two quantities by division, $a:b$; $\frac{a}{b}$; or a to b, where b is not equal to 0 ($b \neq 0$).

  Aaron is making a quilt for a craft fair. The quilt is made with four different fabric colors as shown in the picture.

A. Complete the tape diagram to model the ratio of the number of blue squares to the number of white squares in the quilt.

B. Complete the statements to describe the ratio of blue squares to white squares in Part A.

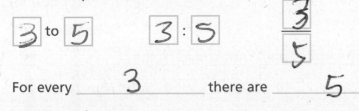

For every _____ 3 _____ there are _____ 5 _____.

C. Write a part-to-whole or whole-to-part comparison about the quilt using symbols and using ratio language, such as "for each," "for every," or "per."

3to15   3:15 $\frac{3}{15}$

D. For every small green square, there are 2 large green squares. Does this mean that 1 out of every 2 green squares is small? Why or why not?

Check Understanding

1. Describe in ratio language and with symbols the relationship between the number of tails and the number of legs on a dog.

2. A recipe that makes 8 cups of limeade uses 2 cups of lime juice. Describe the related ratio 2:8 using ratio language. Does the ratio involve only parts, or does it involve a part and the whole?

On Your Own

In Problems 3 and 4, a bag of trail mix contains 3 ounces of peanuts, 6 ounces of cranberries, 2 ounces of almonds, and 2 ounces of raisins. Write each ratio three different ways.

3. What is the ratio of ounces of peanuts to ounces of almonds?

   3 to 2   3:2 $\frac{3}{2}$

4. What is the ratio of ounces of cranberries to ounces of trail mix?

   6 to 13   6:13 $\frac{6}{13}$

In Problems 5 and 6, a carpenter is buying materials. The carpenter needs 36 screws that are 1.5 inches long, 24 screws that are 2 inches long, and 12 screws that are 2.5 inches long. Write each ratio in three different ways.

5. What is the ratio of 1.5-inch screws to 2.5-inch screws?

   36:12 $\frac{36}{12}$ 36 to 12

2.5"

2"

1.5"

6. What is the ratio of the total length of the 2-inch screws to the total length of all the screws?

_____

7. (MP) Critique Reasoning Alfred mixes 1 part cleanser with 3 parts water to make a cleaning solution. Alfred says that the ratio of cleaning solution to cleanser is 3:1. Is he correct? Why or why not.

_____

_____

_____

8. Open Ended Write a statement using ratio language that could describe the whole ratio of 7:10.

_____

_____

I'm in a Learning Mindset!

How does my mindset affect my confidence with depicting ratios using a tape diagram?

_____

_____

Name _____

Represent Ratios and Rates with Tables and Graphs

(I Can) use a table or graph to find equivalent ratios and use the ratios to solve problems.

Spark Your Learning SMALL GROUPS

Cameron cleans her kitchen with an eco-friendly cleaning solution. She uses 4 tablespoons of baking soda for every 1 quart of warm water. She made a table to help her mix different amounts of the cleaning solution, but the table has faded over time and some of the values are illegible. A copy of the table is shown. Complete the table and describe the strategies you used to fill in the missing quantities.

Water (qt)	Baking soda (Tbsp)
1	4
	8
4	

Turn and Talk What is another method you could use to complete the table.

Build Understanding

1 Hank has a recipe that calls for the ingredients shown per batch. The table shows the amount of sour cream and milk he will need if he doubles the recipe.

1 cup sour cream and 4 cups milk per recipe

A. Describe a pattern you see in the amount of sour cream and the amount of milk when the recipe is doubled.

_____

_____

B. Complete the table for 3 and 4 times the original batch size of the recipe. What did you do to find the answer?

_____

_____

Sour cream (cups)	Milk (cups)
1	4
2	8

C. Write a ratio of cups of sour cream to cups of milk for each batch size of the recipe in the table.

1 Batch　　　**2 Batches**　　　**3 Batches**　　　**4 Batches**

☐　　　☐　　　☐　　　☐
☐　　　☐　　　☐　　　☐

D. Are the ratios you wrote in Part C equivalent ratios? How do you know?

_____

_____

_____

Connect to Vocabulary

Equivalent ratios are ratios that name the same comparison.

E. Complete the statements.

You can _____ both terms of a ratio by the same _____ to find an equivalent ratio. So, equivalent ratios have a

| multiplicative / additive | relationship.

F. Describe a consistent pattern between the number of cups of sour cream and the number of cups of milk. How can you use this pattern to help you find the amount of milk needed for 8 batches?

_____

_____

_____

146

2 ▷ Kim takes dance classes. The dance studio offers classes in blocks.

Number of classes in a block	5	8	10
Cost ($)	90	120	140

A. Kim pays $90 for every block of 5 dance classes. What rate can you write to represent this block of classes?

_____

B. Complete the diagram to find the unit rate for classes in the 5-class block. What is the cost per class?

_____

$$\frac{\$90}{5\ classes} = \frac{\$\ \square}{1\ class}$$

$\div \square$

$\div \square$

C. Explain in words what you did to find the cost per class in Part B.

_____

_____

D. Complete the diagram to find the unit rate for classes in the 8-class block. What is the cost per class?

_____

$$\frac{\$120}{8\ classes} = \frac{\$\ \square}{1\ class}$$

$\div \square$

$\div \square$

E. Draw your own diagram to find the cost per class in the 10-class block. What is the cost per class?

F. Compare the unit rates you found for the blocks of classes.

_____

_____

_____

_____

_____

Turn and Talk Describe the difference between a ratio and a rate. Is a ratio always a rate? Is a rate always a ratio? Explain.

Step It Out

3 Tovah earns money pet sitting for friends and neighbors. She earns the same amount per hour.

A. Complete the table to show how much Tovah earns for different numbers of hours.

Time pet sitting (h)	Money earned ($)
2	40
4	80
6	120

B. Graph the data from the table.

C. What do you notice about the **points** on the graph?

_____

D. Use the graph to predict the unit rate, or amount that Tovah earns per hour. How can you use the table to check your prediction?

20

_____

_____

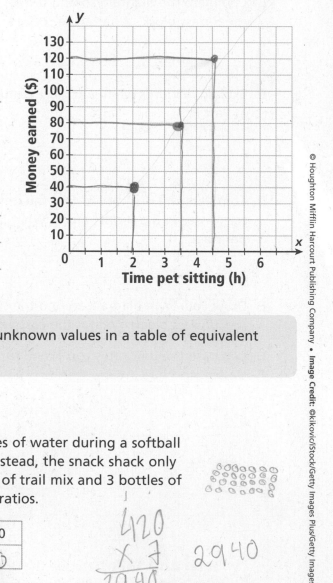

Turn and Talk How can you find unknown values in a table of equivalent ratios?

Check Understanding

1. A snack shack sells trail mix packs and bottles of water during a softball game. The items are not sold individually. Instead, the snack shack only sells a "Snack Special" that contains 2 packs of trail mix and 3 bottles of water. Complete the table using equivalent ratios.

Trail mix packs	2	4	6	20
Bottles of water	3	6	18	30

420
× 7   2940
2940

2. A train travels at a constant speed for 420 miles. If it takes the train 7 hours to travel that distance, what is the unit rate at which the train travels?

2940

_____

© Houghton Mifflin Harcourt Publishing Company • **Image Credit:** ©kikovic/iStock/Getty Images Plus/Getty Images

On Your Own

3. Open Ended A grocery store charges $6 for every 2 boxes of a certain cereal. Complete the table of equivalent ratios.

Boxes	2			
Cost ($)				

4. A hotel advertises vacation packages on its website, and it charges the same amount per night. The table shows the total costs of stays for different numbers of nights.

Length of stay (nights)	Total cost ($)
2	210
3	315
4	420

A. What is the unit rate per night? _____

B. What is the total cost for 5 nights? _____

5. The table shows the number of beads a jeweler used to make bracelets. Each bracelet used the same number of beads.

A. Complete the table. Then graph the data.

Bracelets	2		4
Beads	32	48	

Beads Used for Bracelets

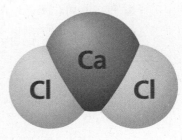

B. Write a ratio to show the number of beads necessary to make one bracelet.

_____

C. How many beads would the jeweler need to make 10 bracelets?

_____

6. STEM Calcium chloride is a salt used in the production of cheese. It consists of calcium (Ca) and chlorine (Cl) atoms. A single calcium chloride molecule is shown in the illustration. Complete the table of equivalent ratios relating the number of calcium atoms to chlorine atoms in 1, 2, 3, 4, and 5 molecules of calcium chloride.

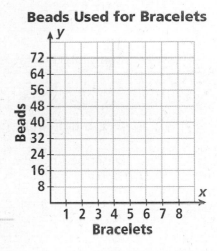

Calcium atoms	1	2	3	4	5
Chlorine atoms					

7. Each week, Sachi has 3 soccer practices that each last 45 minutes. Write the unit rate in minutes per practice. Then find the total time she practices soccer each week.

_____

8. (MP) **Critique Reasoning** Mark bought 2 pounds of apples as shown in the figure. He says that the unit cost is $\frac{2}{3.50} \approx \$0.57$ per pound. Find and correct his error.

2 pounds for $3.50

_____

_____

_____

_____

9. The table shows the number of times a washing machine spins each second when operating at its top speed.

Time (s)	3	6	
Spins	60		180

A. Complete the table. Then find the unit rate.

_____

B. Graph the data from the table.

C. Describe how the graph shows patterns in the table.

_____

_____

_____

_____

_____

For Problems 10–13, find the unit rate.

10. 16 steps for every 2 floors

_____

11. 36 grams for every 4 servings

_____

12. $12 for every 4 containers

_____

13. $960 for 12 months

_____

I'm in a Learning Mindset!

What can I do to increase my understanding of representing ratios?

_____

Name Stephanie paola Hernandez villa

Compare Ratios and Rates

(I Can) compare ratios and rates using a table or a double number line. ·

Step It Out

1 Amari makes orange juice from cans of frozen concentrate and water. The amounts are shown in the picture.

A. Amari wants to make 4 pitchers of orange juice. Complete the table to find how many cups of water and cups of frozen concentrate she will need.

4 ┼ 32
3 ┼ 24
2 ┼ 16
1 ┼ 8
cups ┼ oz

Orange Juice 2 cups Frozen Concentrate

Pitchers	Frozen concentrate (cups)	Water (cups)
1	2	3
2	4	6
3	6	9
4	8	12
5	10	15

B. Amari's friend Gabriela also makes orange juice from the same frozen concentrate. Using the table, write a rate to represent Gabriela's recipe.

4 cups of concentrate

6 cups of water

Pitchers	Frozen concentrate (cups)	Water (cups)
1	3	4
2	6	8
3	9	12
4	12	16
5	15	20

C. Whose orange juice has a weaker flavor, Amari's or Gabriela's?

Step 1 Find a ratio in Gabriela's table that has the same first quantity as a ratio in Amari's table.

Amari: In row _____ , she uses ☐ cups of concentrate.

Gabriela: In row _____ , she uses ☐ cups of concentrate.

Step 2 Compare the number of cups of water used in each ratio.

Amari uses _____ cups of water while Gabriela uses _____ cups of water. _____ uses more water than _____ . So, _____ orange juice will have a weaker flavor.

🗨 **Turn and Talk** Is there another way you could have compared the recipes for orange juice? Explain.

2 Mrs. Morales teaches computer programming. Each
student writes an average of 9 lines of code per hour.

A. Complete the double number line to find how many
lines of code a student could write in a given number
of hours.

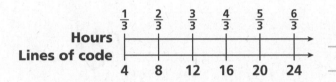

Hours: 1 2 3 4 5 6 7
Lines of code: 9 18 27 36 45 54 63

B. Ms. Sanchez also teaches computer programming. Each of her student
is able to write an average of 4 lines of code every 20 minutes. Write
rate using the quantity 1 hour. Then describe what it means.

Hours: $\frac{1}{3}$ $\frac{2}{3}$ $\frac{3}{3}$ $\frac{4}{3}$ $\frac{5}{3}$ $\frac{6}{3}$
Lines of code: 4 8 12 16 20 24

C. Two ratios can be compared if both have the same amount of one of
the two quantities being compared. Which class writes code faster?
Explain.

$\frac{1}{12}$ is greater then $\frac{1}{9}$

Check Understanding

1. Compare the ratios in the tables. Are they equivalent? Explain.

Sam's Trail Mix	
Cups of peanuts	Cups of raisins
5	3
10	6
15	9

Liam's Trail Mix	
Cups of peanuts	Cups of raisins
3	2
6	4
9	6

Teh is bigger then 9

2. Ms. Markus also teaches computer
programming. Each of her students is
able to write an average of 5 lines of
code every 30 minutes. Which class,
Ms. Markus' class or Ms. Sanchez's class,
writes code faster? Explain.

Hours: $\frac{1}{2}$ $\frac{2}{2}$
Lines of code: 5 10

Name Stephanie paola Hernandez villa

Compare Ratios and Rates

(I Can) compare ratios and rates using a table or a double number line. •

Step It Out

1 ▶ Amari makes orange juice from cans of frozen concentrate and water. The amounts are shown in the picture.

A. Amari wants to make 4 pitchers of orange juice. Complete the table to find how many cups of water and cups of frozen concentrate she will need.

Pitchers	Frozen concentrate (cups)	Water (cups)
1	2	3
2	4	6
3	6	9
4	8	12
5	10	15

B. Amari's friend Gabriela also makes orange juice from the same frozen concentrate. Using the table, write a rate to represent Gabriela's recipe.

4 cups of concentrate
6 cups of water

Pitchers	Frozen concentrate (cups)	Water (cups)
1	3	4
2	6	8
3	9	12
4	12	16
5	15	20

C. Whose orange juice has a weaker flavor, Amari's or Gabriela's?

Step 1 Find a ratio in Gabriela's table that has the same first quantity as a ratio in Amari's table.

Amari: In row _____, she uses ☐ cups of concentrate.

Gabriela: In row _____, she uses ☐ cups of concentrate.

Step 2 Compare the number of cups of water used in each ratio.

Amari uses _____ cups of water while Gabriela uses _____ cups of water. _____ uses more water than _____. So, _____ orange juice will have a weaker flavor.

 Turn and Talk Is there another way you could have compared the recipes for orange juice? Explain.

2 ▶ Mrs. Morales teaches computer programming. Each student writes an average of 9 lines of code per hour.

A. Complete the double number line to find how many lines of code a student could write in a given number of hours.

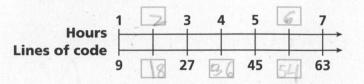

Hours: 1 2 3 4 5 6 7
Lines of code: 9 18 27 36 45 54 63

9 lines of code per hour

B. Ms. Sanchez also teaches computer programming. Each of her students is able to write an average of 4 lines of code every 20 minutes. Write a rate using the quantity 1 hour. Then describe what it means.

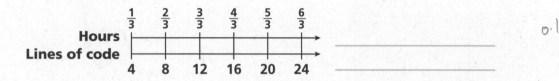

Hours: $\frac{1}{3}$ $\frac{2}{3}$ $\frac{3}{3}$ $\frac{4}{3}$ $\frac{5}{3}$ $\frac{6}{3}$
Lines of code: 4 8 12 16 20 24

o.l

C. Two ratios can be compared if both have the same amount of one of the two quantities being compared. Which class writes code faster? Explain.

$\frac{1}{2}$ is greater then $\frac{1}{9}$

Check Understanding

1. Compare the ratios in the tables. Are they equivalent? Explain.

Sam's Trail Mix	
Cups of peanuts	Cups of raisins
5	3
10	6
15	9

Liam's Trail Mix	
Cups of peanuts	Cups of raisins
3	2
6	4
9	6

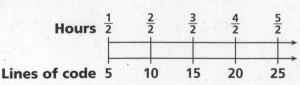

Teh is bigger then 9

2. Ms. Markus also teaches computer programming. Each of her students is able to write an average of 5 lines of code every 30 minutes. Which class, Ms. Markus' class or Ms. Sanchez's class, writes code faster? Explain.

Hours: $\frac{1}{2}$ $\frac{2}{2}$ $\frac{3}{2}$ $\frac{4}{2}$ $\frac{5}{2}$
Lines of code: 5 10 15 20 25

Find and Apply Unit Rates

(**I Can**) find and use unit rates to solve problems.

Step It Out

1 Jack is at the supermarket. He finds a 5-pound bag of flour and a 2-pound bag of flour priced as shown. Which of the two bags of flour is the better buy?

COST **$2.69**

COST **$1.89**

All Purpose Flour

A. Write a rate to represent the cost per pound of the 5-pound bag of flour.

$ ⎡ 5 ⎤
_____
⎡   ⎤ pounds

B. Find the unit cost of the 5-pound bag of flour in dollars per pound. Round your answer to the nearest cent.

$ ⎡   ⎤ ÷ ⎡   ⎤ $ ⎡   ⎤
_____ = _____ = $ ⎡   ⎤ per pound
⎡   ⎤ ÷ ⎡   ⎤   1

C. Find the unit cost of the 2-pound bag of flour in dollars per pound. Round your answer to the nearest cent.

$ ⎡   ⎤ ÷ ⎡   ⎤ $ ⎡   ⎤
_____ = _____ = $ ⎡   ⎤ per pound
⎡   ⎤ ÷ ⎡   ⎤   1

D. Which of the two bags of flour offers the better value? Explain.

_____

_____

_____

Turn and Talk Why is it helpful to use unit rates to compare prices? Explain.

2 ▶ It takes Kendra 27 minutes to run 3 miles.

A. Write a unit rate to represent Kendra's running rate in minutes per mile.

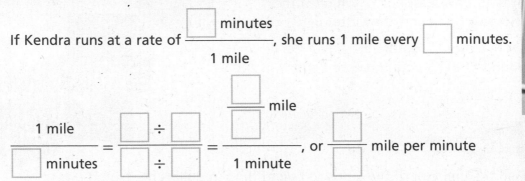

$$\frac{\boxed{27}\ \text{minutes}}{\boxed{3}\ \text{miles}} = \frac{\boxed{3} \div \boxed{}}{\boxed{3} \div \boxed{}} = \frac{\boxed{9}\ \text{minutes}}{1\ \text{mile}}$$

B. Write Kendra's rate as a unit rate in miles per minute.

If Kendra runs at a rate of $\dfrac{\boxed{}\ \text{minutes}}{1\ \text{mile}}$, she runs 1 mile every $\boxed{}$ minutes.

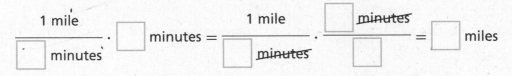

$$\frac{1\ \text{mile}}{\boxed{}\ \text{minutes}} = \frac{\boxed{} \div \boxed{}}{\boxed{} \div \boxed{}} = \frac{\dfrac{\boxed{}}{\boxed{}}\ \text{mile}}{1\ \text{minute}},\ \text{or}\ \frac{\boxed{}}{\boxed{}}\ \text{mile per minute}$$

C. How many miles can Kendra run in 45 minutes?

$$\frac{1\ \text{mile}}{\boxed{}\ \text{minutes}} \cdot \boxed{}\ \text{minutes} = \frac{1\ \text{mile}}{\boxed{}\ \text{minutes}} \cdot \frac{\boxed{}\ \text{minutes}}{\boxed{}} = \boxed{}\ \text{miles}$$

D. How many minutes would it take Kendra to run 7 miles?

$$\frac{\boxed{}\ \text{minutes}}{\boxed{}\ \text{mile}} \cdot \boxed{}\ \text{miles} = \frac{\boxed{}\ \text{minutes}}{\boxed{}\ \text{mile}} \cdot \frac{\boxed{}\ \text{miles}}{\boxed{}} = \boxed{}\ \text{minutes}$$

E. Compare the rates 9 minutes for 1 mile and 63 minutes for 7 miles. Are these rates equivalent? Why or why not?

_____

_____

_____

 Turn and Talk Explain how you can find an equivalent rate given a unit rate. Give an example.

Name Stephanie paola Hernandez Villa

3 ⮞ A potter takes a total of 7.5 hours to mold 12 clay pitchers.

A. Write the rate of the number of pitchers to the number of hours. Is it a unit rate? Explain.

$$\frac{\boxed{12} \text{ pitchers}}{\boxed{7.5} \text{ hours}};\ \underline{\quad 1.6 \text{ of a pitcher} \quad}$$

12 pitchers in 7.5 hours

B. Find the unit rate.

$$\frac{\boxed{} \text{ pitchers} \div \boxed{}}{\boxed{} \text{ hours} \div \boxed{}} = \frac{\boxed{} \text{ pitchers}}{1 \text{ hour}}$$

C. How many pitchers can the potter mold in 70 hours?

$$\frac{\boxed{} \text{ pitchers} \times \boxed{}}{1 \text{ hour} \times \boxed{}} = \frac{\boxed{} \text{ pitchers}}{70 \text{ hours}}$$

D. How can you find how many hours it would take the potter to mold 60 pitchers?

First I need to find $\boxed{60} \div 1.6$, or $\boxed{}$, and then I can use equivalent ratios.

$$\frac{\boxed{} \text{ pitchers} \cdot \boxed{}}{1 \text{ hour} \cdot \boxed{}} = \frac{60 \text{ pitchers}}{\boxed{} \text{ hours}}$$

Check Understanding

1. A recipe for 12 servings of soup calls for 8 cups of chicken broth. How many cups of broth are needed to make 30 servings of the soup?

_____

2. A store sells two different-sized packages of AA batteries. Which package is the better buy? Explain.

Number in package	36	24
Cost in dollars	$19.19	$16.98

_____

_____

_____

On Your Own

3. **STEM** A Rube Goldberg machine consists of a series of devices that perform a simple task. Kate is drawing a scale model of her Rube Goldberg machine, which she plans to build and enter into a contest. A bicycle wheel on the scale model is 2 inches in diameter, while in the actual machine, it will be 28 inches in diameter.

   A. Based on the measures of the wheel diameter, what is the unit rate of inches of machine per inch of the model?

   _____

   B. What would be the actual length of a rope that is 7.25 inches long in the model?

   _____

4. Chen bought a 20-foot chain for $36.50.

   A. What is the unit rate of price per foot? Round the unit rate to the nearest cent.

   _____

   B. At this rate, what would be the price of a 30-foot chain?

   _____

5. **(MP) Reason** A pool is being drained by a pump at a rate of 4 gallons per minute. An identical pump is added to help drain the pool. How does the second pump affect the rate of drainage? Explain.

   _____

   _____

   _____

6. Melanie and her cousin Grace are arguing about who is the faster swimmer. The distance each can swim in a certain number of minutes is shown in the photo.

   A. How fast does Melanie swim?

   _____

   B. How fast does Grace swim?

   _____

   C. Who is the faster swimmer?

   _____

Grace: 325 m in 5.5 min
Melanie: 300 m in 5 min

LESSON 5.4
**More Practice/
Homework**

ONLINE

Video Tutorials and
Interactive Examples

Find and Apply Unit Rates

1. Captain's Lawn Service can mow 8 lawns in 5 hours. At this rate, how long does it take for the service to mow 12 lawns?

   _____

2. **STEM** Density is measured in units of mass per unit of volume. It can be thought of as a unit rate. The mass of a block of aluminum is 9.45 grams. The volume is 3.5 cubic centimeters (cm³). What is the density of the aluminum?

   _____

3. **Math on the Spot** A 3-pack of light bulbs costs $3.45. A 4-pack of the same light bulbs costs $4.20. Which pack is the better value?

   _____

4. It takes Tyreke 28 minutes to bike to his school, which is 7 miles away. If Tyreke continues to pedal at this pace, how long would it take for him to get to the soccer field, which is 8.8 miles away from the school?

   28 minutes to
   bike 7 miles

   _____

5. (MP) **Attend to Precision** Maria and Franco are draining water troughs on their farms. Maria's trough drained 60 gallons of water in 75 minutes. Franco's trough drained 75 gallons of water in an hour and a half. Explain whose trough drained faster.

   _____

   _____

   _____

For Problems 6–9, A) find each unit rate and B) use it to find an equivalent rate.

6. 3 feet in 4 minutes

   A. _____   B. _____ per 16 minutes

7. 473 heartbeats in $5\frac{1}{2}$ minutes

   A. _____   B. _____ per 3 minutes

8. $12.00 for 48 cans

   A. _____   B. _____ per 12 cans

9. $28.00 for 400 square feet

   A. _____   B. _____ per 1,500 sq ft

Test Prep

For Problems 10–11, use the following information.

A store sells two packages of the same brand of water bottles.

Package	48-pack of 8-ounce bottles	28-pack of 10-ounce bottles
Cost ($)	5.88	5.98

10. Which package has the better unit price per bottle?

   _____

11. Which package has the better unit price per ounce?

   _____

12. Deanna will cook a turkey for about 15 minutes per pound of turkey. If she bought an 11-pound turkey, how long should she cook it?

   _____

13. Orlo uses a spool of wire to make 15 necklaces. At this rate, how many spools of the same size would he use to make 50 necklaces?

   _____

14. Preston is buying 1-gallon cans of paint to paint a room. The information on the paint can says that a gallon of paint can cover 400 square feet. The room's walls are 688 square feet combined. How many 1-gallon cans of paint does he need to buy to put 2 coats of paint on the walls?

   (A) 4 cans   (B) 3 cans   (C) 2 cans   (D) 1 can

Spiral Review

15. Juan bought 7.8 pounds of seedless red grapes for $2.85 per pound. How much did Juan spend on seedless red grapes?

   _____

16. Mrs. Kelly bought a bag of flour that holds $16\frac{2}{3}$ cups of flour. Each loaf of banana bread uses $\frac{2}{3}$ cup of flour. How many loaves of banana bread can she make?

   _____

17. The elevation at the top of a mountain is +150 feet. A reef's elevation is −75 feet. Is the top of the mountain or the reef closer to sea level?

   _____

Name

Solve Ratio and Rate Problems Using Proportional Reasoning

(I Can) find and use equivalent ratios using a table, model, or double number line to solve a real-world problem.

Step It Out

1 Lemons are sold in bags of 6 lemons for $4. If you bought 24 lemons, how much would you spend?

LEMONS
6 for $4

A. Write a ratio of 6 lemons to the cost of 6 lemons in dollars.

_____

B. What is the unknown value you are looking for?

_____

C. One way to find the unknown number is to use a table. Complete the table using equivalent ratios.

D. Look at the results in the table. What do you notice about the number of bags of lemons, the number of lemons, and the cost?

_____

_____

_____

Bags of Lemons	Number of Lemons	Cost ($)
1	6	4
2	12	
		12
	24	

E. Another way to find the unknown number is to find a factor that generates the equivalent ratio. When both quantities are multiplied by the same number, the result is an equivalent ratio. Find the unknown number using this method.

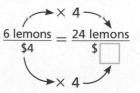

$$\frac{6 \text{ lemons}}{\$4} = \frac{24 \text{ lemons}}{\$\square}$$

$\times 4$

$\times 4$

F. What is the cost of 24 lemons?

_____

Turn and Talk How could you use the relationship between 6 lemons and $4 to find the relationship between 24 lemons and the cost for 24 lemons?

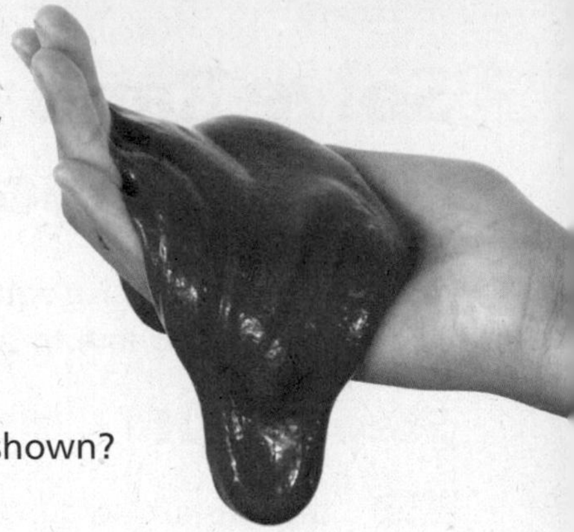

2 Jarrah wants to make a batch of slime. The diagram shows the ratio of hot water to cold water needed to make the slime. He wants to use 18 parts of water in total. How many parts of cold water does he need to make the slime?

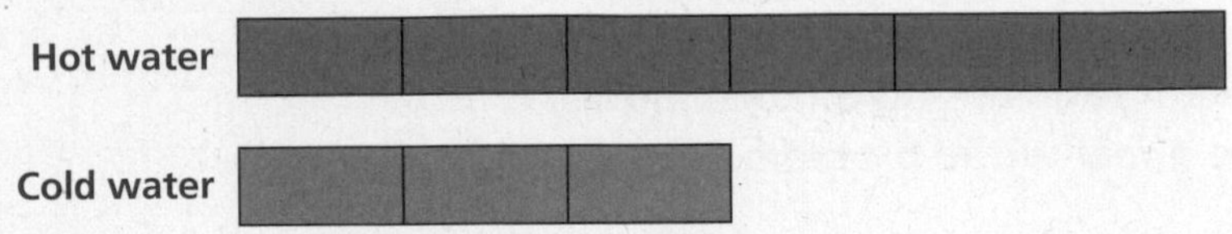

Hot water ▢▢▢▢▢▢

Cold water ▢▢▢

A. Look at the tape diagram. What is the total parts of water shown?

_____

B. Write the ratio of total parts of water to parts of cold water.

▢ total parts of water
▢ parts of cold water

C. What is the relationship between the quantities in the ratio in Part B?

_____

D. How can you use the relationship between the quantities in Part B to find the parts of cold water needed for a total of 18 parts of water?

_____

_____

E. How many parts of cold water will Jarrah need if he has a total of 18 parts of water?

_____

F. If Jarrah wanted to make a larger batch of slime using 36 total parts of water, how many parts of cold water would he need?

_____

G. How many parts of hot water will Jarrah need if he uses a total of 18 parts of water?

_____

H. How many parts of hot water will Jarrah need if he uses 36 total parts of water?

_____

Turn and Talk How can you use the tape diagram to check your answers? Explain.

3 A race car driver completes 5 laps of a race in 3 minutes and 30 seconds. Then the driver continues driving at this rate. How many laps will the driver complete in 17.5 minutes?

A. What is the ratio of laps to minutes? Explain.

_____

_____

B. You can use a double number line to find the unknown quantity. Complete the double number line diagram. Explain how you found the missing numbers of laps and minutes.

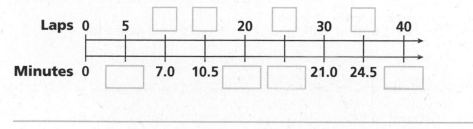

_____

_____

C. Another way to find the unknown quantity is to find a factor that generates the equivalent ratio. What number multiplied by 3.5 minutes will result in 17.5 minutes? _____

Multiply both quantities of the first ratio by this factor to find the quantities of the second, equivalent ratio.

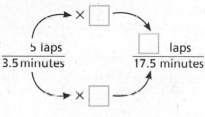

D. How many laps will the race car driver complete in 17.5 minutes? _____

Check Understanding

1. A garden center is running a special on houseplants. A selection of any 2 plants costs $7. If a designer buys 22 plants for new homes, how much does the designer spend on plants?

_____

2. A scale model of the Eiffel Tower uses the scale shown. The Eiffel Tower is 324 meters tall to the tip. What is the height of the model?

_____

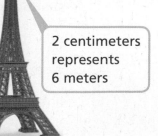

2 centimeters represents 6 meters

3. A hybrid car can drive 53 miles in the city on 1 gallon of gas. How many gallons of gas will it use to drive a total of 371 city miles?

_____

On Your Own

4. The table shows the numbers of water bottles and juice boxes sold at two school events.

Item sold	Event 1	Event 2
Water bottles	24	36
Juice boxes	54	108

   A. What is the ratio of water bottles sold to juice boxes sold at Event 1?

   _____

   B. What is the ratio of water bottles sold to juice boxes sold at Event 2?

   _____

   C. Are the ratios of water bottles sold to juice boxes sold equivalent for each event?

   _____

   _____

5. Elsa builds her own triangular frames for paintings. She has one frame with a length of 60 centimeters and a height of 45 centimeters. She builds a second frame with an equivalent ratio of length to height. If the length of her second frame is 100 centimeters, what is its height?

   _____

6. A court reporter can type 215 words per minute. How many minutes will it take the reporter to type a document that is 1,505 words long?

   _____

7. The ratio of dahlias to sunflowers is the same in all of the flower arrangements at a banquet.

8 dahlias   6 sunflowers

   A. (MP) **Use Structure** Complete the double number line to show the ratios of dahlias to sunflowers in all the flower arrangements at the banquet.

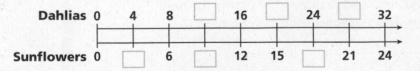

   Dahlias 0   4   8   ☐   16   ☐   24   ☐   32

   Sunflowers 0   ☐   6   ☐   12   15   ☐   21   24

   B. How many dahlias will there be when there are 33 sunflowers? _____

   C. What is the ratio of dahlias to all flowers when there are 21 total

   flowers? _____

   D. What is the ratio of sunflowers to all flowers in a bouquet with

   70 total flowers? _____

8. Nadine shops at three different grocery stores. She uses the ads to determine where to buy certain items. The table shows the cost of a brand of laundry detergent at each store.

48 ounces
$5.76

Store	Detergent size	Cost
Fresh Grocers	48 ounces	$5.76
Jim's Corner Store	26 ounces	$3.38
City Market	54 ounces	$5.94

A. What is the cost per ounce of detergent at each grocery store?

Fresh Grocers: _____

Jim's Corner Store: _____

City Market: _____

B. Where should Nadine shop to get the lowest price per ounce?

_____

9. The tape diagram shows the ratio of hamburgers to veggie burgers served at a family reunion.

Hamburgers

Veggie burgers

A. What is the ratio of veggie burgers served to hamburgers served?

_____

B. If 30 veggie burgers were served, how many hamburgers were served?

_____

10. (MP) **Reason** A sheet of 28 stickers has star and heart stickers. There are 16 heart stickers.

A. How many heart stickers does a pack of 140 stickers have? Write equivalent ratios to show your reasoning.

_____

B. How many star stickers does a pack of 140 stickers have? Write equivalent ratios to show your reasoning.

_____

C. What is another way you could have found the number of star stickers in a pack of 140 stickers?

_____

11. Kyle recorded the results of his basketball free throw practice for three different sessions in the table shown. Any attempt not missed is a free throw he made.

Misses	3	6	9
Attempts	10	20	30

   A. Are the ratios of misses to attempts in the table equivalent ratios? Explain how you know.

   _____

   _____

   _____

   B. If the ratio remains the same, how many free throws would Kyle make if he misses 15 free throws in his next practice session?

   _____

12. Geography On a small island, 63 people live on 21 acres of land.

   A. If the ratio of people to acres is about the same on each acre, how many people would you expect to live on 1 acre of land?

   _____

   B. If another 42 people move to the island and the ratio of people to acres is equivalent to the original ratio, how many acres will the 105 people live on?

   _____

13. The length-to-width ratios of three rectangles are equivalent. One of the rectangles has a width of 2.5 centimeters and a length of 15 centimeters.

   A. The second rectangle has a length of 9 centimeters. What is its width?

   _____

   B. The third rectangle has a width of 6 centimeters. What is its length?

   _____

   C. (MP) **Reason** Write the length and width of two more rectangles whose length-to-width ratios are equivalent to that of the three rectangles. Explain how you found the length and width of each of your rectangles.

   _____

   _____

   _____

   _____

Name

Use Ratio Reasoning With Circle Graphs

(I Can) use reasoning about equivalent ratios to make and interpret a circle graph.

Spark Your Learning

In a music competition, the ratio of guitarists to all musicians is 5:8. There are 64 musicians in the competition. Of the guitarists, 32 play jazz solos and the rest play classical solos. How could you represent the portion of all musicians who play jazz guitar solos and the portion who play classical guitar solos both numerically and visually?

$\frac{1}{2}$ $\frac{1}{2}$

Turn and Talk Is there another visual representation that could be used to display this situation? Explain.

Build Understanding

A circle graph shows how a whole set of data is divided into parts or categories. The size of the angle for a section indicates the portion of the whole that the category makes up. The sum of all the angle measures is 360°, the measure of one full rotation around a circle.

1 Kara conducted a survey of 120 students. She asked how they get to school. The results are shown in the circle graph.

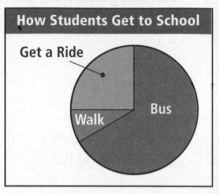

How Students Get to School

A. What do the sizes of the sections tell you about how the number of students who walk to school compares to the number who take the bus?

_____

_____

_____

B. How can you find the angle measure of each section? What are the angle measures?

_____

_____

C. Write part-to-whole ratios comparing the angle measure for each section to the angle measure for the whole **circle**, 360°.

_____

D. Use your part-to-whole ratios from Part C to find the number of students represented by each section.

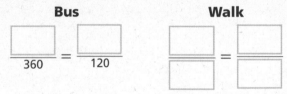

Bus   **Walk**   **Get a Ride**

$$\frac{\boxed{}}{360} = \frac{\boxed{}}{120}$$

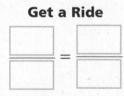

_____   _____   _____

Step It Out

2 There are 45 vehicles in a parking lot. There are 25 cars, 5 trucks, and 15 SUVs. How can you use ratio reasoning to make a circle graph to represent this data?

A. Write a part-to-whole ratio to represent the number of each type of vehicle in the parking lot.

Cars   **Trucks**   **SUVs**

_____   _____   _____

© Houghton Mifflin Harcourt Publishing Company • Image Credit: ©krumanop/Shutterstock

B. Use your part-to-whole ratios from Part A to find the angle measure for each section in the graph.

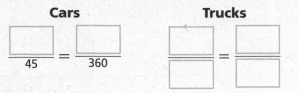

Cars

$$\frac{\boxed{}}{45} = \frac{\boxed{}}{360}$$

Trucks

$$\frac{\boxed{}}{\boxed{}} = \frac{\boxed{}}{\boxed{}}$$

SUVs

$$\frac{\boxed{}}{\boxed{}} = \frac{\boxed{}}{\boxed{}}$$

C. What is the sum of the angle measures you found in Part B? What does this tell you?

_____

_____

D. Make a circle graph of the parking-lot data. Use a protractor to draw each angle using the angle measures from Part B. Label each section with the type of vehicle it represents.

Turn and Talk How does changing the order in which you graph each category affect the circle graph? Explain.

Check Understanding

1. Sara collected information from 60 students in the sixth grade about their pets. She represented the results in a circle graph. How many students own a dog?

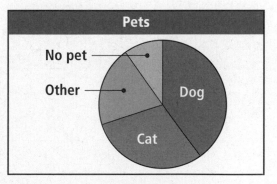

Pets

No pet

Other

Dog

Cat

_____

2. Max conducted a survey of 60 students in which he asked about their favorite school subject. 24 students said math, 12 students said science, 18 students said English, and 6 students said social studies. Max wants to make a circle graph of these data. What angle measure should he use for the English section?

_____

On Your Own

3. **(MP)** **Use Repeated Reasoning** The circle graph shows the preferences of town residents for new playground equipment in a park. If 240 residents responded to the survey, how many residents preferred each type of playground equipment?

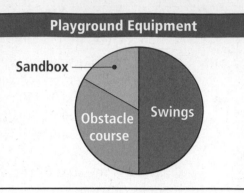

Playground Equipment

Swings: _____   Sandbox: _____

Obstacle Course: _____

4. Mr. Perez's science students conducted a wildlife count in the local forest. The results of their count are shown in the table.

Animal	Count
Squirrel	25
Rabbit	10
Deer	10
Raccoon	5

A. Find the angle measure for each section.

_____

B. Make a circle graph to represent the data.

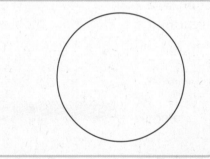

5. Daniela listened to a popular radio station for 1 hour. Then she made the circle graph to summarize what she had heard. Complete the table to show the angle measure for each section and the number of minutes that section represents.

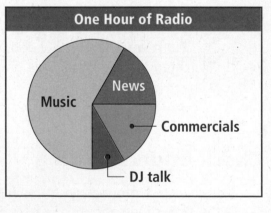

One Hour of Radio

Category	Angle Measure (degrees)	Time (minutes)
Music		
News		
Commercials		
DJ talk		

I'm in a Learning Mindset!

What challenges do I face in trying to master making a circle graph?

_____

LESSON 6.1
**More Practice/
Homework**

ONLINE
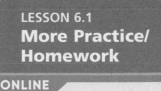
Video Tutorials and
Interactive Examples

Use Ratio Reasoning With Circles

1. **Health and Fitness** Kahlil asks his doctor how much of his daily
   diet should come from carbohydrates, protein, and fat. His
   doctor recommended 900 calories from carbohydrates,
   360 calories from protein, and 540 calories from fat.
   Kahlil wants to make a circle graph of this information.

   A. What is the total number of calories Kahlil should
      have each day?

      _____

   B. What are the angle measures for each section?

      _____

   C. Use your answers from Part B to make a circle graph.

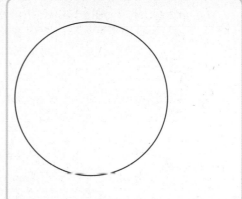

2. (MP) **Attend to Precision** Sara collected information from students in her
   school about their favorite type of movie. She represented the results in a circle
   graph. If 200 students expressed their preference, complete the table below to
   show how many students picked each type of movie. Use a protractor to find
   the angle measure of each section.

Movie Type	Number of People
Comedy	
Action	
Horror	
Romance	
Drama	

Movies

Drama
Romance
Horror
Comedy
Action

3. **Open Ended** Make up your own trail mix recipe.

   A. The trail mix will include nuts, raisins, and two
      ingredients of your choice. Write the ingredients
      you will use in the first column of the table.

   B. Your recipe should make a total of 24 ounces of trail
      mix. In the second column, record the weight, in
      ounces, of each ingredient in your recipe.

   C. Make a circle graph to show the portion of the whole
      recipe each ingredient makes up.

Ingredient	Weight (ounces)
Nuts	
Raisins	

My Trail Mix

Test Prep

4. Jon conducted a survey of 180 people in which he asked about their favorite type of exercise. 60 said jogging, 40 said cycling, and 80 said aerobics. Jon wants to make a circle graph of these data. What angle measure should he use for the aerobics section?

Ⓐ 80°

Ⓒ 160°

Ⓑ 120°

Ⓓ 240°

5. Ms. Hager's math class kept a record of the fruit sold in the school cafeteria over the course of a week. The results are shown in the table.

Fruit	Number sold
Apples	150
Bananas	100
Oranges	200
Peaches	25
Other	25

A. Write the ratio of oranges sold to total pieces of fruit sold.

200+150+100+25+25=500

B. The class wants to make a circle graph of the data. What angle measure should they use to represent the oranges section?

Spiral Review

6. Bob buys some apples for $16.50. If Bob buys 4.4 pounds of apples, what is the price per pound?

7. Sara wants to make dinner for herself. The recipe she will use calls for $13\frac{1}{2}$ ounces of chopped nuts. However, the recipe feeds 6 people. How many ounces of chopped nuts does Sara need for one serving?

8. How many inches are in 8 feet? _____

© Houghton Mifflin Harcourt Publishing Company

Name _____

Use Rate Reasoning to Convert Within Measurement Systems

(I Can) write and use equivalent fractions or conversion factors to convert units within a measurement system.

Spark Your Learning PAIRS

Milo is making $1\frac{1}{2}$ batches of muffins for a bake sale. If each batch of muffins calls for $1\frac{3}{4}$ cups of flour, how much flour will he need?

 Turn and Talk How is multiplying fractions similar to multiplying whole numbers or decimals? How is it different? Explain.

Build Understanding

You can use equivalent rates to convert both customary and metric units. Use the table to convert one unit to another unit within the same measurement system.

Customary Measurements		
Length	**Weight**	**Capacity**
1 ft = 12 in. 1 yd = 36 in. 1 yd = 3 ft 1 mi = 5,280 ft 1 mi = 1,760 yd	1 lb = 16 oz 1 T = 2,000 lb	1 c = 8 fl oz 1 pt = 2 c 1 qt = 2 pt 1 qt = 4 c 1 gal = 4 qt
Metric Measurements		
Length	**Mass**	**Capacity**
1 km = 1,000 m 1 m = 100 cm 1 cm = 10 mm	1 kg = 1,000 g 1 g = 1,000 mg	1 L = 1,000 mL

1 ▶ Heather needs to mail the package shown. The weight on the display is in pounds. The shipping company charges by the ounce. How many ounces does the package weigh?

A. How many ounces are in one pound?

_____

B. What rate could you use to convert 4 pounds into ounces?

_____

C. Use equivalent rates to convert 4 pounds into ounces.

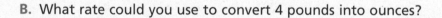

$$\frac{\boxed{} \text{ ounces}}{\boxed{} \text{ pound}} \times \frac{\boxed{}}{\boxed{}} = \frac{\boxed{} \text{ ounces}}{4 \text{ pounds}}$$

D. How many ounces are in 4 pounds?

$\boxed{}$ pounds is equal to $\boxed{}$ ounces.

 Turn and Talk How can you convert units within a measurement system? Explain.

Step It Out

Another way to convert measurements is by using a *conversion factor*.

Connect to Vocabulary

A **conversion factor** is a rate in which two quantities are equal, but use different units.

2 In Paris, the sculpture Long-Term Parking, created by Armand Fernandez, contains 60 cars embedded in 40,000 pounds of concrete. How many tons of concrete are in 40,000 pounds?

A. Find the conversion factor comparing tons to pounds.

$$\frac{\boxed{}\ \text{ton}}{\boxed{}\ \text{pounds}}$$

B. Multiply the conversion factor by 40,000 pounds.

$$\frac{\boxed{}\ \text{ton}}{\boxed{}\ \text{pounds}} \times \boxed{}\ \text{pounds}$$

C. Simplify the expression.

$$\frac{\boxed{}\ \text{ton}}{\boxed{}\ \text{pounds}} \times \frac{\boxed{}\ \text{pounds}}{1} = \frac{\boxed{}\ \text{tons}}{\boxed{}} = \boxed{}\ \text{tons}$$

Long-Term Parking Sculpture by Armand Fernandez

D. How many tons of concrete are in 40,000 pounds?

_____

 Turn and Talk Explain how you know how to set up the conversion factor.

3 A bag of flour has a mass of 4.5 kilograms. How many grams are in 4.5 kilograms?

A. Write a conversion factor comparing kilograms to grams.

$$\frac{\boxed{}\ \text{g}}{\boxed{}\ \text{kg}}$$

B. Multiply the conversion factor by 4.5 kilograms.

$$\frac{\boxed{}\ \text{g}}{\boxed{}\ \text{kg}} \cdot \boxed{}\ \text{kg}$$

C. Simplify the expression.

$$\frac{\boxed{}\ \text{g}}{\boxed{}\ \text{kg}} \cdot \frac{\boxed{}\ \text{kg}}{1} = \boxed{}\ \text{g}$$

D. How many grams are in 4.5 kilograms? _____

4 ▷ A camel can drink 25 gallons of water in 10 minutes. How many cups of water can the camel drink in 10 minutes?

A. I need to find the conversion factor for gallons to cups, but the conversion table does not show this conversion. The table does show that

☐ cups = ☐ quart, and that ☐ quarts = ☐ gallon.

Complete the table of equivalent ratios to compare cups to quarts.

Cups	2	4	8	16
Quarts		1		

B. How many cups are in 1 gallon?

☐ quarts = ☐ gallon, so 1 gallon = ☐ cups

C. Multiply the conversion factor by 25 gallons.

$\dfrac{\boxed{}\ \text{cups}}{\boxed{}\ \text{gallon}} \times \boxed{}$ gallons

D. How many cups are in 25 gallons?

_____

Check Understanding

1. The 1,600-meter race in the Olympics is very close to 1 mile long. How many kilometers is 1,600 meters? Show your work using equivalent ratios.

_____

2. Scott is 72 inches tall. How many feet tall is Scott? Use a conversion factor to show your work.

_____

_____

3. Jill has 15 feet of ribbon. How many yards of ribbon does she have? Use a conversion factor to show your work.

_____

_____

1,600-meter race

On Your Own

4. Karen is preparing 4.5 liters of punch. How many milliliters are in 4.5 liters?

_____

5. Chen's pedometer says he has walked 5,600 meters today. How many kilometers has Chen walked today?

_____

6. (MP) **Critique Reasoning** Doug says that 3,000 kilometers is the same distance as 3 meters. What mistake did he make converting 3 meters to kilometers?

_____

_____

_____

7. (MP) **Reason** A truck weighs 9,000 pounds. A repair shop sends a tow truck that can pull up to 5 tons. Can the tow truck tow the truck? Explain.

_____

_____

_____

8. Morgan has 42 inches of rope, Malcolm has 4 feet of rope, and Roberto has 2 yards of rope. Express the total length of rope the three friends have in inches, feet, and yards.

[   ] inches — [   ] feet — [   ] yards

9. What conversion factor can you use to convert miles to inches? Explain how you found it.

_____

_____

_____

For Problems 10–15, convert the units.

10. 8 ft = [   ] in.

11. 12 yd = [   ] ft

12. [   ] km = 11,250 m

13. [   ] mg = 3.5 g

14. 150 mL = [   ] L

15. [   ] in. = 0.5 ft

16. Open Ended Give an example of an item often measured with customary units and an item often measured with metric units.

_____

_____

17. Aisling runs 5.5 kilometers and Fiona runs 6,250 meters. Who runs farther? Explain how you know.

_____

_____

18. (MP) **Critique Reasoning** Vince and Larry are converting 1 kilogram to milligrams. Larry reports that there are 2,000 milligrams in 1 kilogram, and Vince reports that there are 1,000,000 milligrams in 1 kilogram. Who is correct and why? Explain.

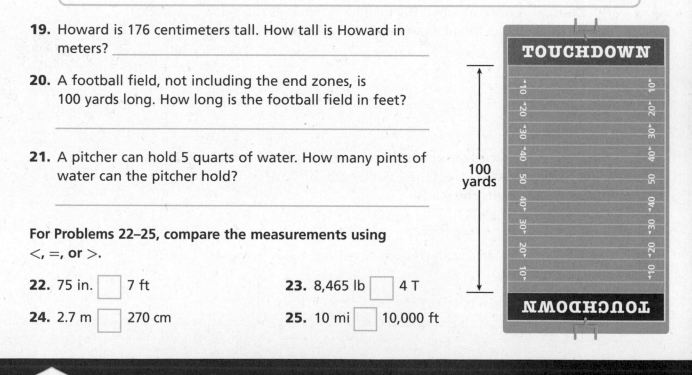

19. Howard is 176 centimeters tall. How tall is Howard in meters? _____

20. A football field, not including the end zones, is 100 yards long. How long is the football field in feet?

_____

21. A pitcher can hold 5 quarts of water. How many pints of water can the pitcher hold?

_____

For Problems 22–25, compare the measurements using <, =, or >.

22. 75 in. ☐ 7 ft

23. 8,465 lb ☐ 4 T

24. 2.7 m ☐ 270 cm

25. 10 mi ☐ 10,000 ft

I'm in a Learning Mindset!

Did I have confidence in my answer for Task 1? What specific evidence do I have that I solved it correctly?

_____

_____

© Houghton Mifflin Harcourt Publishing Company

Name _____

LESSON 6.2
More Practice/ Homework

ONLINE
Video Tutorials and
Interactive Examples

Use Rate Reasoning to Convert Within Measurement Systems

1. Angela has 3 gallons of milk. How many quarts of milk does she have?

_____

Math on the Spot For Problems 2–3, use conversion factors.

2. Convert 40 yards to feet.

_____

3. Convert 20 quarts to gallons.

_____

4. A sink can hold 10 gallons of water. How many quarts of water can the sink hold?

_____

5. A box weighs 64 ounces. What is the weight of the box in pounds?

_____

Sink can hold 10 gallons of water

6. (MP) **Reason** Greg already has 2 gallons of paint to paint his living room. He estimates that he will need 10 quarts of paint. Does he have enough paint? Show your work.

_____

_____

7. Two bottles of water have a mass of 4 kilograms. How many grams is 4 kilograms?

_____

For Problems 8–13, convert to the unit indicated in parentheses. Then compare the measurements using $<$, $=$, or $>$.

8. 5,000 m ☐ 4.9 km; (meters)

9. 4 lb ☐ 60 oz; (ounces)

10. 3 mi ☐ 15,840 ft; (feet)

11. 72 in. ☐ 2 yd; (feet)

12. 0.45 L ☐ 4,200 mL; (milliliters)

13. 1.2 g ☐ 950 mg; (milligrams)

Test Prep

14. Write the following measurements in order from least to greatest:
0.04 kilometer, 420 centimeters, 4,600 millimeters, 4.3 meters

_____

_____

15. Which of the following measurements is equivalent to 528 feet?
Select all that apply.

Ⓐ 176 yards

Ⓑ 5,280 inches

Ⓒ 44 inches

Ⓓ 0.1 mile

Ⓔ 6,336 inches

16. One quart of milk costs $1.05 and 1 gallon of milk costs $3.89. Which is a better buy? Explain.

_____

_____

17. Which of the following measurements is equivalent to 400 grams?

Ⓐ 4 kilograms

Ⓑ 0.4 kilogram

Ⓒ 0.04 kilogram

Ⓓ 0.004 kilogram

18. Mairead jogs 2,700 feet, while Paula jogs 0.5 mile. Who jogs farther, and by how many feet?

_____

Spiral Review

19. Kelly is trying to decide which plan to use to download songs. She can download 8 songs for $9.60 or 15 songs for $15.00. Which plan offers the lowest cost per song? Explain.

_____

20. There are 10 seniors and 15 juniors in a gym class. What is the ratio of seniors to total students?

_____

21. Polly buys 6.8 yards of fabric for $28.90. What is the cost per yard?

_____

22. What is the distance between −7 and its opposite on a number line?

_____

Name _____

Use Rate Reasoning to Convert Between Measurement Systems

(I Can) write and use equivalent rates or conversion factors to convert units between measurement systems.

Spark Your Learning

At Winnie's restaurant, one serving of chicken soup is $1\frac{1}{2}$ cups. The chef makes 48 cups of soup each night. How many servings of chicken soup are in 48 cups? Explain how you know.

 Turn and Talk How is dividing fractions related to multiplying fractions?

Build Understanding

Many countries use only the **metric system** of measurement. In the United States, however, we use measurements in both metric units and customary units. Sometimes we need to convert between the two systems.

The table below shows equivalences between **customary** and metric systems. You can use these equivalences to convert a measurement in one system to a measurement in the other system.

Length	Weight/Mass	Capacity
1 inch = 2.54 centimeters 1 foot ≈ 0.305 meter 1 yard ≈ 0.914 meter 1 mile ≈ 1.61 kilometers	1 ounce ≈ 28.4 grams 1 pound ≈ 0.454 kilogram	1 fluid ounce ≈ 29.6 milliliters 1 quart ≈ 0.946 liter 1 gallon ≈ 3.79 liters

The systems are not related so the conversions are approximate, as indicated by the symbol ≈.

1 Daniel is 6 feet tall. He wants to know how tall he is in meters.

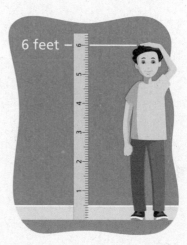

6 feet —

A. One way to solve this problem is to use a bar diagram. Each part represents 1 foot.

1 foot ≈ _____

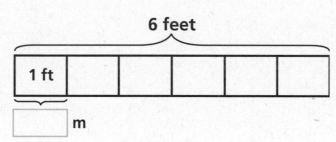

6 feet

1 ft					

[____] m

B. How does the diagram help you solve the problem?

_____

_____

C. You could also use a unit rate as the conversion factor.

$$\frac{\boxed{}\ m}{1\ ft} \times 6\ ft \approx \boxed{}\ m$$

D. There is about [____] meter in 1 foot. There are about [____] meters in 6 feet.

 Turn and Talk How would the steps to solve the problem be different if you converted a metric height to feet? Explain.

© Houghton Mifflin Harcourt Publishing Company

Step It Out

2 In the metric system, 1 gram is the mass of 1 milliliter of water. So, a 2–liter bottle of water has a mass of 2 kilograms. A gallon of water weighs about 8 pounds. What is the mass of a gallon of water to the nearest tenth of a kilogram?

1 gallon

Method 1: Solve using equivalent rates.

A. The first rate is the conversion factor, which is found in the table.

$$\frac{1\ lb}{\boxed{}\ kg}$$

B. The second rate relates the known amount to the unknown converted amount.

$$\frac{\boxed{}\ lb}{x\ kg}$$

C. Set the rates equal to one another.

$$\frac{1\ lb}{\boxed{}\ kg} = \frac{\boxed{}\ lb}{\boxed{}\ kg}$$

D. Multiply both parts of the left rate by a number that will make the number of pounds in the two rates the same.

$$\frac{1\ lb \times \boxed{}}{\boxed{}\ kg \times \boxed{}} = \frac{\boxed{}\ lb}{\boxed{}\ kg}$$

E. A gallon of water has a mass of about $\boxed{}$ kilograms.

Method 2: Solve using the conversion factor.

A. Write the conversion factor as a rate.

$$\frac{\boxed{}\ kg}{\boxed{}\ lb}$$

B. Multiply 8 pounds by the conversion factor. Round the result.

$$\frac{\boxed{}\ kg}{\boxed{}\ lb} \times 8\ lb \approx \boxed{}\ kg$$

C. Notice the _____ units cancel, resulting in an answer given

in _____.

D. When you choose a conversion factor, the unit you are converting to is the

| first / second | quantity in the rate.

> **Turn and Talk** Which method is easier to use, equivalent rates method or the conversion method? Explain.

Many water bottles contain 16 fluid ounces, or 1 pint, of water. Drink labels often show the number of fluid ounces and the number of milliliters in a container. How many milliliters are in a 16-fluid-ounce drink?

16 fluid ounces

Solve using equivalent rates.

A. One rate is the conversion factor.

$$\frac{\boxed{}\ \text{mL}}{1\ \text{fl oz}}$$

B. The other rate relates the known amount to the unknown converted amount.

$$\frac{x\ \text{mL}}{\boxed{}\ \text{fl oz}}$$

C. Set the rates equal to one another.

$$\frac{\boxed{}\ \text{mL}}{1\ \text{fl oz}} = \frac{x\ \text{mL}}{\boxed{}\ \text{fl oz}}$$

D. Multiply both parts of the left rate by a number that will make the number of fluid ounces in the two rates the same.

$$\frac{\boxed{}\ \text{mL} \times \boxed{}}{1\ \text{fl oz} \times \boxed{}} = \frac{\boxed{}\ \text{mL}}{\boxed{}\ \text{fl oz}}$$

There are about $\boxed{}$ milliliters in 16 fluid ounces.

 Turn and Talk When converting units using equivalent rates, does it matter which unit is in the numerator? Explain.

Check Understanding

1. Robert enters a race. The race is 10 kilometers long, but he is more familiar with miles than kilometers. How many miles are in 10 kilometers to the nearest tenth of a mile?

_____

2. Scott is 72 inches tall and Chris is 185 centimeters tall. Who is taller? Show your work.

_____

_____

On Your Own

3. (MP) **Reason** Kathy is following a recipe for punch that calls for 3 liters of juice. She has 3 quarts of juice. Without using an equation, does Kathy have enough juice for the punch? Explain.

_____

_____

4. Simon measures the length of an insect that is 2.5 inches long for a science project. He needs to record his data in centimeters. How long is the insect in centimeters?

_____

5. An Olympic-size swimming pool is 50 meters long. How many yards long is the pool, to the nearest tenth of a yard?

_____

6. How many kilograms are in 1 ton, or 2,000 pounds?

_____

7. Many newborn babies have a mass between 2,500 grams and 4,000 grams. How many pounds does a 2,500-gram baby weigh, to the nearest tenth of a pound? [16 ounces = 1 pound] Show your work.

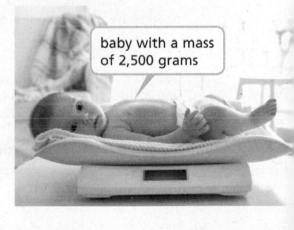

baby with a mass of 2,500 grams

8. Shane is following an English recipe for scones. The recipe calls for 1.2 kilograms of flour. How many pounds of flour, to the nearest tenth of a pound, does he need?

_____

For Problems 9–14, convert the units to the nearest tenth.

9. 10 feet ≈ _____ meters

10. _____ yards ≈ 25 meters

11. _____ kilometers ≈ 50 miles

12. _____ grams ≈ 10 ounces

13. 8 fluid ounces ≈ _____ milliliters

14. 6 inches = _____ centimeters

15. Which distance is longer, 500 kilometers or 250 miles? Explain.

16. The tank of a car holds 10 gallons of gas. How many liters does the tank hold?

17. Wendy drives a car 110 kilometers per hour. What is this rate, in miles per hour, to the nearest tenth?

18. Jim sits on a seesaw. If Jim weighs 100 pounds, what mass in kilograms does the person on the other side need to be for the seesaw to be balanced?

100 pounds

19. Caitlyn is 160 centimeters tall. How tall is she in feet and inches, rounded to the nearest inch?

For Problems 20–25, compare the measurements using <, =, or >.

20. 2 meters ☐ 7 feet

21. 50 pounds ☐ 25 kilograms

22. 100 inches ☐ 254 centimeters

23. 10 miles ☐ 6.2 kilometers

24. 6 liters ☐ 2 gallons

25. 24 ounces ☐ 600 grams

I'm in a Learning Mindset!

What types of decisions did I make when solving Problem 8? Which strategy did I use?

Understand and Apply Percent

TIME TO CLEAN UP

A nature club held a beach cleanup. Four club members described the length of the beach that they each cleaned.

I cleaned 0.16 mile.

I cleaned 0.3 mile.

I cleaned 0.28 mile.

I cleaned 0.2 mile.

Kurt   Maria   Eddie   Celia

Find the total amount of beach the club cleaned.

A. Write a fraction with a denominator of 10 or 100 that is equal to each decimal.

0.16 = _____   0.28 = _____

0.3 = _____   0.2 = _____

B. What length of the beach did the club clean? _____

 **Turn and Talk**

- How does the length of beach cleaned compare with 1 mile? How do you know?

- How would the length of beach cleaned change if Kurt cleaned $\frac{6}{100}$ mile more? Justify your response.

Are You Ready?

Complete these problems to review prior concepts and skills you will need for this module.

Relate Fractions and Decimals

Write each fraction as a decimal.

1. $\frac{7}{10} =$ _____

2. $\frac{3}{10} =$ _____

3. $\frac{9}{10} =$ _____

4. $\frac{5}{10} =$ _____

5. $\frac{12}{100} =$ _____

6. $\frac{73}{100} =$ _____

7. $\frac{45}{100} =$ _____

8. $\frac{90}{100} =$ _____

Write Decimals as Fractions

Write each decimal as a fraction with a denominator of 10 or 100.

9. $0.6 =$ _____

10. $0.8 =$ _____

11. $0.16 =$ _____

12. $0.25 =$ _____

13. $0.3 =$ _____

14. $0.24 =$ _____

15. $0.52 =$ _____

16. $0.44 =$ _____

Name

Understand, Express, and Compare Percent Ratios

(I Can) convert ratios to percents by applying one strategy.

Spark Your Learning
SMALL GROUPS

A race car uses 2 gallons of gas to travel 25 miles. How many miles can the race car travel on 8 gallons of gas?

Turn and Talk How can you use the ratio of 2 gallons of gas to 25 miles to write a ratio for the number of miles the race car travels on 1 gallon of gas? How could this be useful?

Build Understanding

1 ▶ Eleanor, Tillie, and Caleb earn money training dogs to surf. For every dollar they earn, Caleb gets 20 cents, Tillie gets 30 cents, and Eleanor gets 50 cents.

A. Write a ratio that shows how much each trainer earns from a dollar.

Caleb: [ ] : 100

Tillie: [ ] : 100

Eleanor: [ ] : 100

B. Caleb's portion of each dollar earned is shaded on the 10 × 10 grid. How many boxes do you need to shade to represent Tillie's portion? Shade in Tillie's portion of each dollar on the grid.

_____

C. A percent is a part-to-whole ratio with a whole of 100. You can write 25% as 25 : 100 or $\frac{25}{100}$. Write percents to represent the amounts Caleb and Tillie earn from each dollar. Explain how you found them.

_____

_____

_____

_____

_____

D. What does the part of the grid that isn't shaded represent? Write a percent to represent this portion of the grid.

_____

_____

_____

Turn and Talk Devon says that the ratios 2:10, 3:10, and 5:10 represent Caleb's, Tillie's, and Eleanor's portions. Is Devon right? If so, explain how he found these ratios. If not, explain Devon's error.

2 A survey says that 13 out of 20 people have pets. Write this ratio as a percent.

A. One way to write a ratio as a percent is to use a table. Complete the table to write equivalent ratios for the ratio 13:20.

People who have pets	13				
Total number of people	20	40		80	

B. Use the table to write the percent of people who own pets. What is $\frac{13}{20}$ as a percent? Explain.

_____

_____

C. You also can use equivalent ratios to find the percent. What is $\frac{13}{20}$ as a percent?

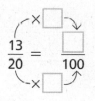

$$\frac{13}{20} = \frac{\square}{100}$$

$$\frac{13}{20} = \underline{\quad\quad} \%$$

Turn and Talk Could you use any of the ratios in the table to find the percent?

3 A recipe for pie crust includes the ingredients shown. Find the ratio of sugar to flour as a percent.

pie crust: 1 cup of sugar per 4 cups of flour

A. What fraction can represent the ratio of sugar to flour? Convert this fraction to a decimal. Explain how you did the conversion.

_____

_____

B. Write the decimal as a percent. Explain how you found the percent.

_____

Step It Out

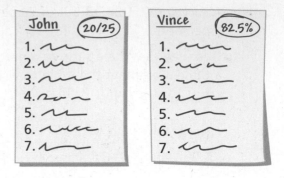

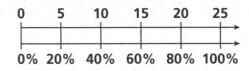

4 ▶ The diagram shows quiz results in red for John and Vince. Who received the higher score, John or Vince?

A. What can you do to solve this problem?

_____

_____

B. Many test scores are written as percents. Use the double number line to convert John's score to a percent. John's score is a ratio with a whole of 25. So the 25 is placed with the 100% on the double number line.

0	5	10	15	20	25
0%	20%	40%	60%	80%	100%

To convert John's score to a percent, what number do you mark on the top number line? _____

What number do you mark on the bottom number line? _____

C. Use your answers in Part B to write $\frac{20}{25}$ as a percent.

$$\frac{20}{25} = \frac{\boxed{}}{100} = \boxed{}\%$$

D. Who received the higher score?

_____

_____

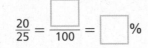 **Turn and Talk** How else could you find out who had the higher score?

Check Understanding

1. A basketball player made 12 out of the 30 shots she attempted. What percent of shots did the basketball player make? Explain.

_____

_____

For Problems 2–7, write each ratio as a percent.

2. 1 to 20 _____

3. $\frac{45}{75}$ _____

4. 160 : 400 _____

5. $\frac{12}{60}$ _____

6. 5 to 250 _____

7. $\frac{1}{8}$ _____

On Your Own

8. Rachel hits one home run every 40 times she bats.

   A. Complete the table to write equivalent ratios for the ratio 1:40.

Number of home runs	1			4	
Number of times at bat	40	80			

   B. Use the table to write the percent of the time Rachel hits a home run after 200 times at bat.

   _____

9. **Financial Literacy** Compared to the money he made last year, Zach made 115% as much this year. Use the 10-by-10 grids to show 115%.

   Did he make more or less money than last year?

   _____

10. (MP) **Construct Arguments** Ryan got 36 out of 40 questions right on a test. Tessa got 92% on the same test. Who got a better score? Explain.

    _____

    _____

11. **Open Ended** Write three ratios that are equivalent to 75% and three ratios that are equivalent to 100%.

    _____

For Problems 12–17, write each number as a percent.

12. $\frac{3}{24}$ _____

13. 0.95 _____

14. 8.37 _____

15. $6\frac{1}{5}$ _____

16. $\frac{70}{50}$ _____

17. 0.340 _____

18. Ricardo threw rings over bottles in a ring-toss competition. The diagram shows the number of bottles Ricardo got rings around.

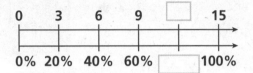

A. Write a ratio of the number of bottles with rings to the total number of bottles.

_____

B. Complete the double number line to show the percentage of rings that successfully landed around a bottle.

```
  0    3    6    9   [ ]   15
  |----|----|----|----|----|--->
                            --->
 0%  20%  40%  60%  [ ]  100%
```

C. What percent of the bottles have rings on them? _____

19. Two marathon runners run the full distance of the marathon, approximately 26 miles, in 4 hours.

A. About how many miles did they run in 1 hour?

_____

B. What percent of the full distance have they run in 1 hour?

_____

20. The ratio of seventh graders to sixth graders on a chess team is 5 to 3.

A. The ratio of seventh graders to total chess players is $\dfrac{5}{\boxed{}}$.

B. What percent of the players on the chess team are seventh graders? _____

21. Kari has one day each week (7-day week) to research the decline in bee populations. Approximately what percent of each week does she have to research this topic? Round your answer to the nearest hundredth of a percent. _____

Bee populations are in decline.

I'm in a Learning Mindset!

What did I learn from Task 2 that I can use in my future learning?

_____

Understand, Express, and Compare Percent Ratios

1. In a Louisiana chili cook-off, 18 of the 40 chilis included two types of beans. What percentage of the chilis did *not* include two types of beans? _____

2. The ratio of roses to lilies in a garden is 3 to 2. If lilies and roses are the only flowers in the garden, what percentage of the garden's flowers are roses? _____

chili cook-off

3. **(MP) Attend to Precision** The picture shows the blue and white tiles of an outdoor patio. What percent of the tiles are blue? Explain.

_____

_____

_____

4. A movie studio keeps 240 dresses in its wardrobe for historical films. Three-fifths of them can be used for movies that take place in the 1700s and 15% of them can be used for movies in the civil war era.

A. What percent of the dresses are for films set in the 1700s? _____

B. What percent of the dresses are for films *not* set in the 1700s? Explain how you found your answer.

_____

_____

C. What percent of the dresses are for films set in the 1700s *or* during the civil war era? Explain how you found your answer.

_____

_____

D. What percent of the dresses are *not* for films set during the civil war era? Explain how you found your answer.

_____

_____

For Problems 5–8, write each number as a percent.

5. $\frac{1}{5}$

6. $\frac{9}{10}$

7. 0.33

8. $\frac{11}{2}$

_____ _____ _____ _____

Test Prep

9. A hotel puts out 3 apples for every 1 orange as the fruit for their breakfast buffet.

    A. Write a ratio of apples compared to all the fruit.

    _____

    B. What percent of the fruit in the breakfast buffet are apples?

    _____

10. On a necklace of 100 beads, 45 of the beads are round. The rest of the beads are rectangular. What percent of the beads are round? What percent are rectangular?

_____

11.

R	S	T	A	E
V	O	A	G	S

What percent of the tiles are vowels?

(A) 25%   (B) 40%   (C) 60%   (D) 400%

12. A chorus has 50 singers. There are 16 altos and 10 tenors. What percent of the singers are altos? What percent of the singers are tenors?

(A) 8%; 5%   (B) 16%; 10%   (C) 32%; 20%   (D) 68%; 80%

Spiral Review

13. On the first move, a game piece is moved ahead two spaces. On the next move, the game piece is moved ahead five spaces. What integer represents the overall result of the two moves?

_____

14. Alex paid $3.59 for 1.35 pounds of chicken. To the nearest cent, how much did Alex pay per pound?

_____

15. One-third of an orchestra's musicians play violin or viola and another one-quarter play cello or contrabass. What fraction of the orchestra's musicians play either violin, viola, cello, or contrabass?

_____

Name _____

Use Strategies to Find a Percent of a Quantity

(I Can) write a percent as a fraction or a decimal and use multiplication to find the percent of a number.

Spark Your Learning

In a school football game, Marcus completes 3 out of 4 pass attempts. Terry completes 7 out of 10 pass attempts. Who has the better record of successful pass attempts? Explain.

x	y

$\frac{1}{2}$	$\frac{1}{2}$

Turn and Talk Is there another way you could have solved this problem?

Build Understanding

1 What is 32% of 25?

A. You can use equivalent ratios to find 32% of 25. The first ratio is the percent. How can you express 32% as a ratio?

_____

B. The second ratio is a part-to-whole ratio. The whole is 25 and the part is unknown. Write the second ratio as a fraction. Use a question mark to represent the unknown part. Then set the ratios equal to each other to find the unknown part.

$$\frac{\square}{\square} ; \frac{\square}{\square} = \frac{\square}{\square}$$

C. What multiplication fact will help you to find the unknown number? Explain how.

_____

_____

_____

D. Use the multiplication fact you wrote in Part C to find equivalent ratios.

32% of 25 is _____.

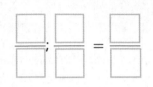

part → $\dfrac{\square}{25}$ = $\dfrac{32}{100}$ ← whole, with ×□ and ×4

2 Bree wants to save 40% of her weekly pay as a lifeguard. How much does she plan to save each week?

A. What number should you enter into the top bar of the model? What number should you enter into each section on the bottom bar? Explain your reasoning.

_____

_____

_____

B. How much money does Bree plan to save each week? Explain.

_____

_____

_____

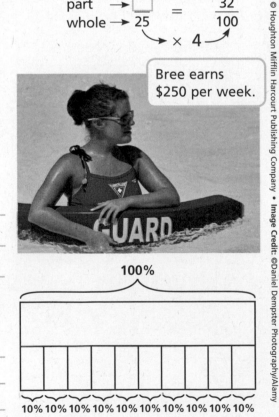

Bree earns $250 per week.

100%

| 10% | 10% | 10% | 10% | 10% | 10% | 10% | 10% | 10% | 10% |

Step It Out

3 ▶ Use multiplication to find 45% of 80.

A. Write 45% as a fraction. ⬚/⬚

B. I can _____ 80 by the fraction in Part A to find 45% percent of 80.

C. Complete the multiplication to show how you can use the fraction from Part A to find 45% of 80.

$$\frac{\square}{100} \text{ of } 80 = \frac{\square}{100} \times 80$$

$$= \frac{\square}{100}$$

$$= \square$$

 Turn and Talk Is there another way to find 45% of 80? Explain.

---

4 ▶ Alyssa has to make 250 invitations for a party. She has completed 72% of them. How many invitations has she completed?

A. Write a ratio to represent the percent. ⬚/⬚

B. What operation does the word "of" indicate?

_____

C. Write a multiplication problem to find the number of completed invitations.

$$\frac{\square}{\square} \times \square = \square$$

D. How many invitations has Alyssa completed? _____

E. Check your answer using decimal multiplication. Write a decimal to represent 72%. _____

F. Write a decimal multiplication problem to find the number of completed invitations.

$$\square \times \square = \square$$

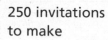
250 invitations to make

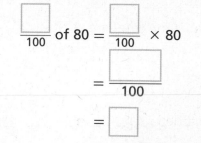
You're Invited

Turn and Talk What is 100% of any amount? What is 50% of any amount?

5 ▶ Scott planted 20% of a garden with roses. What is the area of the part of the garden planted with roses?

10 ft

5 ft

A. How can you find the total area of the garden? What is the total area?

_____

_____

B. You know that the rose garden is 20% of the total garden.

Write 20% as a ratio. $\dfrac{\Box}{100}$

C. Write a ratio to represent the unknown area of the garden planted with roses compared to the total area of the garden. Use a question

mark for the unknown area. $\dfrac{\Box}{\Box}$

D. Use equivalent ratios to find 20% of the rose garden's area.

E. What is the area of the rose garden? _____

 Turn and Talk What percent of the garden is not planted with roses? Explain how you know.

Check Understanding

1. Shonda has $125. She spends 35% of the money she has on a concert ticket. How much did Shonda pay for the concert ticket?

_____

For Problems 2–5, find the percent of each number.

2. 10% of 70 _____   **3.** 75% of 8 _____

4. 55% of 55 _____   **5.** 90% of 20 _____

216

On Your Own

6. A football team scored 70% of a total of 400 points in the first 11 games of the season.

   A. Fill in the model to show 70% of 400.

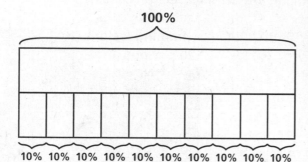

100%

10% 10% 10% 10% 10% 10% 10% 10% 10% 10%

   B. How many points did the football team score in the first 11 games of the season? Explain how you found your answer.

_____

7. Cassie is painting a rectangular wall in her bedroom. The wall is 12 feet by 15 feet. She plans on painting the top 20% of the wall green and the rest of the wall tan. What is the area of the part of the wall that she plans to paint green?

_____

8. **(MP) Reason** Stephon and Marcy are saving money to buy new bikes. If Stephon suddenly has to spend 12% of his savings and Marcy has to spend 8% of her savings, who spent more money? Explain how you found your answer.

Stephon has saved $200.

Marcy has saved $350.

_____

_____

_____

9. The regular price of a pair of sneakers is $40. The sale price is 25% off the regular price. What is the sale price? Explain.

_____

For Problems 10–15, find the percent of each number.

10. 13% of 400 _____

11. 80% of 14,236 _____

12. 60% of 50 _____

13. 30% of 70 _____

14. 45% of 20 _____

15. 75% of 804 _____

16. A quiz has 30 problems. Kamal answered 80% of the problems correctly.

   A. How many problems did Kamal answer correctly? _____

   B. How many problems did Kamal answer incorrectly? _____

   C. What percent of the problems did Kamal answer incorrectly? _____

17. The regular price for swimming lessons for an hour is shown. The sale price for new students is 75% of the regular price. What is the sale price?

swimming lessons $20 per hour

_____

18. Maya has 200 songs on her cell phone. Of these songs, 48 are jazz songs. What percent of Maya's songs are jazz songs?

_____

19. Financial Literacy The sales tax in the town where Gina lives is 8%. Gina wants to buy a table saw that costs $300. How much sales tax will she pay?

_____

20. Parson City Middle School has 1,340 students. About 38% of the students are in the seventh grade. About how many seventh-graders attend Parson City Middle School?

_____

For Problems 21–26, find the percent of each number.

21. 25% of 500 _____

22. 80% of 10 _____

23. 10% of 100 _____

24. 100% of 60 _____

25. 105% of 220 _____

26. 120% of 40 _____

☒ I'm in a Learning Mindset!

What challenges do I face trying to master percent problems?

_____

_____

LESSON 7.2
**More Practice/
Homework**

ONLINE
Video Tutorials and
Interactive Examples

Use Strategies to Find a Percent of a Quantity

1. A football team scored 80% of a total of 500 points in the first 11 games of the season. Fill in the model to show 80% of 500 and then write the number.

_____

2. STEM About 71% of Earth's surface is covered in water.

A. If the surface area of the Earth is about 196,900,000 square miles, about how many square miles are covered in water?

_____

B. About what percent of the Earth's surface is not covered in water? How many square miles is this?

_____

_____

For Problems 3–4, use the following information.

The metal bar shown is an alloy of silver and other metals.

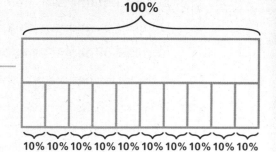

7.5 ounces

3. If the silver accounts for **84%** of the bar's weight, what is the weight of the silver? _____

4. (MP) **Attend to Precision** If 9% of the bar's weight is iron, how much does the iron weigh? _____

5. Math on the Spot Find 30% of 180. _____

6. (MP) **Use Repeated Reasoning** Find 10% of each number. What pattern do you notice?

A. 10% of 30 is _____.   **B.** 10% of 47 is _____.

C. 10% of 240 is _____.   **D.** 10% of 10.8 is _____.

E. Describe the pattern that you notice.

_____

_____

_____

For Problems 7–10, find the percent of each number.

7. 10% of 90   **8.** 50% of 14   **9.** 30% of 90   **10.** 80% of 40

_____   _____   _____   _____

Test Prep

11. Of 140 people at a movie, 40% of the people bought popcorn, 30% of the people bought pretzels, and 10% of the people bought pizza. How many people bought each item?

Number of people who bought popcorn: _____

Number of people who bought pretzels: _____

Number of people who bought pizza: _____

12. The circle graph shows the percent of votes the winning candidate received in a local election. About how many votes did the winning candidate receive?

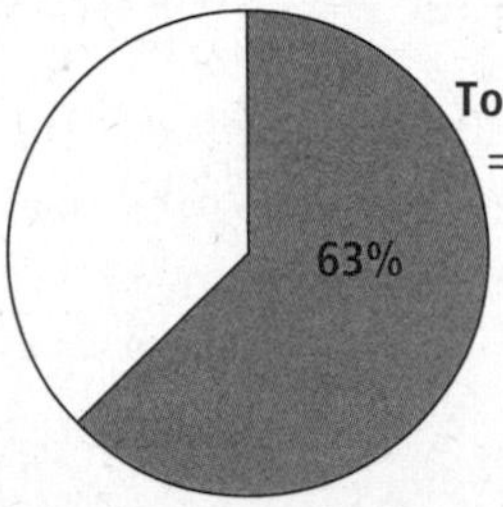

Ⓐ 630 votes

Ⓒ 4,000 votes

Ⓑ 2,350 votes

Ⓓ 6,350 votes

Total votes = 6,350

63%

13. There are 80 marbles in a bag. If 30% of the marbles are green, how many marbles are *not* green?

_____

14. Lamar earns 40% of his money moving furniture. If he earns $150 in total, how much money did he earn moving furniture?

Ⓐ $110

Ⓒ $40

Ⓑ $60

Ⓓ $90

15. Barry entered a singing competition. Three of 15 judges voted for him to go on to the semi-finals. What percent of the judges voted for him?

_____

Spiral Review

16. A bakery packages 868 muffins into 31 boxes. The same number of muffins are put into each box. How many muffins are in each box?

_____

17. Order the numbers 0, 3, −12, and −1 from least to greatest.

_____

Find the quotient. If necessary, round to the nearest thousandth.

18. $560 \div 1.4$ _____

19. $9.5 \div 500$ _____

20. $0.80 \div 46$ _____

21. $10.2 \div 100$ _____

22. $0.72 \div 0.09$ _____

23. $13 \div 0.04$ _____

Name

Solve a Variety of Percent Problems

(I Can) write a percent as a fraction or a decimal and use a variety of strategies to solve real-world problems.

Step It Out

1 ▶ Liz is collecting aluminum cans for a school fundraiser. So far, she has collected 16 cans, which is 20% of her goal. How many cans must she collect to reach her goal?

A. Use a double number line to solve the problem. When Liz reaches 100%, she has reached her goal. Complete the double number line until you reach 100%.

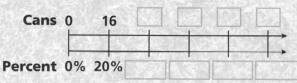

B. For every 16 cans Liz collects, she adds ☐ % toward her goal.

If she reaches 40% of her goal she will have ☐ cans. Liz must

collect ☐ cans to reach her goal.

2 ▶ Jose is in the same class as Liz and he is also collecting aluminum cans. He has collected 36 cans, which is 18% of his goal. How many cans must Jose collect to reach his goal?

A. Use equivalent ratios to solve the problem. One ratio is the percent: $\frac{\Box}{100}$. The second ratio is the number of cans already collected compared to the total number of cans that must be collected. You know the first number, the *part*, of the ratio. You must find the second number, the *whole*, of the ratio. Complete the ratio. The gray box represents

the unknown number. $\dfrac{\Box}{\blacksquare}$

B. Find equivalent ratios: $\dfrac{\Box}{100} = \dfrac{\Box}{\blacksquare}$. Eighteen is multiplied by ☐ to

get ☐. Multiply 100 by the same amount to find the answer.

$100 \times \Box = \Box$. Jose must collect ☐ cans to reach his goal.

Turn and Talk Which method do you think is easier to use: a double number line or finding equivalent ratios? Explain.

3 In Big Bog in Maui, Hawaii, about 400 inches of rain falls during a normal year. It is the 7th wettest place in the world, judging by annual rainfall. If 364 inches of rain have fallen so far and you expect the rainfall to reach the usual yearly amount, what percent of the year's rain has already fallen? Use equivalent ratios to find the solution.

400 inches yearly

364 inches so far

BIG BOG
Maui, Hawaii

A. You know one ratio already, the rainfall so far and the total rainfall expected. Write the ratio in fraction form. $\dfrac{364}{\boxed{}}$.

B. What ratio do we need to solve for? _____

C. Find equivalent ratios. $\dfrac{\boxed{}}{\boxed{}} = \dfrac{\boxed{}}{\boxed{}}$

D. 400 is divided by $\boxed{}$ to get 100. Divide 364 by the same number to find the percent. $364 \div \boxed{} = \boxed{}$

E. $\boxed{}$ % of the annual rain has fallen so far.

Turn and Talk How did you know which ratio to find?

Check Understanding

1. In a city election, 5,000 people voted for mayor. If the new mayor received 60% of the votes, how many people voted for the new mayor? Show how you know.

_____

2. At the King School, 55% of the students take a bus to school. If 220 students take a bus to school, how many students are there in total?

_____

3. When Randy is 3 years old, the doctor tells his parents that Randy will be 180 centimeters tall when he is fully grown. If Randy is 90 centimeters tall now, what percent of his expected adult height is he?

_____

4. On a math test, Janice answers 85% of the questions correctly. If she answered 17 questions correctly, how many questions are on the test?

_____

On Your Own

5. There are 8 equally sized slices in a pizza. If Ken eats 5 of the slices, what percent of the pizza has he eaten? Show your work.

_____

6. An animal shelter offers kittens and puppies each day for adoption. The shelter director wants 40% of the animals offered to be kittens. Fill in the double number line diagram to find out how many kittens should be included if the shelter offers 20 animals for adoption.

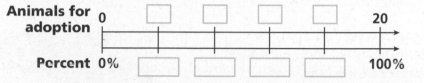

Animals for adoption 0 [ ] [ ] [ ] [ ] 20

Percent 0% [ ] [ ] [ ] [ ] 100%

7. A zoo has the ratio of giraffes to zebras shown. What percent of this grouping of animals are giraffes? What percent of this grouping are zebras?

1 giraffe for every 4 zebras

8. About $\frac{39}{50}$ of Earth's atmosphere is made up of nitrogen. Use equivalent ratios to find about what percent of the atmosphere is nitrogen.

_____

9. (MP) **Critique Reasoning** Andy has read 126 pages of a biography that has 300 pages. He says that he has read 60% of the book. Is this percent reasonable? Why or why not?

_____

_____

10. STEM The average adult is about 60% water. One liter of water has a mass of 1 kilogram. If a person's body contains 45 liters of water, what is the person's mass in kilograms? _____

For Problems 11–16 find the unknown value.

11. 25% of 48 = [ ]   **12.** 75% of 60 = [ ]

13. 40% of 72 = [ ]   **14.** 100% of [ ] = 30

15. 30% of [ ] = 30   **16.** 120% of [ ] = 18

© Houghton Mifflin Harcourt Publishing Company • Image Credit: ©Patryk Kosmider/Shutterstock

17. (MP) **Reason** Lily is using the equivalent ratios $\frac{7}{100} = \frac{77}{\blacksquare}$ to find the unknown whole value. What factor should she multiply 100 by? Explain how you found the factor.

_____

_____

18. If the gas tank in Glen's car can hold 12 gallons and it is 80% full, how many gallons of gas are in the gas tank?

_____

19. A water tank in the shape of a cylinder contains 54,000 gallons of water. If the tank is only 60% filled, how many gallons of water can the tank hold?

_____

60% filled

20. Melinda earned $550 in one month and saved 30% of her earnings. She is saving for a new bicycle which costs $825. How much has Melinda saved so far? At this rate, how long will it take her to save enough money to buy the bicycle?

_____

21. In a survey of 560 students, 35% chose math as their favorite subject. Use multiplication to find the number of students who chose math.

A. Write the percent in fraction form. $35\% = \frac{\boxed{}}{100}$

B. How many students chose math? Show your work.

_____

C. Double-check your answer by converting the percent to a decimal and using decimal multiplication. Write the percent in decimal form. $35\% = $ _____

D. Multiply the decimal by the total number of students surveyed.

_____

E. **Open Ended** Which method do you prefer, converting the percent to a fraction and multiplying or converting the percent to a decimal and multiplying? Why?

_____

_____

_____

Expressions, Equations, and Inequalities

Visual Artist

STEM
POWERING INGENUITY

Edna Andrade was an American artist and educator. She began her teaching career as an elementary school art teacher in Virginia. She later taught at the University of the Arts in Philadelphia and Tulane University in New Orleans. As an artist, Andrade was an early pioneer in the op art movement. Op art features geometric patterns that create optical illusions such as a sense of motion, flashing, or vibration.

STEM Task:

Visual artists may mix paints to match a color they used before or to create new colors. Matthew is an artist. He mixes 4 parts blue paint with 2 parts yellow paint to make a pint of green paint. After he uses all of the green paint, he wants to make 3 more pints of the same shade. How much blue and yellow paint should he mix? Explain.

Learning Mindset
Resilience Monitors Emotions

Artists may be frustrated as they strive to achieve a particular result, or sad when their work receives negative criticism. What emotions do you experience when you are learning something new? Do you feel excited, or do you feel discouraged and want to give up? It's normal to experience negative emotions at times, but learning to recognize and address these feelings will help prevent them from being obstacles to learning. As you work, monitor your thoughts and feelings by asking yourself these questions.

- How am I feeling about this task? Am I frustrated, bored, or tired? Am I worried or embarrassed about how others perceive my work?

- Is there a fixed-mindset voice in my head that is contributing to my negative feelings? If so, what is that voice telling me? What is triggering that voice?

- How can I activate my growth-mindset voice to counter messages from the fixed-mindset voice?

Remember, feelings often shift and change. If you find yourself struggling with negative emotions, take a few deep breaths. You may also want to take a short break or talk to someone about your feelings.

Reflect

Q As you worked on the STEM Task, how did you feel about your learning?

Q Did any part of the STEM Task trigger a fixed-mindset voice in your head? If so, what part? How did you use self-talk to activate a growth-mindset voice?

Numerical and Algebraic Expressions

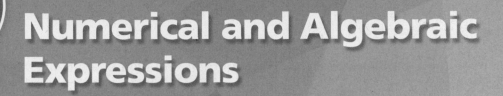

Guess the Number

Follow the directions to see if the number game is true for any number.

Ethan discovered a number game. See if it works for any number.

A. Try Ethan's number game.

> I predict that your final answer is 3!

Think of a number. _____

Add 5. _____

Double the result. _____

Subtract 4. _____

Divide by 2. _____

Subtract the original number.

_____

B. How does your final number compare with Ethan's prediction?

_____

C. Use your original number to write a single numerical expression that represents the steps of the game.

_____

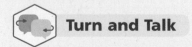 **Turn and Talk**

- How does your expression show the order in which the operations should be performed?

- How could you change your expression so that it would model the game no matter which number you start with?

Are You Ready?

Complete these problems to review prior concepts and skills you will need for this module.

Write and Interpret Numerical Expressions

Write the expression.

1. 3 times the sum of 4 and 9: _____

2. Divide 12 by 4 and add 5: _____

3. Subtract 6 from 13, then multiply by 2: _____

4. The quantity 12 times 5 divided by 7: _____

5. The quantity 32 minus 16 multiplied by 9: _____

Write a statement to represent each expression.

6. $3 \times 2 + 5$: _____

7. $6(5 + 7)$: _____

8. $24 - 8 \div 4$: _____

9. $(9 + 5) \div 7$: _____

Evaluate Simple Numerical Expressions

Find the value of each expression.

10. $4 \times (3 + 5) =$ _____

11. $7 + (3 \times 2) =$ _____

12. $(45 \div 9) \times 2 =$ _____

13. $(3 + 9) \div 3 =$ _____

14. $(12 + 6) \div 2 + 4 =$ _____

15. $(20 - 11) \times 5 + 1 =$ _____

Name

Understand and Apply Exponents

(I Can) write and evaluate numerical expressions involving whole-number exponents.

Spark Your Learning

Brianna needs to contact members of the softball league. She calls 4 members in the morning. Those 4 people each call 4 more people in the afternoon. That evening, those additional people each call 4 others. How many people are called that evening?

Turn and Talk Is there another way to solve this problem? Explain.

© Houghton Mifflin Harcourt Publishing Company • Image Credit: ©Sadeugra/E+/Getty Images

Build Understanding

1 A small company uses a phone tree to notify employees of cancellation due to bad weather. The manager calls 2 people. Then each of those people calls 2 more people, and so on.

Connect to Vocabulary

When a number is raised to a power, the number that is used as a factor is the **base**.
An **exponent** is the number that indicates how many times the base is used as a factor.

Round	Number of Calls
1	2
2	2 × 2
3	2 × 2 × 2
4	2 × 2 × 2 × 2
5	2 × 2 × 2 × 2 × 2

phone tree

A. Complete the table. What pattern(s) do you see?

_____

_____

B. Complete each statement to describe the pattern.

In the 2nd round of calling, the total number of calls in that round is equal to the product of two 2s.

In the 3rd round of calling, the total number of calls in that round is equal to the product of ___3___ 2s.

In the 4th round of calling, the total number of calls in that round is equal to the product of ___4___ 2s.

In the 5th round of calling, the total number of calls in that round is equal to the product of ___5___ 2s.

C. How is the number of the round of calling related to the number of times 2 is used as a factor?

_____

_____

Turn and Talk When is it useful to write an expression using a base and an exponent? Give an example.

Step It Out

A dot is sometimes used instead of the symbol × to represent multiplication.
You can use an exponent and a base to show repeated multiplication of a factor.
The expression shown is read as "7 to the 5th power."

$$7 \cdot 7 \cdot 7 \cdot 7 \cdot 7 = 7^5 \longleftarrow \text{exponent}$$

5 repeated factors   base

There are two specially named powers:

8^2 could be read as "8 to the 2nd power" or as "8 squared."

9^3 could be read as "9 to the 3rd power" or as "9 cubed."

2 ▷ An exponent tells how many times a number is used in an expression.
Look at the expression 5 · 5 · 5 · 5.

A. How many times is the factor 5 used? __4 times__

B. Complete each statement.

$5 \cdot 5 \cdot 5 \cdot 5 = 5^{\boxed{4}}$ $8 \cdot 8 \cdot 8 \cdot 8 \cdot 8 = 8^{\boxed{5}}$

C. Write an equivalent repeated multiplication expression.

$2^3 = \boxed{2} \times \boxed{2} \times \boxed{2}$ $\left(\frac{1}{3}\right)^5 = \boxed{\frac{1}{3}} \times \boxed{\frac{1}{3}} \times \boxed{\frac{1}{3}} \times \boxed{\frac{1}{3}} \times \boxed{\frac{1}{3}}$

3 ▷ Find the value of each expression.

A. $5^3 = \boxed{5} \times \boxed{5} \times \boxed{5} = \boxed{125}$

B. $4^5 = \boxed{4} \times \boxed{4} \times \boxed{4} \times \boxed{4} \times \boxed{4} = \boxed{1024}$

Check Understanding

1. A farming community begins with one resident. Then every year, the number of residents multiplies by 10. Write an expression using an exponent to represent the number of residents in the community after 5 years.

   _____

2. On a tree, the trunk splits into 5 branches. Then each branch splits into 5 smaller branches, and each of those branches splits into 5 very thin branches. How many very thin branches are on the tree?

   _____

3. Explain the expression 2^{10}. Complete the sentences.

   A. The number $\boxed{2}$ is used as a repeated factor $\boxed{10}$ times.

   B. The base of the expression is $\boxed{100}$ and the exponent is $\boxed{1000}$.

   C. The value of 2^{10} is $\boxed{10.000}$

On Your Own

4. **STEM** A certain bacterium splits itself into 2 identical cells in 1 day. Each of those new cells is capable of splitting itself into 2 identical cells in 1 day. So the first day there are 2 cells, the second day there are 2 × 2 cells, and so on. Write and evaluate an expression using a base and an exponent to represent the number of cells present at the end of the 7th day.

Bacterium splitting

128

5. Write each expression in exponential form.

   A. $9 \cdot 9 \cdot 9 \cdot 9 \cdot 9 =$ ___ 9^5 **B.** $\frac{1}{8} \cdot \frac{1}{8} \cdot \frac{1}{8} =$ ___ $\frac{1}{8}^3$

For Problems 6–7, write the exponential expression as an equivalent repeated multiplication expression and then evaluate the expression.

6. $6^3 =$ ___ $6 \cdot 6 \cdot 6$

7. $2^6 =$ ___ $2 \cdot 2 \cdot 2 \cdot 2 \cdot 2 \cdot 2$

8. Explain the expression 10^5. Complete the sentences.

   The number ☐ is used as a repeated factor.

   ☐ is used as a factor ☐ times.

9. **(MP) Use Repeated Reasoning** Carrie recruits 3 of her friends to sell candles to raise money for new playground equipment. The next day each of her 3 friends recruits 3 more friends. This pattern continues for 5 days. Write an exponential expression to represent the number of new recruits on the 5th day.

   A. The number ⟨3⟩ is used as a repeated factor ⟨5⟩ times.

   B. Write the expression as an equivalent repeated multiplication expression. Then write it as an expression with an exponent.

   ⟨3⟩ × ⟨3⟩ × ⟨3⟩ × ⟨3⟩ × ⟨3⟩ = ⟨243⟩

⊟ **I'm in a** Learning Mindset!

What facts about exponents can I talk about?

_____

_____

© Houghton Mifflin Harcourt Publishing Company • **Image Credit:** ©CNRI/Science Source

Name _____

Understand and Apply Exponents

1. Explain the expression 12^8. Complete the sentences.

   The number | 12 | is used as a repeated factor.

   | 12 | is used as a factor | 8 | times.

2. (MP) **Use Repeated Reasoning** At 4 o'clock, Devon called 6 friends to let them know that the weather forecast called for snow. At 6 o'clock, each of his friends called 6 other friends. At 8 o'clock, each of those friends called 6 of their other friends.

   A. Write an expression to represent the number of people called at 6 o'clock using a base and an exponent. 8 _____

   B. Write an expression to represent the number of people called at 8 o'clock using a base and an exponent. 10 _____

   C. How many people were called in all? Explain.
   _____ what _____ 36 _____

3. (MP) **Reason** Compare the expressions 3^8 and $3^5 \times 3^3$ using the properties of multiplication. What do you notice?

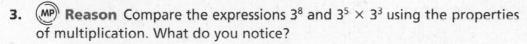

4. **Math on the Spot** Write the expression in exponential form.

   A. $7 \cdot 7 \cdot 7 \cdot 7 =$ _~~7×7~~ 7^4_

   B. $3 \cdot 3 \cdot 3 \cdot 3 \cdot 3 \cdot 3 =$ _3^6_

For Problems 5–6, write the exponential expression as an equivalent repeated multiplication expression and then evaluate the expression.

5. $2^8 =$ _$2 \cdot 2 \cdot 2 \cdot 2 \cdot 2 \cdot 2 \cdot 2 \cdot 2$_

6. $5^5 =$ _$5 \cdot 5 \cdot 5 \cdot 5 \cdot 5$_

For Problems 7 and 8, write the repeated multiplication expression using a single exponent.

7. $8 \cdot 8 \cdot 8 \cdot 8 \cdot 8 =$ _____

8. $4 \cdot 4 \cdot 4 \cdot 4 \cdot 4 \cdot 4 \cdot 4 =$ _____

Test Prep

9. Select all expressions equivalent to $3 \cdot 3 \cdot 3 \cdot 3 \cdot 3 \cdot 3 \cdot 3 \cdot 3$.

   (A) 8^3

   (B) 3^8

   (C) $3^5 \cdot 3^3$

   (D) $3^4 \cdot 3^4$

   (E) $3^7 \cdot 3^2$

10. Select all expressions equivalent to $11 \cdot 11 \cdot 11$.

   (A) 11^3

   (B) 3^{11}

   (C) $11^1 \cdot 11^3$

   (D) $3^5 \cdot 3^6$

   (E) $11^1 \cdot 11^2$

11. Write two equivalent expressions, one exponential and one a product of factors, for "4 to the 5th power." Evaluate the expressions.

12. Select the correct expanded form of 7^5.

   (A) $7 \times 7 \times 7 \times 7 \times 7 \times 7 \times 7$

   (B) $7 \times 7 \times 7 \times 7 \times 7$

   (C) $5 \times 5 \times 5 \times 5 \times 5 \times 5 \times 5$

   (D) $5 \times 5 \times 5 \times 5 \times 5$

Spiral Review

13. Letty answered 15 out of 20 questions correctly on her history quiz. What is her grade as a percent?

14. 1 kilogram is equivalent to about 2.2 pounds. An orangutan weighs 142 pounds. What is its mass in kilograms?

15. Which is the better buy, a 31-ounce bottle of ketchup for $2.53 or a 64-ounce bottle for $5.05?

16. A pancake recipe calls for $4\frac{1}{2}$ cups of whole-wheat flour. If the chef wants to split the recipe into 3 equal batches, how much flour should be in each batch?

Name _____

Write and Evaluate Numerical Expressions for Situations

(I Can) write and evaluate numerical expressions using the order of operations.

Spark Your Learning

Two tour groups are visiting an aquarium. There are 20 children in one group and 22 children in the other. Along with the 2 group leaders, there are 5 additional adults between the two groups. If the cost per child is $9.00 and the total for both groups is $490, what is the cost per adult? Explain your reasoning.

 Turn and Talk If the aquarium gave both groups a 10% discount, what would the total cost be? Explain.

Build Understanding

The parts of an expression that are added or subtracted are called **terms**.

Connect to Vocabulary

A **numerical expression** is an expression that contains only numbers and operations.

$7 + 8 \times 2^2$

$25 - 16 + 9$

are examples of numerical expressions.

 Consider the expressions in Parts A–D.

A. How many terms does the expression $14 + 9$ have? What are they? Explain how you know.

_____

B. How many terms does the expression $6 + 20 - 9$ have? What are they? Explain how you know.

_____

_____

C. The expression $25 + (4 \times 5)$ has _____ terms, namely _____, because it is a _____ of those expressions.

The expression 4×5 has two _____, namely _____, because it is a _____ of those expressions.

D. The expression $\frac{7}{10} - \frac{11}{20}$ has _____ terms, namely,

_____ and _____, because it is a _____ of those expressions.

The fraction expression $\frac{7}{10}$ is also a _____ because it represents

7 _____ 10.

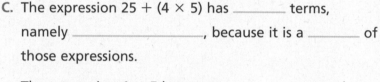

2 ▶ How can you write a numerical expression to represent a phrase?

A. Consider the phrase, "the product of 7 and the sum of 5 and 4."

The sum of 5 and 4 is written as _____.

The product of 7 and the sum of 5 and 4 is written as _____.

B. Consider the phrase, "the square of the difference of 9 and 3."

The difference of 9 and 3 is written as _____.

The square of the difference of 9 and 3 is written as _____.

Turn and Talk Compare and explain the meanings of 2^3 and $2(3)$.

Step It Out

You learned about the **order of operations** in a previous grade. Now we need to add exponents into our order of operations. Exponents are calculated after performing operations in parentheses or brackets.

Connect to Vocabulary

Evaluate means to find the value of a numerical or algebraic expression.

3 The correct order of operations has been used to evaluate the given expressions. Identify the operation used in each step.

A. $3^3 + 12 \times 2$

$27 + 12 \times 2$ Evaluate exponents.

$27 + 24$ _____

51 _____

B. $72 \div (15 - 6) + 3 \times 2^2$

$72 \div 9 + 3 \times 2^2$ _____

     _____

$72 \div 9 + 3 \times 4$ _____

$8 + 3 \times 4$ _____

$8 + 12$ _____

20 _____

C. $15 + 32 - 6 + (5 + 2)^2$

$15 + 32 - 6 + 7^2$ _____

$15 + 32 - 6 + 49$ _____

$47 - 6 + 49$ _____

$41 + 49$ _____

90 _____

Order of Operations

Perform operations in parentheses.
( )

Find the value of numbers with exponents.
exponents

Multiply and divide from left to right.
× ÷

Add and subtract from left to right.
+ −

Turn and Talk Why is it important to follow the order of operations?

4 A staff member is buying beds for all the dogs in a shelter. There are 10 dogs in one building and 14 dogs in another building. The price of a bed is shown.

DOG BED
$12

A. Complete the numerical expression to find the total cost.

☐(☐ + ☐)

B. How many terms are there in the parentheses?

_____

C. What is the first step for evaluating this expression? Complete the step.

_____

D. What is the next step for evaluating the expression using the order of operations? Complete the step.

_____

E. Use the **Distributive Property** to evaluate 12(10 + 14) and show it is equal to your previous evaluation.

F. What is the total cost of the beds?

_____

Check Understanding

1. Consider the expression $20 - (4^2 \div 2)$. How many terms does it have? Identify them. Also identify a quotient in the expression.

_____

2. Write a numerical expression to represent the phrase "the quotient of 12 and the product of 4 and 5".

_____

3. Use the order of operations to evaluate the expression.

$4(7 + 9) + 8^2 - 7$ _____

On Your Own

4. Lamar drinks 8 ounces of water with breakfast, 6 ounces of water with his vitamins, 16 ounces of water with his lunch, 16 ounces of water with his dinner, and 32 ounces of water from a bottle he carries throughout the day. Write and evaluate a numerical expression for the amount of water in ounces that he drinks in a week.

_____

5. (MP) **Use Structure** Kyle rides his bicycle to school 5 days a week. He also rides from school to the soccer field twice a week. Every day, he rides his bicycle home on the same paths. Write and evaluate a numerical expression for the total number of miles Kyle bikes during the week.

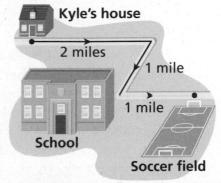

A. Write an expression for the number of miles Kyle rides his bike on a day when he does not go to the soccer field. _____

B. Write an expression for the number of miles Kyle bikes on a day when he does go to the soccer field. _____

C. Write and evaluate an expression for the total number of miles Kyle bikes during the week.

_____

For Problems 6–9, evaluate each expression.

6. $25 - 21 \div 3 -$ _____

7. $8 + 8 \div 8 =$ _____

8. $10 - 4 \times 1 + 7 =$ _____

9. $18 \div 3 - 1 \times 4 =$ _____

For Problems 10–11, complete the sentence using *sum, difference, product, quotient,* or *factors*.

10. The expression $20 + (8 \div 2)$ is the _____ of 20 and $(8 \div 2)$. The expression $8 \div 2$ is the _____ of 8 and 2.

11. The expression 11×6 has two _____, namely 11 and 6, because it is the _____ of those expressions.

For Problems 12–15, write a numerical expression to represent the phrase.

12. the sum of 6 and the square of 12 _____

13. the quotient of 30 and the sum of 5 and 7 _____

14. the difference of 4 cubed and 25 _____

15. 5 more than the product of 12 and 8 _____

© Houghton Mifflin Harcourt Publishing Company

16. (MP) **Critique Reasoning** Aman and Jennifer both evaluated the same numerical expression. They got different answers. Who simplified the expression correctly? Explain.

Aman

$1 + 4 \cdot 3^2$

$5 \cdot 3^2$

15^2

225

Jennifer

$1 + 4 \cdot 3^2$

$1 + 4 \cdot 9$

$1 + 36$

37

17. (MP) **Use Repeated Reasoning** A field has 11 dandelions. Complete the statements by writing numerical expressions to show the total number of dandelions after 1 month, 2 months, 3 months, and 4 months. Use exponents in your answers for Part A.

The number of dandelions doubles every month.

A. After 1 month, there are $11 \cdot \boxed{}$ dandelions.

After 2 months, there are $11 \cdot \boxed{}$ dandelions.

After 3 months, there are _____ dandelions.

After 4 months, there are _____ dandelions.

B. Evaluate the last expression in Part A. Show your work.

For Problems 18–21, evaluate the expression.

18. $7 + 15 \div 3 \cdot 2 - 12$ _____

19. $6(9 - 6) - 2^3 + 4$ _____

20. $(7 - 6) + 9 - 2 \cdot 5$ _____

21. $7 + (2 - 1)^5 \cdot 8$ _____

△ ✕
➕ 👤 ➗ **I'm in a Learning Mindset!**

How did I apply prior knowledge to evaluate numerical expressions using order of operations?

© Houghton Mifflin Harcourt Publishing Company • **Image Credit:** ©Vaclav Volrab/Shutterstock

Write and Evaluate Numerical Expressions for Situations

1. **STEM** Margarite is building 3 prototypes of a robot she designed. Each robot includes a body and a remote control. She needs 450 inches of wire for each body and 120 inches for each remote control. In addition, she is going to build one master remote to run all three robots at once. The master remote will require 380 inches of wire. Write and evaluate a numerical expression to find the total length of wire she will need.

    A. Write an expression for the amount of wire needed for a robot.

    _____

    B. Write an expression for the total amount of wire needed for all 3 robots.

    _____

    C. Write an expression for the amount of wire needed for all 3 robots and the master remote.

    _____

    D. How much wire will Margarite need to complete her project?

    _____

2. For a company picnic, Todd fills 30 paper cups with ketchup and Yuki fills 27 paper cups with ketchup. Each paper cup holds 1 ounce. Later, Todd and Yuki learn that two other company employees completed exactly the same task. How many ounces of ketchup did the four employees prepare?

    _____

3. **MP Reason** At football practice on Monday, Brandon threw a football into the target 5 times. The next Monday, he tripled the number of targets he hit. On the following Monday, his hits doubled that of the week before. Write and evaluate a numerical expression to find how many times he hit the target during those three weeks.

    _____

Math on the Spot For Problems 4–7, evaluate each expression.

4. $25 - 21 \div 3$

    _____

5. $50 + 12 \div 3 \times 5 - 2$

    _____

6. $7 + 3^3 \times 10$

7. $40 - 4^2 \times 2 + 1$

Test Prep

8. Evaluate the expression.

$13 - 2 \times 5 + 7^2$

Ⓐ 104

Ⓑ 594

Ⓒ 100

Ⓓ 52

9. Mr. Kershner is a school nurse. He uses, on average, 24 self-adhesive bandages during each spring month: March, April, and May. He also knows that in June there are several field days and he will need 4 times the number of bandages for that month. How many bandages should he order for March through June? If the bandages cost 3 cents each, what is his total cost for March through June?

10. To evaluate the expression, what is the first step to follow?

$2(7 + 3 \div 3 \times 7)^2 - 100$

Ⓐ Divide $3 \div 3$.

Ⓑ Multiply 3×7.

Ⓒ Multiply by 2.

Ⓓ Add $7 + 3$.

11. Evaluate $15 \times 3 + 7(4 + 1) - 5^2$. What is the second step according to order of operations?

Spiral Review

12. What is 30% of 400?

13. In a circle graph displaying the most popular fruit sold to students in the school cafeteria, the ratio of apples to the total pieces of fruit sold is $\frac{3}{5}$. What is the angle measure of the apples section of the graph?

14. On the last history test, Kim scored 80% and Juan answered 27 out of 30 questions correctly. Who answered more questions correctly?

Name _____

Write Algebraic Expressions to Model Situations

(**I Can**) use variables to write an algebraic expression to represent a real-world problem.

Spark Your Learning

Viola is helping to plant a rectangular community garden. A plant handbook states that 1 plant requires 8 square inches of soil. Given the dimensions of the rectangular garden shown, how many plants can be planted in the garden? Explain.

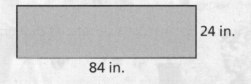

24 in.

84 in.

 Turn and Talk If the width of the garden were increased to 36 inches, how many more plants could be put in the garden? Explain.

Build Understanding

An **algebraic expression** is an expression that contains one or more variables.

A **variable** is a letter or symbol used to represent one or more unknown quantities.

A **constant** is a specific number whose value does not change.

$2x + 75$ is an example of an algebraic expression.

2 is a coefficient.   *x* is a variable.   75 is a constant.

1 A day-care center has 2 baskets of dolls. One basket has 8 dolls, and the other basket has an unknown number of dolls in it. What expression can you use to represent this situation?

A. Can you write a numerical expression to represent this situation? Explain.

_____

B. What do you know about this situation? Complete the sentences.

There are ☐ baskets. One has ☐ dolls in it.

The other basket has _____ number of dolls.

C. If you do not have all the information you need, could you still write an expression to represent this situation? Explain.

_____

_____

D. Complete the bar model to represent this situation. Then write an expression to represent the bar model.

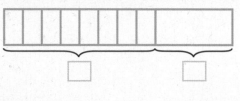

The expression is ☐ + ☐.

E. Explain why the expression in Part D is an algebraic expression. Identify the coefficient.

_____

_____

 Turn and Talk Suppose the number of dolls in both baskets is unknown. Write an expression for the number of dolls. Do the variables you choose make a difference? Explain.

Step It Out

2 ▸ Kristen works at a supermarket. She wants to divide a box of apples equally among 3 displays.

A. Let *f* represent the total number of apples. Complete the bar model to express the number of apples each display will have.

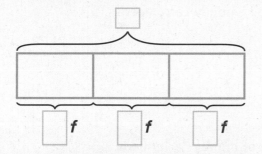

B. Write an algebraic expression that represents the number of apples each display will have. Write your answer as a product and a quotient.

_____

C. Kristen decides to use an additional 12 apples for each display. What is the new algebraic expression that represents the number of apples each display will have?

_____

 Turn and Talk How would the algebraic expression change if, instead of putting an additional 12 apples in each display, Kristen decided to keep 6 apples from the total number before she divided them among the 3 displays? Explain.

Check Understanding

1. Raj is 3 inches taller than Howard. Let *h* represent Howard's height. Write an algebraic expression to represent Raj's height.

_____

2. Marcus has 4 times the sum of 6 and the number of marbles David has. Let *d* represent the number of marbles David has. Write an algebraic expression to represent how many marbles Marcus has.

_____

For Problems 3–4, write an algebraic expression for the words. Identify the coefficient(s).

3. the quotient of *t* and 13

4. the product of *g* and 2 plus *m*

_____   _____

On Your Own

5. **(MP) Use Tools** Larry and Zach have both been hired to do odd jobs. Larry will receive $7 for each of the 3 flower beds he weeds and y dollars to edge a yard. Zach will receive $25 to clean out a garage and y dollars to wash a car. Both Larry and Zach need to make x dollars to meet their goal. Write an expression for the amount each still has to earn to reach his goal.

A. Complete the model to show the amount of money Larry needs.

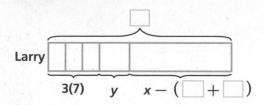

3(7) y $x - (\Box + \Box)$

B. Complete the model to show the amount of money Zach needs.

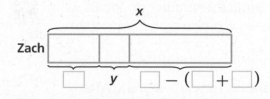

$\Box$ y $\Box - (\Box + \Box)$

C. **(MP) Reason** Who has more money left to earn before meeting his goal? Explain.

_____

_____

6. Jayden begins with 25 cups with soil at the greenhouse. Each day he will fill 5 cups more. Write an algebraic expression to represent the number of cups he will have after n days. Identify the coefficient.

_____

For Problems 7–9, write an algebraic expression for the word expression.

7. 32 divided by b

8. the sum of 112 and m

9. the product of $\frac{1}{2}$ and x

_____   _____   _____

I'm in a Learning Mindset!

What about writing algebraic expressions triggers a fixed-mindset voice in my head?

_____

Write Algebraic Expressions to Model Situations

1. **Financial Literacy** Clyde rents a tuxedo for several days. Let *d* represent the number of additional days Clyde uses the tuxedo. Write an algebraic expression to represent the total cost of the rental after *d* additional days.

TUXEDO RENTAL

First day $75
each additional day $10

_____

2. **Math on the Spot** Sage and Tom started the month with the same number of talk minutes on their cell phone plans. Sage talked for 7 minutes with her dad. Tom talked for 4 minutes with a friend and for 3 minutes with his mom. Do Sage and Tom have the same number of talk minutes left on their cell phone plans?

   A. Complete the models to represent Sage's and Tom's minutes. Then write an algebraic expression to represent the number of minutes each has left.

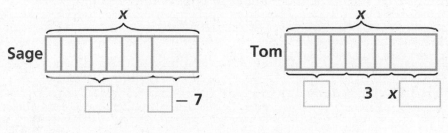

   B. Do Sage and Tom have the same number of talk minutes left on their cell phone plans? Explain your reasoning.

   _____

   _____

3. **Open Ended** Nola fits together *p* pieces a day of a 5,000-piece puzzle. Write an algebraic expression for this situation and explain what it represents.

   _____

   _____

For Problems 4–5, write an algebraic expression for the word expression.

4. the product of 7, and *c* minus 13

5. the quotient of 10 times *m* and 7

   _____   _____

Identify the variable, coefficient, and constant term of the expression.

6. $4b + 24$

   variable:_____

   coefficient:_____

   constant:_____

7. $11y + 4.5$

   variable:_____

   coefficient:_____

   constant:_____

Test Prep

8. Alix has x dollars per week available for lunch. She spends \$3 on lunch every weekday. Write an algebraic expression to represent how much money she has left over at the end of the week.

_____

9. The Color My Room painting company charges a fixed set-up fee of \$20 per job and then \$0.25 per square foot to paint. Let p represent the square footage of a laundry room's walls. Write an algebraic expression to find the total cost to paint the room.

_____

10. A farmer gathered eggs from his chickens. Let e represent the total number of eggs he collected. He gives a third of the eggs to his friend, 7 of the eggs to another friend, and the rest to his cousin. Select all the algebraic expressions that represent the number of eggs he gives to his cousin.

    (A) $\frac{1}{3}e + 7$

    (B) $e - \frac{1}{3}e - 7$

    (C) $e - \frac{e}{3} - 7$

    (D) $\frac{e}{3} - 7$

11. Let g represent the total number of hours Greg will travel on his trip across the country to attend his cousin's wedding. The first day he travels 8 hours. The second day he travels 9 hours. The third day he had mechanical problems and only drove for 4 hours. Write an algebraic expression to represent how much time he has left to drive.

_____

Spiral Review

12. What is 75% of 128?

_____

13. What is 2,220 yards in miles? Round to the nearest tenth of a mile. [Note: 1 mile = 1,760 yards]

_____

14. Haru is putting lace around the edge of a rectangular pillow case that has a length of 12.75 inches and a width of 15.5 inches. How much lace does he need?

_____

Name

Interpret and Evaluate Algebraic Expressions

(I Can) interpret and evaluate algebraic expressions using the order of operations.

Step It Out

You can evaluate an expression with a variable by substituting a known value for the variable.

6 ft

w ft

1 Evaluate each expression for the given value of the variable.

A. The area of a rug can be represented by the expression 6w.

Find the area when $w = 4$ feet.

Substitute 4 for w. $6\left(\boxed{}\right)$

Multiply. $\boxed{}$

When $w = 4$ ft, $6w = \boxed{}$ square feet.

B. Evaluate 18y when $y = \frac{2}{3}$.

Substitute $\frac{2}{3}$ for y. $18\left(\dfrac{\boxed{}}{\boxed{}}\right)$

Multiply. $\boxed{}$

When $y = \frac{2}{3}$, $18y = \boxed{}$.

C. Evaluate $x - 12$ when $x = 18.6$.

Substitute 18.6 for x. $\boxed{} - 12$

Subtract. $\boxed{}$

When $x = 18.6$, $x - 12 = \boxed{}$.

Turn and Talk For the expression in Part A, how is the value of the expression related to the value of the variable? Explain.

Sometimes expressions have more than one variable.

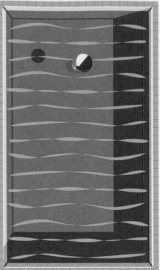

2 The **perimeter** of a rectangular swimming pool can be written as $2l + 2w$, where l is the length and w is the width. Find the perimeter when $l = 7.5$ meters and $w = 4.5$ meters.

Substitute 7.5 for l and 4.5 for w. $2\left(\boxed{}\right) + 2\left(\boxed{}\right)$

Multiply. $\boxed{} + \boxed{}$

Add. $\boxed{}$

When $l = \boxed{}$ and $w = \boxed{}$, $2l + 2w = \boxed{}$ meters.

3 Evaluate each expression for the given values of the variables.

A. Evaluate $4x^3 - 3y$ when $x = 2$ and $y = 10$.

Substitute 2 for x and 10 for y. $4\left(\boxed{}\right)^3 - 3\left(\boxed{}\right)$

Evaluate the exponent. $4\left(\boxed{}\right) - 3\left(\boxed{}\right)$

Multiply. $\boxed{} - \boxed{}$

Subtract. $\boxed{}$

When $x = \boxed{}$ and $y = \boxed{}$, $4x^3 - 3y = \boxed{}$.

B. Evaluate $6s + \dfrac{d}{2}$ when $s = \dfrac{5}{12}$ and $d = 15$.

Substitute $\dfrac{5}{12}$ for s and 15 for d. $6\left(\dfrac{\boxed{}}{\boxed{}}\right) + \dfrac{\boxed{}}{2}$

Multiply. $\dfrac{\boxed{}}{\boxed{}} + \dfrac{\boxed{}}{\boxed{}}$

Add. $\boxed{}$

Divide. $\boxed{}$

When $s = \underline{}$ and $d = 15$, $6s + \dfrac{d}{2} = \boxed{}$.

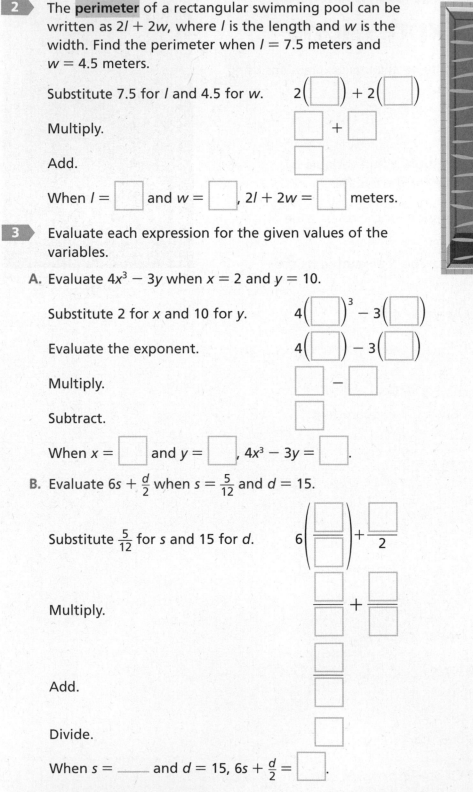

Turn and Talk How is evaluating algebraic expressions similar to evaluating numerical expressions? How is it different? Explain.

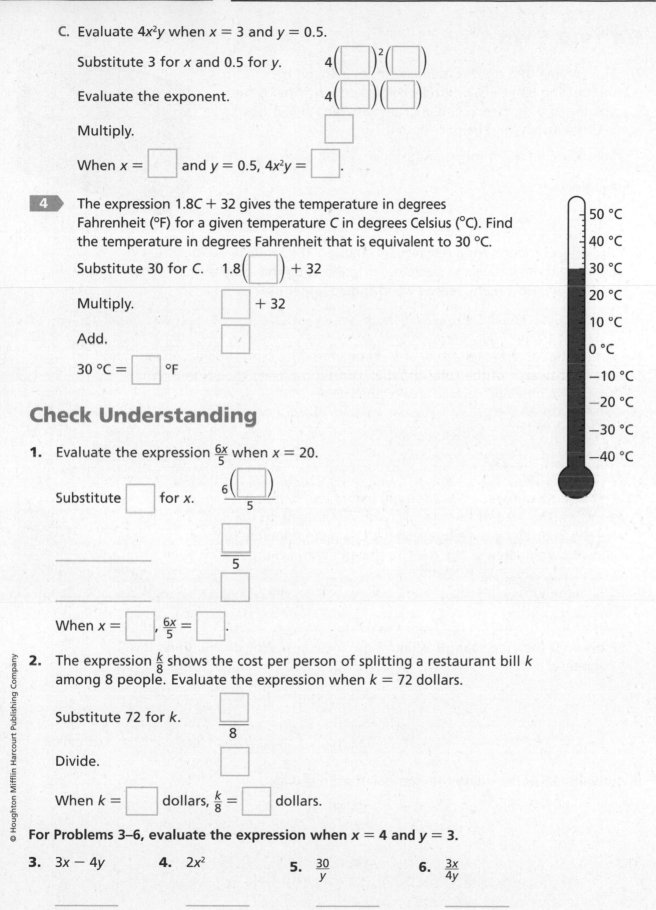

C. Evaluate $4x^2y$ when $x = 3$ and $y = 0.5$.

Substitute 3 for x and 0.5 for y. $\quad 4\left(\boxed{}\right)^2\left(\boxed{}\right)$

Evaluate the exponent. $\quad 4\left(\boxed{}\right)\left(\boxed{}\right)$

Multiply. $\quad \boxed{}$

When $x = \boxed{}$ and $y = 0.5$, $4x^2y = \boxed{}$.

4 The expression $1.8C + 32$ gives the temperature in degrees Fahrenheit (°F) for a given temperature C in degrees Celsius (°C). Find the temperature in degrees Fahrenheit that is equivalent to 30 °C.

Substitute 30 for C. $\quad 1.8\left(\boxed{}\right) + 32$

Multiply. $\quad \boxed{} + 32$

Add. $\quad \boxed{}$

$30\ °C = \boxed{}\ °F$

Check Understanding

1. Evaluate the expression $\frac{6x}{5}$ when $x = 20$.

Substitute $\boxed{}$ for x. $\quad \dfrac{6\left(\boxed{}\right)}{5}$

$\dfrac{\boxed{}}{5}$

$\boxed{}$

When $x = \boxed{}$, $\frac{6x}{5} = \boxed{}$.

2. The expression $\frac{k}{8}$ shows the cost per person of splitting a restaurant bill k among 8 people. Evaluate the expression when $k = 72$ dollars.

Substitute 72 for k. $\quad \dfrac{\boxed{}}{8}$

Divide. $\quad \boxed{}$

When $k = \boxed{}$ dollars, $\frac{k}{8} = \boxed{}$ dollars.

For Problems 3–6, evaluate the expression when $x = 4$ and $y = 3$.

3. $3x - 4y$

4. $2x^2$

5. $\dfrac{30}{y}$

6. $\dfrac{3x}{4y}$

© Houghton Mifflin Harcourt Publishing Company

On Your Own

7. The volume of a right rectangular prism is found by multiplying length by width by height, or *lwh*. What is the volume of a right rectangular prism with length 6 inches, width 4 inches, and height $\frac{3}{4}$ inch?

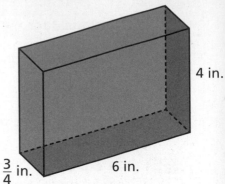

4 in.

$\frac{3}{4}$ in.   6 in.

Substitute 6 for *l*, 4 for *w*, and $\frac{3}{4}$ for *h*.   (___)(___)(___)

Multiply. _____

_____

8. Jasper needs wood for a rectangular sandbox. The sandbox will be 8 feet by 4.5 feet. He knows the perimeter is found using the expression $2l + 2w$, or $2(l + w)$. How many feet of wood should Jasper use?

_____

9. A cube has an edge length, *s*, of 5 centimeters. The expression $6s^2$ gives the surface area of the cube and the expression s^3 gives the volume. What are the volume and surface area of the cube?

surface area = ☐ cm²

volume = ☐ cm³

10. (MP) **Use Structure** A right triangle has a base, *b*, that is 6 inches. The area of the triangle, with *h* representing the height, is given by the expression $\frac{bh}{2}$. Complete the table to show how the area of the triangle changes with height:

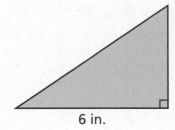

6 in.

Height (in.)	4	5	6	7	8
Area (in²)	12				

How does the area change as the height increases? Why do you think this happens?

_____

_____

_____

In Problems 11–14, evaluate the expression for $n = 0.75$.

11. $4n$

12. $6 - n$

_____

_____

13. $n + 12.5$

14. $0.5n$

_____

_____

15. (MP) **Critique Reasoning** Bill and Tia are trying to evaluate the expression $5x^2$ when $x = 3$. They both agree that 3 should be substituted for x. Tia says they should multiply 3 by 5, and then square the result. Bill says they should square 3 and then multiply by 5. Who is correct and why? What is the value of the expression?

16. **STEM** The expression $(F - 32)\frac{5}{9}$ gives the temperature in degrees Celsius (°C) for a given temperature F in degrees Fahrenheit (°F).

  A. Find the temperature in degrees Celsius that is equivalent to 77 °F.

  B. Water freezes at 32 °F. At what temperature does water freeze in degrees Celsius?

17. To find approximately how many pounds are equivalent to a given number of kilograms, use the expression $2.2k$, where k represents kilograms. How many pounds are equivalent to 6.5 kilograms?

18. To find the perimeter of a regular octagon, use the expression $8s$, where s represents side length. If the side length of a regular octagon is 1.5 feet, what is its perimeter in feet?

1.5 ft

19. A rectangle is twice as long as it is wide. If the width is w, the length is $2w$. The area of the rectangle can be found using the expression $2w^2$. If the rectangle is 10 centimeters wide, what is its area in square centimeters?

For Problems 20−25, evaluate the expression for the given value.

20. $6w$; $w = 0.1$

21. $x + 5\frac{1}{4}$; $x = 3\frac{1}{2}$

22. $1.4y$; $y = 5$

23. $\frac{48}{k}$; $k = 3$

24. z^5; $z = 2$

25. $2.5g^2$; $g = 4$

26. (MP) **Critique Reasoning** To evaluate the expression $(r + 6)^2$ for $r = 7$, Sayid says that r should be squared and 6 should be squared, and then the results should be added. Explain why Sayid is incorrect. Then find the value of the expression when $r = 7$.

_____

_____

_____

27. Evaluate the expression $4a^2 - \frac{b}{6}$ when $a = 6$ and $b = 36$. Show your work.

28. Rosa sells pens. She pays $0.75 for each pen and sells them for $1.25 each. She uses the expression $1.25p - 0.75p$, where p is the number of pens she sells, to calculate her profit. If Rosa sells 48 pens, what is her profit?

_____

29. Steve is playing a carnival game. He wants to win a prize, but he thinks he has about a 20% chance of winning. He uses the expression $0.2t$ to calculate the number of games he can expect to win if he plays t times. If he plays the game 12 times, about how many times can he expect to win?

_____

For Problems 30–35, evaluate the expression s^3 for the given value.

30. $s = 4$

31. $s = \frac{1}{2}$

_____

_____

32. $s = 0.3$

33. $s = 10$

_____

_____

34. $s = 1.2$

35. $s = \frac{1}{6}$

_____

_____

Name _____

LESSON 8.4
**More Practice/
Homework**

ONLINE
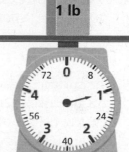
Video Tutorials and
Interactive Examples

Interpret and Evaluate Algebraic Expressions

1. Every day Jin reads for 0.75 hour in the morning and 1.25 hours in the evening. He uses the expression $0.75d + 1.25d$ to keep track of the number of hours he has read for any number of days, *d*. If Jin reads for 20 days, how many hours has he read? Show your work.

2. There are 16 ounces in 1 pound, so the expression $\frac{z}{16}$, where *z* represents the number of ounces, can be used to find the number of pounds for any given number of ounces. How many pounds are in 40 ounces?

   _____

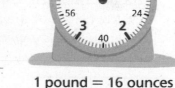

1 pound = 16 ounces

3. Jeffrey is 5 years older than his brother. If *j* represents Jeffrey's age, the expression $j - 5$ can be used to find his brother's age. If Jeffrey is 23, how old is his brother?

   _____

Math on the Spot For Problems 4–6, evaluate each expression.

4. $4x - 5$ for $x = 10$

   _____

5. $w \div 5 + w$ for $w = 20$

   _____

6. $3z^2 - 6z$ for $z = 5$

   _____

For Problems 7–10, evaluate each expression for $b = 5$.

7. $2.1b$ 8. $5b - 12.4$ 9. $7.4b$ 10. $4b^2$

   _____   _____   _____   _____

Test Prep

11. What is the value of the expression $8w - 4j^2$ when $w = 0.25$ and $j = 0.5$?

_____

12. What is the first step in evaluating an expression for given variable values?

_____

_____

13. Match the expression and its value to the value of x that gives the expression its value by filling in the box in the correct column.

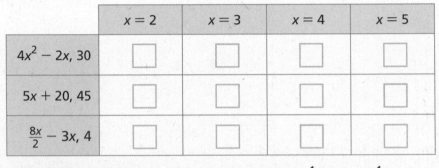

	$x = 2$	$x = 3$	$x = 4$	$x = 5$
$4x^2 - 2x$, 30	☐	☐	☐	☐
$5x + 20$, 45	☐	☐	☐	☐
$\frac{8x}{2} - 3x$, 4	☐	☐	☐	☐

14. Evaluate the expression $4(n + 3) - 5r$ for $n = \frac{1}{4}$ and $r = \frac{1}{5}$.

  Ⓐ 3   Ⓒ 8

  Ⓑ 5   Ⓓ 12

15. The surface area for a rectangular prism with a square base is given by the expression $2s^2 + 4sh$, where s is the side length of the square base and h is the height of the prism. What is the surface area in square feet of a rectangular prism when $s = 4$ feet and $h = 6$ feet?

_____

Spiral Review

16. Write a numerical expression to represent the phrase "the sum of 25 and the cube of 9." Do not evaluate the expression.

_____

17. A customer at a department store has $45.75. How many neckties can the customer buy if each tie costs $15.25?

_____

18. An expression is shown.

$5[8(7 - 4) \div 6]$

What is the value of the expression?

_____

Name

Identify and Generate Equivalent Algebraic Expressions

(I Can) use the properties of operations to determine if two expressions are equivalent and to generate equivalent algebraic expressions.

Step It Out

1 Substitute the given value into both expressions, and determine if the expressions have the same value.

A. Evaluate when $x = 6$.

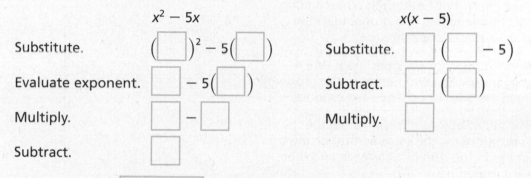

$$x^2 - 5x \qquad\qquad x(x - 5)$$

Substitute.	$(\boxed{})^2 - 5(\boxed{})$	Substitute.	$\boxed{}(\boxed{} - 5)$
Evaluate exponent.	$\boxed{} - 5(\boxed{})$	Subtract.	$\boxed{}(\boxed{})$
Multiply.	$\boxed{} - \boxed{}$	Multiply.	$\boxed{}$
Subtract.	$\boxed{}$		

The expressions | do / do not | have the same value when $x = 6$.

B. For the hexagon shown, Linda says the perimeter can be found using the expression $4\left(\frac{s}{2}\right) + 2s$. David says that he can use the expression $4s$ to find the perimeter. Do the expressions have the same value when $s = 8$?

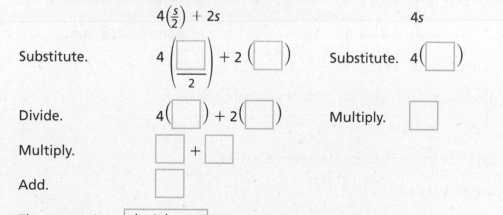

$$4\left(\frac{s}{2}\right) + 2s \qquad\qquad 4s$$

Substitute.	$4\left(\dfrac{\boxed{}}{2}\right) + 2\left(\boxed{}\right)$	Substitute.	$4(\boxed{})$
Divide.	$4(\boxed{}) + 2(\boxed{})$	Multiply.	$\boxed{}$
Multiply.	$\boxed{} + \boxed{}$		
Add.	$\boxed{}$		

The expressions | do / do not | have the same value when $s = 8$.

Turn and Talk How could you compare the expressions in Part A using the Distributive Property?

Equivalent expressions are expressions that have the same value for all possible values of the variable. Of course, you can't check every possible value! Fortunately, there is an easier way to show that expressions are equivalent. You can use the properties of operations. If you can apply the properties to one expression to get the other, then the two expressions are equivalent.

Properties of Operations	Examples
Commutative Property of Addition: When adding, changing the order of the numbers does not change the sum.	$a + b = b + a$
Commutative Property of Multiplication: When multiplying, changing the order of the numbers does not change the product.	$ab = ba$
Associative Property of Addition: When adding more than two numbers, the grouping of the numbers does not change the sum.	$(a + b) + c = a + (b + c)$
Associative Property of Multiplication: When multiplying more than two numbers, the grouping of the numbers does not change the product.	$(ab)c = a(bc)$
Distributive Property: Multiplying a number by a sum or difference is the same as multiplying by each number in the sum or difference and then adding or subtracting.	$a(b + c) = ab + ac$ $a(b - c) = ab - ac$

2 ▶ Identify the properties used to determine if the expressions are equivalent.

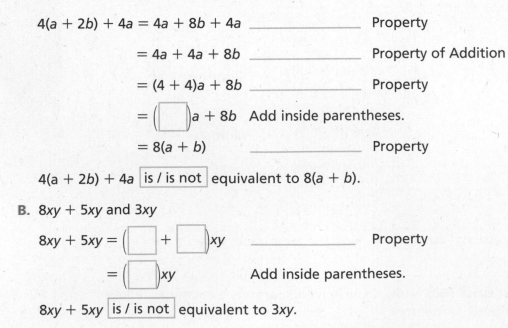

A. $4(a + 2b) + 4a$ and $8(a + b)$

$4(a + 2b) + 4a = 4a + 8b + 4a$ _____ Property

$= 4a + 4a + 8b$ _____ Property of Addition

$= (4 + 4)a + 8b$ _____ Property

$= \left(\boxed{}\right)a + 8b$ Add inside parentheses.

$= 8(a + b)$ _____ Property

$4(a + 2b) + 4a$ is / is not equivalent to $8(a + b)$.

B. $8xy + 5xy$ and $3xy$

$8xy + 5xy = \left(\boxed{} + \boxed{}\right)xy$ _____ Property

$= \left(\boxed{}\right)xy$ Add inside parentheses.

$8xy + 5xy$ is / is not equivalent to $3xy$.

3 A **triangle** is drawn so that starting from the shortest side, each side is one unit longer. The expression $s + (s + 1) + (s + 2)$ gives the perimeter of the triangle. Each of the s terms are like terms and can be combined.

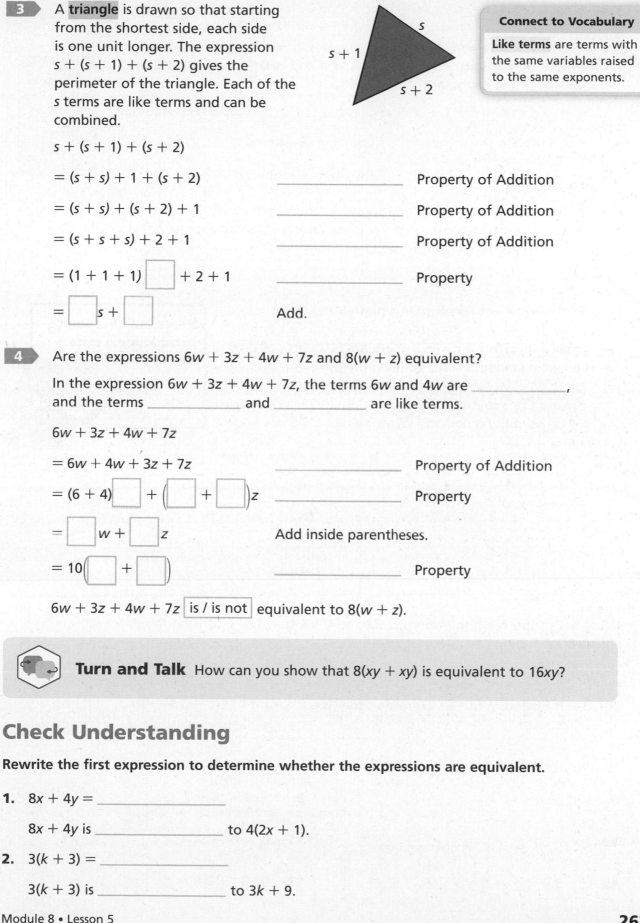

s

$s + 1$

$s + 2$

> **Connect to Vocabulary**
>
> **Like terms** are terms with the same variables raised to the same exponents.

$s + (s + 1) + (s + 2)$

$= (s + s) + 1 + (s + 2)$ _____ Property of Addition

$= (s + s) + (s + 2) + 1$ _____ Property of Addition

$= (s + s + s) + 2 + 1$ _____ Property of Addition

$= (1 + 1 + 1)\boxed{} + 2 + 1$ _____ Property

$= \boxed{}s + \boxed{}$ Add.

4 Are the expressions $6w + 3z + 4w + 7z$ and $8(w + z)$ equivalent?

In the expression $6w + 3z + 4w + 7z$, the terms $6w$ and $4w$ are _____, and the terms _____ and _____ are like terms.

$6w + 3z + 4w + 7z$

$= 6w + 4w + 3z + 7z$ _____ Property of Addition

$= (6 + 4)\boxed{} + \left(\boxed{} + \boxed{}\right)z$ _____ Property

$= \boxed{}w + \boxed{}z$ Add inside parentheses.

$= 10\left(\boxed{} + \boxed{}\right)$ _____ Property

$6w + 3z + 4w + 7z$ [is / is not] equivalent to $8(w + z)$.

> **Turn and Talk** How can you show that $8(xy + xy)$ is equivalent to $16xy$?

Check Understanding

Rewrite the first expression to determine whether the expressions are equivalent.

1. $8x + 4y =$ _____

 $8x + 4y$ is _____ to $4(2x + 1)$.

2. $3(k + 3) =$ _____

 $3(k + 3)$ is _____ to $3k + 9$.

On Your Own

3. (MP) **Use Structure** To find the perimeter of a rectangle, you can use different expressions: $\ell + w + \ell + w$, $2\ell + 2w$, or $2(\ell + w)$. Show that the expressions are equivalent.

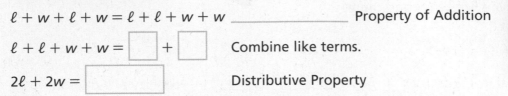

$\ell + w + \ell + w = \ell + \ell + w + w$ _____ Property of Addition

$\ell + \ell + w + w = \boxed{} + \boxed{}$ Combine like terms.

$2\ell + 2w = \boxed{}$ Distributive Property

4. (MP) **Reason** Marcus wrote an expression equivalent to $7(x + 8)$. Liz wrote a different expression that has the same value as Marcus' expression when $x = 2$. What could Liz's expression be?

_____

5. (MP) **Critique Reasoning** On a math test, students earn 4 points for each correct answer and lose 1 point for each incorrect answer. If there are 50 questions on the test, a student's score is shown by the expression $4(50 - w) - w$, where w is the number of wrong answers. Chris says that the expression $5(40 - w)$ could also be used. Is he correct? Why or why not? Show your work.

Today's math test scoring:
Correct answer: 4 points
Incorrect answer: −1 point

6. What property of operations is used to show that $12x + 6y$ is equivalent to $6(2x + y)$?

_____

7. **Open Ended** Write an expression that is equivalent to $5(d + 2f) + 5d$.

_____

For Problems 8–13, combine like terms.

8. $8w^2 - 3w^2 =$ _____

9. $x + 5 + 7x =$ _____

10. $6p^3 + 2p^2 + p^3 =$ _____

11. $2(x + 4) - 5 =$ _____

12. $g + 3 + 4(g + 2) =$ _____

13. $3(x^2 + 2) + 8 =$ _____

14. **(MP) Construct Arguments** Determine whether $6y + 18 + 3y$ is equivalent to $9(y + 2)$. Use properties of operations to justify your answer.

15. $6(4x + 3y)$ and $3(8x + 6y)$ are equivalent expressions. Explain why this is true.

16. Sarah earns $7.50 per hour babysitting and $5.00 per hour walking dogs. Last week she worked h hours babysitting and twice as many hours walking dogs. Write an expression to show the amount of money Sarah earned last week. Then multiply and combine like terms to write the expression as one term.

$7.50 per hour babysitting

17. **(MP) Reason** If $2n$ is added to an expression, it will be equivalent to $6(2n + 3)$. For which expression is this true:

$12n + 21$, $10 + 9$, $2(5n + 9)$, or $12n + 1$? Show how you know.

18. Determine whether the expressions $6x + 2 + 4x$ and $8x + 4$ have the same value when $x = 2$.

$6x + 2 + 4x$ is equal to ☐ when $x = 2$.

$8x + 4$ is equal to ☐ when $x = 2$.

Do $6x + 2 + 4x$ and $8x + 4$ have the same value when $x = 2$? _____

19. Identify the property used in each step.

$6x + (19 + 5x) = 6x + (5x + 19)$ _____ Property of Addition

$= (6x + 5x) + 19$ _____ Property of Addition

$= 11x + 19$

For Problems 20–21, determine if the expressions are equivalent.

20. $4m + 3m$ is _____ to $7m$.

21. $3j + 3k$ is _____ to $\frac{1}{4}(8j + 12k)$.

22. Which expression is NOT equivalent to the others? Explain.

$12p + 8$ $6p + 8 + 6p$ $4(p + 2) + 3p$ $4(3p + 2)$

23. A rectangle is 4 units wide and $6 + x$ units long. Write two expressions to represent the area of the rectangle.

_____

$\frac{3}{4}$ hour morning run

24. Open Ended Each weekday, Ana runs in the morning and the afternoon. Write an expression to show how long Ana runs for any number of days d. Then multiply and combine like terms to write the expression as one term.

$\frac{1}{2}$ hour afternoon run

_____

25. (MP) **Use Structure** Determine if the expressions $4x$ and $3x + 3$ have the same value when $x = 3$ and when $x = 0$.

$4x = \boxed{}$ when $x = 3$. $3x + 3 = \boxed{}$ when $x = 3$.

$4x = \boxed{}$ when $x = 0$. $3x + 3 = \boxed{}$ when $x = 0$.

The expressions have the same value when $x = \boxed{}$, but not when $x = \boxed{}$.

This means that $4x$ and $3x + 3$ _____ equivalent expressions.

For Problems 26–31, find an equivalent expression using the Distributive Property.

26. $25w + 30x$ **27.** $x(4 + y)$ **28.** $0.25(8r - 4m)$

_____   _____   _____

29. $24 + 8k$ **30.** $4xy - 16x$ **31.** $g^3(7 + h)$

_____   _____   _____

For Problems 32–33, determine if the expressions are equivalent.

32. $7(x + 4)$ is _____ to $7x + 4$.

33. $3r + 11 + 5r$ is _____ to $2(4r + 3) + 5$.

LESSON 8.5
**More Practice/
Homework**

ONLINE
Ed Video Tutorials and
Interactive Examples

Identify and Generate Equivalent Algebraic Expressions

1. **MP Use Tools** A pattern of squares is shown. It changes by the same amount in each step. Kwan has determined that he can use the expression $2(n + 1) - 3$ to find the number of squares for any step number n. Find an equivalent expression that Kwan also can use.

_____

2. Determine if the expressions have the same value when $x = 5$.

   $6x + 9$ and $3(2x + 3)$

   The value of $6x + 9$ when $x = 5$ is ⬚.

   The value of $3(2x + 3)$ when $x = 5$ is ⬚.

   Do $6x + 9$ and $3(2x + 3)$ have the same value when $x = 5$?

   _____

3. **MP Critique Reasoning** Trisha says that since $4(3s + 2)$ and $5(7s - 3)$ both equal 20 when $s = 1$, the expressions are equivalent. Is she correct? Explain.

   _____

4. A stained glass sun catcher in the shape of a pentagon is shown. Write and simplify an expression to find the perimeter of the pentagon in inches.

   _____

5. The surface area of a rectangular prism with length ℓ, width w, and height h is given by the expression $2\ell w + 2\ell h + 2wh$. Write an equivalent expression using the Distributive Property.

   _____

Math on the Spot For Problems 6–7, identify the property.

6. $3(6 \cdot 5) = (3 \cdot 6)5$ _____ Property of Multiplication

7. $w + z = z + w$ _____ Property of Addition

For Problems 8–9, determine whether the expressions are equivalent.

8. $6r + 3w - 2r + 5w$ is _____ to $4(r + 2w)$.

9. $12d + 8r$ is _____ to $2(5d + 4r) + 4d$.

© Houghton Mifflin Harcourt Publishing Company

Test Prep

10. What property of operations can be used to justify that the two expressions in this equation are equivalent? $6x^2 + 4x = 4x + 6x^2$

_____

11. Do the expressions $6x - 4x$ and $12x \div 6$ have the same value when $x = 6$?

$6x - 4x = \boxed{}$ when $x = 6$. $12x \div 6 = \boxed{}$ when $x = 6$.

The expressions $6x - 4x$ and $12x \div 6$ $\boxed{\text{do / do not}}$ have the same value when $x = 6$.

12. Fill in the box in the column of the expression that is equivalent to each expression on the side of the chart.

	$2(3x + 2y)$	$2(5x + 4y)$	$3(2x + 3y)$
$2(4x + 3y) - 2x - 2y$	☐	☐	☐
$2(4x + 3y) + 2(x + y)$	☐	☐	☐
$2(4x + 4y) - 2x + y$	☐	☐	☐

13. Which expressions are equivalent to $6(h + 4)$? Select all that apply.

Ⓐ $6h + 4$

Ⓑ $6h + 24$

Ⓒ $h + 10$

Ⓓ $4(h + 4) + 2(h + 4)$

Ⓔ $2(3h + 12)$

14. Write an expression that is equivalent to $24x + 36y$.

_____

Spiral Review

15. Penny is 100 centimeters tall. Jeremy is 38 inches tall. Who is taller? Show how you know. [Note: 1 centimeter $\approx$ 0.394 inches]

_____

16. What integer is the opposite of 12?

_____

17. Write $5 \times 5 \times 5 \times 5 \times 5 \times 5 \times 5$ as an expression with an exponent.

_____

Review

Vocabulary

Complete the following to review your vocabulary for this module.

Vocabulary
algebraic expression
base
coefficient
constant
equivalent expression
evaluate
exponent
like term
numerical expression
term
variable

1. For the expression 6^4:

   A. The _____ is 6 and the _____ is 4.

   B. A(n) _____ using repeated multiplication is $6 \times 6 \times 6 \times 6$.

2. A(n) _____ expression contains at least one variable, while a(n) _____ expression contains only numbers and operations.

3. For the expression $4x + 7$, the _____ is 4, the _____ is x, and the _____ is 7.

4. To _____ an algebraic or numerical expression, find its value.

5. _____ are terms with the same variables raised to the same exponents.

Concepts and Skills

For Problems 6–9, write an equivalent expression and evaluate.

6. $5 \times 5 \times 5 \times 5 =$ _____ = _____

7. _____ $= 4^3 =$ _____

8. _____ $= 2^5 =$ _____

9. $3 \times 3 \times 3 \times 3 \times 3 =$ _____ = _____

10. (MP) **Use Tools** Howard buys 5 pounds of apples at $2.50 per pound and 3 pounds of grapes at $1.50 per pound. What is the total cost of the fruit. State what strategy and tool you will use to answer the question, explain your choice, and then find the answer.

   _____

   _____

For Problems 11–12, identify the variable, coefficient, and constant term of the expression.

11. $12p + 47$

   variable: _____

   coefficient: _____

   constant: _____

12. $m + 7.5$

   variable: _____

   coefficient: _____

   constant: _____

13. Write an equivalent expression using the Distributive Property.

$$35 + 21 = 7\left(\boxed{} + \boxed{}\right)$$

14. Write an algebraic expression for 24 more than the product of 2 and x.

_____

15. Barbara has b bags that each contain 4 pounds of rice. She has another bag that has 3 pounds of rice. Write an algebraic expression that shows how many pounds of rice Barbara has.

_____

16. Evaluate the expression $5(m - 2) + 10w$ when $m = 8.4$ and $w = 1.25$.

(A) 8.75

(B) 44.5

(C) 80.25

(D) 52.5

17. Evaluate the expression $6x + \frac{2}{3} - 4y + \frac{1}{2}$ when $x = \frac{3}{4}$ and $y = \frac{1}{6}$.

(A) $2\frac{2}{3}$

(B) 5

(C) $1\frac{1}{2}$

(D) 4

18. Which expressions are equivalent to $8(2s + 6)$? Select all that apply.

(A) $16s + 6$

(B) $16s + 48$

(C) $10s + 48$

(D) $4(4s + 12)$

(E) $2(4s + 1) + 4(2s + 1)$

19. Write three expressions that are equivalent to $24k + 12k$.

_____

_____

20. A bag of plums costs $3 per pound and a bag of oranges costs $2 per pound. If Cammie buys x pounds of plums and y pounds of oranges, what expression could she write to find the total amount she will spend?

_____

Solve Problems Using Equations and Inequalities

EXPRESSION DARTS

Write expressions to match the scenario given.

The dartboard has sections numbered 1 to 20. You can "hit" a number on the dartboard by writing an expression equal to the number. Each expression must include each of the numbers 1, 2, 3, and 4 exactly once, but no other numbers. Try to get as many hits as you can. An example is shown.

1. $(4 + 2) \div 3 - 1 = 1$

2. _____

3. _____

4. _____

5. _____

6. _____

7. _____

8. _____

9. _____

10. _____

11. _____

12. _____

13. _____

14. _____

15. _____

16. _____

17. _____

18. _____

19. _____

20. _____

Turn and Talk

- Describe a strategy you used to hit different numbers

- How did grouping symbols help you hit different numbers?

Are You Ready?

Complete these problems to review prior concepts and skills you will need for this module.

Expressions with Variables

For Problems 1–10, find the value of the expression. Show your work.

1. $25 - m$ if $m = 9$

2. $50 + t$ if $t = 18$

3. $105 - a$ if $a = 75$

4. $112 + c$ if $c = 35$

5. $15 \times x$ if $x = 5$

6. $36 \div y$ if $y = 3$

7. $64 \div d$ if $d = 4$

8. $24 \times n$ if $n = 8$

9. $125 \div k$ if $k = 25$

10. $120 \times b$ if $b = 10$

Plot Points on a Number Line

For Problems 11–16, plot and label each integer on the number line.

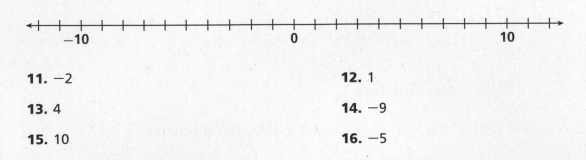

11. -2

12. 1

13. 4

14. -9

15. 10

16. -5

Write Equations to Represent Situations

I Can write and solve equations that model real-world situations involving all four operations.

Spark Your Learning SMALL GROUPS

Bella and Tia began the week with the same amount of money. Bella paid $9 to go to the movies. Tia spent $2 on snacks and $7 on a new T-shirt. Do Bella and Tia have the same amount of money left? Explain how you know.

| $\frac{1}{2}$ | $\frac{1}{2}$ |

Turn and Talk How would your representation of the problem change if both people earned money instead of spending money?

Build Understanding

Connect to Vocabulary

An **equation** is a mathematical sentence that shows that two expressions are equivalent.

1 ▶ You can think of an equation as a balance scale that is level with equal weight on both sides. The scale shows two quantities that have equal weight.

A. What does the left side of the scale show? Write your answer in words. Then write a mathematical expression using addition that represents the weight on the left side.

_____

_____

B. What does the right side of the scale show? Write your answer in words. Then write an integer that represents the weight on the right side.

_____

_____

C. What equation does the scale represent? _____

D. If the 2-unit weight is removed, will the scale remain balanced? What would the scale show if the 2-unit weight were removed?

_____

_____

2 ▶ If a scale is balanced but a value is unknown, you can solve for the unknown value.

A. What equation does the scale represent?

_____

B. How can you solve for x?

_____

_____

_____

C. Would other values of x keep the scale balanced? Explain.

_____

_____

_____

_____

 Turn and Talk Do you think an equation with one variable can have more than one solution? Explain.

Name _____

Step It Out

> 4 tickets to
> skate = $72

3 Ben buys tickets for the outdoor skating rink as shown. Each ticket costs the same amount. How much does 1 ticket cost?

A. What information do you know?

Ben bought ☐ tickets. Ben spent $ ☐ .

B. What do you need to find out?

_____

C. You can represent the cost of a ticket with the variable *c*. How are the unknown amount *c* and the amount Ben spent related?

_____

D. Model the situation using an equation, thinking about the different parts. Write the value or variable for each part of the model.

Number of tickets bought	×	Cost per ticket	=	Total amount spent

☐ × ☐ = 72

E. Substitute values for *c* to find the solution. Try $c = 20$.

When $c = 20$, the left side of the equation is _____ 72,

so $c = 20$ | is / is not | a *solution of the equation*.

> **Connect to Vocabulary**
>
> A **solution of an equation** is a value that makes the equation true.

F. Try other values for *c*, thinking about how close your result is to 72. What is the solution for the equation? How much does a ticket cost?

When $c = $ ☐ , $4 \times c = 72$. Each ticket costs ☐ .

Check Understanding

1. There are 30 students in a class. Today, 26 students are present. Write and solve an equation to show how many students are absent.

_____

For Problems 2–4, determine whether the given value is a solution for the equation. Answer *yes* or *no*.

2. $x - 8 = 12$, $x = 4$ 3. $12w = 36$, $w = 3$ 4. $\frac{y}{8} = 40$, $y = 5$

_____

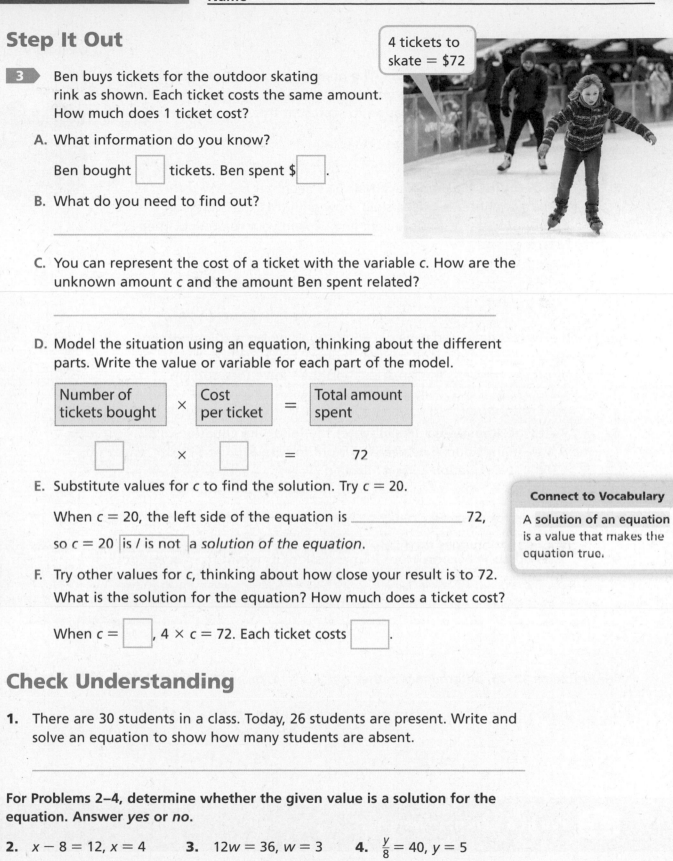

On Your Own

5. **MP Model with Mathematics** The number of red marbles in a jar is 3 times the number of blue marbles. There are 27 red marbles and *b* blue marbles. Write an equation to represent this situation. How many blue marbles are there?

6. **MP Model with Mathematics** Martha's daughter is $\frac{1}{4}$ Martha's age. If Martha's daughter is 12 years old, how old is Martha? Write an equation to represent this problem and explain your reasoning. Then find Martha's age.

7. Shan exercises daily. Today he did 85 pushups, which is 20 more than he usually does. How many pushups *p* does Shan usually do? Write an equation to represent this situation, and then solve the problem.

8. **MP Critique Reasoning** Phillip writes the following equation to show how many hours *h* he needs to work to earn $108 at $12 per hour: $\frac{h}{12} = 108$. Is his equation correct? Explain.

9. **MP Attend to Precision** How are expressions different from equations?

For Problems 10–15, determine whether $x = 3$, $x = 4$, or $x = 5$ is the solution.

10. $8x = 32$, $x =$ ☐

11. $42 - x = 37$, $x =$ ☐

12. $\frac{20}{x} = 4$, $x =$ ☐

13. $0.5x = 2$, $x =$ ☐

14. $\frac{x}{3} = 1$, $x =$ ☐

15. $x + 13 = 16$, $x =$ ☐

I'm in a Learning Mindset!

How do I keep myself motivated to write equations for real-world situations?

LESSON 9.1
**More Practice/
Homework**

ONLINE

Video Tutorials and
Interactive Examples

Write Equations to Represent Situations

1. **Math on the Spot** At Glencliff High School, the photography club has 23 members., which is 12 fewer than the hacky sack club. Does the hacky sack club have 35 members or 11 members? Write an equation to model the problem.

   _____

   _____

2. (MP) **Model with Mathematics** Tilda buys a shirt for d dollars. She uses a $50 gift card and receives the change shown. Write an equation for this situation.

   _____

$22.50 in change

3. **Open Ended** Write an equation that has a solution of 4. Use the variable n and multiplication.

   _____

4. (MP) **Model with Mathematics** One pound is equal to 0.454 kilogram. If Jim has a mass of 50 kilograms, write an equation to represent how many pounds p he weighs.

   _____

5. **Open Ended** Write a word problem that could be modeled by the equation $x + 5 = 12$.

   _____

   _____

   _____

6. (MP) **Model with Mathematics** Jon bought a pizza as shown. Write an equation to find the cost per slice c.

   _____

BIG DEAL! Large pizza
$20

For Problems 7–12, write whether the given value *is* or *is not* a solution for the equation.

7. $9x = 45$, $x = 5$

   5 _____ a solution.

8. $k - 6 = 8$, $k = 2$

   2 _____ a solution.

9. $n + 12 = 20$, $n = 32$

   32 _____ a solution.

10. $\frac{r}{5} = 25$, $r = 125$

    125 _____ a solution.

11. $\frac{16}{a} = \frac{1}{2}$, $a = 8$

    8 _____ a solution.

12. $24x = 6$, $x = \frac{1}{4}$

    $\frac{1}{4}$ _____ a solution.

Test Prep

13. Jennifer reads p pages every day. After 15 days, she has read 300 pages. Write an equation to represent this situation.

$P(15) = 300$

14. Jermaine has t trading cards. Jasmine has 7 trading cards. Together, Jermaine and Jasmine have 13 trading cards. Which equation could represent the problem? Select all that apply.

- Ⓐ $t + 7 = 13$
- Ⓑ $7 + t = 7$
- Ⓒ $7t = 13$
- Ⓓ $7 + t = 13$
- Ⓔ $13 \div t = 7$
- Ⓕ $13 - 7 = t$

15. Lily is 5 inches shorter than Dan. If Dan is 67 inches tall, how tall is Lily? Write an equation to model the problem using h for Lily's height.

$67 - h = 5$

16. Which value is a solution for the equation $\frac{m}{4} = 16$?

- Ⓐ $m = 4$
- Ⓑ $m = 12$
- Ⓒ $m = 20$
- Ⓓ $m = 64$

17. Derrick has 72 inches of ribbon to make bows. He uses all of his ribbon to make 9 bows of equal length ℓ. How many inches of ribbon does each bow use? Write an equation to model the situation. Then solve the problem.

$L = 72 \div 9$

Spiral Review

18. Walter's sink can hold 12 gallons of water. If it is 85% full, how many gallons of water are in the sink?

10.2

19. A rectangular stage is 6.25 feet long and 12 feet wide. What is the area of the stage in square feet?

20. Turkey hot dogs come in packages of 6 and buns come in packages of 8. What is the least number of packages that can be bought of each so that there are the same number of hot dogs and buns?

For Problems 21–23, find each quotient.

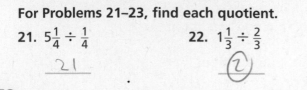

21. $5\frac{1}{4} \div \frac{1}{4}$

21

22. $1\frac{1}{3} \div \frac{2}{3}$

2

23. $9\frac{3}{4} \div 3\frac{1}{4}$

Name

Use Addition and Subtraction Equations to Solve Problems

(I Can) write and solve equations using addition and subtraction to represent real-world situations involving an unknown.

Spark Your Learning

Thomas has four jugs of different sizes. One holds 1.2 liters, one holds 1.3 liters, one holds 2.3 liters, and one holds 2.6 liters. He has to fill a large barrel with exactly 5 liters of water. How can he use the jugs to pour this amount into the barrel? Find as many ways as possible.

Turn and Talk Explain how you could measure exactly 0.1 liter, exactly 1 liter, and exactly 1.4 liters by pouring water from one jug to another.

Build Understanding

When solving an addition equation, you can model the equation on a balance scale. For the equation to remain true, both sides must remain equal or, in the case of a balance scale, be the same weight. If you remove something from one side, you must remove the same amount from the other side.

1 Weights are shown on the scale. Each square is 1 unit, but the value of the triangle x is unknown. The scale sides are balanced.

A. Describe the weights on the left side of the scale and on the right side of the scale using both words and mathematical expressions.

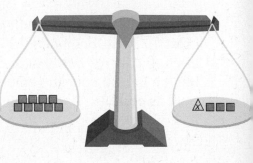

_____

_____

_____

_____

B. What equation represents the weights shown on the scale?

_____

C. How could you remove weights, making sure that the scale is still balanced, and use that to find the value of x?

_____

_____

_____

_____

D. As if you were removing weights from both sides of the scale, cross out the same number of weights on both sides of the scale until x is by itself. How much must the weight labeled x weigh? Explain how you know.

_____

_____

E. Check your answer by substituting the value of x into the equation from Part B. Explain your work.

_____

_____

 Turn and Talk If one side of a balance is lower than the other side, what mathematical symbol could you use to describe what the balance shows?

Step It Out

2 ▶ A plant is 6 inches tall. After 2 weeks, the plant is 14 inches tall. How many inches did the plant grow?

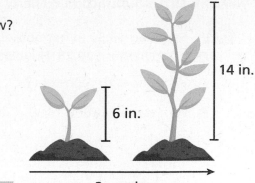

14 in.

6 in.

2 weeks

A. What information do you know?

The plant starts at ☐ inches.

The plant grows to ☐ inches.

B. What do you need to find out?

_____

_____

C. You can represent how many inches the plant grew in two weeks with a variable *x*. How can you describe the relationship between the unknown amount *x* and the height of the plant at the start?

_____

_____

D. Write an equation you can solve in order to answer the problem.

☐ + ☐ = ☐

E. You can also model the problem using algebra tiles. The sets of tiles on both sides of the gray rule are equal. Just like with a scale, if you remove one tile from one side, you must also remove one tile from the other side. Cross out tiles until *x* is by itself. How many tiles did you cross out on each side? How many tiles remain on the right side of the model?

☐ 1-tiles were crossed out on each side.

☐ 1-tiles are left on the right side.

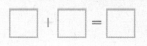

F. What is the solution to the equation?

_____

G. Check your answer by substituting the value for *x* into the equation from Part D and combine like terms then solve. Is your answer correct?

_____

🔄 **Turn and Talk** Which model do you prefer, the scale or algebra tiles? Explain.

Instead of using a scale or algebra tiles, you can subtract the same amount from both sides of an equation and the two sides will remain equal. This is known as the **Subtraction Property of Equality**.

3 ▸ Sara had $8.50 in her pocket. She earned *m* dollars babysitting and now she has $20.25. How much did she earn babysitting?

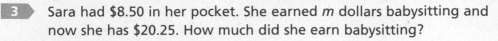

A. What does *m* represent? _____

B. Write an equation for this situation.

   $ [ ]   +   [ ]   = $ [ ]

C. How much do you need to subtract from both sides of the equation to get an equation with only *m* on the left side? _____

D. Subtract [ ] from both sides to isolate *m*. $8.50 + m = 20.25$

   $\begin{array}{r} - [\ ] \quad - [\ ] \\ \hline [\ ] = [\ ] \end{array}$

E. Sara earned $ [ ] babysitting.

4 ▸ You can also add the same amount to both sides of an equation and the two sides will remain equal. This is the **Addition Property of Equality**.

A. Solve the equation $x - 7 = 12$ by adding [ ] to each side.

B. $x - 7 = 12$

   $\begin{array}{cc} [\ ] & [\ ] \\ [\ ] & = [\ ] \end{array}$

Check Understanding

1. Jerry has two dogs. The older one weighs 95 pounds. Their combined weight is 120 pounds. Write and solve an equation to find the younger dog's weight *d*. What number did you subtract from both sides?

   _____

   _____

For Problems 2–4, add or subtract to solve the equation, circle the correct word, and state the number that you added or subtracted.

2. $x - 15 = 29$, $x =$ [ ]   I added / subtracted [ ] .

3. $12.26 + w = 39$, $w =$ [ ]   I added / subtracted [ ] .

4. $y - \frac{3}{4} = 4\frac{1}{4}$, $y =$ [ ]   I added / subtracted [ ] .

On Your Own

5. **(MP) Model with Mathematics** Annie is the height shown. She is 49 centimeters taller than her brother. Write and solve an equation to find her brother's height b in centimeters.

Annie is 152.5 cm. tall.

_____

6. **(MP) Critique Reasoning** For the equation $z - 14 = 29$, Juan says that the solution is 33. Check whether Juan's solution works by substituting it into the equation and combining like terms. Is his solution correct?

_____

7. William buys a book for $14.85. If he pays with a $20 bill, what will his change c be? Write and solve an equation to find out.

_____

8. Yan had 5 trading cards, and then his friend gave him more cards. Now he has 16 trading cards. Let t represent the number of cards his friend gave him. Write both an addition equation and a subtraction equation to model the problem.

$\boxed{} + t = \boxed{}$ $\boxed{} - \boxed{} = t$

9. The scale shows the equation $7 = r + 5$. Cross out the same number of tiles on each side to get r by itself. What is the value of r?

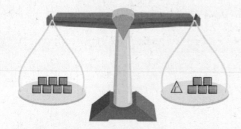

$r = \underline{\hspace{2cm}}$

For Problems 10–15, circle whether you add or subtract to solve the equation. Then find the value.

10. $8 + x = 42$, add / subtract, $x = \boxed{}$ 11. $w - 61 = 14$, add / subtract, $w = \boxed{}$

12. $n - 81 = 67$, add / subtract, $n = \boxed{}$ 13. $m + 3.89 = 9.02$, add / subtract, $m = \boxed{}$

14. $y + 2.4 = 6.75$, add / subtract, $y = \boxed{}$ 15. $c + \frac{5}{9} = \frac{8}{9}$, add / subtract, $c = \boxed{}$

16.  **Model with Mathematics** Jasmine is training for a race. Her goal is to cover 28 miles this week. So far this week, she has gone the distances shown. Write and solve an equation to find the number of miles *m* Jasmine has left to meet her goal.

_____

_____

17. Aviva has collected 56 cans of food for disaster relief. Her goal is to collect 200 cans. Write and solve an equation to show how many more cans *c* she needs to reach her goal.

_____

_____

Monday	⟶ 6 miles
Tuesday	⟶ 8 miles
Wednesday	⟶ 6 miles

18. The Gateway Arch in St. Louis, Missouri, is 630 feet tall. It is 75 feet taller than the Washington Monument in Washington, D.C. Write and solve an equation to find the height *h* of the Washington Monument.

_____

19. Show that 1.27 is not a solution for the equation $g + 3.74 = 5.1$. Then find the correct solution and show why it is correct.

_____

_____

20. The balance shows the equation $b + 6 = 10$. What is the value of *b*?

$b = $ _____

For Problems 21–22, add or subtract to solve the equation.

21. $8.7 + x = 12.05$, $x = $ _____   **22.** $a - 34 = 60$, $a = $ _____

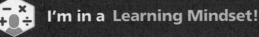 **I'm in a Learning Mindset!**

How do I know when solving addition and subtraction equations triggered a fixed-mindset response in a classmate?

_____

_____

© Houghton Mifflin Harcourt Publishing Company • **Image Credit:** ©Clark Brennan/Alamy

LESSON 9.2
**More Practice/
Homework**

ONLINE

Video Tutorials and
Interactive Examples

Use Addition and Subtraction Equations to Solve Problems

Math on the Spot For Problems 1–3, solve each equation. Check your answer.

1. $s - 5 = 12$ _____

2. $35 = y - 6$ _____

3. $x - 22 = 44$ _____

4. (MP) **Model with Mathematics** Mary compares the heights of two trees. Their heights are shown. Write and solve an equation to find the height h of the taller tree.

_____

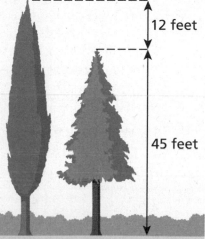

12 feet

45 feet

5. **Open Ended** Write an equation with a solution of 25. Use the variable x and addition.

_____

6. Each small square on this scale weighs 1 unit. Each larger square weighs 10 units. The weight of the triangle x is unknown. The scale is balanced. What is the weight of the triangle?

A. (MP) **Model with Mathematics** Write an equation to represent the weights shown on the scale.

_____

B. Cross out the same weights on each side until x is alone. What is the total weight that you crossed out on each side?

_____

C. Write the simplified equation represented by the scale now. What is the weight of the triangle?

_____

For Problems 7–8, determine whether the given value is a solution for the equation. Write *is* or *is not* on the line.

7. $x - 14 = 42$, $x = 56$

56 _____ a solution.

8. $k + 66 = 98$, $k = 28$

28 _____ a solution.

For Problems 9–10, solve the equation.

9. $55 + s = 110$, $s =$ _____

10. $n - 52 = 12$, $n =$ _____

Test Prep

11. What value for *w* makes the equation $76 + w = 100$ true?

_____

12. Which equations have $x = 15$ as a solution? Select all that apply.

(A) $x + 14 = 29$ (D) $x + 17 = 32$

(B) $25 + x = 10$ (E) $x - 8 = 7$

(C) $x - 38 = 23$ (F) $35 - x = 25$

13. What must you do to both sides to solve the equation $g - 24 = 36$? Circle the correct response and fill in the blank.

| Add / Subtract | ☐ | to / from | both sides.

14. Which value is a solution to the equation $\frac{7}{12} + n = \frac{5}{6}$?

(A) $n = \frac{10}{7}$ (C) $n = \frac{1}{3}$

(B) $n = \frac{1}{4}$ (D) $n = \frac{17}{12}$

15. Mr. Renner drove 18 miles to work. He drove home a different way and saw that he had driven a total of 41 miles that day. How many miles was the drive home?

_____

Spiral Review

16. What is the value of $\frac{4}{5} \times \frac{3}{4}$ in simplest form?

_____

17. Which is a lower price per pound, 4 pounds for $1.40 or 3 pounds for $1.20? Show each as a unit rate.

_____

_____

Evaluate the expression.

18. 2^3 _____

19. 3^4 _____

20. 1^{10} _____

21. 10^3 _____

Name

Use Multiplication and Division Equations to Solve Problems

(I Can) write and solve equations using multiplication and division to represent real-world situations involving an unknown.

Spark Your Learning

Diana is preparing lunch for her friends. She has 0.75 pound of ham and 0.5 pound of cheese. She uses 0.15 pound of ham and 0.08 pound of cheese to make a ham and cheese sandwich. Is there enough ham and cheese to make 5 sandwiches if she uses the same amount of ham and cheese for each sandwich? Explain.

$\frac{1}{2}$	$\frac{1}{2}$

Turn and Talk If ham costs $5.79 per pound and cheese costs $4.29 per pound, how can you find the total amount you pay for the ham and cheese in each sandwich? Can you stay within a budget of $1.50 per sandwich? Explain.

Build Understanding

In the previous lesson, you learned to solve addition equations with a variable by subtracting. How can you solve a multiplication equation?

1 A group of 4 people goes apple picking. They pick the amount shown. If they share the apples equally, how many pounds of apples does each person get? Let x represent the weight in pounds of apples that each person receives.

20 lb of apples

A. Complete the diagram.

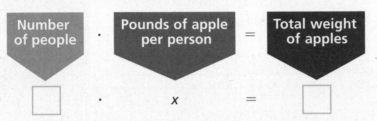

| Number of people | · | Pounds of apple per person | = | Total weight of apples |

☐ · x = ☐

B. Write an equation to represent this problem.

_____

C. Model the equation using algebra tiles. How many x-tiles are in your model? How many 1-tiles?

D. How many equal groups do you need to divide your model into to solve for x? Explain.

_____

E. Draw circles around the tiles you drew for Part C to separate the tiles into equal groups.

F. How many 1-tiles are in each group? How many pounds of apples does each person get?

_____

 Turn and Talk What other method can you use to find how many pounds of apples each person gets? Explain.

Name _____

Step It Out

The **Division Property of Equality** states that you can divide both sides of an equation by the same nonzero number and the two sides will remain equal.

2 ▶ What is the value of x in the equation $7x = 119$?

A. Divide both sides of the equation by the same nonzero number to get x alone on one side.

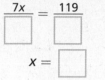

B. To check the solution, substitute your answer in the original equation.

7(⬜) $\overset{?}{=}$ 119

⬜ = ⬜

Does your solution check? _____

The **Multiplication Property of Equality** states that you can multiply both sides of an equation by the same number and the two sides will remain equal.

3 ▶ What is the value of x in the equation $\frac{x}{6} = 9$?

A. Multiply both sides of the equation by the same number to get x alone on one side.

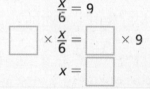

$$\frac{x}{6} = 9$$

$$⬜ \times \frac{x}{6} = ⬜ \times 9$$

$$x = ⬜$$

D. To check the solution, substitute your answer in the original equation.

$$\frac{⬜}{6} \overset{?}{=} 9$$

⬜ = ⬜

Does your solution check? _____

C. Find the value of x if you know that $\frac{x}{10} = 9$. Describe how you found the solution.

_____

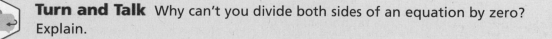

Turn and Talk Why can't you divide both sides of an equation by zero? Explain.

© Houghton Mifflin Harcourt Publishing Company

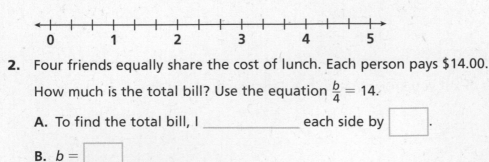

$1.85 per pound

4. A bag of 5 plum tomatoes weighs 1 pound. If each tomato weighs the same amount, what is the cost of one tomato? Use the equation $5x = 1.85$.

A. To solve the equation $5x = 1.85$, _____ both sides of the equation by the number ☐.

B. The result of performing the same operation to both sides of the equation leads to the solution $x = $ ☐.

C. Graph your solution on the number line.

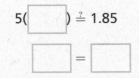

| | | | | | | | | | | |
|0|0.05|0.1|0.15|0.2|0.25|0.3|0.35|0.4|0.45|0.5|

D. To check the solution, put your answer into the original equation.

$5(☐) \stackrel{?}{=} 1.85$

☐ $=$ ☐   Does your solution check? _____

E. Interpret your answer.

_____

Turn and Talk How is solving a multiplication equation with decimals like solving a multiplication equation with whole numbers?

Check Understanding

1. Mr. Poyser uses $4\frac{2}{3}$ cups of flour to make 7 dozen oatmeal-raisin cookies. How many cups of flour does he need to make a dozen cookies? Use the equation $7c = 4\frac{2}{3}$. Graph the solution on a number line.

_____

| | | | | | |
|0|1|2|3|4|5|

2. Four friends equally share the cost of lunch. Each person pays $14.00. How much is the total bill? Use the equation $\frac{b}{4} = 14$.

A. To find the total bill, I _____ each side by ☐.

B. $b = $ ☐

C. Graph the solution on a number line.

| | | | | | | | | | | | | |
|0|5|10|15|20|25|30|35|40|45|50|55|60|

On Your Own

3. Preston earns $33.00 for babysitting his neighbor's children for 2.4 hours.

    A. (MP) **Model with Mathematics** Write an equation you can use to find out how much Preston earns per hour.

    _____

    B. How much does Preston earn in one hour? _____

4. Henri has exactly enough quarters to wash 3 loads of laundry. It takes 8 quarters to wash one load of laundry. How many quarters does Henri have? Use the equation $\frac{x}{3} = 8$.

5. (MP) **Use Tools** Carlos has 6 mugs on a shelf as shown. The mugs all have the same weight. The equation $6x = 84$ represents this situation.

Total weight = 84 ounces

    A. What visual model could you use to solve the equation $6x = 84$? Explain.

    _____

    _____

    _____

    B. How much does each mug weigh? _____

For Problems 6–9, find each solution and graph it on the number line.

6. $\frac{x}{3} = 4$

    $x = \boxed{}$

    0 2 4 6 8 10 12 14 16 18 20

7. $1.9x = 4.75$

    $x = \boxed{}$

    0 1 2 3 4 5

8. $12x = 60$

    $x = \boxed{}$

    0 2 4 6 8 10

9. $\frac{x}{5} = 3$

    $x = \boxed{}$

    0 2 4 6 8 10 12 14 16 18 20

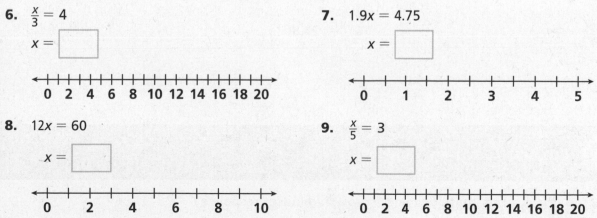

10. Glenn is 5 feet tall. He is $\frac{4}{5}$ as tall as his brother. How tall is Glenn's brother?

$5\frac{4}{5}$

A. (MP) **Model with Mathematics** Write an equation to find Glenn's brother's height, using *x* to represent the height.

$5\frac{4}{2} \times x =$

_____

B. How can you solve this equation for *x*?

$x \times 67 = 180$

_____

_____

C. How tall is Glenn's brother in feet?

_____

11. Iris made bracelets with string and beads. She used x centimeters of string and made 7 bracelets. She used 17.8 centimeters of string for each bracelet. How much string did she use in all? Write an equation and use it to solve this problem.

_____

12. (MP) **Model with Mathematics** The price of a can of beans is shown. Jason has $8.69 to spend on beans. Write an equation to represent the situation and solve the equation to find number of cans Jason can buy.

COST
$0.79

_____

For Problems 13–16, find each solution.

13. $9x = 171$

14. $\frac{x}{6} = 15$

_____   _____

15. $\frac{9}{5}x = 2\frac{7}{10}$

16. $\frac{x}{4} = 28.80$

_____   _____

I'm in a Learning Mindset!

How can I help a classmate develop a growth-mindset response?

_____

_____

Name _stephanie paola Hernandez villa_

Write and Graph Inequalities

(**I Can**) write and graph the solution of an inequality to represent a condition in a real-world or mathematical problem.

Step it Out

You can write inequalities using inequality symbols and variables to describe quantities that have many values.

Symbol	Meaning	Word phrases
<	Is less than	Fewer than, below
>	Is greater than	More than, above
≤	Is less than or equal to	At most, no more than
≥	Is greater than or equal to	At least, no less than

Connect to Vocabulary

An **inequality** is a mathematical sentence that shows the relationship between quantities that are not equal.

1 ▷ A record-breaking low temperature of −23 °F was recorded in Seminole, Texas, on February 8, 1933.

   A. Find −23 and graph it on the number line.

<!-- number line: -->
−24 −22 −20 −18 −16 −14 −12 −10 −8 −6 −4 −2 0 2 4

   B. The temperatures 4 °F, −3 °F, −14 °F, 1 °F, and −19 °F have also been recorded in Texas. How do these temperatures compare to −23 °F?

   _____

   C. Give examples of other numbers that are greater than −23. How many of these numbers exist?

   _____

   _____

   D. Let x represent the temperatures greater than −23 °F. Complete the inequality to describe these temperatures.

   x [   ] −23

🗨 **Turn and Talk** How is a number line not like a thermometer? Explain.

The solution of the inequality $x > 2$ is all numbers greater than 2, not including 2.

An inequality such as $x > 2$ represents a **constraint**. A constraint is a condition that restricts the values of a quantity or variable to a given value or range of values. For the inequality $x > 2$, the values of x must be greater than 2. So, 2 and numbers less than 2 are not solutions of $x > 2$.

For the inequality $x \leq 4$, the values of x must be less than or equal to 4. So, 4 is a solution of $x \leq 4$, but numbers greater than 4 are not solutions.

The constraint of this ride is that you must be 54 inches or taller.

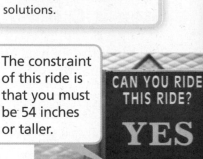

CAN YOU RIDE THIS RIDE? **YES** 54"

2 ▶ Graph the inequalities.

A. $y \leq -3$

Step 1 Draw a solid circle at -3 to show that -3 is a solution.

$$\xleftarrow{\hspace{1cm}}\underset{-5\ -4\ -3\ -2\ -1\ \ 0\ \ 1\ \ 2\ \ 3\ \ 4\ \ 5}{|\quad|\quad|\quad|\quad|\quad|\quad|\quad|\quad|\quad|\quad|}\xrightarrow{\hspace{1cm}}$$

Step 2 Shade the number line to the left of -3 to show that numbers less than -3 are also solutions.

Step 3 Check your solution. Choose a number that is on the shaded section of the number line, such as -4. Substitute -4 for y. Since the inequality $-4 \leq -3$ is true, the solution graphed on the number line appears to be correct. You can never check all the possible values for the variable but checking one or two values helps assure you have shaded the correct side of the number line.

B. $1 < m$

Step 1 Draw an open circle at 1 to show that 1 is *not* a solution.

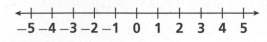

$$\xleftarrow{\hspace{1cm}}\underset{-5\ -4\ -3\ -2\ -1\ \ 0\ \ 1\ \ 2\ \ 3\ \ 4\ \ 5}{|\quad|\quad|\quad|\quad|\quad|\quad|\quad|\quad|\quad|\quad|}\xrightarrow{\hspace{1cm}}$$

Step 2 Shade the number line to the right of 1 to show that numbers greater than 1 are solutions.

Step 3 Check your solution. Pick any number for m that falls on the shaded section of the number line. $1 < \boxed{}$. If the inequality you have just written is true, then you have shaded the correct side of the number line.

Turn and Talk Think of a situation you have faced where something must be greater than a certain amount. Think of a second situation where something must be greater than or equal to a certain amount. Explain each scenario and then write an inequality to represent each situation.

You can write inequalities to represent certain real-world situations.

3 ▶ Use inequalities to solve these problems.

A. The temperature is at most −2 °F. What could be the temperature *t*?

Are numbers less than −2 part of the solution? _____

Are numbers greater than −2 part of the solution? _____

Is −2 included as a solution? _____

Write the inequality. *t* ☐ −2

B. Raphael needs to buy more than 4 concert tickets. How many tickets *t* could he buy?

Are numbers less than 4 part of the solution? _____

Are numbers greater than 4 part of the solution? _____

Is 4 included as a solution? _____

Write the inequality. *t* ☐ 4

Graph the inequality. Use an open circle because the value 4 is not part of the solution.

How many tickets can Raphael buy?

```
<-+---+---+---+---+---+---+---+---+---+---+->
 -1  0   1   2   3   4   5   6   7   8   9
```

Check Understanding

1. Camille wants to become a pilot. A pilot needs to log at least 500 flying hours before earning a pilot's license. Write and graph an inequality to show the number of flying hours *h* Camille needs to get a license.

```
<-+---+---+---+---+---+---+---+---+---+---+->
-100    0  100 200 300 400 500 600 700 800
```

_____

For Problems 2–3, graph each inequality.

2. $r \leq 8$

```
<-+-+-+-+-+-+-+-+-+-+-+->
 -1 0 1 2 3 4 5 6 7 8 9
```

3. $z < -3$

```
<-+--+--+--+--+--+--+--+--+->
 -7 -6 -5 -4 -3 -2 -1  0  1
```

On Your Own

4. When cooking chicken, the recommended internal temperature of the chicken is shown. A lower internal temperature will undercook the chicken. Write an inequality to describe the temperatures *t* at which the chicken will be undercooked. _____

internal temp. 165 °F

Graph the inequality.

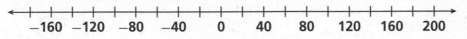

$$-160 \quad -120 \quad -80 \quad -40 \quad 0 \quad 40 \quad 80 \quad 120 \quad 160 \quad 200$$

5. **STEM** The speed of sound is approximately 761 miles per hour. For an object to produce a sonic boom, it must travel faster than the speed of sound. Write an inequality to describe the speeds *s* at which a moving object will produce a sonic boom. _____

6. To find the area *A* of a rectangle, the length *ℓ* must be multiplied by the width *w*. A farmer needs to build a fence to enclose a chicken pen with an area greater than or equal to 50 square feet. The length of the fence must be 10 feet.

ℓ = 10 feet

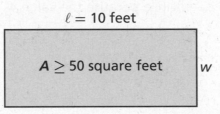

$A \geq 50$ square feet

w

A. Write an inequality to describe the widths *w* that will yield a fenced-in area of at least 50 square feet. _____

B. Graph the inequality.

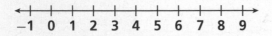

$$-1 \quad 0 \quad 1 \quad 2 \quad 3 \quad 4 \quad 5 \quad 6 \quad 7 \quad 8 \quad 9$$

7. The temperature in Minneapolis was −9 °F. The next day, the temperature in Minneapolis was warmer than −9 °F.

A. Write an inequality which is true only for temperatures *t* that are warmer than −9 °F.

_____

B. Could the temperature have been −12 °F in Minneapolis on the next day? Why or why not?

_____

_____

8. **A.** Graph the inequality $d \leq -2$.

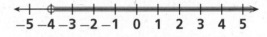

$$\begin{array}{ccccccccccc} -5 & -4 & -3 & -2 & -1 & 0 & 1 & 2 & 3 & 4 & 5 \end{array}$$

B. (MP) **Reason** Name three solutions for d. How many possible solutions does this inequality have?

_____

9. Write an inequality to represent the graph. Use y for the solution.

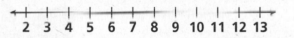

$$\begin{array}{ccccccccccc} -5 & -4 & -3 & -2 & -1 & 0 & 1 & 2 & 3 & 4 & 5 \end{array}$$

_____

10. To have enough orange juice for all the campers, the camp cook will need at least 9 gallons.

A. Write an inequality that is true only for the number of gallons g the cook needs.

_____

B. Graph the inequality.

$$\begin{array}{cccccccccccc} 2 & 3 & 4 & 5 & 6 & 7 & 8 & 9 & 10 & 11 & 12 & 13 \end{array}$$

C. If the cook buys 4 gallons, will there be enough
orange juice? _____

11. According to government guidelines, drones are limited to
how high they can legally fly above the ground as shown.

Drones may not fly higher than 400 feet.

A. Write an inequality that is true only for the height h a
drone can fly above the ground.

_____

B. If a drone flies 430 feet above the ground, will it violate
government guidelines? Explain.

_____

_____

12. Write an inequality that represents the graph. Use x for the variable.

$$\begin{array}{ccccccccccc} -5 & -4 & -3 & -2 & -1 & 0 & 1 & 2 & 3 & 4 & 5 \end{array}$$

_____

13. A. Write an inequality that represents the graph. Use *x* for the variable.

```
←—+—+—+—+—+—+—+—+—+—+—+—+—+—+—→
 -160 -120  -80  -40   0   40   80  120  160  200
```

_____

B. Choose a number from the shaded area of the graph to check your inequality. State the number you picked and explain why it is a possible solution.

_____

_____

14. Graph the inequality on the number line: $b \geq -14$.

```
←—+—+—+—+—+—+—+—+—+—+—+—→
 -16 -14 -12 -10 -8  -6  -4  -2   0   2   4
```

15. Graph the inequality on the number line: $d < 25$.

```
←—+—+—+—+—+—+—+—+—+—+—+—→
 -15 -10 -5   0   5   10  15  20  25  30  35  40
```

16. A dog weighs less than 15 pounds.

A. List three possible weights for the dog.

_____

B. Write an inequality that describes the possible weights *w* the dog can weigh. _____

C. Some puppies can be born with a weight of $\frac{1}{5}$ of a pound. Can any dog ever weigh 0 pounds or less? _____

D. An inequality can be written with a variable between two numbers if that variable must be greater than one number and less than another number. Write a new, more accurate inequality to describe the dog's possible weight by writing an inequality symbol in each blank.

0 ☐ *w* ☐ 15

less than 15 pounds

E. Graph this new inequality.

```
←—+—+—+—+—+—+—+—+—+—+—+—→
 -2   0   2   4   6   8  10  12  14  16  18
```

17. Open Ended Write a situation that can be modeled by $x < 7$.

_____

_____

Name _____

LESSON 9.5
More Practice/ Homework

ONLINE
Video Tutorials and
Interactive Examples

Write and Graph Inequalities

1. Regan won the grand prize at a store giveaway. The grand prize winner is guaranteed to win at least $500 in cash and prizes.

   A. List three possible dollar amounts in cash and prizes Regan can win.

   _____

   B. Write an inequality to represent the dollar amounts d in cash and prizes Regan can win. _____

   C. Graph the inequality.

   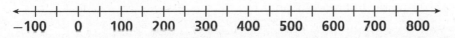

2. **STEM** Alonso uses the table to help him identify an unknown mineral. He finds the specific gravity of the mineral and discovers it is less than 3.

   A. List three possible minerals the unknown mineral could be.

   _____

   B. Write an inequality to represent the specific gravity g of the unknown mineral. _____

Specific gravity	Mineral
2.16	halite
2.31 to 2.33	gypsum
2.65	quartz
2.7	calcite
3.0 to 3.3	fluorite
3.4 to 3.6	topaz
3.5 to 4	chalcopyrite
4.9 to 5.2	pyrite

Math on the Spot For Problems 3–4, graph each inequality on a number line.

3. $x > -7$

   -10 8 6 4 2 0 2 4 6 8 10

4. $y \leq -5$

   ← | | | | | | | | | | | | | | | | | | | | | →
   -10 -8 -6 -4 -2 0 2 4 6 8 10

5. **MP** **Reason** When two numbers are added together, the sum is at least 100. One of the numbers is 77.

   A. Which of these could be the other number? Circle the correct number or numbers.

   15   9   23   41   50   20   25

   B. Write an inequality to represent the possible values of the other number n.

   _____

Test Prep

6. Children 12 and under eat free at a local restaurant. If x represents age, write an inequality to represent the ages of people who do **not** get a discount.

_____

7. It is colder than $-7\ °F$ outside. Which inequality represents the temperature t?

Ⓐ $7 < t$ Ⓑ $t > -7$ Ⓒ $-7 > t$ Ⓓ $t < 7$

8. An online retailer charges an additional fee to ship orders that weigh over 48 pounds. Write and graph an inequality which represents the weight x of online orders that result in an additional fee.

$$\longleftarrow\!\!+\!\!+\!\!+\!\!+\!\!+\!\!+\!\!+\!\!+\!\!\longrightarrow$$
−12   0   12 24 36 48 60 72 84   _____

9. Draw a line to match each graph with the inequality that it represents.

$-5 > x$ •

$x < -3$ •

$x > 4$ •

$x > 2$ •

Spiral Review

10. Benjamin bought 4 goldfish. Each goldfish cost $1.29. How much did Benjamin spend? _____

11. A youth league soccer team has 20 students who play defender positions and 23 students who play midfielder positions. Write a ratio of students who play defender positions to the total number of students who play defender or midfielder positions. _____

For Problems 12–15, find each quotient or product.

12. $0.2 \div 4$ ☐   **13.** $3.1 \div 4$ ☐

14. 0.2×0.25 ☐   **15.** 3.1×0.25 ☐

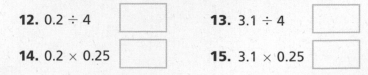

Review

Vocabulary

Choose the correct term from the Vocabulary box.

1. a mathematical sentence that shows the relationship between quantities that are not equal _____

2. a mathematical sentence that shows that two expressions are equivalent _____

3. 3 is the _____ of the equation $b + 2 = 5$

4. 8 is a _____ $x < 10$

Concepts and Skills

5. (MP) **Use Tools** A Komodo dragon can grow to be 120 inches long. One Komodo dragon is 92 inches long. Write and solve an equation to find the number of inches x the Komodo dragon still needs to grow to be 120 inches long. State what strategy and tool you will use to answer the question, explain your choice, and then find the answer.

_____

_____

6. Dakota has been assigned 80 math problems that are due in 5 days.

   A. Write an equation to determine how many problems she should do each day if she wants to do the same number each day. Choose any letter for the variable and explain what it represents.

   _____

   _____

   _____

   B. Solve the equation. How many problems should Dakota do each day?

   _____

7. Karen used one-third of her total stamps on a campaign for charity. Karen used 60 stamps on the charity campaign.

   A. Write an equation you could use to find how many stamps she had at the start. Choose any letter for the variable and explain what it represents.

   _____

   _____

   B. Solve the equation. How many stamps did Karen start with?

   _____

8. Denise used 22.5 gallons of water in the shower. This amount is 7.5 gallons less than the amount she used for washing clothes. Write and solve an equation to find the amount of water x Denise used to wash clothes.

   _____

   _____

9. In a visit to Glacier National Park in Montana, Vera hiked a total of 138 miles in 12 days. She hiked the same distance each day. Write and solve an equation to find the number of miles m she hiked each day.

   _____

10. The temperature dropped 20 degrees from noon to midnight. The temperature at midnight was 24 °F. Write and solve an equation to find the temperature at noon.

    _____

For Problems 11–13, write and graph an inequality for each situation.

11. The width w is less than 10 inches.

    _____

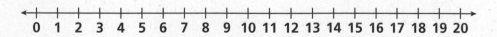

0 1 2 3 4 5 6 7 8 9 10 11 12 13 14 15 16 17 18 19 20

12. The truck has a weight t of more than 2 tons.

    _____

0 1 2 3 4 5 6 7 8 9 10 11 12 13 14 15 16 17 18 19 20

13. The temperature t was below 20 °C.

    _____

0 1 2 3 4 5 6 7 8 9 10 11 12 13 14 15 16 17 18 19 20

Real-World Relationships Between Variables

Which Relationship Does NOT Belong?

Describe the pattern shown by each relationship.

A.

Number of markers	Cost ($)
5	3
10	6
15	9

_____

_____

_____

C.

Cost ($) vs Number of markers

3.00, 2.40, 1.80, 1.20, 0.60, 0

0 1 2 3 4 5
Number of markers

_____

_____

_____

B.

Package of 8 markers: $4
Package of 16 markers: $8

_____

_____

_____

D.

$3.60
Markers 6 markers

$7.20
Markers 12 markers

_____

_____

_____

Turn and Talk

- Which relationship does not belong? Explain why.

- Which relationship represents the best deal? Explain your reasoning.

Are You Ready?

Complete these problems to review prior concepts and skills you will need for this module.

Generate Patterns and Find Relationships

Describe a pattern you see in each table. Use the pattern to complete each table.

1.

x	y
0	0
1	6
2	12
3	
4	

2.

x	y
0	8
1	13
2	18
3	
4	

_____

_____

_____

_____

Identify Points on a Coordinate Grid

Write the ordered pair for each point.

3. A _____

4. B _____

5. C _____

6. D _____

7. E _____

8. F _____

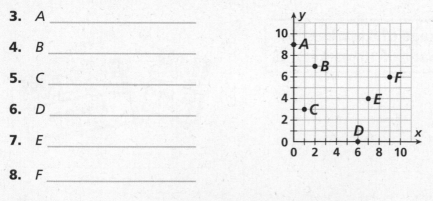

Graph and label each ordered pair on the coordinate grid.

9. G(0, 7)

10. H(3, 8)

11. I(5, 5)

12. J(1, 0)

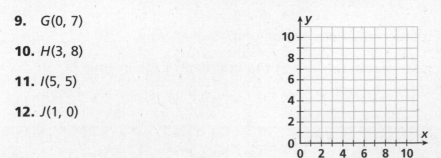

Name _____

Represent Equations in Tables and Graphs

(**I Can**) represent a situation using a table, equation, or graph.

Spark Your Learning

PAIRS

A baby gorilla had a mass of 2,620 grams at birth, 2,960 grams after 10 days, and 3,300 grams after 20 days. What is the average number of grams that the baby gorilla grew each day during the first 10 days and during the next 10 days? Show your work.

x	y

 Turn and Talk If the baby gorilla continued to grow at the same rate for the first month after birth, what would be the baby gorilla's mass 26 days after birth? Explain how you found your answer.

Build Understanding

Many real-world situations involve two variable quantities in which one quantity depends on the other. The quantity that depends on the other quantity is the **dependent variable**, and the quantity that it depends on is the **independent variable**. In general, the dependent variable is typically recorded on the *y*-axis.

1 ▶ The Jackson family is driving to visit family members who live out of state. They record the following information about their trip.

Hours	Miles
2	130
3	195
4	260
5	325

A. Which of the two quantities is the independent quantity, and which is the dependent quantity? Explain.

_____

_____

_____

B. How far does the car travel each hour? How do you know?

_____

_____

C. Suppose that *d* represents the distance traveled by the car in miles and that *t* represents the time in hours the car has been traveling. How can you model the relationship between the distance traveled, in miles, by the car and the time, in hours, using an equation? Use *d* for distance and *t* for time in hours.

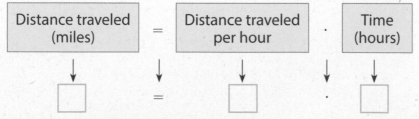

D. A student represented this relationship as $65t = d$. Is this student correct? Why or why not?

_____

_____

Turn and Talk Describe how the table and the equation are related.

Name _____

Step It Out

When one variable depends on a second variable, the relationship between the variables can be represented in a table or by an equation. An equation can be used to express the dependent variable in terms of the independent variable.

Pablo walks dogs to earn money

2 Pablo walks dogs after school. His earnings e, in dollars, are represented by the equation $e = 24h$, where h is the number of hours he works.

A. Complete the table.

Hours worked, h	1	2	3	4
Earnings, e			$72	

B. To determine values to the table, multiply each value of the independent variable, ☐, by ☐ to find each corresponding value of the dependent variable, ☐.

3 Each egg carton holds one dozen eggs. The equation $n = 12c$ shows the number of eggs n in 1 carton.

A. Use the equation to complete the table.

Number of cartons, c	1		5	
Number of eggs, n	12	24		96

B. To find the missing values in the table, sometimes I multiplied a value of the independent variable, ☐, by ☐ to get each corresponding value of the dependent variable, ☐. Other times I divided a value of the dependent variable by ☐ to get the value of the independent variable, c.

 Turn and Talk Do the equations and the tables describe the same relationships? Explain how you know.

4 The distance in meters that Kaycia hikes in *x* minutes is represented by the equation $y = 75x$.

A. Complete the table.

Minutes, *x*	Meters, *y*
5	
15	
	1,500
	2,250

75 meters per minute

B. How did you find the value of *y* when *x* = 5?

_____

_____

C. How did you find the value of *x* when *y* = 1,500?

_____

_____

D. Write the ordered pairs from the table.

(___ , ___), (___ , ___), (___ , ___),

(___ , ___)

Kaycia's Hiking

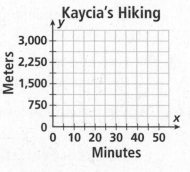

E. Graph the ordered pairs on the coordinate grid.

F. Your points should follow a straight line pattern. Because Kaycia is hiking between the times represented by points, you can draw a line through the points. Draw this line on the graph.

Turn and Talk Why might graphing a set of paired values be better than displaying them in a table?

Check Understanding

1. The equation $p = \frac{2}{5}m$ relates the number of book pages *p* Ellen reads in *m* minutes. What is the dependent variable? What is the independent variable?

Complete the table. _____

m	*p*
10	
	8
	12
60	

2. A store sells a box of breakfast cereal for $3. Write an equation to relate the number of boxes *b* to total sales *T*. _____

On Your Own

3. The total cost C, in dollars, to dry clean a certain number of shirts s is given by the equation $C = 3.25s$.

   A. What is the dependent variable? _____

   What is the independent variable? _____

   B. Complete the table to relate the total cost to the number of shirts dry cleaned.

Shirts, s	3			10
Cost, C		$16.25	$26.00	

   C. Plot the points on a graph.

   D. (MP) **Reason** Should you draw a straight line through the points on the graph, or should you leave them as separate points? Explain.

   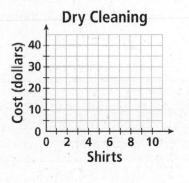
   Dry Cleaning

   _____

   _____

4. (MP) **Model with Mathematics** Dennis is floating down the river on a raft. The table shows the distance he travels over time. Write an equation that represents the number of kilometers k he travels in h hours.

Hours, h	0.5	2	3	5
Kilometers, k	0.75	3	4.5	7.5

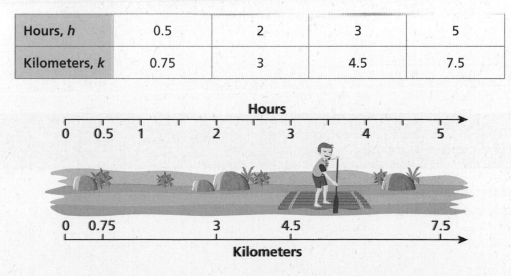

_____

5. Gary has a sister Tina. Their ages are related by the equation $G = T + 4.5$ where G stands for Gary's age and T stands for Tina's age.

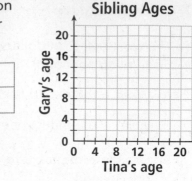

Sibling Ages

(graph with y-axis "Gary's age" 0–20 and x-axis "Tina's age" 0–20)

Tina			7	10
Gary	7	10		

A. Complete the table to show Gary's and Tina's ages over time.

B. Write the ordered pairs from the table.

(___ , ___), (___ , ___), (___ , ___), (___ , ___),

C. Graph the ordered pairs on the coordinate grid.

D. (MP) **Reason** Should you draw a straight line through the points on the graph, or should you leave them as separate points? Explain.

_____

_____

6. The equation $y = 1.19x$, gives the cost y, in dollars, of x boxes of pasta. Complete the table to represent the relationship.

x	2	3	5	8
y				

PASTA
$1.19
PER POUND

(MP) **Model with Mathematics** For Problems 7–8, write an equation to represent each table of values.

7.

t	4	6	9	15
d	228	342	513	855

_____

8.

x	3.8	4.2	5.1	7.3
y	0	0.4	1.3	3.5

_____

I'm in a Learning Mindset!

How does understanding of independent and dependent variables impact my ability to complete a table and graph?

_____

_____

Name _____

LESSON 10.1
More Practice/ Homework

ONLINE
😊Ed
Video Tutorials and Interactive Examples

Represent Equations in Tables and Graphs

1. The price of green beans at a supermarket is shown in the table. Write an equation for the total cost C, in dollars, of p pounds of green beans.

Pounds of green beans, p	0.8	1.2	1.5	0.6
Total cost, C	$2.40	$3.60	$4.50	$1.80

_____

2. **STEM** Joules and calories are two different units of energy. The equation $j = 0.239c$ relates the measures, where c stands for calories and j stands for joules. Complete the table.

c	3	7	10	50
j				

3. **Math on the Spot** A car wash attendant counted the number of cars washed and the total amount of money earned. The company charged the same price for each car washed and earned $165 for 15 cars, $231 for 21 cars, and $275 for 25 cars. Write an equation for the relationship between the number of cars washed, n, and the number of dollars earned, m.

n	15	21	25
m	165	231	275

4. Data for the fastest long-distance train in the United States as of 2018 are shown, where t is the time in minutes, and d is the distance in miles.

$d = 2.5t$

A. What is the dependent variable? What is the independent variable? _____

B. Complete the table.

t	3		10	
d		15		28

(MP) **Model with Mathematics** For Problems 5–6, write an equation representing each table of values.

5.

x	17	14	29
y	25	22	37

6.

d	9	12	16
g	135	180	240

© Houghton Mifflin Harcourt Publishing Company • Image Credit: ©ssuaphotos/Shutterstock

Test Prep

7. The perimeter p of a regular hexagon is found using the equation $p = 6s$. The length of each side is s. Complete the table to represent the relationship.

s	5	12		
p		72	21	54

8. Does the graph match the values in the table?

x	4	8	12	16
y	12	24	36	48

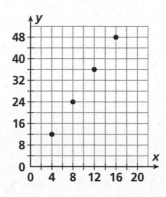

The graph does / does not match the values in the table.

9. The distance m in miles, traveled by an airplane in h hours of flying is shown in the table. What equation represents the situation?

h	1.5	2.5	4	7
m	810	1,350	2,160	3,780

_____

10. Write an equation to represent the values in the table.

n	2.5	3.2	4.5	5.4
p	3.0	3.7	5.0	5.9

_____

Spiral Review

11. Write an inequality that represents the sentence, *"y is less than 3."* Then graph the inequality.

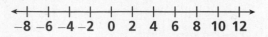

_____

12. Sally pays $50.00 for a meal that costs $38.13. She tells the server to keep the difference as a tip. How much is the tip?

_____

Name _____

Write Equations from Verbal Descriptions

(I Can) identify the dependent and independent variables, write equations to represent a real-world situation, and use the equations to solve problems.

Step It Out

Tutoring rate: $25.50 per hour

1 Ms. Tran tutors students in mathematics. Her rate is shown. How much does Ms. Tran earn tutoring for any number of hours?

A. Identify the independent and dependent variables.

Let x represent the number of hours Ms. Tran tutors.

Let y represent the number of dollars per hour Ms. Tran earns for tutoring.

☐ is the independent variable.

☐ is the dependent variable.

B. Write an equation to represent the situation.

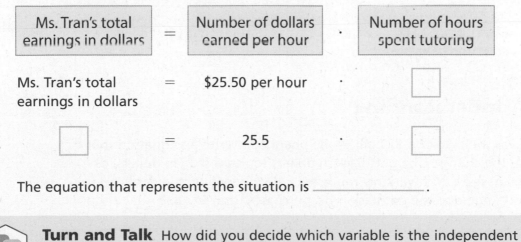

| Ms. Tran's total earnings in dollars | = | Number of dollars earned per hour | · | Number of hours spent tutoring |

Ms. Tran's total   = $25.50 per hour   ·   ☐
earnings in dollars

☐   =   25.5   ·   ☐

The equation that represents the situation is _____ .

Turn and Talk How did you decide which variable is the independent variable?

2 An orchestra will give a concert. There are 1,500 seats in the concert hall. Some tickets have been sold. How many tickets remain?

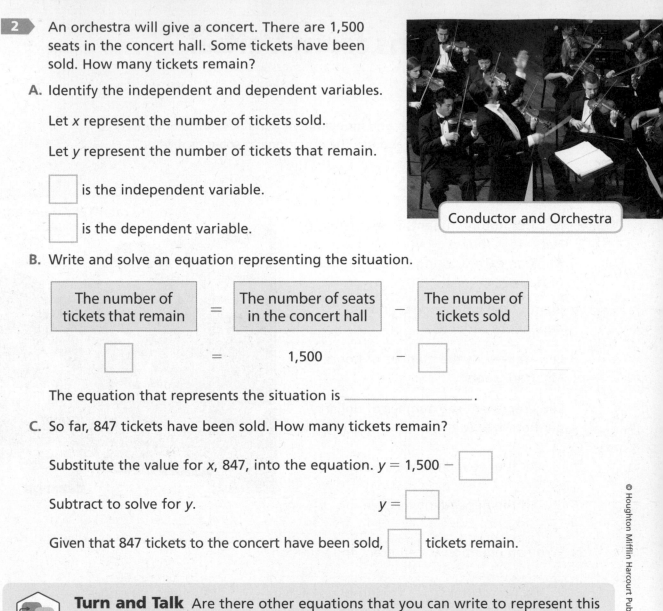

Conductor and Orchestra

A. Identify the independent and dependent variables.

Let *x* represent the number of tickets sold.

Let *y* represent the number of tickets that remain.

☐ is the independent variable.

☐ is the dependent variable.

B. Write and solve an equation representing the situation.

The number of tickets that remain	=	The number of seats in the concert hall	−	The number of tickets sold

☐ = 1,500 − ☐

The equation that represents the situation is _____.

C. So far, 847 tickets have been sold. How many tickets remain?

Substitute the value for *x*, 847, into the equation. $y = 1{,}500 -$ ☐

Subtract to solve for *y*. $y =$ ☐

Given that 847 tickets to the concert have been sold, ☐ tickets remain.

Turn and Talk Are there other equations that you can write to represent this situation? Explain.

Check Understanding

1. Jim gives the cashier a $20 bill at the pharmacy. Write an equation that relates the change *c* he gets back in dollars to the cost *b*, in dollars, of his purchases. Which variable represents the independent variable? How much change does he get back if his purchases total $12.83?

_____

2. A hot-air balloon is 45 meters above the top of the tallest building in a city. Write an equation to show the height *b* of the balloon if the tallest building is *t* meters tall.

_____

322

On Your Own

3. Rosa earns $12.25 per hour working at an ice-cream shop.

A. Write an equation that shows Rosa's earnings e, in dollars, for h hours of working at the ice-cream shop.

_____

B. How much does Rosa earn for working $19\frac{1}{2}$ hours? Round your answer to the nearest cent.

_____

4. Lin is running a marathon.

A. Write an equation that shows the number of miles y she has left after running x miles.

_____

B. If Lin has already run 19.6 miles of the marathon, how many miles does she have left?

_____

> A marathon is 26.2 miles long.

5. (MP) **Use Structure** You want to make $2\frac{1}{2}$ times as many muffins as your friend's recipe makes. Write an equation that shows how to find the amount of each ingredient you will need for the adjusted recipe. Let x represent the amount of each ingredient in the original recipe and y represent the amount of each ingredient in the adjusted recipe.

_____

(MP) **Model with Mathematics** For Problems 6–9, write an equation to represent each situation.

6. Neil pays $19.99 for each shirt he buys. How many total dollars p does he pay for s shirts?

7. Omar has been practicing violin for $4\frac{1}{2}$ years longer than his sister. If his sister has been practicing for x years, how many years y has Omar been practicing violin?

8. A coupon discounts the total grocery bill by $3.50. How many dollars g is the bill after the discount if the bill before the discount is b dollars?

9. Tickets for a local dog show cost $9.75 each. What is the total cost c, in dollars, for t tickets?

10. **STEM** Scientists measure temperature in degrees Celsius and in kelvin. A temperature in kelvin is 273.15 greater than the temperature in degrees Celsius.

A. (MP) **Model with Mathematics** What is an equation that relates the temperature K, in kelvin, to the temperature C, in degrees Celsius?

_____

B. What is the temperature in kelvin of a gas that has a temperature of 5 °C?

_____

11. **Open Ended** Describe a scenario that matches the equation $y = \frac{3}{2}x$.

_____

_____

12. A giraffe is 3 times as tall as a person. Write an equation for the height g, in meters, of a giraffe if a person is t meters tall. How tall is the giraffe if the person is 1.85 meters tall?

_____

13. Kayla walked 1,392 fewer steps than her mother walked. Write an equation for the number of steps w Kayla walked if her mother walked s steps. If her mother walked 11,258 steps, how many steps did Kayla walk?

_____

14. The diameter of a tree increases by about $\frac{1}{8}$ inch each year. Write an equation that represents x, the increase in the diameter of the tree, in the last y years. How much has the diameter increased in the last 15 years?

_____

15. (MP) **Model with Mathematics** Ramon wants to collect $250 in donations to support his favorite charity. He has collected f dollars from his friends and family but has not reached his goal. Write an equation that describes the number of dollars d Ramon still needs to collect to meet his goal. Which variable represents the independent variable?

_____

16. Ms. Quinn pays $16.99 per person to take several friends to lunch. Write an equation that represents the cost C, in dollars, Ms. Quinn pays for f friends. How much does she pay for 7 friends?

_____

Write Equations from Verbal Descriptions

1. (MP) **Model with Mathematics** The area of a floor in square yards is one-ninth the area of the floor in square feet. Write the equation representing y, the area in square yards, to f, the area in square feet.

   _____

2. An object's height is measured in centimeters and inches. Write an equation that relates the number of centimeters c to the number of inches i. Determine the height in centimeters of a chair that is 32 inches tall.

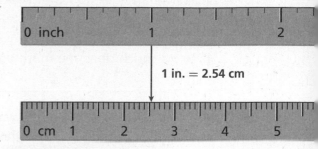

1 in. = 2.54 cm

   _____

3. (MP) **Model with Mathematics** Michael practiced his harmonica 3 times as long as Timothy did. Michael practiced for 126 minutes. Write an equation that represents the relationship between the amount of time Timothy practiced x and the amount of time Michael practiced.

   _____

4. Caleb has read 17 more books than his friend Liana. Write an equation that represents the relationship between n, the number of books Caleb has read, and p, the number of books Liana has read.

   _____

(MP) **Model with Mathematics** For Problems 5–10, write an equation for each description.

5. Felix sold 35 fewer raffle tickets than Helene. How many tickets F did Felix sell if Helene sold H tickets?

   _____

6. Sloane works $7\frac{1}{2}$ hours each day. How many hours h does Sloane work in d days?

   _____

7. A grocery store charges $2.49 per pound for organic apples. What is the cost c, in dollars, of p pounds of organic apples?

   _____

8. Paula used $1\frac{3}{4}$ cups of flour for a recipe. How many cups y of flour did Paula have if she had x cups before making the recipe?

   _____

9. Each crate holds 135 avocados. How many avocados a are in c crates?

   _____

10. Every delivery order from a pizzeria has a delivery charge of $1.50. How many dollars b is the total bill for a delivery of one pizza if the pizza costs p dollars?

   _____

Test Prep

11. Edith bought a science book and a math book for her college classes. The cost s, in dollars, of the science book is $28.75 more than the cost m, in dollars, of the math book.

A. Write an equation that relates the prices of the two books.

_____

B. How much does the math book cost if the science book cost $78.50?

_____

12. A machine fills 75 bottles of water each minute. Write an equation to represent the number of bottles b of water the machine can fill in m minutes.

_____

13. Ken said he would sell 30 tickets to the school play. Write an equation to relate the number of tickets t he has left to sell to the number of tickets s he has already sold. Which variable is the dependent variable?

_____

14. Viola is making bracelets to sell at a craft fair. Each bracelet will have 20 beads. Write an equation to relate the number of beads b she has to the number of bracelets x she can make.

_____

Spiral Review

15. Roberto paid $35.75 for dinner at a restaurant, plus an additional $7.15 tip. What percent of the bill did he pay as a tip? Round to the nearest percent, if necessary.

_____

16. Write an equation to represent the values in the table.

x	3	8	13	18
y	0	5	10	15

_____

17. A 5-pound bag of organic brown rice costs $12.99. A 12-pound bag of the same type of rice costs $31.99. Which represents the better buy? Explain.

_____

_____

_____

Name

Write Equations from Tables and Graphs

(I Can) identify patterns in tables and graphs and use the patterns to write equations to represent real-world situations.

Step It Out

1 ▶ Use the table to complete each statement.

x	y
2	10
3.25	11.25
4.5	12.5
5.75	13.75
7	15

A. Look at the table for patterns. Describe the patterns found in the table.

As x increases by _____, y increases by _____.

Each value of y is _____ units _____ than the corresponding value of x.

B. Write a verbal model describing an equation in the form $y = x + p$ to represent the relationship between the values in the table.

_____

C. Write an equation using the verbal model.

_____

 Turn and Talk What would be the value of x in the table if the corresponding value of y were 25.2? Explain.

2 ▶ Mara is making bracelets. For every red bead, she uses 4 green beads. The graph represents this situation. Use the graph to complete each part.

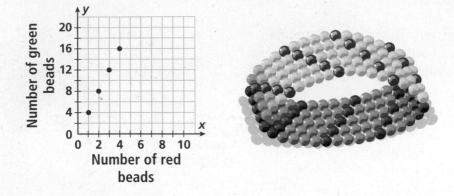

A. Read the ordered pairs from the graph. Use them to complete the table.

Red beads, x	Green beads, y

B. Look at the table for patterns. Describe the patterns found in the table.

As x increases by _____, y increases by _____.

Each value of y is _____ the corresponding value of x.

C. Write a verbal model of the form y = px to represent the relationship between the values in the table

_____

D. Write an equation using the verbal model.

_____

 Turn and Talk In Task 2, should the dots be connected in the graph? Explain why or why not.

© Houghton Mifflin Harcourt Publishing Company

You can model real-world situations using an equation.

3 The graph shows the distance *d*, in miles, a car traveled over time *t*, in hours.

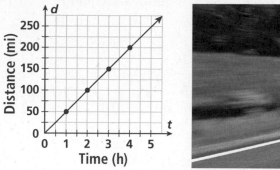

A. Write the coordinates of the points on the graph as ordered pairs.

(☐ , ☐), (☐ , ☐), (☐ , ☐), and (☐ , ☐)

B. Complete the sentence to describe the pattern shown in the graph.

As the first coordinate of each of the points increases by _____,

the second coordinate of each of the points increases by _____.

C. The value of the distance *d*, in miles, is always _____

_____ the value of the time *t*, in hours. So the equation

that models the relationship is _____.

Turn and Talk Why does it make sense to have the line connecting the points on the graph in Task 3 but not in Task 2. Explain.

Check Understanding

Write an equation representing each table or graph.

1.

x	y
0	12
1	13
2	14
3	15
4	16

2.

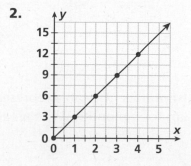

_____   _____

On Your Own

3. **(MP) Construct Arguments** The table represents the distance driven using various amounts of gas. Write an equation that models the distance d, in miles, with respect to gas g, in gallons. Explain your answer by describing patterns in the table.

Distance (d) in miles	120	144	168	192	216
Gas (g) in gallons	5	6	7	8	9

_____

_____

_____

4. The graph represents the relationship between the total cost, in dollars, of a city taxi and the number of miles driven.

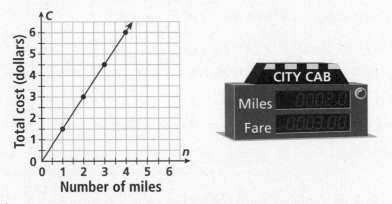

A. Write an equation that relates C, the cost in dollars, to n, the miles driven.

_____

B. **(MP) Reason** Suppose the points in the graph are all increased by three dollars. Write an equation that relates C, the new cost in dollars, to n, the miles driven. If the number of miles driven is 6, what would the cost be? Explain how you found the new equation.

_____

_____

_____

5. **(MP) Model with Mathematics** The table represents the cost C, in dollars, of a cell phone data plan for n months. Write an equation that represents the data in the table.

n	1	2	3	4
C	45.25	90.50	135.75	181.00

6. (MP) **Model with Mathematics** Write an equation representing each table or graph.

A.

x	y
0	14
1	15
2	16
3	17
4	18

B.

x	y
0	0
1	13
2	26
3	39
4	52

_____

_____

C.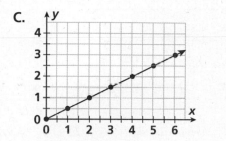

_____

D.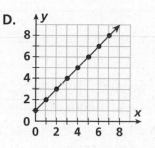

_____

E.

x	y
0	16
1	17
2	18
3	19
4	20

F.

x	y
0	0
1	14
2	28
3	42
4	56

_____

_____

G. (MP) **Look for Repeated Reasoning** Examine the tables and graphs. What do you notice about the equations for the tables and graphs that include the point (0, 0)? What do you notice about the equations for the tables and graphs that do not include the point (0, 0)?

_____

_____

_____

_____

7. The table shows the monthly costs for a smartphone plan with Company A. The advertisement shows the cost of Company B's plan.

n	1	2	3	4
C	32.50	65.00	97.50	130.00

NEW   CELL PHONE PLAN

$7.50 lower per month than our competition!

START-UP FEE: $35.00

A. (MP) **Use Structure** Write an equation that models the total cost C, in dollars, for n months of Company B's plan. Explain.

_____

_____

_____

_____

B. Complete the table for Company B's plan.

n	1	2	3	4
C				

C. After how many months will Company B's plan cost less than Company A's plan? Explain how you arrived at your answer.

_____

_____

_____

(MP) **Model with Mathematics** For Problems 8–9, write an equation representing each table or graph.

8.

x	y
0	0
2	12
5	30
8	48
12	72

9.

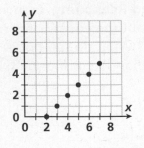

_____   _____

Write Equations from Tables and Graphs

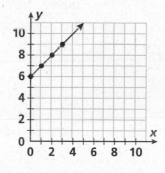
1. The graph shows the total sales of tickets to a school performance.

   A. Write an equation that relates the total sales to the number of tickets sold. Use T for the total sales and n for the number of tickets.

   _____

   B. If the number of tickets sold is 125, what will be the total sales? _____

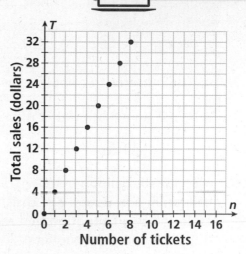

2. **STEM** The table shows the relationship between the mass m and the force w of weights on the ground. Write an equation representing this relationship.

Force (newtons)	9.8	19.6	29.4	39.2
Mass (kilograms)	1	2	3	4

(MP) **Model with Mathematics** For Problems 3–6, write an equation representing each graph or table.

3.
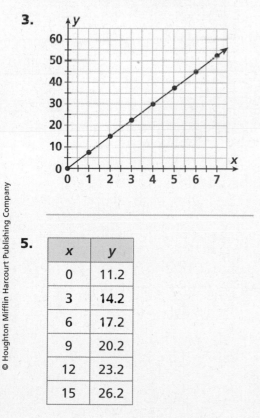

4.

_____

_____

5.

x	y
0	11.2
3	14.2
6	17.2
9	20.2
12	23.2
15	26.2

6.

x	y
0	0
2	17
4	34
6	51
8	68
10	85

_____

_____

Test Prep

7. The partially completed table contains some values for x and y.

x	1	3	5		9
y	7		35		

  A. Use patterns to complete the table.

  B. Write an equation that models the relationship between x and y.

  _____

8. Brenda sells balloon bouquets. She charges the same price for each balloon in a bouquet. The costs for several bouquets are shown in the table. Write an equation that relates the cost of a bouquet to the number of balloons in the bouquet.

Number of balloons, x	6	9	12
Cost ($), y	3	4.50	6

  _____

9. Which equation represents the relationship between x and y shown in the graph?

  Ⓐ $y = 0.25x$

  Ⓑ $y = 0.5x$

  Ⓒ $y = 2x$

  Ⓓ $y = 4x$

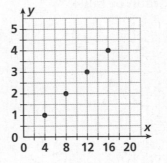

Spiral Review

10. Evaluate the expression for $a = 3$ and $b = \frac{1}{4}$.

  $5a - 16b + 7$

  _____

11. What is the opposite of -3.5?

  _____

12. Combine like terms: $4(x^2 - 3) + 2x^2 + 8$

  _____

Review

Vocabulary

Identify the dependent and independent variables.

1. For every hour of reading, Cameron earns 10 minutes on the computer.

	Dependent	Independent
Hours of reading	☐	☐
Minutes of computer time	☐	☐

Concepts and Skills

2. A community center offers yoga classes for $8 per month plus an additional $0.25 per center floor mat used. Write an equation to express this relationship and complete the table.

1	
2	
3	
4	

_____

_____

3. Becka can make a bracelet in 2 minutes. Write an equation to express the relationship between the number of bracelets made and the amount of time it took, in minutes, to make them. Let x represent the number of bracelets made and let y represent the time, in minutes, it took to make the bracelets. Complete the table and graph.

1	
2	
3	
4	

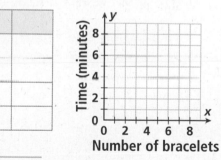

_____

4. (MP) **Use Tools** Renee bought 6 tickets to a football game. She paid a total of $216. Write an equation to represent the situation. What is the cost per ticket? State what strategy and tool you will use to answer the question, explain your choice, and then find the answer.

_____

_____

5. Tag's uncle gave him 25 baseball cards to start his collection. Every week, Tag buys 5 more cards. Write an equation that represents the total number of baseball cards Tag has in his collection. Let x represent the number of weeks Tag bought cards, and let y represent the total number of cards Tag has. Complete the table and the graph.

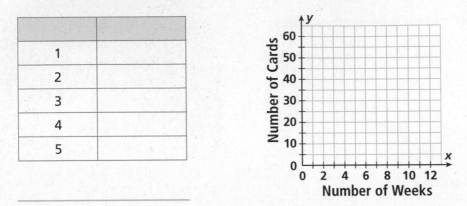

1	
2	
3	
4	
5	

_____

For Problems 6–8, write an equation representing the given graph.

6.

7.

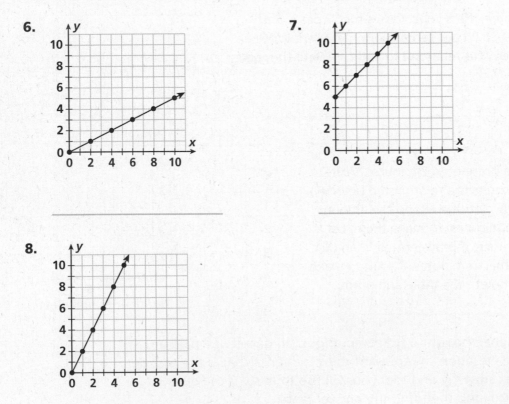

_____   _____

8.

_____

9. Willow works at a grocery store. Her hourly wage is $10.50 per hour. Write an equation to represent Willow's earnings s if she works t hours. What are Willow's earnings if she works 12 hours?

_____

Marketing Manager

STEM
POWERING INGENUITY

Marketing managers are responsible for making a company's products appeal to customers. They often do this using information gathered from focus groups and surveys. To do their job effectively, marketing managers must analyze not only *how* people react to products and advertising, but also *why* they react the way they do. The managers then use their analyses to develop and implement marketing strategies.

STEM Task:

Market researchers study people's reactions to product logos. One study found that circular logos suggest softness and comfort, while angular logos convey strength and durability. RunWalk, an athletic shoe company, found that consumers think their shoes do not last very long. Design a logo for RunWalk to address this issue. Explain your thinking.

Learning Mindset

Strategic Help-Seeking Identifies Need for Help

Do you ask for help when you need it? Sometimes, struggling with a concept or task is the best way to learn. But other times, you may find that you are unable to make progress despite your efforts. When this happens, you may need to seek help from other people or resources. No one knows better than you do when your effort is unproductive, so it is important to recognize when to ask for help. Here are some questions to consider when you are struggling with a new concept.

- Do you understand enough of the concept to keep moving forward on your own? How do you know?

- What parts of the concept are you struggling with? What resources can you use to increase your understanding?

- Who might be able to help you? Who can you go to with questions?

Reflect

Q Were there any parts of the STEM Task that you did not understand? If so, how did you get the help you needed to complete the task?

Q Think about times you have asked for and received help in the past. What kinds of help best support your learning? How do you communicate the kind of help you need?

Polygons on the Coordinate Plane

Polygon Seek and Find

Find an example of each polygon in the design.

In this figure, assume that what appear to be right angles, parallel lines, or segments with equal lengths are actually so.

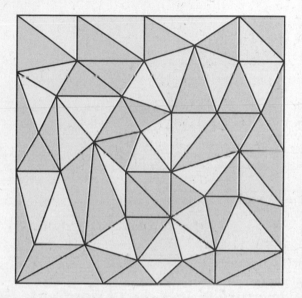

A. square

B. rectangle
(that is not a square)

C. rhombus
(that is not a square)

D. parallelogram
(that is not a rectangle
or a rhombus)

E. quadrilateral
(that is not a parallelogram)

F. isosceles triangle
(that is not equilateral)

G. right triangle

H. acute triangle

I. obtuse triangle

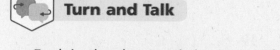 **Turn and Talk**

- Explain the characteristics you used to identify a rhombus that is not a square.

- Explain the characteristics you used to identify a quadrilateral that is not a parallelogram.

Are You Ready?

Complete these problems to review prior concepts and skills you will need for this module.

Quadrilaterals

Classify each figure using the most specific term from the list.

quadrilateral, parallelogram, rectangle, square

1.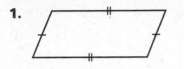

_____

2.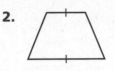

_____

3.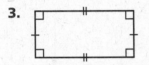

_____

4.

_____

Identify Points on a Coordinate Grid

Graph and label each ordered pair on the coordinate grid.

5. *A*(3, 4)

6. *B*(1, 1)

7. *C*(5, 2)

8. *D*(6, 7)

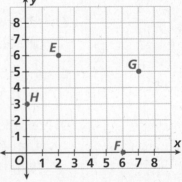

Write the ordered pair for each point shown on the coordinate grid shown.

9. *E* _____

10. *F* _____

11. *G* _____

12. *H* _____

Name _____

Graph Rational Numbers on the Coordinate Plane

(I Can) identify and graph rational number ordered pairs in all four quadrants on a coordinate plane.

Spark Your Learning

The Robinsons' family home is located at (3, 7) on the coordinate grid, where the units are miles. They begin their vacation by leaving home and driving to a restaurant located at (3, 1). From the restaurant, the family drives to a campground located 5 miles due west of the restaurant. After spending five days at the campground, the family drives 6 miles due south to visit their grandparents. What are the coordinates of the campground and their grandparents' home? Explain how you found the coordinates of each location.

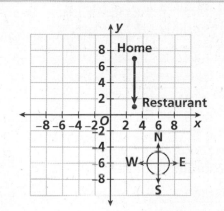

Turn and Talk Explain how the coordinate grid relates to the number lines you used in Module 1.

Build Understanding

A **coordinate plane** is formed by the intersection of two number lines called **axes**. The horizontal number line is called the **x-axis**, and the vertical number line is called the **y-axis**. The **origin** is the point where the x-axis and y-axis intersect. Notice that the coordinate plane is divided into four regions called **quadrants**. Remember that an **ordered pair** is two numbers in the form (x, y) used to locate a point on a coordinate plane.

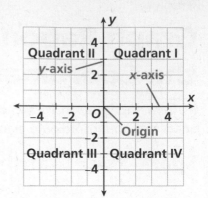

1 How do you identify the **coordinates** of a point on a coordinate plane?

A. The **x-coordinate** and the **y-coordinate** of an ordered pair in Quadrant I will both be positive numbers. What are the coordinates of Point A? How can you describe the location of Point A?

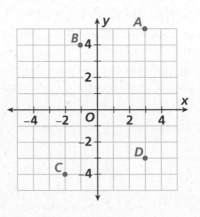

_____

_____

B. Look at Quadrant II. What values can the x-coordinate of an ordered pair in this quadrant have? What values can the y-coordinate have?

_____

_____

C. Look at Quadrant III. What values can the x-coordinate of an ordered pair in this quadrant have? What values can the y-coordinate have?

_____

_____

D. Look at Quadrant IV. What values can the x-coordinate of an ordered pair in this quadrant have? What values can the y-coordinate have?

_____

_____

E. What are the coordinates of Points B, C, and D?

_____

 Turn and Talk Suppose one number in an ordered pair is zero. Is it possible to graph that point? Explain.

© Houghton Mifflin Harcourt Publishing Company

Step It Out

2 ▶ A city mayor wants to build a fence around a community garden. The fence will be in the shape of a **rectangle**. Three fence posts are placed at Points *A*, *B*, and *C*, which are corners of the rectangle. The fourth fence post will be placed at Point *D*, which is not shown.

A. What are the coordinates of Points *A*, *B*, and *C*?

$A\left(\boxed{}, \boxed{}\right)$, $B\left(\boxed{}, \boxed{}\right)$, $C\left(\boxed{}, \boxed{}\right)$

B. To complete the rectangle, which quadrant must Point *D* be in?

_____

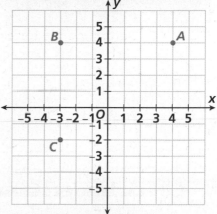

C. What are the coordinates of Point *D*?

$D\left(\boxed{}, \boxed{}\right)$

D. Graph Point *D* on the coordinate plane shown. Then connect the points to form the rectangle.

3 ▶ Coordinates for points graphed on a coordinate plane can be any rational number, including decimals.

A. The interval for the *x*- and *y*-axes is _____ on the coordinate plane shown.

B. Graph the ordered pairs on the coordinate plane shown.

$G(-0.3, 0.4)$, $H(0.4, 0.1)$, $J(0.2, -0.5)$

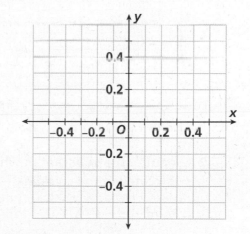

C. In which quadrant is Point *G* located?

_____

D. In which quadrant is Point *H* located?

_____

E. In which quadrant is Point *J* located?

_____

F. Plot a new Point *K* in Quadrant IV and write the point's coordinates.

_____

 Turn and Talk Explain why the ordered pair $(-0.4, -0.5)$ represents a different location than the ordered pair $(0.4, 0.5)$.

4 Coordinates for points graphed on a coordinate plane can be any rational number, including fractions.

A. The interval for the x- and y-axes is

_____ on the coordinate plane.

B. Graph the points with fractional coordinates.

$P\left(1\frac{1}{2}, -\frac{3}{4}\right)$, $Q\left(-1\frac{1}{4}, -1\right)$, $R\left(-\frac{1}{2}, 1\frac{1}{4}\right)$

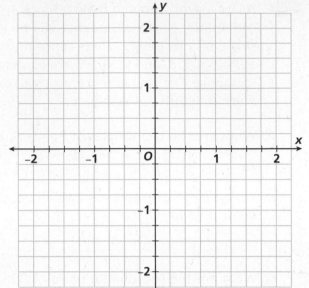

C. Determine the quadrant in which each point is located.

Point P _____

Point Q _____

Point R _____

Check Understanding

1. A grocery store is located at (−5, −4) on a coordinate plane. Shawn says it is located in Quadrant IV. Wren says it is located in Quadrant III. Who is correct? Explain why.

_____

_____

_____

_____

_____

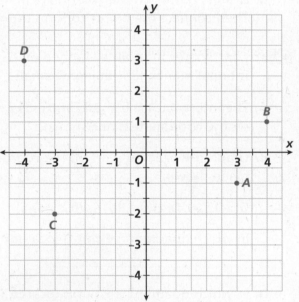

2. Identify the quadrant in which each point is located in the coordinate plane shown.

Point A _____

Point B _____

Point C _____

Point D _____

3. Graph and label the points on the coordinate plane shown.

$M\left(-2\frac{1}{2}, -3\right)$, $N(-1.5, 3.5)$,

$P\left(-3\frac{1}{2}, \frac{3}{4}\right)$, $Q(0.5, -3.5)$, $R\left(2\frac{3}{4}, -1\frac{1}{2}\right)$

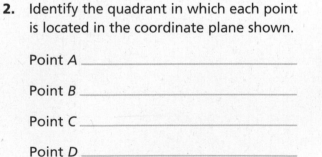

© Houghton Mifflin Harcourt Publishing Company

On Your Own

4. Terrell's house is plotted on a coordinate plane at $(-3, -1)$.

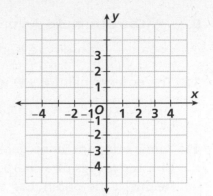

   A. In which quadrant is Terrell's house located?

   _____

   B. To get to Annie's house from Terrell's house, you have to move 5 units directly north and 2 units directly east. In which quadrant is Annie's house?

   _____

   C. What are the coordinates of Annie's house?

   _____

Terrell's house

   D. Graph the locations of Terrell's house, Point T, and Annie's house, Point A, on the coordinate plane.

5. (MP) **Attend to Precision** Alex is making a blueprint of Kite *QRST* on a coordinate plane. Each corner of the kite will lie directly on the *x*- or *y*-axis. The top of the kite, Point *Q*, is at $(0, 2.5)$. The left corner, Point *R*, is at $(-3.5, 0)$. The kite is 7 units from bottom to top and 7 units across from left to right. What are the coordinates of Points *S* and *T*? Explain how you know. Then draw and label the kite on the coordinate plane shown.

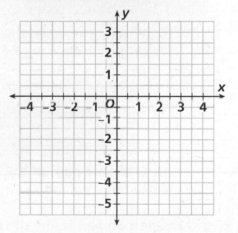

   _____
   _____
   _____
   _____
   _____
   _____
   _____

6. In which quadrant is the point $\left(\frac{13}{48}, -\frac{1}{16}\right)$ located? _____

7. In which quadrant is the point $(-1.7, 4.9)$ located? _____

8. **Open Ended** Name the coordinates of one point in Quadrant I, one point in Quadrant II, one point in Quadrant III, and one point in Quadrant IV.

   _____
   _____

9. (MP) **Use Structure** An ordered pair with a negative *x*-coordinate and a negative *y*-coordinate is in which quadrant? _____

10. The ordered pair (4, −8) is in Quadrant _____. If the coordinates are switched so that it is (−8, 4), it will now be in Quadrant _____.

11. Tamara designs video games. She uses a coordinate plane to plot the moves of a character in the game. The character begins at the origin. Use the coordinate plane to find the character's position.

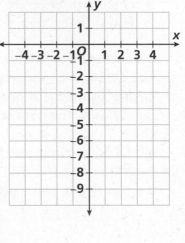

   A. The character moves 3 units left and 2 units down. What are the coordinates of the character after this move? In which quadrant is the character located?

   _____

   B. The character then moves 6 units right and 6 units down. What are the coordinates of the character now? In which quadrant is the character located now?

   _____

   C. What move could the character make to return to the origin? Explain.

   _____

   _____

   _____

   D. Draw the path of the character on the coordinate plane, using *A* and *B* to label the places where the character stopped.

12. **Open Ended** Name the coordinates of two points so that the line segment drawn from one to the other will intersect the *y*-axis.

   _____

I'm in a Learning Mindset!

What is challenging about graphing rational numbers on the coordinate plane? Can I work through it on my own, or do I need help?

_____

_____

LESSON 11.1
**More Practice/
Homework**

ONLINE
Ed   Video Tutorials and
Interactive Examples

Graph Rational Numbers on the Coordinate Plane

1. Graph each of the following ordered pairs on the coordinate plane and name the quadrant in which they are located.

   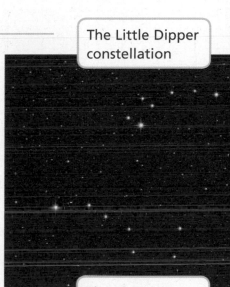

   (2, 1), Quadrant _____

   (−2, 1), Quadrant _____

   (−2, −1), Quadrant _____

   (2, −1), Quadrant _____

   What shape can you make by connecting the four points? _____

2. **STEM** A constellation is a group of stars that form a noticeable pattern in the night sky. It is often named after its form or identified with a mythological figure.

   The Little Dipper constellation

   A. Graph each point. Then connect the points in alphabetical order to form a constellation.

   $A(-6, 2)$, $B(-4, 2.5)$, $C(-3, 2)$,

   $D(-1.5, 1.5)$, $E(-1, 0.5)$, $F(1, 0.5)$,

   $G(1.5, 2)$

   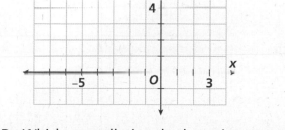

   The Big Dipper constellation

   B. Which constellation do the points resemble the Big Dipper or the Little Dipper?

   _____

3. **Math on the Spot** Give the coordinates of each point on the coordinate plane shown.

   $E\left(\boxed{}, \boxed{}\right)$, $F\left(\boxed{}, \boxed{}\right)$, $G\left(\boxed{}, \boxed{}\right)$

   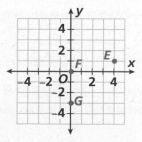

4. In which quadrant is the point $\left(-4\frac{1}{8}, -\frac{5}{8}\right)$ located?

   _____

Test Prep

5. Which ordered pairs are in Quadrant IV? Select all that apply.

   (A) $(-3.7, 4.1)$ (D) $(6.3, -17.25)$

   (B) $\left(2\frac{2}{5}, -\frac{24}{75}\right)$ (E) $(-33, -42)$

   (C) $(5.11, 4.1)$ (F) $(0.1, -0.25)$

6. Match the ordered pair with the quadrant by filling in the correct boxes in the table.

	Quadrant I	Quadrant II	Quadrant III	Quadrant IV
$(-2, -4)$	☐	☐	☐	☐
$\left(\frac{1}{2}, \frac{1}{3}\right)$	☐	☐	☐	☐
$(-1.254, 3.6)$	☐	☐	☐	☐
$(14, -0.254)$	☐	☐	☐	☐

7. Draw a line to match each label to the correct ordered pair.

   Point A •   • $(-2.25, 2)$

   Point B •   • $(2, 1)$

   Point C •   • $\left(-1\frac{3}{4}, -2\right)$

   Point D •   • $(-1.75, 0.75)$

   Point E •   • $(1.5, -1.75)$

   Point F •   • $(0.75, -1)$

   Point G •   • $\left(1\frac{1}{2}, 2\frac{1}{4}\right)$

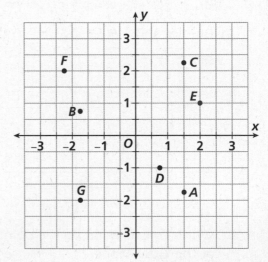

Spiral Review

8. Plot the points on the number line. 2.1, −0.4, 1.3, −1.8

9. In order to ride a roller coaster at Amazing Rides Fair, a person must be at least 42 inches tall. Write an inequality to express this situation.

Name _____

Graph Polygons on the Coordinate Plane

(I Can) graph the given vertices of a figure and determine the coordinates of an unknown vertex to complete the figure given the classification of the polygon.

Spark Your Learning

Marisol is designing a vegetable garden. The coordinate plane shows the area where the garden will be planted where 1 grid square equals 1 square meter. She has 24 meters of fencing to put around her garden. The garden can be any shape as long as she uses all of the fencing to make a border around the garden. Use the coordinate plane to show a possible design for her vegetable garden. Name the coordinates of the corners of the garden. Explain your reasoning.

Turn and Talk What do you notice about the coordinates of the corners of the rectangles? Explain.

Build Understanding

A **vertex** is the point where two sides of a *polygon* intersect. The plural of vertex is *vertices*.

A **polygon** is a closed plane figure formed by three or more line segments that intersect only at their endpoints.

Connect to Vocabulary

1 Look at the figures shown.

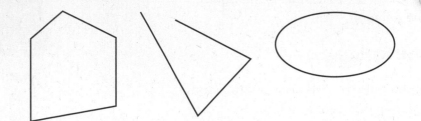

A. What do you notice about the first figure? Is it a polygon?

_____

_____

B. What do you notice about the second figure? Is it a polygon?

_____

_____

C. What do you notice about the third figure? Is it a polygon?

_____

_____

You can classify polygons by the number of sides they have. Triangles, **quadrilaterals**, **pentagons**, and **hexagons** are all examples of polygons.

2 Describe the polygon with vertices $F(2, 5)$, $G(7, 1)$, $H(2, -6)$, and $J(-3, 1)$.

A. Plot the points on the coordinate plane.

B. Connect the points drawing straight lines from F to G, G to H, H to J, and J to F. Classify the polygon you drew by the number of sides.

_____

C. How many vertices does it have?

_____

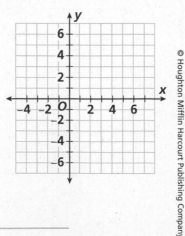

 Turn and Talk Is there another way to classify the figure you drew in Part B? Explain.

© Houghton Mifflin Harcourt Publishing Company

Step It Out

right triangle

3 ▶ An architect is drawing a plan for part of a bridge that makes a **right triangle**. The coordinates of two vertices of the right triangle are A(−3, 5) and B(2, 4). Sides AC and BC will form the right angle of the triangle. What are the coordinates of Vertex C?

A. Plot Points A and B on the coordinate plane.

B. What must be true about a right triangle?

_____

C. Is there more than one possible location for Vertex C? What are the possible coordinates of C?

_____

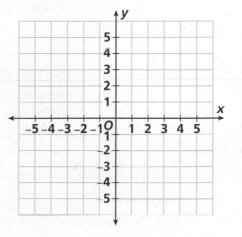

D. Plot Point C and draw Triangle ABC.

E. At which vertex is the right angle?

_____

F. Draw a second right triangle in the fourth quadrant of the coordinate plane. What are the coordinates of each vertex of the triangle?

_____

_____

G. Label the vertices of your triangle with letters. What is the vertex of the right angle in your triangle?

_____

H. Are the right triangles you drew polygons? Explain.

_____

_____

_____

I. Can you plot three points on a coordinate plane that cannot be the vertices of a triangle? If so, how?

_____

_____

_____

Turn and Talk Can you make a right triangle ABC with a right angle at Vertex B instead of at Vertex C? How could you find where to place Point C?

4 An architect is designing a plan for a new building inspired by the NyKredit Krystallen building in Copenhagen, Denmark. The building will have faces that are parallelograms without right angles. The architect plots three of the four corners of one face at $Q(-5, -2)$, $R(1, -2)$ and $S(-2, 3)$. What are the coordinates of Point T if T is the fourth corner of that face of the building?

NyKredit Krystallen building, Copenhagen, Denmark

A. Plot Points Q, R, and S on the coordinate plane.

B. What must be true about a parallelogram?

_____

_____

C. Is there more than one possible location for Point T? What are the possible coordinates of T?

_____

_____

D. Plot Point T and draw the parallelogram.

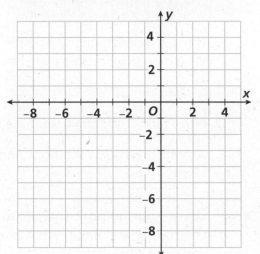

Check Understanding

1. You can classify polygons by the number of sides they have.

A. Graph the points $A(-3, 4)$, $B(-4, -2)$, $C(1, -2)$, and $D(0, 4)$. Connect A to B to C to D to A. What names can you use to describe this polygon? Explain.

_____

_____

_____

_____

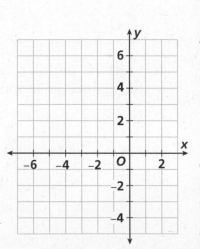

B. Use the points you graphed in Part A. What are the possible coordinates of a Point E if ADE is a right triangle where Angle D is the right angle? Explain.

_____

_____

_____

On Your Own

2. Wesley designs a shark fin for a costume. He chooses the points $K(1, 7)$, $L(3, 5)$, $M(6, -3)$, $N(-5, -2)$, and $P(-1, 1)$ to model the fin.

   A. Graph the points on the coordinate plane.

   B. Connect the points in order from K to L to M to N to P, and back to K.

   C. How many sides does the polygon that you drew have? Classify the polygon by the number of sides.

   _____

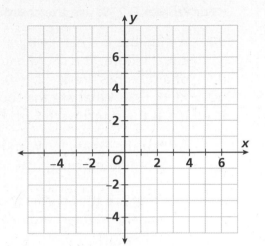

MP Construct Arguments For Problems 3–4, tell whether the figure is a polygon. If it is a polygon, give the number of sides and classify it. If it is not, explain why not.

3.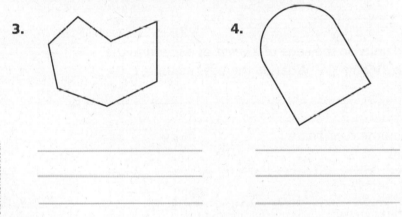

   _____
   _____
   _____

4.

   _____
   _____
   _____

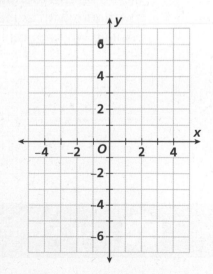

For Problems 5–6, use the coordinate plane.

5. Consider the points $K(1, 2)$ and $L(3, 5)$. What possible coordinates for Point J will make Figure JKL a right triangle with the right angle at Point J? Graph Triangle JKL on the coordinate plane shown.

   _____

6. **MP Use Tools** An isosceles triangle has two sides of the same length. Isosceles triangle DEF has vertices $D(4, -5)$ and $E(-2, -5)$. What are possible coordinates for Point F in section of Quadrant IV shown in the coordinate plane? Explain how you could use a ruler to check your answer.

   _____
   _____
   _____
   _____

For Problems 7–8, use the coordinate plane.

7. A rhombus is a parallelogram with sides of equal length. The coordinates of three vertices of a rhombus are $V(-2, -4)$, $W(3, -4)$ and $X(-6, -1)$. What are the coordinates of Point Y if Y is the fourth vertex of the rhombus?

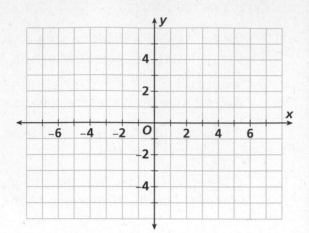

   A. Plot the Points V, W, and X on the coordinate plane.

   B. What are the coordinates of Point Y? Plot Point Y on the coordinate plane.

   _____

   C. To check that all four sides are the same length, first use the coordinate plane to find the lengths of Sides VW and XY. What do the sides measure?

   _____

   D. Next, mark off a scale of grid units on the edge of a sheet of paper and use it to find the lengths of Sides XV and YW. What do the sides measure?

   _____

8. **Open Ended** Graph a square on the coordinate plane with sides of length 3 units.

   _____

9. (MP) **Construct Arguments** Carla drew the figure on the coordinate plane shown. Classify the figure with as many terms as possible. Explain why you can use each term.

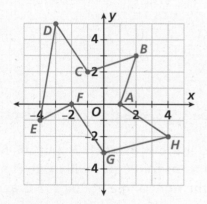

   _____

   _____

   _____

   _____

   _____

I'm in a Learning Mindset!

What tools can I use to solve Problem 6?

_____

_____

Graph Polygons on the Coordinate Plane

(MP) Construct Arguments For Problems 1–2, tell whether the figure is a polygon. If it is a polygon, give the number of sides and classify it. If it is not, explain why not.

1.

2.

_____

_____

3. Points $A(3, 3)$, $B(-6, 1)$, and $C(-3, 1)$ are three vertices of a parallelogram.

  A. Plot the points on the coordinate plane.

  B. Find one possible point in the part of the coordinate plane shown that could be the fourth Vertex D of the parallelogram. Give its coordinates.

  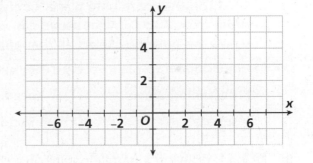

  _____

  C. Plot Point D and draw the parallelogram on the coordinate plane.

  _____

4. **(MP) Reason** Suppose you want to give the coordinates of three points that are vertices of a right triangle. How can you do this without looking at a coordinate plane?

_____

_____

_____

5. A right Triangle *XYZ* has Vertices $X(-2, -1)$ and $Y(1, 1)$ and a right angle at Vertex *Z*. What could the coordinates of Vertex *Z* be? Use the coordinate plane provided.

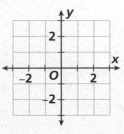

_____

Test Prep

6. Graph the points (1, 3), (5, −4), and (−4, 2) and connect them to form a polygon.

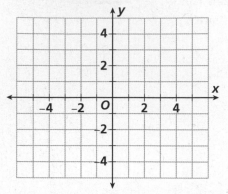

7. Graph the points A(−3, −1), B(−3, −3), C(4, −3), and D(4, −1) on the coordinate plane. Connect the points in order from A to D. What names can you use to describe this polygon? Select all that apply.

(A) quadrilateral

(B) parallelogram

(C) square

(D) rectangle

(E) trapezoid

(F) pentagon

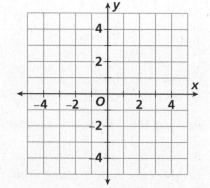

8. Diana is drawing a parallelogram on a coordinate plane. She plots vertices at (−2, −2), (2, −2), and (0, 1). Select all the possible coordinates for the fourth vertex.

(A) (4, 1)

(B) (1, 0)

(C) (−3, 1)

(D) (−4, 1)

(E) (0, −5)

(F) (2, −5)

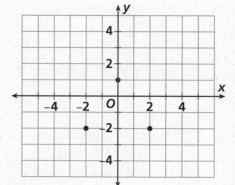

Spiral Review

9. The population of a certain bacteria doubles every 24 hours. How many times as great is the population after 5 days as the population at the start?

_____

10. A farmer gets paid $3.75 per bushel of corn. How much does the farmer get paid for c bushels of corn? Use p to represent the farmer's pay and write an equation that represents this situation.

_____

Name _____

Find Distance on the Coordinate Plane

(**I Can**) find the distance between two points with the same *x*- or *y*-coordinate across quadrants and use a scale in real-world problems to find actual distances.

Spark Your Learning

Nestor is bicycling around the city. All the streets in his neighborhood are in a grid. The grid provided shows the locations of several landmarks. Each side of a square on the grid represents 200 meters. Nestor wants to ride from the library to the coffee shop, staying on the roads. What is the length of the shortest route he can take?

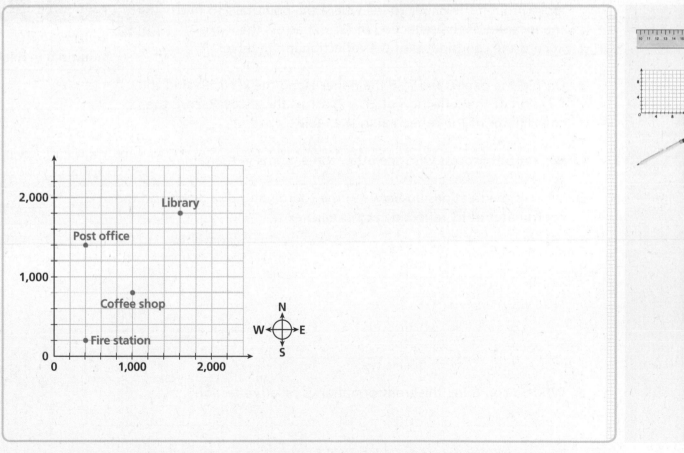

Turn and Talk Explain how you can find the total distance that Nestor needs to bicycle to get from the post office to the library.

Build Understanding

A point on a coordinate plane can be *reflected* across an axis. The *reflection* is located on the opposite side of the axis, at the same distance from the axis.

Connect to Vocabulary

A **reflection** of a figure is a **transformation** of the figure that flips the figure across a line.

1 ▶ Use the table to record your work.

Point	Reflection across y-axis	Reflection across x-axis
(3, −2)		
(−5, 1)		
(2, 4)		
(−1, −3)		

Reflection of a mountain in a lake

A. Draw a coordinate plane on graph paper. Graph the point (3, −2) on your grid. Fold the paper along the y-axis and look through the paper to see where the point falls to find the location of the reflection of (3, −2) across the y-axis. Record the coordinates of the reflection in the table.

B. Unfold the paper, and fold the paper along the x-axis to find the location of the reflection of (3, −2) across the x-axis. Record the coordinates of the reflection in the table.

C. Repeat this process with the other three points in the table.

D. What is the relationship between the coordinates of a point and the coordinates of its reflection across each axis?

_____

_____

_____

_____

E. Why do you think this transformation is called *reflection*?

_____

_____

 Turn and Talk A point is reflected first across the x-axis and then across the y-axis. How will the coordinates of the final point be related to the coordinates of the original point? Explain.

Step It Out

2   What is the distance between the two points on the coordinate plane, measured by units of the coordinate plane?

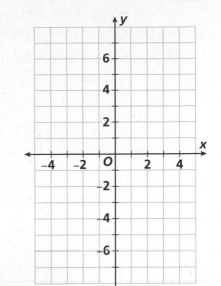

A. Plot and label Points *F*(3, 6) and *G*(3, −2) on the coordinate plane.

B. The *x*-coordinate of Point *F* is _____ as the *x*-coordinate of Point *G*.

C. Draw a line segment that connects the two points. What is the distance between Point *F* and the point where the line intersects the *x*-axis?

_____

D. What is the absolute value of the *y*-coordinate of Point *F*?

_____

E. What is the distance between Point *G* and the *x*-axis? What is the absolute value of the *y*-coordinate of Point *G*?

_____

F. What do you notice about the absolute value of each point's *y*-coordinate and the distance of the point to the *x*-axis?

_____

G. The points ⎢are / aren't⎥ in the same quadrant.

H. Because the points are in different quadrants, add the absolute values of the points' *y*-coordinates to find the distance between Points *F* and *G*.

[ ] + [ ] = [ ]

 Turn and Talk Explain how you might find the distance between two points with the same *x*-coordinate that were both in Quadrant I.

3 ▶ A wholesale chain has two stores as shown on the graph. Each unit represents 10 miles. How far apart are the stores?

A. What are the coordinates of each store?

Store A: (⬚ , ⬚); Store B: (⬚ , ⬚)

B. The y-coordinate of Store A is _____ as the y-coordinate of Store B.

C. Find the distance between Store A and the y-axis using absolute value.

Distance: | ⬚ | = ⬚ units

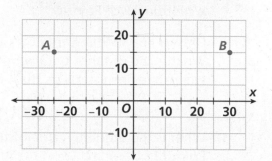

D. Find the distance between Store B and the y-axis using absolute value.

Distance: | ⬚ | = ⬚ units

E. Find the distance, in miles, between the two stores.

Distance (units): ⬚ + ⬚ = ⬚ units

Distance (in miles): ⬚ × ⬚ = ⬚ miles

Turn and Talk How would you find the distance between two points in the same quadrant using absolute value? Explain.

Check Understanding

1. Amy is making a map. She wants to reflect Point (−6, 5) across the y-axis. What are the coordinates of its reflection? _____

2. Are the points P(80, −75) and Q(−35, −75) in the same quadrant or different quadrants? What is the distance between the points? Explain how you found the distance.

_____

_____

3. Are the points A(−4, −10) and B(−4, −2) in the same quadrant or different quadrants? What is the distance between the points? Explain how you found the distance.

_____

_____

_____

Name _____

On Your Own

4. The positions of two neighboring train stations are shown. Each unit on the coordinate plane is equal to 1 mile. How far apart are the two stations?

A. What are the coordinates of each station?

Station *M*: (☐ , ☐); Station *N*: (☐ , ☐)

B. What is the distance in miles between Station *M* and the *x*-axis?

_____

C. What is the distance in miles between Station *N* and the *x*-axis?

_____

D. What is the distance in miles between the two stations?

_____

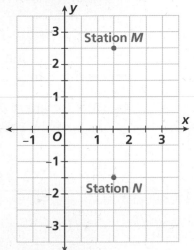

For Problems 5–8, use the coordinate plane.

5. Name two points that have the same *y*-coordinate.

_____

_____

6. What is the distance between Points *S* and *T*? Are they in the same quadrant?

_____

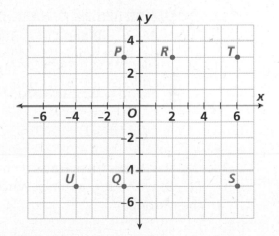

7. What is the distance between Points *R* and *T*? Are they in the same quadrant?

_____

8. What is the distance between Points *Q* and *U*? Are they in the same quadrant?

_____

9. (MP) **Critique Reasoning** Theo says that the point (−5, 7) and its reflection are always 10 units apart. Is he correct? Explain.

_____

_____

_____

_____

Module 11 • Lesson 3

10. (MP) **Use Repeated Reasoning** Write the coordinates of each point after each reflection.

Point	Reflection across x-axis	Reflection across y-axis
(2, −5)		
(−6, −3)		
(−4, 1)		
(1, 9)		

11. The graph shows the positions of two movie theaters. Each unit of the coordinate plane represents 8 miles.

    A. How far apart are the movie theaters in units of the coordinate plane?

    _____

    B. How far apart are the movie theaters in miles?

    _____

Theater A

Theater B

12. (MP) **Use Structure** Find the distance between Points B(−2, −8) and C(−2, 3) without graphing. How did you find the distance?

    _____

    _____

13. (MP) **Use Structure** Find the distance between Points P(3, 9) and R(7, 9) without graphing. Why do you subtract instead of add to find the distance?

    _____

    _____

    _____

- ×
+ ● ÷   **I'm in a Learning Mindset!**

What is challenging about finding distance in a coordinate plane? Can I work through it on my own or do I need help?

_____

_____

Find Distance on the Coordinate Plane

1. On the coordinate plane provided each unit represents 20 miles. Use the coordinate plane to find how far apart two airports are from each other.

   A. Plot and label the points to represent the locations of Airport *A*(125, −325) and Airport *B*(125, 125). Then connect the points.

   B. What is the distance between Airport *A* and the *x*-axis in units and in miles?

   _____

   C. What is the distance between Airport *B* and the *x*-axis in units and in miles?

   _____

   D. What is the distance between the two airports in miles?

   _____

2. What are the coordinates of Point *Z*(−3.9, −9.3) after a reflection across the *y*-axis?

   _____

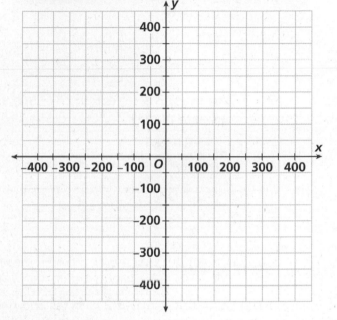

Math on the Spot For Problems 3–4, find the distance between the points.

3.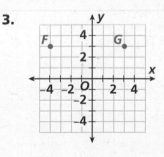

4.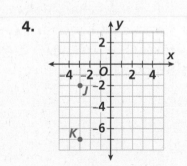

5. (MP) **Use Structure** Find the distance between Points *D*(−5, −3) and *E*(9, −3) without graphing. How did you find the distance?

   _____

   _____

Test Prep

6. What is the distance between the points (−2.5, 6.5) and (2.5, 6.5)?

_____ units

7. What is the distance between the points (3, 4.1) and (3, 1.2)?

_____ units

8. Which point is a reflection of (−3, 8) across the *x*-axis on a coordinate plane?

Ⓐ (−8, 3)

Ⓑ (−3, −8)

Ⓒ (3, 8)

Ⓓ (3, −8)

9. Which point is a reflection of (−5.2, 9.5) across the *y*-axis on a coordinate plane?

Ⓐ (−5.2, −9.5)

Ⓑ (5.2, 9.5)

Ⓒ (5.2, −9.5)

Ⓓ (9.5, −5.2)

Spiral Review

10. A truck driver drives 245 miles and needs to drive *m* miles in all. Write an equation for the number of miles *d* the driver has left to drive.

_____

11. Draw the polygon with vertices (3, −1), (3, 4), (−2, 4), and (−2, −1) on the coordinate plane. Classify the polygon.

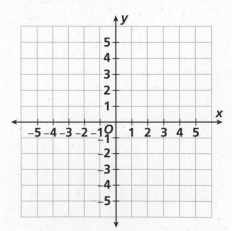

Name _____

Find Perimeter and Area on the Coordinate Plane

(I Can) find the perimeter and area of polygons in the coordinate plane.

Step It Out

You can use what you learned about finding the distance between points to find areas and perimeters of figures on the coordinate plane.

1 ▷ Find the perimeter of the rectangle on the city grid shown.

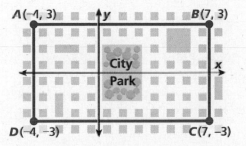

A. To find the perimeter of Rectangle *ABCD*, _____ the lengths of the sides.

B. The coordinates of Point *A* are _____ . The coordinates of

Point *B* are _____ . The length of Side *AB* is _____ units.

C. The coordinates of Point *B* are _____ . The coordinates of Point *C* are

_____ . The length of Side *BC* is _____ units.

D. The coordinates of Point *C* are _____ . The coordinates of Point *D*

are _____ . The length of Side *CD* is _____ units.

E. The coordinates of Point *D* are _____ . The coordinates of Point *A*

are _____ . The length of Side *DA* is _____ units.

F. The perimeter of Rectangle *ABCD* is ⬚ + ⬚ + ⬚ + ⬚ = ⬚ units.

Turn and Talk Explain how you can find the perimeter of a rectangle on the coordinate plane without using the coordinates of the points.

2 ▶ Recall that the formula for the **area** of a rectangle is $A = b \times h$, where b is the length of the **base** and h is the **height**.

A. If we consider Side *EF* to be the base of the rectangle, which side's length is the height?

_____

B. To find the length of the rectangle's base, add the absolute value of the _____-coordinates of Point *E* and Point *F*: $\left|\ \Box\ \right| + \left|\ \Box\ \right|$

The length of the rectangle's base is

$\Box + \Box = \Box$ units.

C. Count the units on the coordinate plane between Point *E* and Point *F* to check the length from Part B. Is the length correct? How many units did you count?

_____

D. To find the rectangle's height, add the absolute value of the

_____-coordinates of Point *E* and Point *D*: $\left|\ \Box\ \right| + \left|\ \Box\ \right|$.

The rectangle's height is $\Box + \Box = \Box$ units.

E. Count the units on the coordinate plane between Point *E* and Point *D* to check the length from Part D. Is the length correct? How many units did you count?

_____

F. Find the area of the rectangle.

$A = b \times h$

$= \Box \times \Box$

$= \Box$ square units

Turn and Talk What are two ways to find the area of a rectangle on a coordinate plane? Explain.

© Houghton Mifflin Harcourt Publishing Company

3 ▶ Alex is designing a rectangular piece of art. He uses the points (1, −1), (4, −1), (4, −8), and (1, −8) to draw the a rectangle on a coordinate plane to begin the piece.

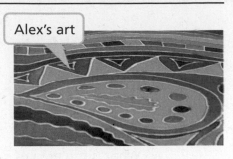
Alex's art

A. Graph the points on the coordinate plane. Then connect the points in the order they were given to draw the rectangle.

B. What are the length and width of the rectangle?

_____

C. Find the perimeter of the rectangle.

$P = \boxed{} + \boxed{} + \boxed{} + \boxed{} = \boxed{}$ units

D. Find the area of the rectangle.

$A = \boxed{} \times \boxed{} = \boxed{}$ square units

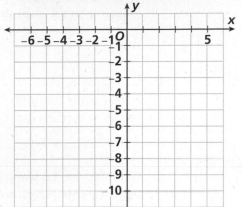

4 ▶ Figures *PQRS* and *TUVW* are squares. Find the shaded area.

A. Find the length of side *PS*.

$\boxed{} + \boxed{} = \boxed{}$ units

B. Find the length of side *TW*.

$\boxed{} \mid \boxed{} = \boxed{}$ units

C. Find the shaded area.

Shaded area = Area of *PQRS* − Area of *TUVW*

$= \boxed{} - \boxed{}$

$= \boxed{} - \boxed{}$

$= \boxed{}$ square units

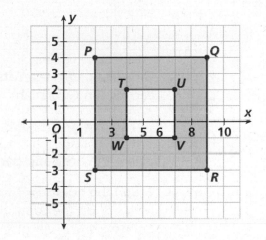

Check Understanding

1. A blueprint of a rectangular pool is shown. What are the area and perimeter of the pool?

_____

_____

2. What is the area of a rectangle *ABCD* with vertices at *A*(−8, 5), *B*(−8, −4), *C*(3, −4), and *D*(3, 5)?

_____

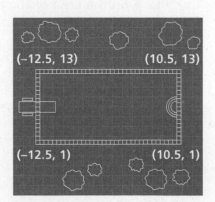
(−12.5, 13)   (10.5, 13)

(−12.5, 1)   (10.5, 1)

On Your Own

3. Gina is growing lettuce in a section of a garden. She represents this section with Rectangle *JKLM*. Each unit in the coordinate plane represents 1 foot.

   A. What is the area of the section where lettuce grows?

   $A = \boxed{} \times \boxed{} = \boxed{}$ square feet

   B. Each head of lettuce needs a 2-foot-square region. How many heads of lettuce can Gina plant?

   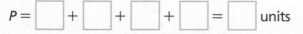

   C. Gina decides to use a section of the lettuce region to plant carrots. Rectangle *MNOP* represents this section of the garden. Find the area of this section of the garden.

   $A = \boxed{} \times \boxed{} = \boxed{}$ square feet

   D. Gina can plant 8 carrots per square foot. How many carrots can Gina plant in the garden?

   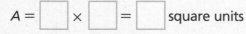

lettuce plants

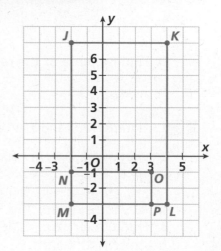

4. What are the area and perimeter of the quadrilateral?

   A. Graph the points (−4, −1), (−1, −1), (−1, −5), and (−4, −5) on the coordinate plane. Then connect the points in the order given.

   B. Find the perimeter of the quadrilateral.

   $P = \boxed{} + \boxed{} + \boxed{} + \boxed{} = \boxed{}$ units

   C. Find the area of the quadrilateral.

   $A = \boxed{} \times \boxed{} = \boxed{}$ square units

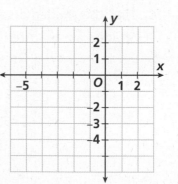

5. **(MP) Reason** The length of one rectangle in a quilt is 6 inches. Its width is 3 inches. About how many of these rectangles do you need to cover an area of 7,500 square inches? Explain.

6. Use the figure on the coordinate plane.

A. What is the area of Rectangle *FGHK*?

_____

B. What is the area of Rectangle *PQRS*?

_____

C. What is the area of the shaded region? Explain how you found your answer.

_____

_____

_____

_____

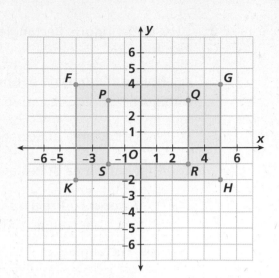

7. (MP) **Use Structure** Wendy needs to make a sheet cake for a party. She draws a plan for the sheet cake on a coordinate plane. One piece of cake is shown in green.

A. What is the perimeter of the sheet cake?

_____

B. What is the area of the sheet cake?

_____

C. Given the size of the first piece of cake cut from the sheet cake, can the cake be cut into pieces of the same size with no cake left over? Explain.

_____

_____

D. **Open Ended** On the coordinate plane, draw two more ways to cut the cake so that the cake can be divided into equal pieces with nothing left over. Name how many people you can feed each time.

_____

_____

_____

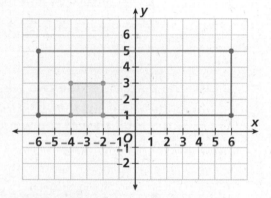

8. Look at the figure. Rectangles *A* and *B* partly cover Rectangle *C*.

    A. What is the outside perimeter of the entire figure? _____

    B. What is the area of Rectangle *A*? _____

    C. What is the area of Rectangle *B*? _____

    D. (MP) **Attend to Precision** What is the area of the part of Rectangle *C* that is not covered by the other rectangles? _____

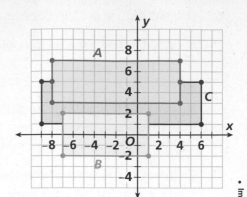

9. **Open Ended** Draw a rectangle on the coordinate plane with an area of 12 square units. What is the rectangle's perimeter?

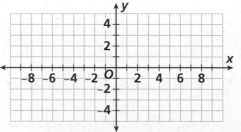

_____

10. The pattern for the two wings of a hang glider is shown on the grid. The unit is inches. What is the total area of the wings? What is the area of each wing?

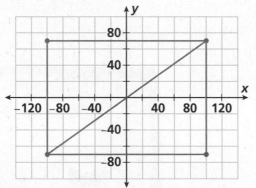

_____

11. What is the area of the rectangle shown on the coordinate plane?

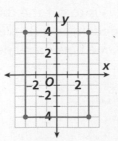

_____

© Houghton Mifflin Harcourt Publishing Company • **Image Credit:** Max Earey/Alamy

Name _____

LESSON 11.4
More Practice/ Homework

ONLINE

Video Tutorials and
Interactive Examples

Find Perimeter and Area on the Coordinate Plane

For Problems 1–2, use the following information.

An engineer is tasked with doubling the length and width of a city park. The engineer draws the park on a coordinate plane and labels it *ABCD*.

1. Find the area of the park before and after the expansion.

   A. What is the area of the park before the expansion? _____

   B. What is the area of the park after the length and width are doubled? _____

   C. By what factor did the area change? _____

Dimensions of park are being doubled.

2. Find the perimeter of the park before and after the expansion.

   A. What is the perimeter of the park before the length and width are doubled? _____

   B. What is the perimeter of the park after the length and width are doubled? _____

   C. By what factor did the perimeter change? _____

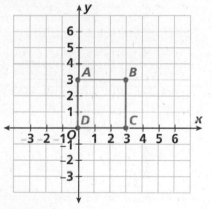

3. **Math on the Spot** What is the perimeter of the rectangle shown?

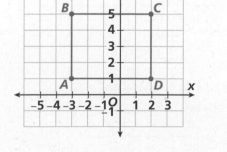

_____

For Problems 4–7, find the length of the segment with the given endpoints.

4. $(-12, 4)$, $(21, 4)$

_____

5. $(-6, 9)$, $(-6, 13)$

_____

6. $(17.1, 3)$, $(21.4, 3)$

_____

7. $(-3, -12.5)$, $(-3, 16.5)$

_____

Test Prep

8. Find the area of the shaded region in square units.

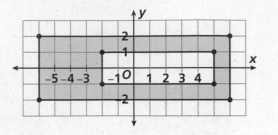

_____

9. Rectangle *ABCD* has a perimeter of 22 units. The coordinates of the rectangle's vertices are *A*(−4, 5), *B*(3, 5), *C*(3, *x*), and *D*(−4, *x*). Which could be the value of *x*?

Ⓐ 7 Ⓒ 1

Ⓑ 4 Ⓓ −9

10. Line segment *DE* is drawn on the coordinate plane. Which ordered pair could be the vertex of a rectangle with Segment *DE* as one side and an area of 28 square units? Select all that apply.

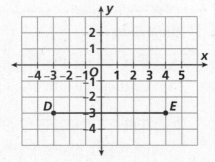

Ⓐ (0, 1) Ⓑ (2, 0) Ⓒ (−3, 1)

Ⓓ (−2, −2) Ⓔ (4, 4) Ⓕ (4, 1)

Spiral Review

11. A triangle has vertices at *A*(−2, −1), *B*(−2, 4), and *C*(7, −1). In what quadrant is Vertex *A* located? _____

12. A dozen donuts cost $2.99. To the nearest cent, what is the cost of 1 donut? _____

13. Mr. Lee had $67. He bought a concert ticket and now has $11. Write an equation that can be used to find the price *c* of the concert ticket.

_____

14. List three possible solutions for the inequality $h < 34$.

_____

Module 11 Review

Vocabulary

Choose the correct term from the Vocabulary box to complete each statement.

Vocabulary
coordinate plane
axes
x-axis
y-axis
origin
quadrant
coordinates
polygon
vertex
reflection

1. A(n) _____ is a closed plane figure formed by three or more line segments that intersect only at their endpoints.

2. An ordered pair describes a point on a _____. The first number in an ordered pair describes the distance from the origin along the _____. The second number in an ordered pair describes the distance from the origin along the _____.

3. The numbers of an ordered pair that locate a point on a coordinate plane are called _____.

4. The point (0, 0) on the coordinate plane is called the _____.

5. A(n) _____ of a figure is a transformation that flips the figure across a line.

6. The point on a polygon where two sides intersect is called a _____.

7. The point (1, 1) is located in _____ I of the coordinate plane.

Concepts and Skills

Use the coordinate plane to answer Problems 8–12.

8. What type of figure has vertices at *R*, *S*, *T*, and *U*?

   _____

9. What is the area of Figure *RSTU*? _____

10. What is the perimeter of Figure *RSTU*? _____

11. Graph the following points: $M(0, -1)$, $N\left(3\frac{1}{2}, 0\right)$, $P(-4, 0)$.

12. (MP) **Use Tools** What is the distance between Points $C(4, 6)$ and $D(-5, 6)$? State what strategy and tool you will use to answer the question, explain your choice, and then find the answer.

   _____

   _____

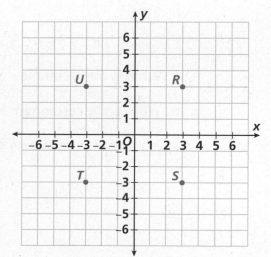

Use the coordinate plane to answer Problems 13–16.

13. Write the ordered pair for each of the points on the graph.

Point *G:* _____

Point *H:* _____

Point *L:* _____

Point *J:* _____

14. Point *K* is reflected across the *x*-axis. What are the coordinates of its image after the reflection?

_____

15. What is the distance from *J* to *G*?

[ ] grid units, which equals [ ]

16. What is the distance from *L* to *H*?

[ ] grid units, which equals [ ]

17. Find the distance between Points *V*(12, 14) and *W*(12, −16) without using a coordinate plane. _____

18. The vertices of Rectangle *DEFG* have these coordinates: *D*(4, 6), *E*(4, 1), *F*(0, 1), and *G*(0, 6). What is the area of Rectangle *DEFG* in square units?

_____

19. The vertices of Rectangle *RSTU* have these coordinates: *R*(−8, 2), *S*(−8, −4), *T*(−2, −4), and *U*(−2, 2). What is the area of Rectangle *RSTU* in square units?

_____

20. The points *M*(−3, 2), *N*(−3, −4), *P*(2, −4) and *Q*(2, 2) form a rectangle.

A. What is the rectangle's perimeter? _____

B. What is the rectangle's area in square units? _____

21. Which point is a reflection of (−5, 1.8) across the *y*-axis on a coordinate plane?

(A) (5, 1.8)

(B) (−5, −1.8)

(C) (−5, 1.8)

(D) (5, −1.8)

Area of Triangles and Special Quadrilaterals

A zoo is adding three new cages to its bird exhibit. The floors of the cages will be rectangles with the same perimeters but different areas. The floor plan for one of the cages is shown on the grid.

Draw possible floor plans for the other two cages with the same perimeter.

A. Each unit on the grid represents 5 feet.

What is the perimeter of the floor of each cage?

_____

B. Label the floor plan for each cage with its area.

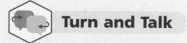

Cage 1

Turn and Talk

- What happens to the floor area of a cage as the difference between the length and width decreases?

- What is the largest possible floor area for one of the new cages?

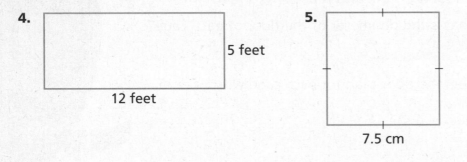

Are You Ready?

Complete these problems to review prior concepts and skills you will need for this module.

Triangles

Complete each statement.

1. A triangle that has three acute angles is called a(n) _____ triangle.

2. A triangle that has one obtuse angle is called a(n) _____ triangle.

3. A triangle with a 90° angle is called a(n) _____ triangle.

Estimate and Find Area

For Problems 4–5, find the area of each rectangle.

4.

5 feet

12 feet

_____

5.

7.5 cm

_____

6. A rectangular swimming pool has a length of 25 meters and a width of 12 meters. Find the area of the pool.

_____

7. A high school basketball court is a rectangle with a length of 84 feet and a width of 50 feet. Find the area of the basketball court.

_____

8. Find the area of a rectangular painting that has a length of 7.2 feet and a width of 4.5 feet.

_____

Name _____

Develop and Use the Formula for Area of Parallelograms

(I Can) understand the area formula for a parallelogram and use it to find area or to find unknown dimensions given the area.

Spark Your Learning

The tabletops in a restaurant are parallelograms and rectangles with the same distance between parallel sides. The approximate side lengths are shown. Is the area of a parallelogram-shaped tabletop the same as the area of a rectangular one? Explain.

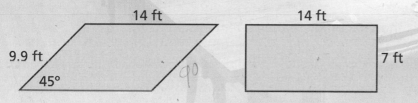

14 ft

9.9 ft

45°   90

14 ft

7 ft

$a = \frac{1}{2} bh$

© Houghton Mifflin Harcourt Publishing Company • Image Credit: ©August_08012/Shutterstock

Turn and Talk Suppose the restaurant also has square tabletops. What are the approximate side lengths of one of the square tabletops if it has the same area as the rectangular tabletop? Explain.

Build Understanding

A quadrilateral is a polygon with four sides and four angles. If it has two pairs of sides that are parallel, it is a **parallelogram**.

How can you find the area of a parallelogram?

A. Look at the parallelogram shown. If you draw a line to make a right triangle and then move the right triangle as shown, it forms a new figure. What is the new figure?

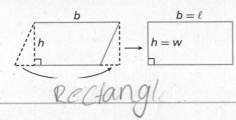

Rectangle

B. Look at the quadrilaterals shown. Complete the statements.

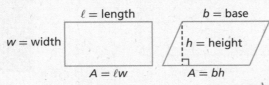

To find the area of a rectangle, multiply its __lighthen__ by its

_____. The area of a parallelogram is found by multiplying

its _____ by its _____.

C. Why are the area equations in Part B so alike?

In the quadrilaterals in Part B, the length of the rectangle is equal

to the _____ of the parallelogram, and the width of the

rectangle is equal to the _____ of the parallelogram.

D. Since $b = \boxed{\ell}$ and $h = \boxed{w}$, and since $A = \ell w$ for a rectangle, then

$A = \boxed{B} \times \boxed{h}$ for a parallelogram.

E. What is the area of the parallelogram shown?

$A = bh$

$A = \boxed{3}$ cm $\times$ $\boxed{}$ cm

$A = \boxed{18}$ cm²

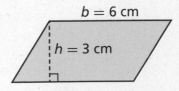

Turn and Talk Explain how the area of the rectangle and the area of the parallelogram in Part B compare.

Name _____

Develop and Use the Formula for Area of Triangles

(I Can) use the area formula for a triangle given either the base and height or the area and the height or the base.

Spark Your Learning
SMALL GROUPS

A farmer has a rectangular paddock for his horses, as shown. He wants to reconfigure his fields and change the paddock so that it is square. However, he wants it to have the same area as the rectangular paddock. What should the side length of the square paddock be? Justify your answer.

$8\frac{1}{4}$ ft | 289 sq ft

33 ft

$8\frac{1}{4} \times 33$ 　　$\begin{array}{r} 33 \\ 35 \end{array}$ 　　$\frac{33}{1} \times \frac{33}{1} = \begin{array}{r} 199 \\ 990 \\ \hline 289 \end{array}$

area = 289 sq ft

Turn and Talk Will the rectangular paddock and the square paddock use the same amount of fencing? Explain.

Build Understanding

A **diagonal** is a line segment that connects two nonadjacent vertices of a polygon.

1 How can you find the area of a right triangle?

A. Recall that a rectangle is a quadrilateral with four right angles. The length and width of a rectangle also can be called the base and height.

You can put together two copies of a right triangle to form a rectangle as shown. What is the relationship between the rectangle and each right triangle?

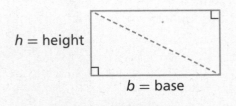

h = height

b = base

each right Tranglenis is ~~#tline~~ haft size a square

B. What is the area formula for a rectangle in terms of b and h?

$a = b \times h$

C. How can you use the area formula for a rectangle to write an area formula for a right triangle?

I can the right side of the rectangle in haft.

D. Write the area formula for a right triangle.

$$A = \frac{b \times h}{2} = \frac{1}{2}bh$$

E. What is the area of the right triangle shown?

$A = \frac{1}{2}bh$

$A = \frac{1}{2}\left(\boxed{4} \times \boxed{16} \right)$

$A = \boxed{32} \text{ cm}^2$

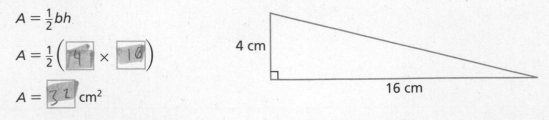

4 cm

16 cm

 Turn and Talk Do you need to know the angle measures of a triangle to find its area? Explain.

2 ▸ How can you find the area of a non-right triangle?

A. Recall that a parallelogram is a quadrilateral with two pairs of parallel sides. You can put together two copies of a non-right triangle to form a parallelogram as shown. What is the relationship between the parallelogram and each non-right triangle?

h = height

b = base

H = Hight
b = base

B. What is the area formula for a parallelogram?

C. How can you use the area formula for a parallelogram to write an area formula for a triangle?

D. Write the area formula for a triangle.

$$A = \frac{\boxed{b} \times \boxed{h}}{\boxed{2}}$$

$$= \frac{\boxed{1}}{\boxed{2}}$$

$$= \frac{\boxed{1}}{\boxed{2}}\left(\boxed{b} \times \boxed{h}\right)$$

$$\frac{b \times h}{2}$$

E. What is the area of the triangle shown?

$A = \frac{1}{2}bh$

$A = \frac{1}{2}\left(\boxed{} \times \boxed{}\right)$

$A = \boxed{}$ in²

6 in.

10 in.

Step It Out

3 The height of a triangle is perpendicular to the base. Sometimes it is shown outside of the triangle. Find the length of the base in meters.

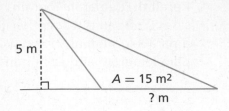

5 m

A = 15 m²

? m

A. Substitute the known values into the formula for the area of a triangle.

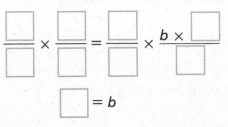

$$\boxed{} = \frac{b \times \boxed{}}{\boxed{}}$$

B. To solve for b, _____ each side of the equation by $\frac{2}{5}$.

$$\frac{\boxed{}}{\boxed{}} \times \frac{\boxed{}}{\boxed{}} = \frac{\boxed{}}{\boxed{}} \times \frac{b \times \boxed{}}{\boxed{}}$$

$$\boxed{} = b$$

The base is _____ meters long.

4 Many cities are planned with a grid pattern for the streets. Often there are one or more diagonal streets that cut across the grid, forming right triangles. What is the area within the triangle, in square feet?

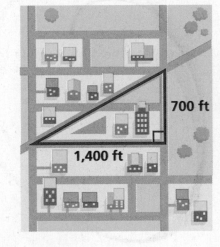

700 ft

1,400 ft

A. What are the dimensions of the triangle?

$b = \boxed{}$ ft, $h = \boxed{}$ ft

B. Substitute the values for b and h into the formula for the area of a triangle. Then find the area.

$$A = \frac{\boxed{}}{\boxed{}} \left(\boxed{} \times \boxed{} \right) = \boxed{} \ \text{ft}^2$$

C. The area of the triangle is _____ square feet.

Check Understanding

1. An isosceles right triangle has a base and height of 5 inches. Find its area.

_____

2. Find the height of a triangle with an area of 12 square centimeters and a base of 8 centimeters.

_____

On Your Own

3. (MP) **Reason** Doug is making square tiles as shown. What is the area of the smaller square in the figure? Explain.

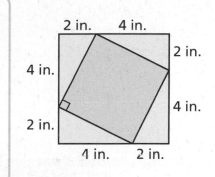

2 in.   4 in.

2 in.

4 in.

2 in.

4 in.

2 in.

4 in.   2 in.

4. A triangle has a base measuring $8\frac{1}{2}$ inches. If its height is $4\frac{1}{2}$ inches, what is the area of the triangle?

5. Walt is designing a school pennant in the shape of a triangle. The pennant must have a height of 11 inches and an area of 66 square inches. What must the length of the base be?

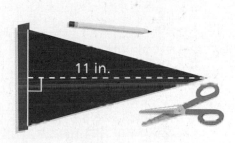

11 in.

6. A rectangle has a length of 8 feet and a width of 3 feet. If a right triangle has a height of 3 feet, what length would its base be if it has the same area as the rectangle?

7. A triangular roof is built so that its height is half its base. If the base of the roof is 32 feet long, what is the area of the roof?

8. A triangle has a height of 7 inches and an area of 35 square inches. What is the length of the base?

For Problems 9–12, find the area of a triangle with the given base and height.

9. $b = 12$ m, $h = 6.5$ m

10. $b = 4\frac{1}{4}$ in., $h = 8$ in.

11. $b = 8$ ft, $h = 7$ ft

12. $b = 4.4$ cm, $h = 6.5$ cm

13.  **Critique Reasoning** For the two triangles shown, Clara says that the triangle on the right has a larger area because the triangle on the left is narrower. Prisha says that both triangles have the same area. Who is correct? Why?

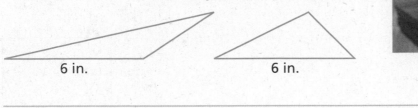

6 in.   6 in.

Who is correct?

_____

_____

14. Open Ended Draw two different triangles so that each has an area of 10 square units.

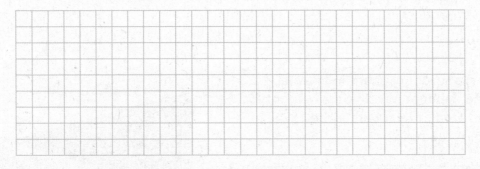

15. A triangle has an area of 7 square feet. What could be the length of the base and the height?

_____

For Problems 16–19, find the unknown base length for each triangle.

16. $A = 44$ cm^2, $h = 11$ cm

_____

17. $A = 34$ ft^2, $h = 8.5$ ft

_____

18. $A = 49$ m^2, $h = 7$ m

_____

19. $A = 31.5$ in^2, $h = 7$ in.

_____

I'm in a Learning Mindset!

What questions can I ask to help me understand how to find the area of a right triangle?

_____

_____

Name _____

Develop and Use the Formula for Area of Trapezoids

(I Can) use the area formula for a trapezoid given the lengths of its bases and its height.

Spark Your Learning

Quinn is putting sod in a yard, but is leaving part of the area without grass for a patio. He needs to know how many square feet of sod to buy. The shaded area shown is the part of the yard that will have grass. How many square feet of sod does Quinn need?

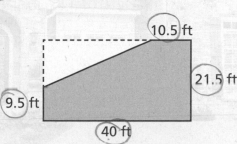

10.5 ft

21.5 ft

9.5 ft

40 ft

FO

5.

7.

3.5

Turn and Talk How does knowing the formulas for the areas of rectangles and triangles help in finding the areas of other figures?

Build Understanding

Trapezoids have two bases. Any pair of parallel sides of a trapezoid can be the **bases** of the trapezoid. The **height of a trapezoid** is the perpendicular distance from the base to the opposite vertex or side.

1 ▶ How can you find the area of a trapezoid?

A. Notice that two copies of the same trapezoid fit together to form a parallelogram. How does the area of the trapezoids compare to the area of the parallelogram?

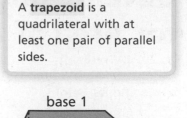

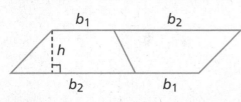

_____

B. How does the height of the trapezoid compare to the height of the parallelogram in Part A?

_____

C. How can you find the length of the base of the parallelogram in Part A?

The length of the base of the parallelogram is the _____

of the _____ of the trapezoid.

D. How can you use the area formula for a parallelogram to write an area formula for a trapezoid?

Area of parallelogram = bh

$$= \left(\boxed{} + \boxed{} \right) \times h \qquad \text{Substitute the sum of the two bases for } b.$$

$$\text{Area of trapezoid} = \frac{\left(\boxed{} + \boxed{} \right)}{\boxed{}} \times h \qquad \text{Divide by 2.}$$

So, the area formula for a trapezoid can be written as

$$A = \frac{\boxed{}}{\boxed{}} h \left(\boxed{} + \boxed{} \right).$$

 Turn and Talk Will this area formula work for all trapezoids regardless of size? Explain.

Step It Out

2 ▶ What is the area of the trapezoidal cactus garden shown?

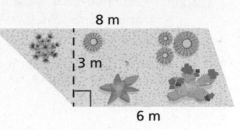

8 m

3 m

6 m

A. What is the formula for the area of a trapezoid?

_____

B. What are the dimensions of the trapezoid?

$b_1 = \boxed{}$ m $b_2 = \boxed{}$ m $h = \boxed{}$ m

C. Substitute the values for b_1, b_2, and h into the formula.

$A = \frac{1}{2}\left(\boxed{}\right)\left(\boxed{} + \boxed{}\right)$

D. Add inside the parentheses.

$A = \frac{1}{2}\left(\boxed{}\right)\left(\boxed{}\right)$

E. Multiply.

$A = \frac{1}{2}\left(\boxed{}\right)$

F. Divide.

$A = \boxed{}$ square meters

G. The area of the cactus garden is $\boxed{}$ square meters.

3 ▶ What is the area of the trapezoid shown?
Remember, the bases are the two parallel sides.

A. What is the formula for the area of a trapezoid?

_____

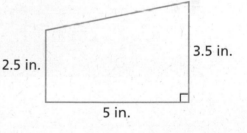

2.5 in.

3.5 in.

5 in.

B. What are the dimensions of the trapezoid?

$b_1 = \boxed{}$ in. $b_2 = \boxed{}$ in. $h = \boxed{}$ in.

C. Substitute the values for b_1, b_2, and h into the formula.

$A = \frac{1}{2}\left(\boxed{}\right)\left(\boxed{} + \boxed{}\right)$

D. Simplify.

$A = \boxed{}$ square inches

E. The trapezoid has an area of _____ square inches.

Turn and Talk Could you find the area of a trapezoid using triangles? Explain.

A teacher has a table in the shape of the trapezoid shown. What is the height of the tabletop in feet?

A. What is the formula for the area of a trapezoid?

_____

B. Substitute the given values in the formula.

$$\boxed{} = \tfrac{1}{2}h \left(\boxed{} + \boxed{} \right)$$

C. Simplify.

$$\boxed{} = \boxed{}\, h$$

D. Divide.

$$h = \boxed{}$$

E. The height of the tabletop is $\boxed{}$ feet.

Check Understanding

1. A patch on a denim jacket is in the shape of the trapezoid shown. Find its area.

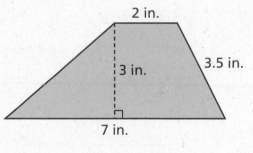

_____

2. In a trapezoid, the length of one base is equal to the height and the length of the other base is twice the height. If the height is 10 centimeters, what is the area of the trapezoid? Explain how you found your answer.

_____

_____

_____

3. A trapezoid has an area of 24 square feet. If the height is 6 feet, what is the sum of the lengths of the bases in feet?

_____

Develop and Use the Formula for Area of Trapezoids

1. The Shanghai World Financial Center is one of the tallest buildings in the world. It features a large trapezoidal opening to allow wind to pass through. The opening is about 35 meters tall. It is about 40 meters along the bottom and 50 meters along the top. What is the approximate area of the opening?

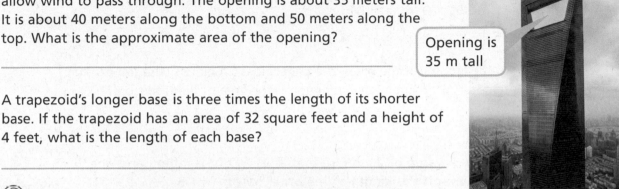

Opening is 35 m tall

_____

2. A trapezoid's longer base is three times the length of its shorter base. If the trapezoid has an area of 32 square feet and a height of 4 feet, what is the length of each base?

_____

3. (MP) **Reason** One base of a trapezoid is 4 inches long, and the other base is 6 inches long. The trapezoid's area is 25 square inches. Do the measurements describe a unique trapezoid? Explain.

_____

_____

4. **Math on the Spot** Find the area of the trapezoid shown.

_____

5. The area of a trapezoid is 18 square feet. If the height is 3 feet, what is the sum of the lengths of the bases?

_____

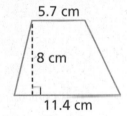

5.7 cm

8 cm

11.4 cm

For Problems 6–9, find the area of each trapezoid.

6.

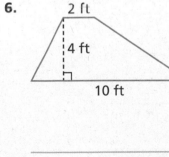

2 ft

4 ft

10 ft

7.

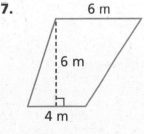

6 m

6 m

4 m

8.

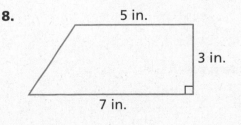

5 in.

3 in.

7 in.

9.

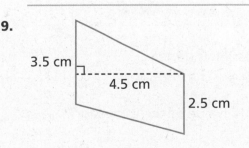

3.5 cm

4.5 cm

2.5 cm

Test Prep

10. A trapezoid with which of these dimensions has the largest area?

(A) $b_1 = 4$ in., $b_2 = 6$ in., $h = 8$ in.

(B) $b_1 = 8$ in., $b_2 = 3$ in., $h = 7$ in.

(C) $b_1 = 5$ in., $b_2 = 8$ in., $h = 6$ in.

(D) $b_1 = 6$ in., $b_2 = 9$ in., $h = 5$ in.

11. The sum of the lengths of the bases of a trapezoid is 6.4 meters. The trapezoid's height is 4 meters. How many square meters is the area of the trapezoid?

_____

12. A trapezoid has an area of 36 square feet. If its height is 8 feet, and one base is 4 feet, what is the length of the other base?

_____

13. Which of the following statements about a trapezoid with a height of 3 inches and an area of 54 square inches are true? Select all that apply.

(A) If one base is 6 inches long, the other base is 30 inches long.

(B) If one base is 9 inches long, the other base is 27 inches long.

(C) If one base is 12 inches long, the other base is 24 inches long.

(D) If one base is 18 inches long, the other base is 2 inches long.

(E) If one base is 36 inches long, the other base is 1 inch long.

Spiral Review

14. An expression is shown.

$\frac{3}{8} \div \frac{9}{16}$

What is the value of the expression?

_____

15. Sue downloaded 20 songs for $25.00. What was the cost per song?

_____

16. An expression is shown.

$11.57 - 6.2$

What is the value of the expression? _____

Name

Find Area of Composite Figures

(I Can) **find the area of any composite figure.**

Step It Out

You can find the area of *composite figures* by breaking them into familiar figures such as triangles or quadrilaterals.

1 ▶ The figure shown gives the dimensions of a city park. What is the area of the city park?

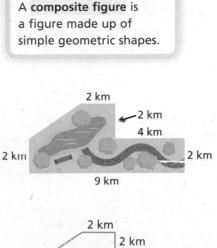

A. What different shapes could the figure be divided into?

_____

_____

B. There are several ways to divide the figure. The figure is divided into two quadrilaterals with a horizontal line. What are the two quadrilaterals?

_____

_____

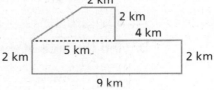

C. Find the area of the top shape.

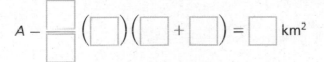
$A = \dfrac{\boxed{}}{\boxed{}} \left(\boxed{}\right)\left(\boxed{} + \boxed{}\right) = \boxed{}$ km²

D. Find the area of the bottom shape.

$A = \boxed{} \times \boxed{} = \boxed{}$ km²

E. Total area = Area of top shape + Area of bottom shape

$= \boxed{}$ km² $+ \boxed{}$ km²

$= \boxed{}$ km²

The area of the park is _____ square kilometers.

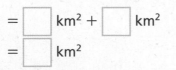 **Turn and Talk** In what other ways could you divide the figure? Explain.

2 The roof of a building is shown. What is its area?

A. What different shapes could the roof be divided into?

_____

_____

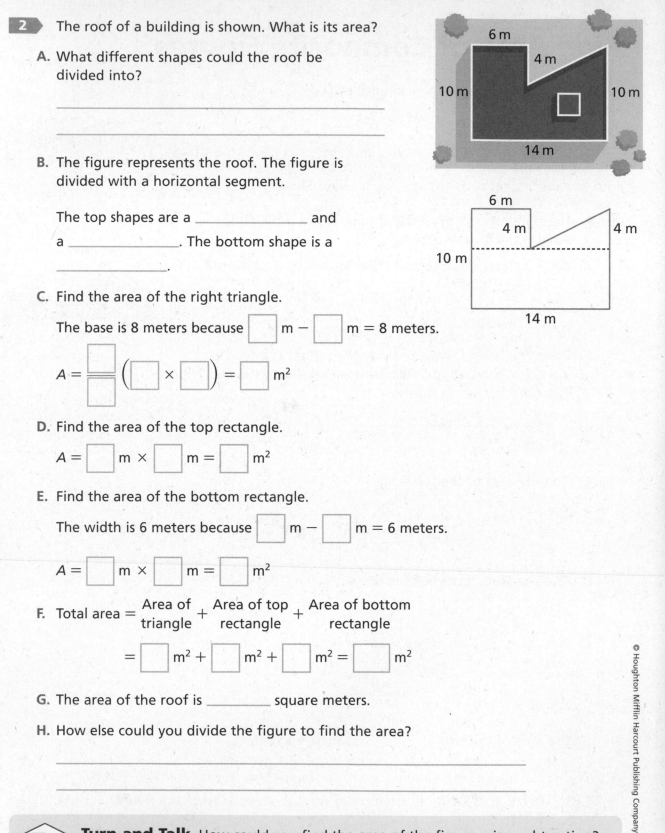

B. The figure represents the roof. The figure is divided with a horizontal segment.

The top shapes are a _____ and a _____. The bottom shape is a _____.

C. Find the area of the right triangle.

The base is 8 meters because ☐ m − ☐ m = 8 meters.

$A = \dfrac{☐}{☐} (☐ × ☐) = ☐ \text{ m}^2$

D. Find the area of the top rectangle.

$A = ☐ \text{ m} × ☐ \text{ m} = ☐ \text{ m}^2$

E. Find the area of the bottom rectangle.

The width is 6 meters because ☐ m − ☐ m = 6 meters.

$A = ☐ \text{ m} × ☐ \text{ m} = ☐ \text{ m}^2$

F. Total area = $\dfrac{\text{Area of}}{\text{triangle}} + \dfrac{\text{Area of top}}{\text{rectangle}} + \dfrac{\text{Area of bottom}}{\text{rectangle}}$

= ☐ m² + ☐ m² + ☐ m² = ☐ m²

G. The area of the roof is _____ square meters.

H. How else could you divide the figure to find the area?

_____

_____

Turn and Talk How could you find the area of the figure using subtraction? What figures would you use? Explain.

3 ▶ Paula is painting the side of a house and needs to know how much paint to buy. Each gallon of paint will cover a certain number of square feet. What is the area, in square feet, of the side of the house?

A. The side of the house is divided into two shapes. The top shape is a _____, and the bottom shape is a _____.

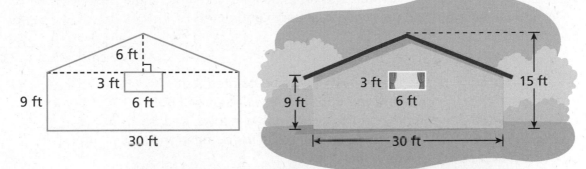

B. Find the area of the rectangle.

$A =$ ⬚ ft × ⬚ ft = ⬚ ft²

C. Find the area of the triangle.

The triangle has a height of 6 feet because $15 -$ ⬚ $= 6$.

$A = \dfrac{⬚}{⬚} \left(⬚ × ⬚ \right) = ⬚$ ft²

D. Find the area of the rectangular window.

$A =$ ⬚ ft × ⬚ ft = ⬚ ft²

E. Total area = Area of rectangle + Area of triangle − Area of window

$=$ ⬚ ft² $+$ ⬚ ft² ⬚ ft² $-$ ⬚ ft²

Check Understanding

1. Find the area of the figure shown.

_____

2. What is the area of the picture frame in square inches? Show how you solved the problem.

_____

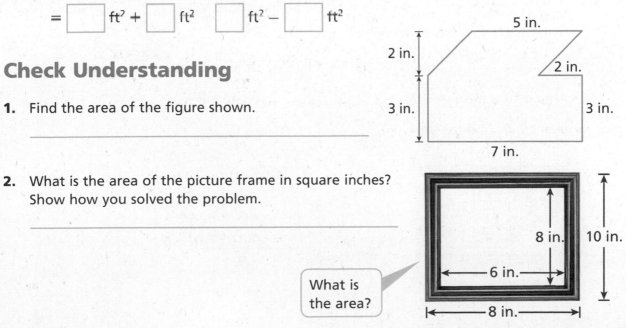

What is the area?

On Your Own

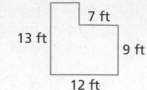

3. The outline of Sara's family room, including the entry, is shown. Sara wants to carpet the family room. How many square feet of carpet does she need? _____

4. The pentagon shown is divided into four triangles and a rectangle. What is the area of the pentagon in square centimeters?

_____

5. **Open Ended** A rectangular wall needs to be painted, but there are two windows and one door in the wall that will not be painted. Given the dimensions of the wall, windows, and door, how would you find the area to be painted? Do you need to know the location of the windows and door?

_____

_____

_____

_____

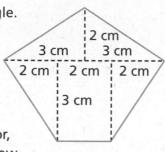

6. **Geography** The state of Utah is shown. All the angles measure 90°. What is the area, in square miles, of the state?

A. Find the area of the larger rectangle that contains the state. Show the equation you used.

_____ square miles

B. Find the area of the rectangle that is missing from the top-right corner of the larger rectangle. Show the equation you used.

_____ square miles

C. Area of the state of Utah ≈ _____ square miles

For Problems 7–8, find the area.

7.

8.

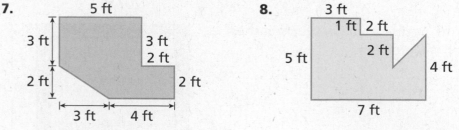

9. (MP) **Construct Arguments** The two figures shown have the same area. Without calculating the area, explain why this is so.

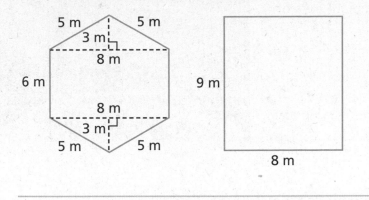

_____

_____

_____

10. In the compass rose shown, each triangle has the same area, and the center is a square. What is the area of the figure in square inches?

_____

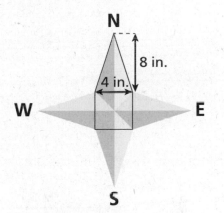

11. Sandy has built a triangular pool and wants to add a rectangular deck around it as shown in the figure. How many square feet of wood does Sandy need for the deck?

_____

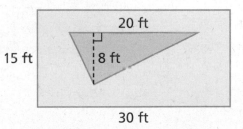

For Problems 12–13, find the area of the figure.

12.
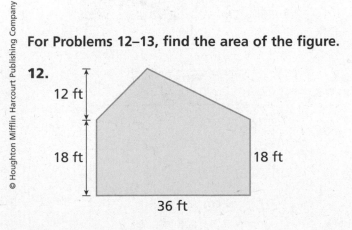

13.
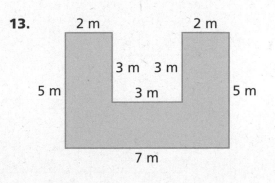

_____   _____

© Houghton Mifflin Harcourt Publishing Company

14. **(MP) Reason** Piazza San Marco is a famous open plaza in Venice, Italy. Its shape is shown. How would you find the approximate area of the plaza?

Piazza San Marco

_____
_____
_____
_____

15. **Open Ended** Draw a composite figure with at least one slanted side and an area of 24 square units.

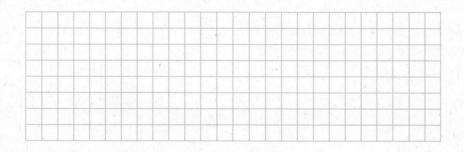

For Problems 16–19, find the area of the figure.

16.

7 cm
3 cm
7 cm
8 cm
5 cm
14 cm

17.

9 cm
3 cm
3 cm
8 cm 3 cm
5 cm
12 cm

18.

5 cm
3 cm
8 cm
8 cm
5 cm
5 cm 8 cm

19.

13 cm
3 cm
5 cm
5 cm
5 cm 5 cm
3 cm
3 cm

Find Area of Composite Figures

1. The floor plan for a house is shown. Vertical lengths and horizontal lengths are given. What is the floor area in square feet?

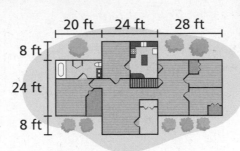

_____

2. On a baseball field, home plate is where the batter stands to hit and where a runner scores a run. What is the area of the home plate diagram shown in square inches?

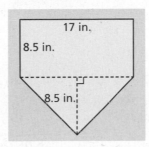

_____

3. **Math on the Spot** Kirsten wants to buy wooden flooring for her bedroom. The diagram shows the bedroom's shape and dimensions. One case of flooring will cover 25 square feet. How many cases of flooring will Kirsten need to buy? Explain.

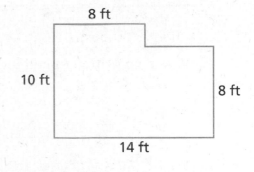

_____

_____

_____

4. (MP) **Attend to Precision** Robert is designing hexagonal tiles that are made up of 12 identical right triangles, as shown. Write three equations Robert can use to find the area A of the hexagonal tile in square centimeters.

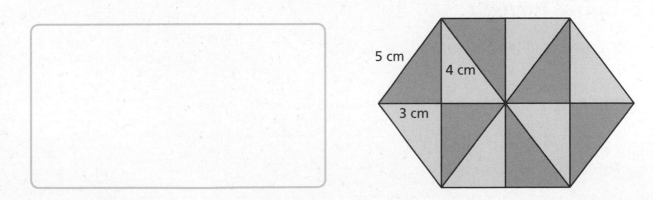

Test Prep

5. A figure is shown.

Which equations could be used to find the area A of the figure in square centimeters? Select all that apply.

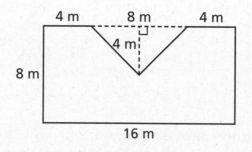

7 cm
6 cm
4 cm
11 cm

Ⓐ $A = 6 \times 11$

Ⓑ $A = 7 \times 6 + 4 \times 4$

Ⓒ $A = 4 \times 11 + 2 \times 7$

Ⓓ $A = 7 \times 6 + 4 \times 11$

Ⓔ $A = 6 \times 11 - 4 \times 2$

6. A figure is shown.

What is the area of the figure in square meters?

_____

_____

4 m   8 m   4 m
4 m
8 m
16 m

7. A figure is shown.

Write an equation to find the area A of the figure in square feet.

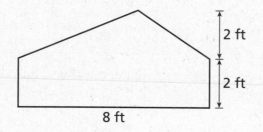

2 ft
2 ft
8 ft

_____

Spiral Review

8. An expression is shown.

2.54×5.5

What is the value of the expression?

_____

9. Write $\frac{12}{15}$ as a decimal.

_____

Review

Vocabulary

Choose the correct term from the Vocabulary box.

Vocabulary
parallelogram
trapezoid
composite figure

1. A _____ is a shape that can be divided into more than one of the basic shapes.

2. A _____ is a four-sided figure with opposite sides that are parallel.

3. A _____ is a four-sided figure with at least one pair of parallel sides.

Concepts and Skills

4. What is the area of the parallelogram?

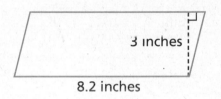

3 inches

8.2 inches

_____

5. A square stepping stone has a side length of $10\frac{1}{4}$ inches. What is the area of the stepping stone?

_____

6. Tamara's backyard pool needs a cover for the winter. The pool is rectangular with a length of 12 feet and an area of 196.8 square feet. What is the width of the pool cover Tamara's pool will need?

_____

7. (MP) **Use Tools** A rectangular flag consists of two right triangles. The area of each triangle is 6.6 square feet. What are the length and area of the flag? State what strategy and tool you will use to answer the question, explain your choice, and then find the answer.

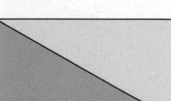

2.2 feet

_____

_____

8. A tile maker makes triangular tiles for a mosaic. Two triangular tiles form a square. What is the area of one of the triangular tiles?

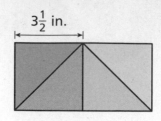

$3\frac{1}{2}$ in.

_____

9. The top of a school work table is in the shape of a trapezoid. What is the area of the tabletop?

Ⓐ 7 ft²

Ⓑ 12 ft²

Ⓒ 14 ft²

Ⓓ 24 ft²

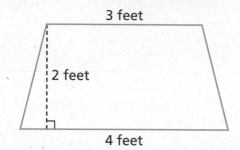

3 feet

2 feet

4 feet

10. A tangram is a puzzle consisting of pieces that are put together to form shapes. One such shape is shown. What is the area of the figure shape?

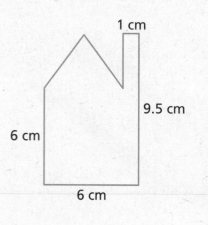

1 cm

9.5 cm

6 cm

6 cm

_____

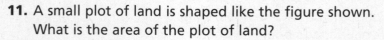

11. A small plot of land is shaped like the figure shown. What is the area of the plot of land?

Ⓐ   43 yd²

Ⓑ   153 yd²

Ⓒ   306 yd²

Ⓓ 1,188 yd²

12 yd

9 yd

22 yd

12. An artwork consists of the triangles shown, where the shaded triangle is cut out of the larger triangle. What is the area of the remaining unshaded portion?

_____

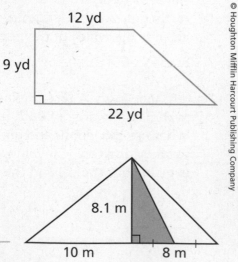

8.1 m

10 m

8 m

Pass the Popcorn

A company that makes microwave popcorn is redesigning its boxes. The diagram shows the company's current box size, with each face marked off in squares with a side length of 1 inch.

Use the diagram to answer the questions.

A. What is the volume of the company's current popcorn box? _____ cubic inches

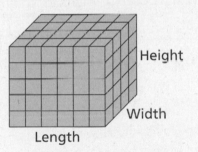

Height

Width

Length

B. The company wants to keep the volume of its popcorn boxes the same, but decrease the width from 4 inches to 3 inches. What are a possible length and a possible height for the new box design?

Length: _____ inches   Height: _____ inches

Turn and Talk

• Explain how you determined the volume of the company's current popcorn box.

• Explain how you determined a possible length and height for the new box design.

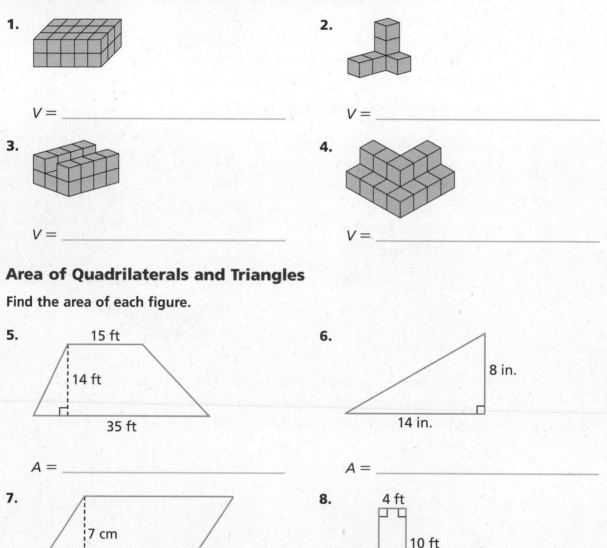

Are You Ready?

Complete these problems to review prior concepts and skills you will need for this module.

Explore Volume

Find the volume of each prism by counting cubic units.

1.

$V =$ _____

2.

$V =$ _____

3.

$V =$ _____

4.

$V =$ _____

Area of Quadrilaterals and Triangles

Find the area of each figure.

5.

15 ft

14 ft

35 ft

$A =$ _____

6.

8 in.

14 in.

$A =$ _____

7.

7 cm

14 cm

$A =$ _____

8.

4 ft

10 ft

14 ft

18 ft

$A =$ _____

9. The height of a parallelogram is 36 meters and the base is 6 meters. Find the area of the parallelogram.

_____

Name _____

Explore Nets and Surface Area

(**I Can**) make and use nets to find the surface areas of
rectangular and triangular prisms and pyramids.

Spark Your Learning

Caleb built a rectangular box to store his cast iron oven when
camping. He wants to paint the outside of the box, and has enough
paint to cover an area of 14 square feet. Does Caleb have enough
paint? Explain.

1 ft

2.5 ft   1.5 ft

Turn and Talk If Caleb decides not to paint the bottom of the storage box,
will he have enough paint to paint the storage box? Explain.

Build Understanding

1 A **solid figure** is a three-dimensional figure because it has three dimensions: length, width, and height.

A. A cube is a closed three-dimensional figure. Look at the cube at the right. How many faces does a cube have?

_____

B. A *net* is the pattern made when the surface of a closed three-dimensional figure is laid out flat, showing each face of the figure. Look at the two nets shown. What do you notice about the nets? What three-dimensional figures might they represent? Explain.

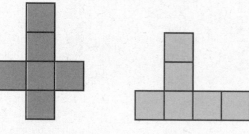

_____

_____

_____

C. Trace both nets in Part B on a separate sheet of paper. Cut out each net. Then fold the nets. Which net will fold into a closed three-dimensional figure? What is the three-dimensional figure?

_____

D. Write an equation to represent the area of one face of the cube.

_____

E. If the edge of the cube measures 4 centimeters, what is the area of one face of the cube?

_____

F. What is the total area of all 6 faces of the cube?

_____

 Turn and Talk What do all six faces of the cube have in common? Is there another way to calculate the total area of the faces?

© Houghton Mifflin Harcourt Publishing Company

2 Look at the square pyramid shown. How many faces does the pyramid have? Explain how you know.

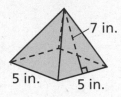

7 in.

5 in.   5 in.

_____

_____

_____

A. Fill in the boxes of the net for the square pyramid shown with the correct dimensions.

B. What formula can you use to find the area of one triangular face?

_____

_____

_____

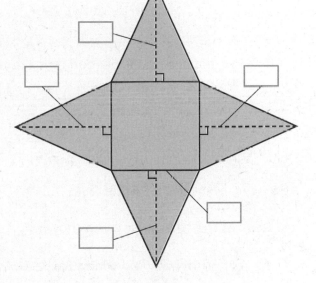

C. What is the area of one triangular face?

_____

D. What is the area of the square base?

_____

E. How can you find the surface area of the square pyramid?

_____

_____

F. What is the surface area of the square pyramid?

_____

Turn and Talk Is there another way to solve for the surface area? Explain.

3 Chandra is making a jewelry box and needs to know how much wood to buy.

A. Use the dimensions shown to label the side lengths of each face of the net.

B. Find the area of its right and left faces.

[ ] in. × [ ] in. = [ ] in²

C. Find the area of its top and bottom faces.

[ ] in. × [ ] in. = [ ] in²

D. Find the area of its front and back faces.

[ ] in. × [ ] in. = [ ] in²

E. How much wood is needed to make the jewelry box?

2 ([ ]) + 2 ([ ]) + 2 ([ ]) = [ ] square inches

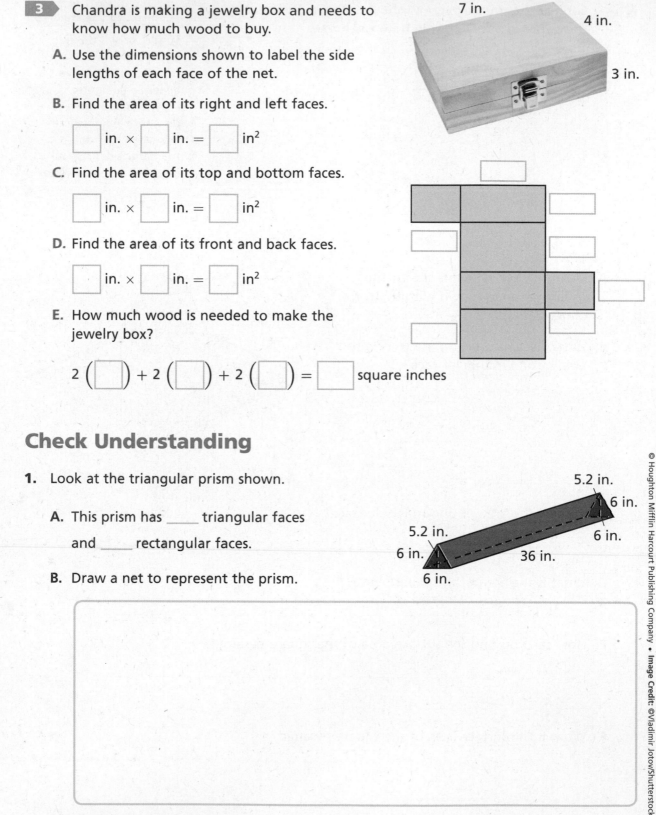

7 in. 4 in. 3 in.

Check Understanding

1. Look at the triangular prism shown.

A. This prism has _____ triangular faces and _____ rectangular faces.

B. Draw a net to represent the prism.

5.2 in. 6 in.
5.2 in. 6 in.
6 in. 36 in.
6 in.

C. Find the surface area of the triangular prism.

$2\left[\frac{1}{2}()()\right] + 3\left[\cdot \right] = $ in²

On Your Own

2. Keisha is helping her sister build triangular pyramids as containers to package her bracelets.

A. Draw and label a net that Keisha can use to fold and make the container.

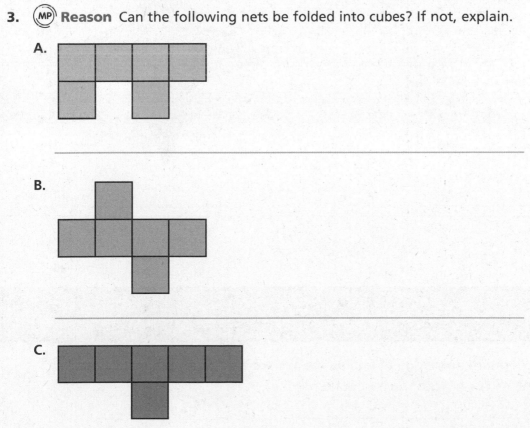

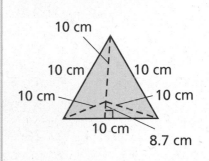

B. How much cardboard do they need for each container?

3. (MP) **Reason** Can the following nets be folded into cubes? If not, explain.

A.

B.

C.

For Problems 4–7, identify what solid figure the net folds into. Then find the surface area of the net.

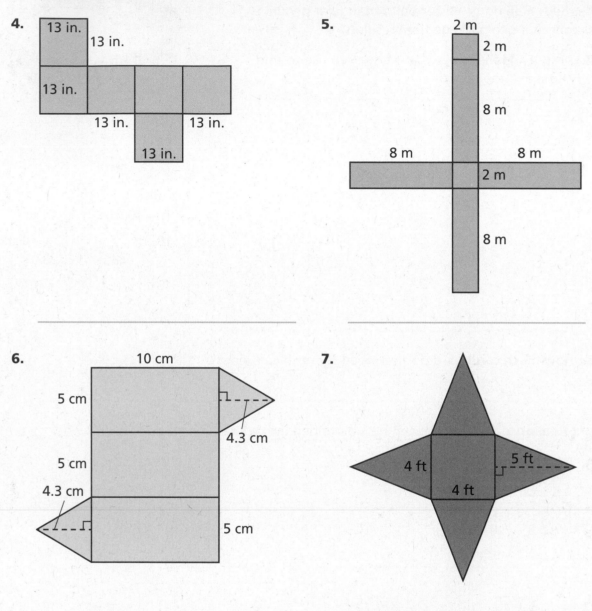

4. 13 in. 13 in. 13 in. 13 in. 13 in. 13 in.

5. 2 m 2 m 8 m 8 m 8 m 2 m 8 m

6. 10 cm 5 cm 4.3 cm 5 cm 4.3 cm 5 cm

7. 4 ft 5 ft 4 ft

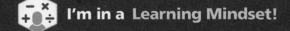

I'm in a **Learning Mindset!**

How did I apply prior knowledge to finding the surface area of a square pyramid in Task 2?

_____

_____

Explore Nets and Surface Area

1. (MP) **Reason** George is building flower boxes to sell as gifts. Draw and label a net to represent a flower box. Then find the amount of material George needs for each box. Explain why you drew the net the way you did.

2. **Math on the Spot** Find the surface area of the prism.

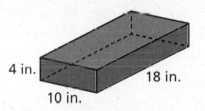

4 in. 10 in. 18 in.

For Problems 3–4, identify what solid figure the net folds into. Then find the surface area of the figure.

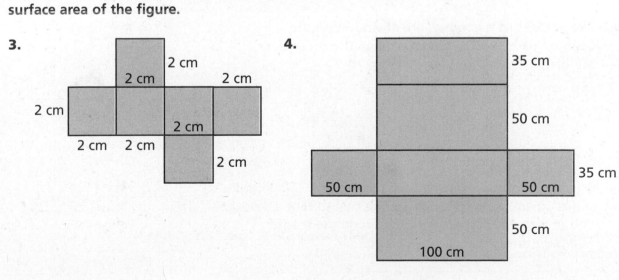

3.
2 cm 2 cm 2 cm
2 cm
2 cm
2 cm 2 cm
2 cm

4.
35 cm
50 cm
35 cm
50 cm 50 cm
50 cm
100 cm

Test Prep

5. Match the net to its three-dimensional figure.

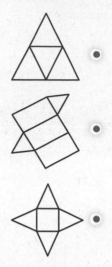

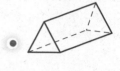

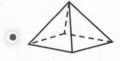

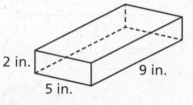

6. Assume that the box has no top. What is the surface area of the box shown?

(A) 64 in²

(B) 73 in²

(C) 90 in²

(D) 101 in²

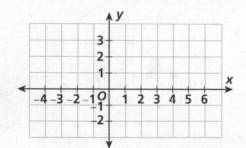

2 in.
9 in.
5 in.

Spiral Review

7. Jem is carpeting a room. A drawing of the floor is shown. How much carpet will she use?

_____

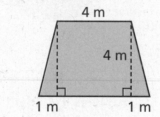

4 m

4 m

1 m   1 m

8. The vertices of a polygon are given. Graph the ordered pairs. Connect the points in the order they are given. Then identify the figure.

(−4, −2), (4, −2), (6, 3), (−2, 3)

_____

9. Brianna can rent a scooter for $15.00 plus $0.50 per mile. Write an equation in which *t* is the cost to rent a scooter and *m* is the number of miles she rode the scooter. Complete the table.

_____

m	t
5	
10	
15	
20	

Name _____

Find Volume of Rectangular Prisms

(I Can) find the volume of a rectangular prism using the formula $V = \ell wh$ or $V = Bh$.

Spark Your Learning

The truck shown is delivering sand for a sand sculpture competition. How many trips must the truck make to deliver 15 cubic yards of sand? Explain your reasoning.

5 ft

12 ft

3 ft

x	y

| $\frac{1}{2}$ | $\frac{1}{2}$ |

 Turn and Talk Is there another formula that you could have used to find the volume of the bed of the truck? Explain.

Build Understanding

1 A cube with edge length 1 unit and volume 1 cubic unit is filled with smaller cubes as shown. Find the **volume** of one small cube.

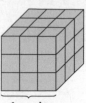

1 unit

A. How many small cubes are there? Explain how you know.

_____

B. How does the combined volume of the small cubes compare to the volume of the large cube?

_____

C. Complete the model.

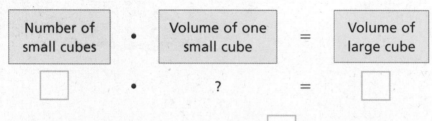

| Number of small cubes | • | Volume of one small cube | = | Volume of large cube |

☐ • ? = ☐

What is the volume of one small cube? ☐ cubic unit(s)

D. Complete the model.

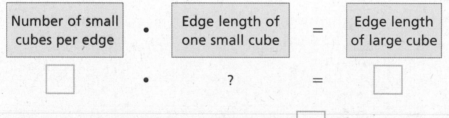

| Number of small cubes per edge | • | Edge length of one small cube | = | Edge length of large cube |

☐ • ? = ☐

What is the edge length of one small cube? ☐ unit(s)

E. The formula for volume of a rectangular prism is $V = \ell wh$, where ℓ and w are the length and width of the base and h is the height. Find the volume of one small cube using this formula.

$V =$ _____ = _____ cubic unit(s)

F. A cube with edge length $\frac{2}{3}$ unit is shown. The cube is filled with the same smaller cubes as used in Parts A–E. Find the volume of the cube shown.

$V =$ _____ = _____ cubic unit(s)

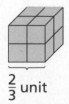

$\frac{2}{3}$ unit

 Turn and Talk What is true about the edge lengths of a cube? How can you use this information to write a formula that uses exponents to find the volume of a cube?

Step It Out

You can find the volume of a rectangular prism using the following formulas:
$V = \ell wh$ or $V = Bh$ (where B represents the area of the prism's base, $B = \ell w$).

2 ▶ Josh would like to know how much flour his container can hold.

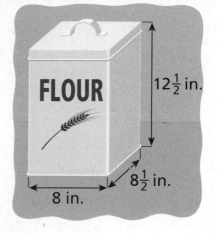

A. The length is _____ in. The width is _____ in. The height

is _____ in.

B. Substitute for the given variables and find the volume
of the flour container.

$V = \ell wh$

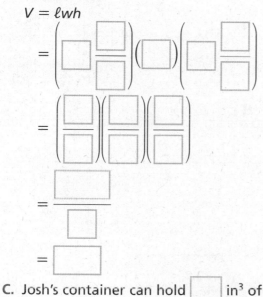

C. Josh's container can hold ☐ in³ of flour.

> 🗨 **Turn and Talk** Use the formula $V = Bh$ to find the area of the flour container.
> What do you notice? Will this always be true? Explain why you think so.

Check Understanding

1. What is the volume of the rectangular prism? Show your work.

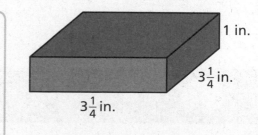

2. What is the volume of a rectangular prism that has a base area of $\frac{1}{8}$ in² and a height of $\frac{3}{4}$ in.?

On Your Own

How much cement does Trent need?

3. Trent is putting in a sidewalk that is $\frac{1}{18}$ yard thick, 9 yards long, and 1 yard wide. How many cubic yards of cement does he need?

_____

4. (MP) **Reason** Explain how to find the volume of the cinder block wall with the window removed.

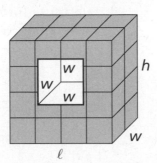

For Problems 5–8, find the volume of each figure.

5.

7 cm
7 cm
7 cm

_____

6.

$20\frac{1}{4}$ in.
$89\frac{1}{10}$ in.
72 in.

_____

7.

$6\frac{1}{3}$ ft
18 ft
15 ft

_____

8.

$1\frac{1}{4}$ ft
$4\frac{1}{4}$ ft
$6\frac{1}{3}$ ft

_____

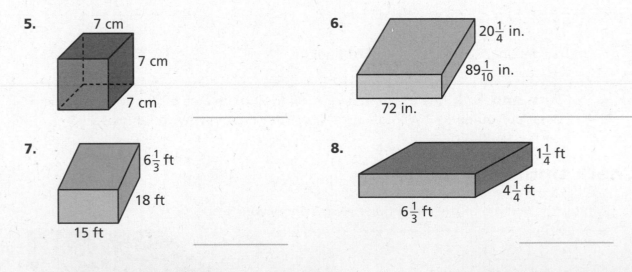

⬡ I'm in a Learning Mindset!

How did I use my prior knowledge of multiplying mixed numbers to find the volume of a rectangular prism?

_____

_____

Find Volume of Rectangular Prisms

1. **Open Ended** Keesha is building a raised flower bed around a tree. Explain how to find the volume of soil she needs in order to fill the flower bed. Then find the volume.

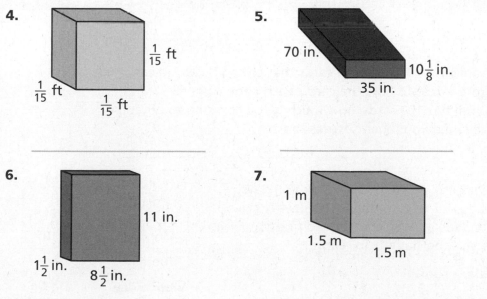

2. **Math on the Spot** An aquarium is shaped like a rectangular prism. The prism is $24\frac{1}{4}$ inches long, $12\frac{1}{2}$ inches wide, and 20 inches high. What is the volume of the aquarium?

3. (MP) **Reason** Ray has 9 identical shoe boxes like the one shown. What is the total volume of all 9 shoe boxes?

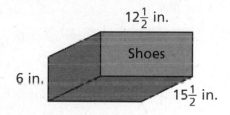

For Problems 4–7, find the volume of each figure.

4.

$\frac{1}{15}$ ft

$\frac{1}{15}$ ft $\frac{1}{15}$ ft

5.

70 in.

35 in. $10\frac{1}{8}$ in.

6.

11 in.

$1\frac{1}{2}$ in. $8\frac{1}{2}$ in.

7.

1 m

1.5 m   1.5 m

Test Prep

8. Anton is filling a fish tank with water. What volume of water does he need?

Ⓐ 19,125 in³

Ⓑ 18,375 in³

Ⓒ 4,815 in³

Ⓓ 90$\frac{1}{2}$ in³

The tank dimensions: 25$\frac{1}{2}$ in., 15 in., 50 in.

9. Jordan needs to carry drinking water to help people in a flooded area. One jug has the dimensions shown.

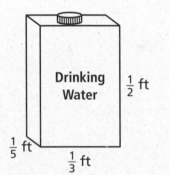

Drinking Water — $\frac{1}{2}$ ft, $\frac{1}{5}$ ft, $\frac{1}{3}$ ft

What is the volume of one jug of drinking water?

_____

Spiral Review

10. 42 is 60% of what number?

_____

11. Tyrell buys an organizer for his baseball cards that costs $12.99. He can add pages to the organizer to hold the cards. Each page costs $2.75 and holds 9 cards. If Tyrell has 100 cards, how much will it cost him to organize them? Write and evaluate a numeric expression.

_____

12. Greg has a goal to read 529 pages of a book in 6 days. The number of pages he read on the first 3 days is given in the table. Write and solve an equation to find the number of pages, p, Greg has left to read.

Day	Number of pages
Monday	110
Tuesday	92
Wednesday	117

_____

Name _____

Solve Volume Problems

(I Can) use the formula $V = lwh$ to find the volume or an unknown dimension of a rectangular prism.

Step It Out

1 ▶ Lyon is making a toolbox as shown.

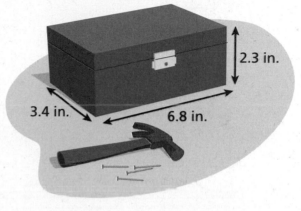

A. What are the dimensions of the box?

Length: _____

Width: _____

Height: _____

B. Complete the volume equation.

$V = \ell \times w \times h = \boxed{} \times \boxed{} \times \boxed{}$

C. What is the volume of the box?

$\boxed{}$ cubic inches, or $\boxed{}$ in³

D. Lyon wants to paint the toolbox. To do so, he needs to know the **surface area** of the toolbox. Find the surface area of the toolbox.

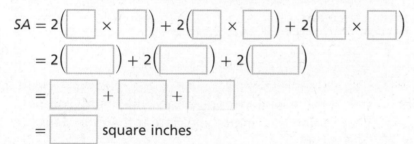

$SA = 2\left(\boxed{} \times \boxed{}\right) + 2\left(\boxed{} \times \boxed{}\right) + 2\left(\boxed{} \times \boxed{}\right)$

$= 2\left(\boxed{}\right) + 2\left(\boxed{}\right) + 2\left(\boxed{}\right)$

$= \boxed{} + \boxed{} + \boxed{}$

$= \boxed{}$ square inches

E. A tube of paint covers 40 square inches. How many tubes of paint should Lyon buy? Explain.

_____

_____

Turn and Talk Why do you think volume is measured in cubic units?

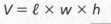 **2** A company makes cereal boxes with a volume of $432\frac{1}{4}$ cubic inches. The dimensions of one of the cereal boxes is shown. What is the width of the box?

A. How can you find the volume of the cereal box?

_____

9 $\frac{1}{2}$ in.

14 in.

w in.

B. Complete the equation to find the volume of the cereal box.

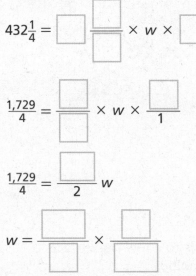

$V = \ell \times w \times h$

$432\frac{1}{4} = \boxed{}\dfrac{\boxed{}}{\boxed{}} \times w \times \boxed{}$

$\dfrac{1{,}729}{4} = \dfrac{\boxed{}}{\boxed{}} \times w \times \dfrac{\boxed{}}{1}$

$\dfrac{1{,}729}{4} = \dfrac{\boxed{}}{2}\, w$

$w = \dfrac{\boxed{}}{\boxed{}} \times \dfrac{\boxed{}}{\boxed{}}$

C. What is the width of the cereal box?

_____

Turn and Talk In Task 2, if the width was given and the length was not, would the steps you used to find the length be different than the steps you used to find the width? Explain.

Check Understanding

1. A right rectangular prism is 10.25 yards long, 5.5 yards wide, and 2 yards tall. What is the volume of the prism?

_____

2. A large rectangular shipping container has a volume of $12\frac{3}{8}$ cubic feet. The shipping container is $2\frac{1}{5}$ feet long and $2\frac{1}{2}$ feet wide. What is the height of the shipping container?

_____

On Your Own

3. What is the volume of the puzzle cube?

_____

4. A fish tank is filled halfway with water.

   A. What is the volume of the tank?

   _____

   B. What is the volume of the water in the tank?

   _____

5. A concert poster is shipped in the box shown.

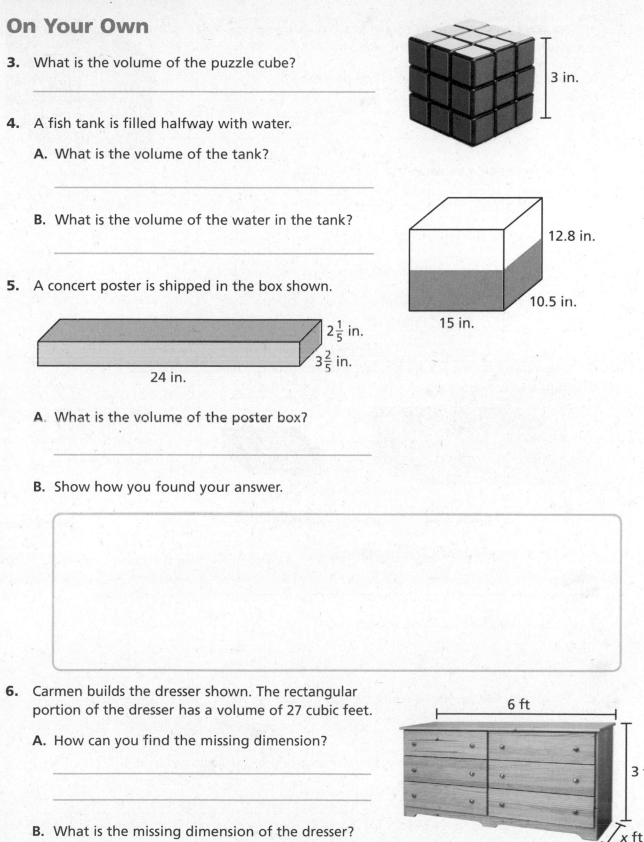

$2\frac{1}{5}$ in.

$3\frac{2}{5}$ in.

24 in.

   A. What is the volume of the poster box?

   _____

   B. Show how you found your answer.

3 in.

12.8 in.

10.5 in.

15 in.

6. Carmen builds the dresser shown. The rectangular portion of the dresser has a volume of 27 cubic feet.

   A. How can you find the missing dimension?

   _____

   _____

   B. What is the missing dimension of the dresser?

   _____

6 ft

3 ft

x ft

7. (MP) **Reason** A set of dishes comes in a cube-shaped box that has a surface area of 600 square inches.

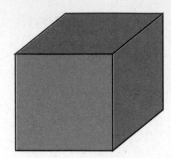

A. How do you find the surface area of a cube?

_____

_____

B. What is the area of each face of the cube?

_____

C. What are the dimensions of the cube?

_____

D. What is the volume of the cube?

_____

8. A toy company ships packages in large boxes. The toy package and the shipping box are shown.

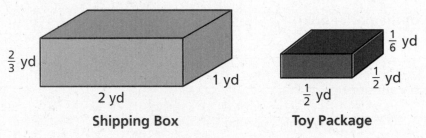

Shipping Box   **Toy Package**

A. What is the volume of the shipping box?

_____

B. What is the volume of the toy package?

_____

C. How many toy packages could fit in the shipping box?

_____

D. **Open Ended** Describe one way you can arrange the packages in the shipping box.

_____

_____

_____

_____

Solve Volume Problems

1. **(MP) Reason** A cube-shaped box can be wrapped completely in gift wrap that measures 384 square inches. What is the volume of the box?

_____

2. **STEM** An architect builds a house like the one shown. What is the total volume of the house?

_____

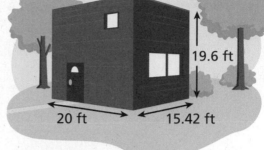

19.6 ft

20 ft   15.42 ft

3. An aquarium has a large fish tank with the dimensions shown. The tank has a volume of 585 cubic meters.

   What is the depth of the tank?

_____

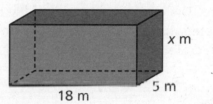

x m

18 m   5 m

4. Joshua is organizing a garage using stackable containers like the one shown. He has a total of 12 containers. What is the combined total volume of the containers?

_____

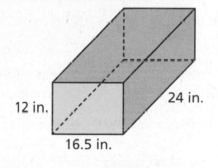

12 in.   24 in.

16.5 in.

5. **Math on the Spot** Aubrey has a suitcase with a volume of 2,200 cubic inches. The length of the suitcase is 25 inches and the width is 11 inches. What is the height of Aubrey's suitcase?

_____

6. A rectangular prism has a length of $2\frac{3}{5}$ inches and a width of $1\frac{2}{5}$ inches. If the prism has a volume of $10\frac{23}{25}$ cubic inches, what is the height of the prism? Explain how you found your answer.

_____
| |
| |
| |
| |
| |
| |
| |
_____

Test Prep

7. Students in an art class are given boxes to use for storage for their materials for the year. Shaun's box has a volume of 72 cubic inches. What is the unknown dimension?

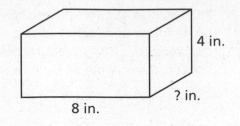

8 in. 4 in. ? in.

Ⓐ $2\frac{1}{4}$ in.

Ⓑ 9 in.

Ⓒ 18 in.

Ⓓ 60 in.

8. A sculptor buys a block of marble shaped like a rectangular prism to use for a sculpture. The original block of marble had a length of 3.5 meters, a width of 4 meters, and a height of 2.8 meters. If the sculptor chisels away a volume of marble that equals 12.2 cubic meters, what is the volume of the resulting sculpture?

Ⓐ 51.4 m^3

Ⓑ 39.2 m^3

Ⓒ 27.0 m^3

Ⓓ 3.21 m^3

9. Angelee buys a decorative photo box as shown. What is the volume of the photo box?

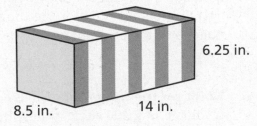

8.5 in. 14 in. 6.25 in.

_____

Spiral Review

10. What is the area of the triangle?

_____

$1\frac{1}{4}$ ft

$\frac{3}{4}$ ft

11. Evaluate the expression.

$3^2 - 2^2 + 1$

_____

12. Amanda earns $12 an hour babysitting. She spends $8 of her earnings on dinner later that evening. Write an expression to represent her total profit after babysitting for x hours and then eating dinner.

_____

Review

Vocabulary

Choose the correct term from the vocabulary box.

1. The total area of the faces of a three-dimensional object is the _____ .

2. A _____ is a pattern that you can cut and fold to make a model of a solid shape.

3. A _____ is a solid with a polygon base and triangular faces that meet at the top.

Concepts and Skills

4. The net shown can be used to form a cube. What is the surface area of the cube formed by the net?

   _____

2 ft

2 ft

5. A cube has a surface area of 54 square centimeters. What is the volume of the cube?

   _____

6. A painting set is shipped in the box shown. The surface area is printed with advertisements. What is the total area covered by advertisements?

   _____

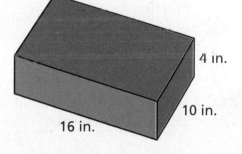

4 in.

10 in.

16 in.

7. **(MP) Use Tools** A rectangular prism is 8 cm long, 11 cm wide, and 5.8 cm tall. What is the volume of the prism? State what strategy and tool you will use to answer the question, explain your choice, and then find the answer.

   _____

   _____

8. A box company makes cardboard boxes using flat templates like the one shown. Both squares are congruent, and the remaining four rectangular faces are congruent. What is the surface area of the cardboard box?

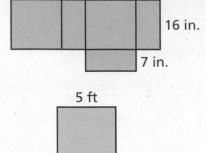

16 in.

16 in.

7 in.

_____

9. What is the volume of the rectangular prism formed by the net?

Ⓐ 10 ft³

Ⓑ 50 ft³

Ⓒ 60 ft³

Ⓓ 90 ft³

5 ft

2 ft

5 ft

10. What are the surface area and volume of the prism?

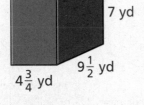

7 yd

$9\frac{1}{2}$ yd

$4\frac{3}{4}$ yd

The surface area is _____.

The volume is _____.

11. A casserole dish is in the shape of a rectangular prism. The dish is 6 inches wide, 12 inches long, and 5 inches deep. What is the volume of the dish?

_____

12. Jerome is painting a rectangular toolbox that is 20 inches by 10 inches by 8 inches. A tube of paint covers 300 square inches.

A. What is the surface area of the toolbox?

_____

B. How many tubes of paint should Jerome buy?

_____

13. A planter in the shape of a rectangular prism is 24 inches by 4 inches by 5 inches. How much dirt is needed to fill the planter?

_____

© Houghton Mifflin Harcourt Publishing Company • Image Credits: (t) ©Dmitriy Shironosov/Alamy; (b) ©Baimieng/Shutterstock

Data Collection and Analysis

Sales Director

A sales director manages a company's salespeople. The director helps develop strategies to increase sales of the company's products. For example, a sales director may help determine the best price to charge for a product by considering the company's cost to manufacture the product, the amount of profit the company hopes to earn, and the prices charged by other companies for similar products.

STEM Task:

The dot plot shows the total amounts of sales made so far this year by the four salespeople at a small wind turbine company. The company's sales goal for the year is $8 million. How much more is needed to reach the goal? Explain.

Sales (millions of dollars)

Learning Mindset

Resilience Monitors Knowledge and Skills

How do you know that you are learning? Whenever you approach a new topic or skill, it is important to pay attention to your understanding. Checking in with yourself before, during, and after learning keeps you focused and helps you identify and address difficulties before they become serious problems. Here are some questions you can ask yourself to monitor your learning.

- What have I learned from this effort?

- Can I explain or demonstrate to someone else what I have learned?

- What am I trying to learn? What is the goal or objective?

- Why am I learning this? What will I know or be able to do after I learn this?

- How is the new topic connected to something I already know? What is the new information?

- What am I learning that I can use next time?

Reflect

Q How did you first make sense of the STEM Task? Did your understanding change as you worked on the Task? If so, explain.

Q What did you learn from the STEM Task that you can use in your future learning?

Data Collection and Displays

GOING FISHING

Fry, or baby fish, are measured at the hatchery. The weights of 12 fry are shown, in pounds:

$1\frac{1}{4}$, 1, $1\frac{3}{4}$, 2, $1\frac{1}{4}$, $1\frac{1}{2}$, $1\frac{1}{4}$, $1\frac{1}{2}$, $1\frac{1}{4}$, $\frac{3}{4}$, $2\frac{1}{4}$, 1

Make a line plot to show the data.

A. Organize the data from least to greatest.

_____

B. Use the data to make a line plot.

> young trout at a California fish hatchery

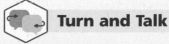 **Turn and Talk**

• Explain how you made the line plot.

• Compare reading the data from a list to reading the data on the line plot. Describe a strength and weakness for each type of display.

Are You Ready?

Complete these problems to review prior concepts and skills you will need for this module.

Make and Interpret Line Plots

1. William has a collection of paint jars. He measures the amount of paint in each jar, in cups. Use the data to complete the line plot.

$1\frac{1}{4}$, $1\frac{3}{4}$, $2\frac{1}{2}$, $\frac{5}{8}$, $1\frac{1}{2}$, $2\frac{3}{8}$, $2\frac{1}{2}$, $1\frac{3}{4}$, $2\frac{1}{2}$, $\frac{5}{8}$, $1\frac{1}{2}$, $\frac{5}{8}$

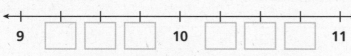

$\frac{5}{8}$ $\frac{3}{4}$ $\frac{7}{8}$ 1 $1\frac{1}{8}$ $1\frac{1}{4}$ $1\frac{3}{8}$ $1\frac{1}{2}$ $1\frac{5}{8}$ $1\frac{3}{4}$ $1\frac{7}{8}$ 2 $2\frac{1}{8}$ $2\frac{1}{4}$ $2\frac{3}{8}$ $2\frac{1}{2}$

Amount of Paint (in cups)

2. The table shows the widths of different stepping stones, in inches, used to build a path. Complete the line plot to represent the data from the table.

Stepping Stone Widths (in inches)	
$10\frac{1}{4}$	$9\frac{3}{4}$
$10\frac{1}{2}$	11
$9\frac{1}{2}$	$10\frac{3}{4}$
10	$9\frac{1}{2}$
$10\frac{1}{4}$	$10\frac{1}{2}$

9 ☐ ☐ ☐ 10 ☐ ☐ ☐ 11

Widths of Stepping Stones (in inches)

Plot Points on a Number Line

3. Plot and label each integer.

−10 −9 −8 −7 −6 −5 −4 −3 −2 −1 0 1 2 3 4 5 6 7 8 9 10

A. −8   D. 0

B. 3   E. 9

C. −5   F. −2

Name _____

Explore Statistical Data Collection

(I Can) identify statistical questions, describe the nature of attributes under investigation, and report the number of observations.

Spark Your Learning

Rani measured the heights of the seedlings she is growing. The heights were $\frac{3}{4}$ inch, $\frac{7}{8}$ inch, $\frac{1}{2}$ inch, $\frac{3}{4}$ inch, $\frac{5}{8}$ inch, $\frac{3}{4}$ inch, $\frac{7}{8}$ inch, $\frac{5}{8}$ inch, $\frac{1}{2}$ inch, $\frac{3}{4}$ inch, $\frac{1}{2}$ inch, and $\frac{1}{2}$ inch. How can Rani organize the information to present it to her science class?

 Turn and Talk What are some other ways you could describe or organize the information shown in the list, such as by least height?

Build Understanding

When you measure the heights of your classmates, you are collecting *data*.

"What are the heights of my classmates?" is a *statistical question*, because height usually varies within a group of people. The data set will have multiple values, such as 54 inches, 48 inches, 51 inches, and so on. Statistical questions require multiple measurements in order to describe data sets, that can be both numeric and non-numeric quantities.

"What is Zoya's height?" is not a statistical question because it asks for only one piece of information. The data set will only have a single value, such as 54 inches.

1 Read the question shown.

"How many hours do sixth-grade students typically spend on homework each week?"

A. Could this question yield a variety of different answers? Explain.

_____

_____

B. Is this a statistical question? Explain how you know.

_____

_____

2 Read the question shown.

"How many siblings does Deion have?"

A. Could this question yield a variety of different answers? Explain.

_____

_____

B. Is this a statistical question? Explain how you know.

_____

_____

 Turn and Talk Is the question "How much does Alvin's cat weigh?" a statistical question? Explain. If it is not a statistical question, how can you change it to make it a statistical question?

One way to describe a set of data is by stating the number of observations, or measurements, that were made. Another method of describing data is to list the attributes or characteristics that were measured, such as color or length.

3 The table shows the results for some female runners in one semifinal heat of the 100-meter hurdles at the 2016 Summer Olympics.

Women's 100-meter hurdles, Summer Olympics, 2016

Runner	Time (in seconds)
Castlin	12.63
Simmonds	12.95
Billaud	13.03
Ofili	12.71
Pedersen	12.88

A. What attribute is being measured by the data in the table?

_____

_____

B. What is the unit of measurement for the data? _____

C. To what fraction of a second are the results given?

_____

D. How do you think the data was measured?

_____

E. How many runners are represented in the table? _____

F. How many observations, or measurements, were made? _____

Check Understanding

1. Is the following question a statistical question? Explain.

   "Did it rain more in Miami or Orlando last month?"

   _____

2. The table shows the masses of students' pets.

Dog	Beagle	Basset hound	Plott hound	Rat terrier	Pug
Mass (kilograms)	11.34	24.04	21.77	4.08	7.26

   A. How many observations were made? _____

   B. What attribute is being measured? _____

   C. What is the unit of measurement for the data? _____

On Your Own

3. (MP) **Construct Arguments** Carrie asks the following questions:

"How many players on the soccer team scored goals during the season?"

"How many players per team in the soccer league scored more than 3 goals during the soccer season?"

Which is a statistical question and which is not? Explain your reasoning.

_____

_____

_____

4. (MP) **Reason** Mr. Garcia has students design an experiment that will result in variable data. Which of the following situations could result in a variety of data? Explain.

- measuring the temperature every day for a week
- measuring the average temperature of one week
- measuring the number of high tides for a day

_____

_____

5. The table shows information about buildings in Rome, Italy. Complete each statement about the data.

The Colosseum
Rome, Italy

Building	Colosseum	Il Vittoriano	Pantheon
Height (meters)	157	230	43.28
Approx. age (hundreds of years)	19.38	1.07	18.92

There are [ ] attributes.

The data were measured using _____.

There are [ ] observations.

⬡ **I'm in a Learning Mindset!**

How do I explain the difference between statistical questions and non-statistical questions?

_____

© Houghton Mifflin Harcourt Publishing Company • Image Credit: ©Marco Rubino/Shutterstock

Explore Statistical Data Collection

1. Which of the following is not a statistical question? Explain.
   - What is the distance from home to places you regularly go?
   - What are the ages of your neighbor's pets?
   - How many days are there in March?
   - What is the time it takes each runner to finish a race at a track meet?

   _____

   _____

2. Light bulbs are labeled with the number of watts of electricity they use as shown by the table. What are the attributes, measurements used, and observations of the data?

Light bulb	A	B	C	D	E	F
Elect. used (watts)	6	18	40	100	60	20

   Attributes: _____

   Measurements Used: _____

   Observations: _____

3. **Open Ended** Write two statistical questions that you could use to gather data about your family.

   _____

   _____

4. **(MP) Reason** Kate asks her friend what her favorite class at school is. How could she change her questioning so that she can collect statistical data?

   _____

   _____

5. Hector collected the data shown in the table for a basketball league. What are the attributes, measurements used, and observations of the data?

Team	A	B	C	D	E	F
Players	12	15	14	17	11	16
Average score (per game)	74	50	63	38	51	60
Average age of players	13.5	12.8	12.2	13.1	12.7	11.9

   Attributes: _____

   Measurements used: _____

   Observations: _____

Test Prep

6. Which of the following are statistical questions? Select all that apply.

(A) How many total tomato plants are in a large garden pot?

(B) How many cucumber plants are in each backyard garden in a neighborhood?

(C) What was the low temperature in my town in December in 2000?

(D) What percent of sixth grade students at a school don't like apple juice?

(E) How many flights were delayed at the airport each day last year?

7. The data shown in the table were collected during an evaporation experiment. Which statement best describes the data collected?

Day	1	2	3	4	5	6	7
Water depth (inches)	18	17.5	16.25	14	10.6	8.7	5.3

(A) There are 7 observations and 1 attribute. The attribute was likely measured using a measuring cup.

(B) There are 7 observations and 1 attribute. The attribute was likely measured using a ruler.

(C) There is 1 observation and 7 attributes. The attributes were likely measured using a measuring cup.

(D) There is 1 observation and 7 attributes. The attributes were likely measured using a ruler.

Spiral Review

8. A right triangle has an area of 54 square inches and a base of 12 inches. What is the height of the triangle?

_____

9. What is the volume of a cube with an edge length of 7 centimeters?

_____

10. Write an equation that can be described by the statement: y is equal to $\frac{1}{3}$ of x.

_____

Name _____

Display Data in Dot Plots

(I Can) construct and analyze a dot plot.

Step It Out

Statistical questions are answered by collecting and analyzing data. One way to understand a set of data is to make a visual display. A *dot plot* is a type of **line plot** that shows the *frequency* of each data value using a dot.

Connect to Vocabulary

A **dot plot** is a visual display in which each piece of data is represented by a dot above a number line. The number of times a data value occurs is called the **frequency**.

1 ▶ A pulse rate is the number of times a heart beats in a minute. The pulse rate for a group of 12-year-olds is taken before physical education class. The results are shown in the table. Which pulse rate is the most common among the group?

Pulse Rates						
65	58	67	72	85	59	66
79	70	75	65	63	55	75
82	56	69	75	57	60	75

A. Complete the number line with an appropriate scale.

Pulse rates vary from ☐ to ☐ , so I should

use a scale from ☐ to ☐ .

☐ ☐ 59 ☐ ☐ ☐ 67 ☐ ☐ ☐ ☐ ☐ 79 ☐ ☐ ☐

B. For each piece of data, plot a dot above the number that corresponds to that data value.

C. Which pulse rate is the most common among the group of 12-year-olds? Explain how you know.

_____

_____

Turn and Talk Are dot plots useful for a large volume of data? Explain.

2 A company's employees are rated for their customer service on a scale of 1–10, with 1 being very unhappy and 10 being very happy with the service. The customer service ratings for one day are shown in the dot plot. Use the dot plot to describe the data.

Daily Customer Service Ratings

A. What is the most common rating for the day? Explain how you know.

_____

B. What is the least common rating for the day? Explain how you know.

_____

C. How many observations are shown in the dot plot? _____

D. If a rating of 6 or higher is considered acceptable by the company, what percent of the ratings are unacceptable?

There are ☐ total ratings and ☐ ratings below 6. So, $\dfrac{\square}{\square}$, or

☐ % of the ratings, are considered unacceptable by the company.

E. If a rating of greater than 8 is considered excellent, what percent of the ratings for the day are excellent?

There are ☐ total ratings and ☐ ratings greater than 8. So $\dfrac{\square}{\square}$,

or ☐ % of the ratings, are considered excellent.

F. There are 5 additional customer ratings at the end of the day, each a rating of 10. Will this change your answers to Parts A–E? Explain.

_____

_____

_____

 Turn and Talk How is a dot plot different from a number line? Explain.

Name _____

3 ▶ The recommended amount of water that each person should drink per day is shown. Students are asked to track how much water they actually drink in a day. The number of glasses of water they drank on a specific day is shown in the following list.

5, 7, 9, 7, 6, 1, 4, 2, 3, 0, 8, 5, 2, 5, 6, 7, 4, 8, 5, 6, 4, 3, 8, 6, 5

A. Complete the dot plot to show the amount of water students drank per day.

Drink 8 glasses of water per day.

0 1 2 3 4 5 6 7 8 9
Water Students Drank Per Day (glasses)

B. What is the most common number of glasses of water students drank?

_____

C. How many students drank at least the recommended amount of water per day?

_____

D. How many observations are shown in the dot plot? _____

E. What percentage of students did not drink at least the recommended amount of water per day?

_____

Check Understanding

1. The shoe sizes of the players on a soccer team are shown in the list.

10.5, 11.5, 10, 9, 10.5, 10, 8, 9, 7.5, 8, 10.5, 11, 10, 10.5, 9.5, 8.5, 7, 8.5, 9, 9.5, 10, 10.5, 11

Complete the dot plot to show the shoe sizes of the players.

7 7.5 8 8.5 9 9.5 10 10.5 11 11.5
Soccer Player Shoe Size

2. A student is asked to make a dot plot with the list shown.

8, 11, 16, 27, 8, 10, 19, 21, 7, 12, 15, 16, 22, 13

How many observations will be shown in the dot plot?

_____

On Your Own

3. **(MP) Attend to Precision** The dot plot shows the thicknesses of sheets of cardstock, a type of paper.

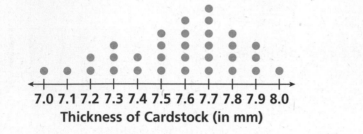

Thickness of Cardstock (in mm)

   A. What is the least thickness measured? _____

   B. What is the greatest thickness measured? _____

   C. What is the most common thickness measured? _____

4. A group of people is asked to count the number of coins in their pockets or wallets. The number of coins each person has is shown in the list.

   7, 10, 2, 0, 6, 8, 5, 3, 4, 0, 9, 1, 8, 7, 10, 0, 5, 7

   A. Complete the dot plot for the number of coins each person had.

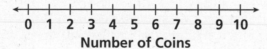

Number of Coins

   B. What is the most common number of coins in a person's pockets?

   _____

   C. How many observations are shown in the dot plot?

   _____

   D. What percentage of people had more than 5 coins in their pockets?

   _____

   E. What percentage of people had fewer than 7 coins in their pockets?

   _____

5. A basketball team tracks the number of three-point shots it makes per game during a season of games, as shown in the dot plot.

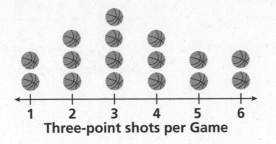

Three-point shots per Game

A. In how many games did the team score at least 3 three-point shots?

_____

B. In how many games did the team score exactly 9 points from three-point shots?

_____

C. What is the most three-point shots made in a game? _____

D. What percent of the games did the team score

at least 3 three-point shots? _____

6. The masses of a set of gemstones a jeweler has for jewelry are listed.

Gemstone masses (in grams): 0.2, 0.5, 0.1, 0.4, 0.7, 0.5, 0.3, 0.2, 0.1, 0.4, 0.2, 0.5, 0.2, 0.3, 0.1, 0.2, 0.6, 0.2, 0.6, 0.1

A. Make a dot plot to show the masses of the gemstones.

B. How many observations are shown in the dot plot? _____

C. What is the most common mass of gemstone? _____

D. Which gemstone mass is the least common? _____

7. **(MP) Reason** The dot plot shows the numbers of pages students in a class read during their dedicated reading time.

Pages Read During Dedicated Reading Time

A. How many students are in the class? _____

B. What percent of students read more than 6 pages? Explain your reasoning.

_____

_____

C. What fraction of the students read fewer than 5 pages? _____

D. How many total pages did all of the students read? Show your work.

8. The table shows the heights of trees at a tree farm, to the nearest foot. Make a dot plot for the tree heights.

Tree type	Height (in feet)
Fraser fir	6, 7, 10, 11, 14, 8, 10, 13, 12, 7
Douglas fir	15, 14, 12, 16, 13, 11, 12, 15, 16, 18
Blue spruce	10, 12, 14, 9, 10, 8, 11, 12, 8, 10

Fraser Fir   Douglas Fir   Blue Spruce

© Houghton Mifflin Harcourt Publishing Company • **Image Credits:** (l) ©bestofgreenscreen/Shutterstock; (c) ©blickwinkel/Alamy; (r) ©Leonid Shtandel/Alamy

Name _____

LESSON 14.2
**More Practice/
Homework**

ONLINE
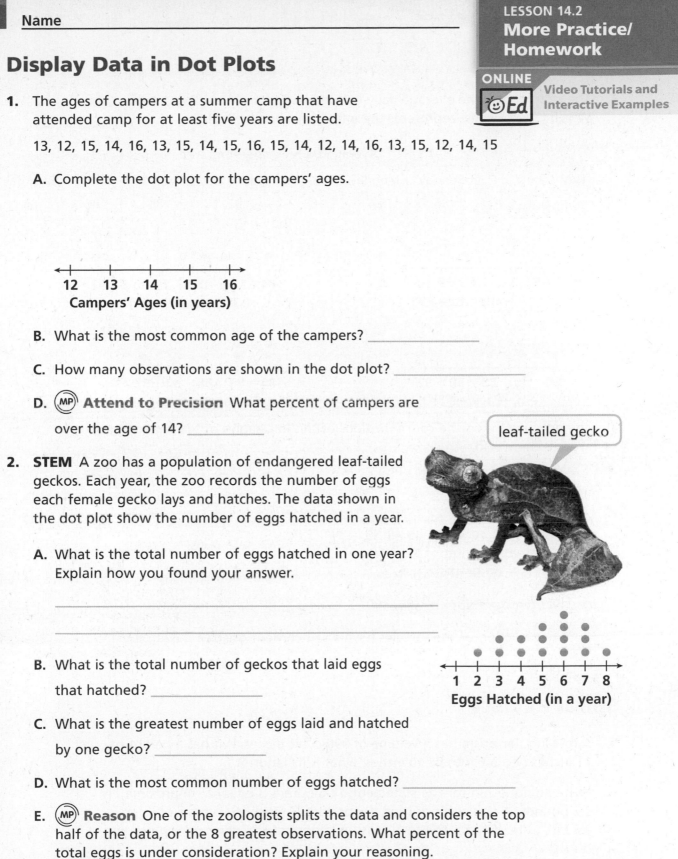
Ⓔd   Video Tutorials and
         Interactive Examples

Display Data in Dot Plots

1. The ages of campers at a summer camp that have attended camp for at least five years are listed.

13, 12, 15, 14, 16, 13, 15, 14, 15, 16, 15, 14, 12, 14, 16, 13, 15, 12, 14, 15

A. Complete the dot plot for the campers' ages.

```
←——+———+———+———+———+——→
   12    13    14    15    16
```
Campers' Ages (in years)

B. What is the most common age of the campers? _____

C. How many observations are shown in the dot plot? _____

D. (MP) **Attend to Precision** What percent of campers are over the age of 14? _____

leaf-tailed gecko

2. **STEM** A zoo has a population of endangered leaf-tailed geckos. Each year, the zoo records the number of eggs each female gecko lays and hatches. The data shown in the dot plot show the number of eggs hatched in a year.

A. What is the total number of eggs hatched in one year? Explain how you found your answer.

_____

_____

B. What is the total number of geckos that laid eggs that hatched? _____

```
            •           •
      •     •     •     •
•     •     •     •     •     •
←—+——+——+——+——+——+——+——+——→
  1  2  3  4  5  6  7  8
```
Eggs Hatched (in a year)

C. What is the greatest number of eggs laid and hatched by one gecko? _____

D. What is the most common number of eggs hatched? _____

E. (MP) **Reason** One of the zoologists splits the data and considers the top half of the data, or the 8 greatest observations. What percent of the total eggs is under consideration? Explain your reasoning.

_____

_____

Test Prep

3. The chart shows the average daily temperatures for a week in a town. Which dot plot best represents the information in the table?

Average Daily Temperature							
Day	Sunday	Monday	Tuesday	Wednesday	Thursday	Friday	Saturday
Temperature (°F)	86	84	88	92	88	86	86

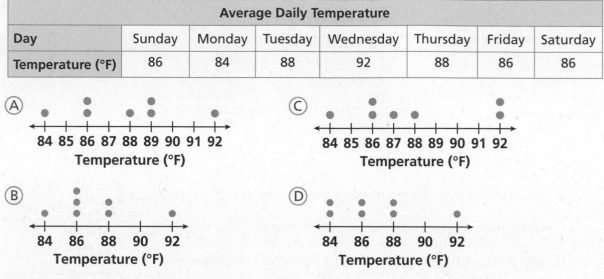

4. The dot plot shows the concentrations of salt in samples of sea water from around the world.

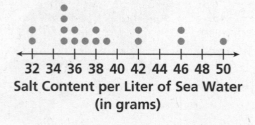

Salt Content per Liter of Sea Water
(in grams)

A. How many samples were taken? _____

B. What fraction of the samples have a salt content greater

than 38 grams? _____

Spiral Review

5. A rectangular prism has a volume of 990 cubic inches. If it has a height of 11 inches and a width of 10 inches, what is its length? _____

6. Write an equation for the statement: A kilogram is equal to approximately 2.2 pounds. A cinder block weighs x pounds. A brick has a mass of 0.6 kilogram. What is the total mass in kilograms y of the cinder block and brick?

_____

7. Evaluate the expression $3x^2 + 4x^3$ when $x = 4$. _____

Name _____

Make Histograms and Frequency Tables

(I Can) determine an appropriate interval for the data and construct a frequency table or histogram.

Connect to Vocabulary

A **histogram** is a **bar graph** whose bars represent the frequencies of numeric data within equal **intervals**.

Step It Out

When there is a large number of data values, it is helpful to group data into intervals. A histogram is a way to show the frequency of numeric data.

1 A tae kwon do school teaches many ages of students. The ages of the students are shown in the histogram.

A. The height of each bar represents the

_____

in each age group.

B. You can find the total number of students that were included in the data set by finding the

_____ of each bar

and _____ those values together.

C. There are _____ students in the range from 25 to 28 years old.

D. There are _____ students ages 9–16 years old.

E. The age range of _____ years old has the greatest number of students.

F. The difference between the number of students in the 13–16 year age range and the number of students in the 17–20 year age range is

_____ students.

Turn and Talk Can you make a dot plot from a histogram? Explain.

A frequency table is used to organize data.

2   A salesperson hands out samples during work. The number of samples handed out each hour during the work week are tracked. Make a frequency table to represent the data.

Samples per Hour
7, 12, 15, 23, 8, 11, 10,
19, 21, 10, 16, 22, 13, 16,
27, 8, 12, 18, 24, 20

A. Write the data in order from least to greatest.

_____

_____

_____

Salesperson handing out food samples

B. The numbers vary from _____ to _____, so use a scale from 1 to 30.

C. Divide the data into six equal-sized intervals.

The first interval is 1 − ☐.

The second interval is ☐ − ☐.

The third interval is ☐ − ☐.

The fourth interval is ☐ − ☐.

The fifth interval is ☐ − ☐.

The sixth interval is ☐ − ☐.

D. Complete the frequency table.

Interval	1—5	6—10				
Frequency	0					

 Turn and Talk What is another way you could display the data from the frequency table?

3 ▸ A movie theater records the number of pretzels it sells per day for 2 weeks. The pretzel sales data are shown in the list. Make a histogram to represent the data.

11, 8, 21, 15, 28, 43, 37, 9, 12, 13, 17, 31, 50, 34

A. Order the data from least to greatest.

_____

B. The numbers vary from _____ to _____, so use a scale from 1 to 50.

C. Divide the data into five equal-sized intervals.

The first interval is 1–10.   The second interval is ☐ – ☐.

The third interval is ☐ – ☐.   The fourth interval is ☐ – ☐.

The fifth interval is ☐ – ☐.

D. Complete the frequency table.

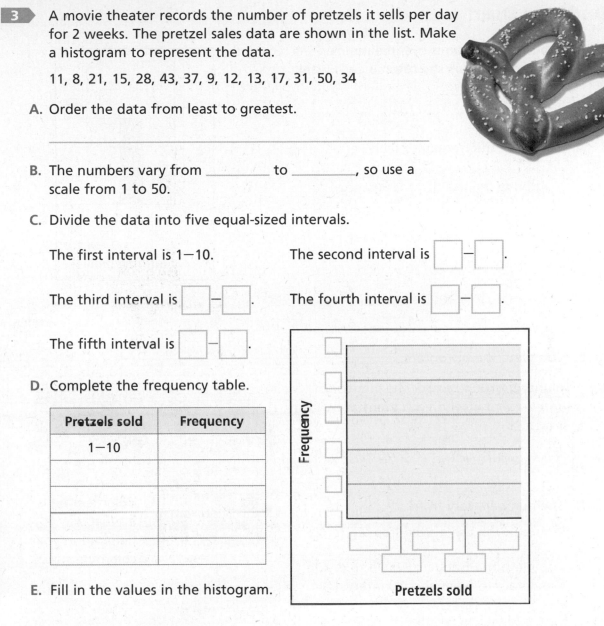

Pretzels sold	Frequency
1–10	

E. Fill in the values in the histogram.

Check Understanding

1. A restaurant records the numbers of people who come in for breakfast for 15 days. Use the data to complete the frequency table.

38, 59, 61, 33, 48, 54, 67, 29, 35, 49, 53, 21, 40, 66, 55

2. Describe how the histogram in Task 3 would look if the intervals were 0–20, 21–40, and 41–60.

_____

_____

Interval	Frequency
11–20	0
21–30	
	4
41–50	
51–60	

On Your Own

3. Jimena tutored students over the summer. She recorded the number of hours she tutored each week. Here are her data:

   15, 24, 18, 26, 18, 21, 23, 12, 24, 25

   A. Complete the frequency table.

Tutoring (hours)	Frequency
10—14	
	3
20—24	

   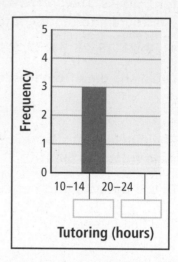

   B. Complete the histogram.

4. A volunteer group records the number of volunteers that attend each event they host, as shown.

   19, 30, 27, 16, 25, 38, 24, 17, 22, 40, 39, 26, 18, 37, 16

   A. The numbers vary from _____ to _____, so use a scale from 16 to 40.

   Volunteering is a great way to help out in your community.

   B. Complete the frequency table to divide the data into 5 equal-sized intervals.

   First interval: 16—☐

   Second interval: ☐—☐

   Third interval: ☐—☐

   Fourth interval: ☐—☐

   Fifth interval: ☐—☐

Volunteers	Frequency

   C. Complete the frequency table.

   D. (MP) **Use Structure** If you drew a histogram for this data, which interval would have the shortest bar? _____

5. Each team in a Hawaiian canoe racing regatta gains points for its finish times. The points each team earned are shown.

2, 6, 7, 5, 3, 4, 1, 8, 2, 9, 8, 6, 3, 5, 2, 4, 6

A. Use the data to complete the frequency table.

Interval	Frequency
1–3	
4–6	

B. How many bars will be used to represent the intervals in a histogram of the team points? _____

C. What is the height of the tallest bar in the histogram?

_____

D. Complete the histogram.

E. (MP) **Reason** Three other teams that competed were accidentally not included in the list. They earned 3, 2, and 8 points. How does this new information change the histogram? Is the second interval still the tallest bar? Explain.

_____

_____

_____

_____

_____

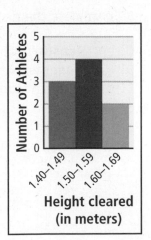

Frequency

1–3   4–6

Regatta team points

6. In the high jump, athletes run and jump over a bar without knocking it down. The histogram shows the heights of the jumps of the top athletes in a state competition.

A. Which height range did the most athletes clear?

_____

B. How many athletes participated in the state competition?

_____

Number of Athletes

1.40–1.49   1.50–1.59   1.60–1.69

Height cleared (in meters)

7. A florist delivers flowers each day. The table shows the numbers of flower deliveries for a two-week period.

Flower Deliveries		
Day	Deliveries (week 1)	Deliveries (week 2)
Monday	38	31
Tuesday	53	47
Wednesday	44	53
Thursday	35	39
Friday	51	48
Saturday	46	52
Sunday	32	35

A. Use the data from the table of delivery information to complete the frequency table.

Deliveries	Frequency
31–35	
36–40	
41–45	
46–50	
51–55	

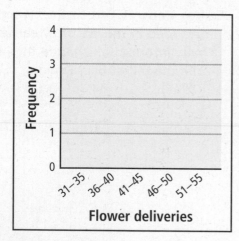

B. Complete the histogram.

C. (MP) **Reason** If the florist makes the same number of deliveries each day in weeks 3 and 4 as in weeks 1 and 2, how does this change the bars in the histogram? Explain.

_____

_____

_____

_____

LESSON 14.3
**More Practice/
Homework**

ONLINE
Video Tutorials and
Interactive Examples

Make Histograms and Frequency Tables

1. A bakery records the number of loaves of bread it sells per hour for one day as shown.

15, 17, 20, 22, 23, 25, 11, 12, 26, 13, 18, 21, 24, 28, 23, 18, 29, 24, 16

A. Write the data in order from least to greatest.

_____

B. Complete the frequency table.

Number of loaves sold (per hour)	Frequency
11–15	

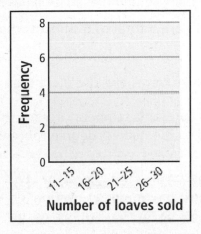

Number of loaves sold

C. Complete the histogam.

2. **Math on the Spot** The table shows survey results about the number of hours a week students spend studying. Make a histogram of the data.

	Number of Hours Spent Studying											
Hours	1	2	3	4	5	6	7	8	9	10	11	12
Number of students	1	1	4	2	6	8	10	10	12	7	2	3

A. Make a frequency table of the data.

B. Draw a bar for each interval from the frequency table.

Hours	Number of students
1–2	2
3–4	
5–6	
7–8	
9–10	
11–12	

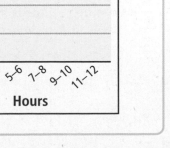

© Houghton Mifflin Harcourt Publishing Company

Test Prep

3. The histogram shows the amounts of time students spend exercising per day, rounded to the nearest hour. Which statements about the histogram are correct? Select all that apply.

Ⓐ The least common amount of time spent exercising was 76–90 minutes.

Ⓑ The most common exercise times are 1–15 minutes.

Ⓒ There are a total of 6 students that exercise.

Ⓓ There are 36 students that were surveyed.

Ⓔ Most students exercise more than 60 minutes per day.

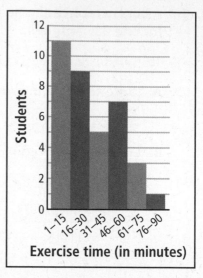

4. The list represents temperatures for the month of June, rounded to the nearest degree Fahrenheit. Complete the frequency table.

93, 85, 97, 79, 104, 88, 92, 94, 97, 87,
78, 95, 101, 93, 97, 99, 87, 103, 90, 95,
102, 97, 99, 91, 95, 92, 101, 89, 99, 98

Temperature (°F)	Days
71–80	

Spiral Review

5. Gustus bought three pairs of shoes. Each pair costs $19.98. What is the total amount he spent on shoes, before tax? _____

6. A car travels 220 miles in 4 hours. If the car travels at the same speed, how far will it have traveled after 6 hours? _____

7. A bucket can hold a total of 5 gallons of water. If the bucket is 45% full, how much water is in the bucket? _____

Name _____

Review

Vocabulary

Choose the correct term from the Vocabulary box.

1. a graph that has bars that represent frequencies of numeric data within equal measures _____

2. a question that has many different, or variable answers

   _____

3. a set of information collected about people or things, often to draw conclusions about them _____

4. a graph in which each piece of data is represented by a dot above a number line _____

5. a table that lists items together according to the number of times that the items occur _____

Concepts and Skills

6. The times, in seconds, that it takes barrel racers to complete their barrel runs at a rodeo are shown.

Time (seconds)						
11	11	12	12	12	12	13
13	14	14	15	15	15	16

   A. What attribute is being measured by the data in table?

   _____

   B. What is the unit of measurement for the data? _____

   C. How many observations were made? _____

   D. (MP) **Use Tools** State what strategy and tool you would use to make a dot plot of the data? Explain your choice.

   _____

7. The dot plot shows the amount each customer spent during a 1-hour period at a coffee shop. How many customers made a purchase at the coffee shop during that 1-hour period?

   _____

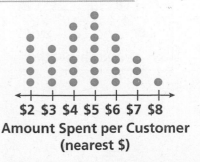

Amount Spent per Customer (nearest $)

8. Which of the following is an example of a statistical question? Select all that apply.

- Ⓐ How many days are in the month of August?
- Ⓑ How many students, in each class, like watermelon?
- Ⓒ What is the temperature at 4:00 p.m. every Saturday?
- Ⓓ What is the time it took each student to read the same chapter?
- Ⓔ How many years did it take to build the oldest building in town?

9. Which histogram correctly represents the data from the frequency table?

Age (in months)	Students
132–138	14
139–145	13
146–152	8
153–159	6

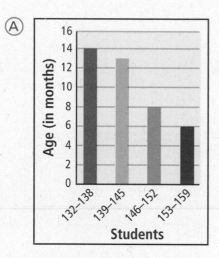

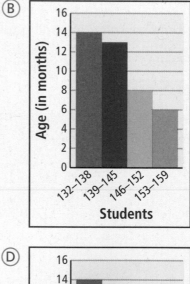

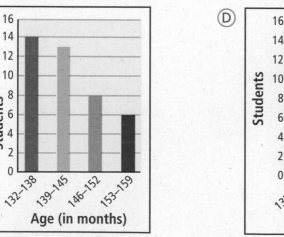

Measures of Center

DOT PLOT LOGIC

The dot plot shows the lengths of eight hiking trails in a park.

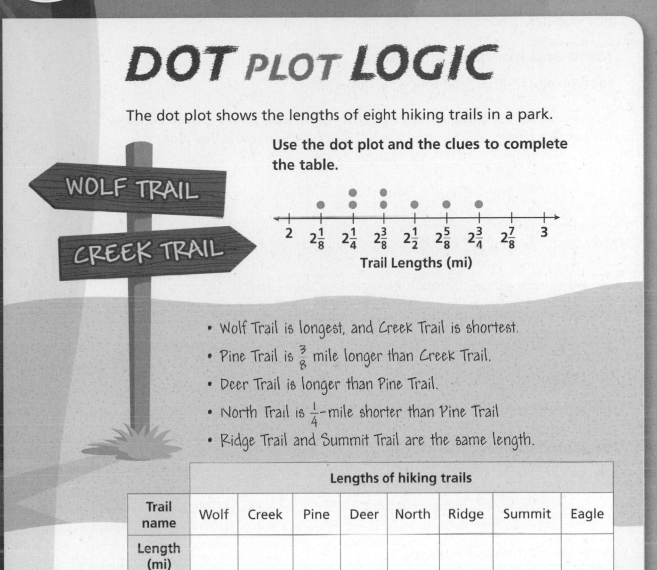

Use the dot plot and the clues to complete the table.

Trail Lengths (mi)

WOLF TRAIL

CREEK TRAIL

- Wolf Trail is longest, and Creek Trail is shortest.
- Pine Trail is $\frac{3}{8}$ mile longer than Creek Trail.
- Deer Trail is longer than Pine Trail.
- North Trail is $\frac{1}{4}$-mile shorter than Pine Trail
- Ridge Trail and Summit Trail are the same length.

Lengths of hiking trails							
Trail name	Wolf	Creek	Pine	Deer	North	Ridge	Summit	Eagle
Length (mi)								

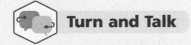 **Turn and Talk**

- Explain how you determined the length of Deer Trail.
- Explain how you determined the lengths of Ridge Trail and Summit Trail.

Are You Ready?

Complete these problems to review prior concepts and skills you will need for this module.

Make and Interpret Line Plots

For Problems 1–4, use the following information.

An art teacher has a bag of ribbon pieces. The ribbon pieces are measured to the nearest $\frac{1}{8}$ foot. The length of each piece is shown in the line plot.

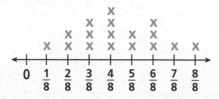

1. How many pieces of ribbon measure less than $\frac{1}{2}$ foot? _____

2. How many pieces of ribbon measure greater than $\frac{1}{2}$ foot? _____

3. What is the difference in length between the longest and the shortest piece of ribbon? _____

4. How many pieces of ribbon measure at least $\frac{3}{4}$ foot? _____

Division Involving Decimals

Divide.

5. $4)\overline{\$8.24}$ _____   6. $7)\overline{\$15.61}$ _____   7. $14)\overline{\$79.80}$ _____

Write the fraction as a decimal.

8. $\frac{40}{16}$ _____   9. $\frac{108}{16}$ _____   10. $\frac{115}{8}$ _____

Write the mixed number as a decimal.

11. $80\frac{2}{5}$ _____   12. $20\frac{4}{16}$ _____   13. $110\frac{9}{12}$ _____

Name _____

Explore Mean as Fair Share

(I Can) find both the fair share and the balance point of a
data set using a model or a number line.

Spark Your Learning

A florist needs to make 10 bouquets with 40 carnations,
36 red roses, 24 yellow roses, and 24 lilies. How many flowers
should there be in each bouquet, so that each bouquet has
the same number of flowers? Justify your answer.

Turn and Talk Suppose the florist has to put the same number of each type
of flower in each bouquet. How many total flowers should there be in each
bouquet, and how many will be left over? Explain.

© Houghton Mifflin Harcourt Publishing Company • Image Credit: ©Volodymyr Melnyk/Alamy

Build Understanding

If everyone has a *fair share* of a group of items, they all have the same number of items.

1 ▶ While at the beach, three friends found 6, 1, and 5 sea shells. The friends agreed to divide the shells evenly. How many shells should each person get?

A. Look at the model shown. For each friend to have the same number of shells, or a fair share of shells, what needs to happen?

_____

_____

B. Explain how you could rearrange the shells in Part A so that each friend has the same number of shells. Then sketch the fair shares.

C. Suppose the three friends had found 9, 1, and 5 sea shells. How many shells would each person get? Explain your reasoning

 Turn and Talk Describe another way to find the fair share of shells each friend should have in Part C.

2 How can you find the balance point of a data set?

A. Look back at the data in Task 1, Part A. Complete the dot plot to represent the data.

```
←—+——+——+——+——+——+——+——+——→
   0   1   2   3   4   5   6   7
```
Number of Sea Shells

B. Now, circle the number that represents the fair share number from Task 1 on the dot plot in Part A. What is the distance from each data point to the fair share number?

The distance from 1 to ☐ is ☐. The distance from 5 to ☐ is ☐.

The distance from 6 to ☐ is ☐.

C. What do you notice about the total distances from the data points on the left side and the right side of the fair share number? Explain.

_____

_____

_____

_____

D. A *balance point* of a data set is the point on a number line where the data distribution is balanced. What number from the dot plot in Part A represents the balance point for the data set 6 shells, 1 shell, and 5 shells? Explain.

_____

_____

_____

Turn and Talk How are fair share and balance point related? Explain.

Check Understanding

1. Three friends have 7, 5, and 9 marbles. The friends agreed to divide the marbles evenly. How many marbles should each person get?

_____

2. What is the balance point for the data set 3, 7, 8? _____

On Your Own

3. Felipe has a bowl of fruit with 2 apples, 7 bananas, 2 oranges, 3 pears, and 1 plum. He wants to share the fruit with 4 friends.

> What is each person's fair share?

   A. How many pieces of fruit will each person get? _____

   B. How should Felipe distribute the fruit so everyone gets a fair share? Show your work.

4. (MP) **Attend to Precision** What is the balance point for the set of data 3, 1, 8, 4, 6, 8?

   A. Make a dot plot for the data.

   ```
   <---+---+---+---+---+---+---+---+---+---+---+--->
       0   1   2   3   4   5   6   7   8   9   10
   ```
   Number of Sea Shells

   B. What is the balance point? _____

   C. Explain how you found the balance point.

   _____

   _____

   _____

   _____

5. **Open Ended** Make a data set that has 5 numbers and a balance point of 12. _____

I'm in a Learning Mindset!

What strategies for representing a fair share can I talk about?

_____

_____

© Houghton Mifflin Harcourt Publishing Company • Image Credit: ©Barbara Lechner/Shutterstock

LESSON 15.1
**More Practice/
Homework**

ONLINE
⊙Ed **Video Tutorials and
Interactive Examples**

Explore Mean as Fair Share

1. Four friends fished for crabs. They caught 5, 9, 8, and 6 crabs.
    The friends agreed to divide the crabs evenly.

    A. How many crabs should each person get? _____

    B. Describe how the crabs should be distributed among the four people.

2. (MP) **Reason** Five pages of a photo album contain 6, 7, 9, 10, and 13
    pictures. Can the pictures be rearranged so that there is an equal number
    of pictures on each page? Explain why or why not.

    _____

3. **Open Ended** How could the cubes be stacked so there is the same
    number of cubes in each stack?

    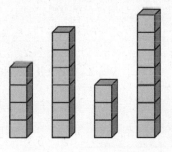

    _____

    _____

4. Tatiana has three dogs. She has the following amounts of dog food left.

    17 cups of Brand A dog food

    12 cups of Brand B dog food

    13 cups of Brand C dog food

    If the food is to be distributed evenly to the three dogs, how many cups of
    dog food should each dog get?

    _____

Test Prep

5. In which ways could the cubes be stacked so there is the same number of cubes in each stack? Select all that apply.

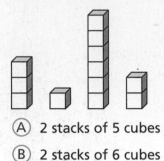

(A) 2 stacks of 5 cubes

(B) 2 stacks of 6 cubes

(C) 3 stacks of 4 cubes

(D) 4 stacks of 3 cubes

(E) 2 stacks of 12 cubes

6. Alex has 36 pennies. He wants to stack them in equal rows. Select all the stacks that Alex can make.

(A) 3 stacks of 10 pennies

(B) 3 stacks of 12 pennies

(C) 5 stacks of 7 pennies

(D) 6 stacks of 6 pennies

(E) 8 stacks of 4 pennies

7. What is the balance point for the data set?

1, 5, 7, 3, 4

Spiral Review

8. Find the volume of a rectangular prism with a length of $6\frac{1}{2}$ feet, a width of $4\frac{3}{4}$ feet, and a height of $3\frac{1}{2}$ feet.

9. Ms. Castillo spent $87.75 on shrimp. The shrimp cost $9.75 per pound. How many pounds of shrimp did Ms. Castillo buy?

10. Janelle earns $12 per hour. What equation can be used to find how many hours Janelle worked if she earned $360?

© Houghton Mifflin Harcourt Publishing Company

Name

Find Measures of Center

(I Can) find and interpret the mean, median, and mode of a set of data.

Spark Your Learning

The list shows the heights, in inches, of the players on a high school basketball team. How can you describe the typical height of this data with a single value?

69, 73, 68, 72, 75, 72, 78, 74, 74, 80, 69, 70, 72

Turn and Talk How would the center change if the tallest player left the team and was replaced by a player who is 66 inches tall? Explain.

Build Understanding

Connect to Vocabulary

Mean is the sum of the items in a set of data divided by the number of items in the set; also called **average**.
Median is the middle number or mean (average) of the two middle numbers in an ordered set of data.
Mode is the number or numbers that occur most frequently in a set of data; when all numbers occur with the same frequency, we say there is no mode.

A **measure of center** is used to describe the middle of a data set.

1 Look at the stacks of counters. The heights of the stacks from left to right are 8, 3, 7, 5, and 7.

A. Arrange the stacks in a row from shortest to greatest. What is the height of the middle stack?

_____

B. What is the measure of center represented by the middle stack?

_____

C. Look at the stacks of counters in Part A. What is the most common height for the stacks? Explain why it is the most common.

_____

_____

D. What is the measure of center represented by the most common stack height?

_____

E. Rearrange the counters so that all of the stacks have the same number of counters. Now how many counters are in each stack? Show your work.

F. What measure of center is represented when all the stacks have the same number of counters?

_____

 Turn and Talk How do you know which measure of center best represents a set of data? Give an example.

Step It Out

2 The data show the average price of gas (in dollars and cents) at some gas stations around the world. Find the mean, median, and mode of the data.

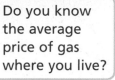

3.50	7.99	3.25	4.00	3.50	7.50	3.65	3.50	4.00

A. Complete the dot plot to represent the data.

Average Price of Gas (in dollars)

> Do you know the average price of gas where you live?

B. Complete the equations to find the mean.

$$3.50 + 3.65 + 3.50 + 3.25 + 7.50 + 4.00 + 7.99 + 3.50 + 4.00 = \boxed{}$$

$$\frac{\boxed{}}{9} \approx \$ \boxed{}$$

C. Write the data in order from least to greatest and circle the median.

_____

D. What is the mode of the data?

_____

Turn and Talk Suppose the average gas prices had been given in a histogram instead of a table. Could you have found the mean, median, or mode?

Check Understanding

1. Zayn surveyed a group of people about how many times they ate at a restaurant last month. The results are: 4, 0, 21, 14, 12, 30, 8, 7, 8, 7, 7, 10, 14, 12. Find the mean, median, and mode of the data.

   Mean: _____   Median: _____   Mode: _____

2. Find the mean, median, and mode of the data:
   2.4, 1.9, 3.3, 3.5, 3.2, 2.7, 1.1, 20.9, 2.4.

   Mean: _____   Median: _____   Mode: _____

On Your Own

3. Eric recorded the temperature (in °F) for 10 days and displayed the information in a table.

10 Day Forecast

SAT	SUN	MON	TUE	WED	THU	FRI	SAT	SUN	MON
21	27	31	21	57	23	25	24	19	16

21	27	31	21	57	23	25	24	19	16

A. Complete the dot plot to represent the data.

```
 ◄─┼┼┼┼┼┼┼┼┼┼┼┼┼┼┼┼┼┼┼┼┼┼┼┼┼┼┼┼┼┼┼┼┼┼┼┼┼┼┼┼┼┼┼┼┼┼┼┼┼─►
    15        25        35        45        55        65
```
Temperature (in degrees Fahrenheit)

B. What is the mean of the data? _____

C. What is the median of the data? _____

D. What is the mode of the data? _____

4. (MP) **Attend to Precision** The 40-yard dash times, in seconds, for 7 runners are shown.

4.8, 5.3, 5.2, 6.4, 5.4, 5.3, 5.4

A. What is the mean of the data? _____

B. What is the median of the data? _____

C. What is the mode of the data? _____

D. Which of the measures of center has more than one possible value?

_____

5. (MP) **Reason** Look at the data. 0, 1, 2, 1, 2, 0, 1, 2, 0, 2, 1, 2, 1, 2. Which measure of center could best be used to describe the data? Explain.

_____

_____

6. **Open Ended** Describe a set of data that has no mode, 1 mode, and more than one mode. _____

I'm in a Learning Mindset!

What differences between the three measures of center can I talk about?

_____

Find Measures of Center

ONLINE
☺Ed
Video Tutorials and Interactive Examples

1. Summer wants to know which cat food her cats prefer. She fed the cats and recorded the number of grams of food the cats ate each day. The results are: 60 grams, 63 grams, 61 grams, 58 grams, 65 grams, 60 grams, and 60 grams.

   Which food do the cats prefer?

   A. How many days did Summer log the amount of food her cats ate? _____

   B. On average, how many grams of food did her cats eat each day? _____

   C. Which amount represents the mode of the data? _____

   D. What is the median of the data? _____

   E. Which measures of center are the same? _____

2. (MP) **Reason** Jackson recorded the following data: 2, 5, *x*, 2, 4, 3. If the mean of the data is 3, what is the value of *x*? Explain how you found your answer.

   _____

   _____

   _____

3. **Math on the Spot** Find the mean, median, and mode of the data set: 10, 6, 2, 3, 1, and 2.

   _____

For Problems 4–7, find the mean, median, and mode of each data set.

4. 17, 25, 23, 200, 14

   Mean _____

   Median _____

   Mode _____

5. 0.5, 1.4, 3.0, 7.0, 0.5, 1.8, 0.5

   Mean _____

   Median _____

   Mode _____

6. 1, 8, 5, 4, 1, 8, 5, 4

   Mean _____

   Median _____

   Mode _____

7. 0, 78, 99, 58, 65, 0, 47, 38, 227

   Mean _____

   Median _____

   Mode _____

Test Prep

8. The ages of dogs (in years) at a dog shelter are shown.

7, 4, 6, 8, 8, 7, 3, 5, 4, 2

What is the mode of the data? Select all that apply.

(A) 2 years

(B) 3 years

(C) 4 years

(D) 7 years

(E) 8 years

9. In their most recent tournament, the winning team's 6 members had the scores shown.

70, 72, 74, 76, 80, 132

Which statement is correct?

(A) The median is 74.

(B) The mean is 75.

(C) The median is 76.

(D) The mean is 84.

10. What is the median of the data?

3, 5, 6, 7, 9, 6, 8, 7, 8, 12

(A) 6

(B) 7

(C) 7.1

(D) 8

Spiral Review

11. A parallelogram has a base of 13 centimeters and a height of 9.2 centimeters. What is the area of the parallelogram?

_____

12. In which quadrant is the point (−5, 1.7) located?

_____

Name

Choose a Measure of Center

(I Can) find the mean, median, and mode for a given data set and determine the best measure of center to describe the data set.

Step It Out

1 ▶ The table shows the numbers of songs downloaded in one week by some students.

12	13	10	9
13	44	15	12

A. What do you notice about the data in the table?

The data value of _____ is much _____ than the other data values in the table.

> **Connect to Vocabulary**
>
> An **outlier** is a value much greater or much less than the other values in a data set. A set of data can have more than 1 outlier.

B. Complete the dot plot to represent the data.

```
  0    5   10   15   20   25   30   35   40   45   50
```
Number of Songs Downloaded

C. Which value in the data set is an outlier? Explain how you know.

_____

D. Find the mean, median, and mode with and without the outlier. Then complete the sentences.

The mean with the outlier is _____, and the mean without the outlier is _____. The outlier makes the mean _____.

The median with the outlier is _____, and the median without the outlier is _____. The outlier makes the median _____.

The mode with the outlier is _____, and the mode without the outlier is _____. The outlier _____ the mode.

> **Turn and Talk** When the outlier is included, which measure of center is least representative of the data set? Why?

Step It Out

2 A group of friends decide to see who can balance themselves the longest on one foot with their eyes closed. The results, in seconds, are listed.

21, 21, 23, 11, 48, 21, 16, 15, 13

21 s   21 s   23 s

A. Complete the dot plot of the data.

Balancing Time (in seconds)

B. Use the dot plot to complete the sentences.

The data value of _____ is an outlier.

The mean with the outlier is _____, and the mean without the outlier is about _____. The outlier made the mean _____.

The median with the outlier is _____, and the median without the outlier is _____. The outlier made the median _____.

The mode with the outlier is _____, and the mode without the outlier is _____. The outlier _____ the mode.

C. The best measure of center for this data set is the median or the _____ , because the _____ with the outlier is too high.

Check Understanding

1. Xavier drew 10 cards at random from a deck of numbered cards. The deck is composed of 3 sets of cards numbered 1 through 10 and three cards numbered 50. He recorded the numbers he drew: 8, 7, 9, 1, 10, 10, 50, 2, 5, 3. Find the mean, median, and mode of the data. What would happen to the mean, median, and mode if Xavier drew a 4 card instead of the 50 card?

_____

_____

2. Find the mean, median, and mode of the data: 0, 100, 25, 25, 25. Which outlier, 0 or 100, affects the data more? Why?

_____

_____

_____

On Your Own

3. The table shows the masses (in kilograms) of eight gorillas.

155	157	160	158
44	160	156	154

A. What are the mean, median, and mode of the data?

_____

B. Which mass is the outlier of the data? _____

C. How does the outlier affect the mean, median, and mode?

_____

_____

_____

Adult male gorillas can have a mass of up to 220 kilograms.

D. Which measure of center best represents the data? Why?

_____

_____

4. (MP) **Attend to Precision** The circumference of a pumpkin is the distance around it. The following are circumferences (in inches) of some pumpkins growing in a pumpkin patch: 16, 12, 14, 17, 15, 9, 8, 5.

A. Make a dot plot of the data.

B. What is the mean of the data? _____

C. What is the median of the data? _____

D. What is the mode of the data? _____

E. Which measure of center best represent this data? Explain.

_____

_____

_____

5. Simone's grandmother likes to give sweaters as gifts. She has eight grandchildren. The prices of the first seven sweaters she buys are shown.

- $42   - $40   - $35   - $30

- $40   - $38   - $50   - ?

  A. How much does the 8th sweater cost if the mean price of all the sweaters is $40? _____

  B. Complete the dot plot to represent the prices of the sweaters.

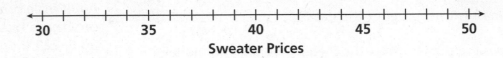

30   35   40   45   50

Sweater Prices

  C. What are the mean, median, and mode of all sweaters?

  _____

  D. Which measure of center best represents the data? Explain.

  _____

  _____

6. The numbers of questions out of 20 that the students in a class got correct on a quiz are shown in the table.

Number of questions answered correctly						
16	15	16	14	12	18	18
19	20	18	17	18	20	15
16	15	0	12	10	10	

  A. Complete the dot plot of the data.

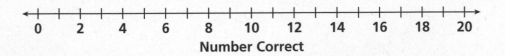

0   2   4   6   8   10   12   14   16   18   20

Number Correct

  B. How does the outlier affect the data? Explain.

  _____

  _____

  C. Which measure of center best represents the data? Why?

  _____

  _____

7. **Open Ended** Describe a data set that has the same mean, median, and mode.

  _____

Choose a Measure of Center

1. **STEM** Rachel launched several model rockets and calculated the height, in feet, of each launch. The heights were: 75, 70, 80, 72, 84, 37, 65, 67, and 80.

   A. Complete the dot plot to represent the data.

   ←┼┼→
   　30　　　40　　　50　　　60　　　70　　　80　　　90
   Rocket Height (in feet)

   B. Find the mean, median, and mode of the heights.

   Mean: _____ Median: _____ Mode: _____

   C. How are the data affected by the outlier?

   _____

   _____

   _____

   D. Which measure of center best represents the data? Why?

   _____

   _____

   _____

   Rachel's best rocket launch reached 84 feet in height!

2. **(MP) Reason** Hayden recorded the following measurements, in centimeters. He noted he was missing one measurement. If the mean is 1 centimeter, what is the value of the missing measurement? Explain.

   0.1, 0.2, 0.1, 0.2, 0.3, 0.1, 0.2.

   _____

   _____

3. **Math on the Spot** The dot plot shows the numbers of hours 15 people spent on the telephone in one week. Which measure of center best describes these data? Justify your answers.

   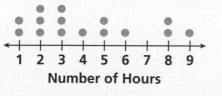
   Number of Hours

   _____

   _____

Test Prep

4. Identify any outliers in the data. Select all that apply.

3, 8, 4, 7, 62, 10, 9, 59, 12

(A) 3

(B) 8

(C) 10

(D) 59

(E) 62

5. The monthly rents for 8 apartments are shown.

$650, $600, $800, $700, $600, $600, $750, $2,000

Which measure of center best represents the data?

_____

6. What is the mode of the data?

0, 5, 8, 12, 14, 19, 11, 3

(A) 0   (C) 5

(B) 3   (D) No mode

7. A basketball team has scored the following numbers of points in games this season.

65, 60, 58, 52, 50, and 51

Find the mean, median, and mode of the data.

_____

Spiral Review

8. Find the surface area of a rectangular prism with a length of 6.1 centimeters, a width of 5.2 centimeters, and a height of 4 centimeters.

_____

9. Write an equation to represent the data in the table.

x	−2	2	4
y	−4	4	8

_____

15 Review

Vocabulary

Choose the correct term from the Vocabulary box.

Vocabulary
measures of center
mean
median
mode
outlier

1. The _____ is the number or numbers that occur most frequently in a set of data.

2. The _____ is the sum of the items in a data set divided by the number of items in the set.

3. A value much greater or much less than the others in a data set is called an _____.

4. The middle number or mean of the two middle numbers in an ordered data set is called the _____.

5. The _____ are used to describe the middle of a data set.

Concepts and Skills

6. (MP) **Use Tools** The table shows the weights of 8 boxes on a postal truck. If the weights of the items in the boxes were shared equally among the boxes, how much would a box weigh? State what strategy and tool you will use to answer the question, explain your choice, and then find the answer.

Weight (in pounds)	
3	9
7	5
4	12
10	8

_____

_____

For Problems 7–9, use the following information.

A city bus driver counts the number of passengers that board the bus at each bus stop. The table shows the numbers of passengers.

Bus stop	Boarding passengers
Elm	8
Sycamore	10
Oak	11
Spruce	8
Hawthorne	13

7. What is the median of the numbers of boarding passengers? _____

8. What is the mode of the numbers of boarding passengers? _____

9. What is the mean number of passengers that board per stop? _____

10. George works with his dad in a yard to help get it ready for a new patio. The times, in minutes, he works each day are listed:

45, 58, 34, 65, 30, 46, 51

What is the mean of the times George worked in the yard?

_____

For Problems 11–13, use the following information.

For a beach trip, D'Marion spends $9 on sunscreen, $18 on beach towels, $22 on food, $9 on a first aid kit, and $11 on sand toys.

11. Which measure of center is represented by $9?

Ⓐ mean   Ⓒ mode

Ⓑ median   Ⓓ outlier

12. Which measure of center will help D'Marion determine the average cost of the types of items he bought?

Ⓐ mean   Ⓒ mode

Ⓑ median   Ⓓ outlier

13. What is the median cost of the different types of items that D'Marion purchased? _____

For Problems 14–17, use the dot plot shown.

14. What is the mode of the data? _____

15. What is the median of the data? _____

16. What is the mean of the data? _____

17. Suppose one more data point is added to the dot plot at 19. Which statement best describes how this would change the measures of center?

Ⓐ The measures of center would be unchanged by the addition of the data point at 19.

Ⓑ The only measure of center that would change is the mean, which would increase.

Ⓒ The median is the only measure that would change.

Ⓓ The mean and median would both increase.

Variability and Data Distribution

Player Stats

Norah looked up her favorite college basketball player online. The player has played in 5 games so far this season. The information Norah found is shown.

PLAYER BIO	POINTS PER GAME
Player Name: S. Palmer	**Mean:** 22 points
Position: Guard	**Median:** 24 points
Height: 5 ft 8 in.	**Range:** 20 points
Class: Junior	

Use the player's data to make a data set with a possible number of points the player could have scored in each game. Your data set should match the information Norah found about the player.

Game 1: _____ points   Game 2: _____ points

Game 3: _____ points   Game 4: _____ points

Game 5: _____ points

 **Turn and Talk**

- Explain how you chose the values for your data set.

- Could the player have scored 0 points in one of the games? Explain your reasoning.

Are You Ready?

Complete these problems to review prior concepts and skills
you will need for this module.

Compare and Order Whole Numbers

Order the numbers from least to greatest.

1. 21, 17, 7, 11, 20, 19, 10

_____

2. 87, 78, 90, 85, 79, 82, 95

_____

3. 101, 110, 107, 97, 111, 105, 102

_____

4. 521, 518, 508, 512, 510, 501, 515

_____

Mean

Find the mean for each set of data.

5. 14, 10, 9, 7, 14, 16, 14, 4

_____

6. 42, 37, 25, 33, 25, 18, 37

_____

7. 30, 75, 60, 10, 50, 85, 25, 45

_____

8. 12, 20, 22, 15, 17, 18, 11, 23

_____

9. The data show the heights, in inches,
of the players on a basketball team.
Find the mean of the heights.

74, 76, 67, 70, 76, 68, 73, 66, 70, 66, 64

_____

Opposites and Absolute Value

Find the absolute value of the expression.

10. $|-6|$

_____

11. $|26|$

_____

12. $|-115|$

_____

13. $|0|$

_____

14. $|-100|$

_____

15. $|134|$

_____

Name

Explore Patterns of Data

(I Can) describe data distributions by their shapes.

Spark Your Learning

Sharice is collecting data on the lengths of crocodiles for a science project. She thinks it would help to make a poster for her class so the students can understand her data at a glance. How should she display her data?

American crocodiles: 5.0 m, 4.5 m, 3.0 m, 4.5 m
Australian freshwater crocodiles: 2.5 m, 2.0 m, 2.0 m, 1.5 m
Orinoco crocodiles: 4.5 m, 4.5 m, 2.5 m, 2.5 m

 Turn and Talk What are the advantages of visually organizing data?

Build Understanding

Seeing data sets represented as dot plots and histograms can help you find and understand overall patterns in the data.

1 Mr. Ortega surveyed one of his classes to determine the number of siblings each of his students has. The results are summarized in the dot plot. What conclusions can you draw from the distribution of the data?

A. How many students did Mr. Ortega survey?

_____

Students' Siblings

B. A *cluster* is a group of data points that lie within a small interval. Does the dot plot have a cluster? If so, where?

_____

_____

C. A *gap* is an interval that contains no data. Does the dot plot have any gaps or deviations from the overall pattern? If so, where?

_____

_____

D. A *peak* is a data value which is higher than the values on either side. Does the dot plot have a peak? If so, where?

_____

E. Calculate the median of the data. How does it relate to the overall pattern?

_____

_____

F. Draw two conclusions from the survey results. Explain whether you used a cluster, gap, a peak, or a mode to reach each conclusion.

_____

_____

_____

 Turn and Talk Suppose Mr. Ortega surveys all of his classes and summarizes the number of siblings in dot plots for each class. Would you expect the plots to look similar to the dot plot in Task 1 with respect to clusters and gaps? Explain.

2 The histogram shows the fuel efficiency, in miles per gallon, for cars sold at Max's Dealership.

A. Is there a peak in the distribution? If so, where?

_____

B. Describe the pattern in how the data change across the intervals.

_____

_____

_____

C. If you draw a vertical line through the middle of the interval 20–24, the two sides of the histogram are close to mirror images. So the histogram is nearly symmetric. Is the pattern in Part B an indicator of symmetry? Does the data deviate from the overall pattern? Explain.

_____

_____

_____

_____

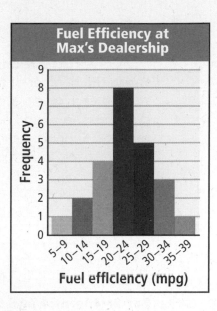

Fuel Efficiency at Max's Dealership

Check Understanding

For Problems 1–2, describe the data set by identifying clusters, peaks, gaps, and symmetry. Draw one conclusion and explain how you reached it.

1.

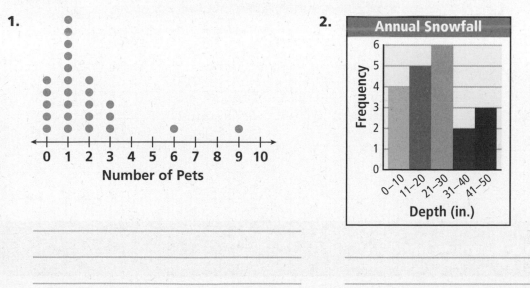

2. **Annual Snowfall**

_____

_____

_____

_____

On Your Own

3. **(MP) Construct Arguments** The dot plot shows the number of hours that 40 students studied each week. Make a statement that describes the overall pattern of the data in the plot. Support your statement by describing clusters, gaps, and/or peaks.

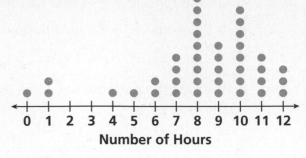

Number of Hours

_____

_____

_____

For Problems 4 and 5, describe any clusters, symmetry, peaks, and gaps or deviations from the overall pattern for the given distributions. Draw one conclusion about the data and explain how you reached it.

4.

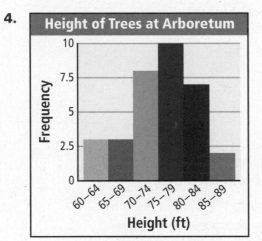

Height of Trees at Arboretum

5. **Times for 100-meter Sprint**

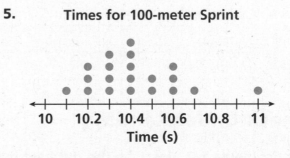

Time (s)

_____   _____

_____   _____

_____   _____

_____   _____

_____   _____

I'm in a Learning Mindset!

What can I apply from previous work to better understand patterns of data?

_____

LESSON 16.1
**More Practice/
Homework**

ONLINE
Video Tutorials and
Interactive Examples

Explore Patterns of Data

1. (MP) **Use Structure** The histogram shows the fuel efficiency (in miles per gallon) for some automobiles. Make a statement that describes the overall pattern and the shape of the distribution. What conclusion can you draw?

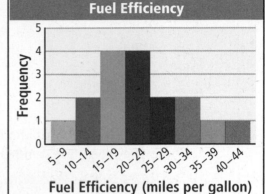

Fuel Efficiency

_____

_____

_____

_____

_____

2. Describe any clusters, gaps, deviations from the overall pattern, and peaks. State the mode. Draw a conclusion based on these patterns in the data.

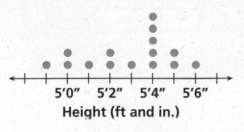

Softball Players' Heights

_____

_____

_____

3. **Math on the Spot** The data set and dot plot display the grades of Professor Burger's students. Describe the shape of the data distribution.

Data set	78	76	80	70	79	82	79	79	88
	74	78	82	79	75	80	83	84	76

Grades of Students

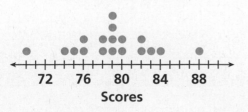

Test Prep

4. The dot plot shows the distribution of books read last summer by students at the Parks School. Which pattern in the data helps you conclude that most students read four books?

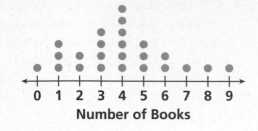

Number of Books

- Ⓐ a cluster
- Ⓑ a peak
- Ⓒ a gap
- Ⓓ no symmetry

5. In the survey from Problem 4, how many people were asked how many books they read last summer?

_____

6. The histogram shows the distribution of petal lengths for flowers in a botanical garden. What statement best summarizes the data distribution?

- Ⓐ Most petal lengths are clustered at 1–1.9 centimeters.
- Ⓑ There is a symmetry between the short and long petal lengths.
- Ⓒ The majority of petal lengths are greater than 3.9 centimeters.
- Ⓓ There is a gap between 2 and 3.4 centimeters.

Petal Length of Flowers

(histogram: Frequency vs Petal Length (cm), categories 0.5–0.9, 1–1.4, 1.5–1.9, 2.0–2.4, 2.5–2.9, 3.0–3.4, 3.5–3.9, 4.0–4.4, 4.5–4.9, 5.0–5.4, 5.5–5.9, 6.0–6.4, 6.5–6.9)

Spiral Review

7. Evaluate the expression for $x = 4$ and $y = 6$.

$4x - y + 15$

_____

8. Write an equation that models the data in the table.

x	1	2	3	4	5
y	7	14	21	28	35

9. Simplify the expression: $4a + 8 - 2a - 4 + 7b$.

_____

Name _____

Display Data in Box Plots

(I Can) draw and interpret box plots.

Spark Your Learning

Slavik is looking to buy new clothes for his best friend's weekend-long celebration. He wants to get the most for his money. He has gone to 7 stores and made a list of the prices for jeans, dress shirts, and sports jackets. He has $160 to spend. He needs to buy 1 of each item. What combination of items best fits his budget?

Store	Jeans	Dress shirt	Sports jacket
Addy's Fashions	$48	$38	$78
Garth's Warehouse	$39	$33	$69
Chester's Menswear	$29	$29	$54
L&P	$57	$45	$95
Dress to Impress	$68	$49	$89
Hallie's Superstore	$25	$20	$40
Kevin's Kicks and More	$33	$44	$85

x	y

 Turn and Talk Why might it be better for Slavik to buy clothes that cost more, instead of buying all of his clothes at Hallie's Superstore?

Build Understanding

A **box plot** is a graph that shows how data are distributed by using the median, quartiles, least value and greatest value.

Connect to Vocabulary

The **lower quartile** is the median of the lower half of the data.
The **upper quartile** is the median of the upper half of the data.

1 ▷ Consider the prices for sports jackets that Slavik found: $78, $69, $54, $95, $89, $40, $85. Find the median, the lower quartile, and the upper quartile of the prices.

A. Explain how to find the median, then find the median.

_____

_____

_____

_____

_____

B. The lower quartile is the median of the lower half of the data or data to the left of the median. What is the lower half of the data? What is the lower quartile?

_____

_____

C. The upper quartile is the median of the upper half of the data or data to the right of the median. What is the upper half of the data? What is the upper quartile?

_____

_____

D. You can do Parts A to C by using the following display. Fill in the boxes with the prices in order from least to greatest.

Least value   Median   Greatest value

Lower quartile   Upper quartile

E. So, the median is ☐, the lower quartile is ☐, and the upper quartile is ☐.

Turn and Talk How would this process change if the data set had 8 values?

© Houghton Mifflin Harcourt Publishing Company

Name _____

Step It Out

A box plot uses boxes to show how the values in a data set are distributed, or spread out. It shows the data set divided into quarters, based on the quartiles and median.

2 The heights in feet of 10 roller coasters are 76, 35, 60, 42.5, 81, 79, 60, 78, 42, and 100. Make a box plot of this data.

A. Find the median, the lower and upper quartiles, the least value, and the greatest value. Start by ordering the data.

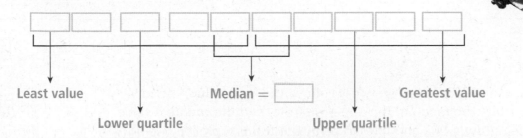

Least value

Lower quartile

Median = ☐

Upper quartile

Greatest value

B. Draw the box plot above the number line. Start by putting dots above the least value, the lower quartile, the median, the upper quartile, and the greatest value. Then draw the box connecting the quartiles.

Draw a box connecting the quartiles.

Roller Coaster Heights

Draw a vertical line through the median.

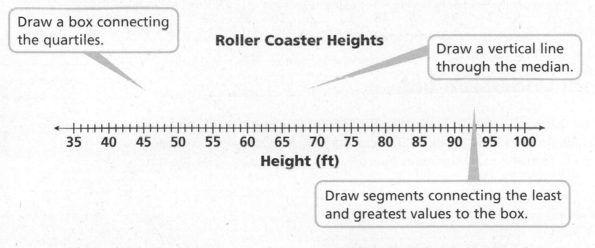

Height (ft)

Draw segments connecting the least and greatest values to the box.

C. If the heights 122 feet and 127 feet were added to the data, how would the box plot change? Draw a new box plot to show the changes.

_____

_____

Roller Coaster Heights

```
← |++++++++++++++++++++++++++++++++++++++++++++++++++++++++++++++++++++++++++| →
  35  40  45  50  55  60  65  70  75  80  85  90  95 100 105 110 115 120 125 130
```
Height (ft)

3 ▷ The daily high temperatures for Cleveland, Ohio, for 15 days in December are: 66, 57, 56, 41, 34, 32, 35, 31, 34, 28, 23, 34, 30, 37, and 39 degrees Fahrenheit. Make a box plot to display the data.

Cleveland, Ohio

A. Find the median, the lower and upper quartiles, the least value, and the greatest value. Start by ordering the data.

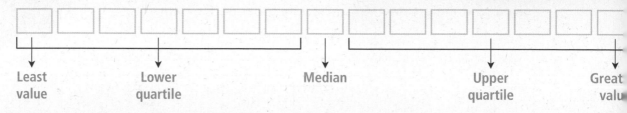

Least value   Lower quartile   Median   Upper quartile   Great valu

B. On the number line, draw dots above the least value, the lower quartile, the median, the upper quartile, and the greatest value. Then draw a box and lines to complete the box plot.

December Temperatures in Cleveland, OH

```
<--|||||||||||||||||||||||||||||||||||||||||||||||||||-->
   20   25   30   35   40   45   50   55   60   65   70
```
Temperature (°F)

Check Understanding

1. The prices of a quart of soy milk at different stores are as listed: $2.99, $3.29, $3.09, $3.79, $3.59, $3.39, $3.59, $3.89, $3.19, $3.49, $3.69, and $3.29. Find the median, lower quartile, and upper quartile of the data.

_____

_____

2. The daily low temperature in degrees Farenheit for a week in Denver, Colorado, were 37, 14, 23, 21, 27, 39, and 34. Make a box plot of the data.

```
<--|||||||||||||||||||||||||||||||||||||||||-->
   10   15   20   25   30   35   40
```
Temperature (°F)

3. The number of customers who entered a store each hour was recorded one Saturday: 5, 9, 15, 23, 27, 20, 16, 12, 14, and 18. Make a box plot of the data.

```
<--|||||||||||||||||||||||||||||||||||||||||||-->
   0    5    10   15   20   25   30
```
Number of Customers

On Your Own

4. **Geography** The heights (to the nearest foot) of coastal redwood trees over 340 feet tall are given below.

    359, 361, 363, 358, 368, 361, 366, 360,
    358, 359, 358, 366, 363, 364, 358, 363

    Giant sequoias in Kings Canyon National Park, CA

    A. Order the numbers from least to greatest.

    _____

    _____

    B. Find the median, lower quartile and upper quartile of the data set.

    Median: _____   Lower quartile: _____   Upper quartile: _____

5. The number of points a basketball player scored in each game this season so far are 16, 26, 23, 32, 19, 36, 18, 25, 30, 23, 47, 30, 16, 25, and 19.

    A. Find the median, lower quartile, and upper quartile of the data set.

    _____

    B. Make a box plot for the data set.

    ```
    ←+++++++++++++++||||||++++++++++++++++++++++++→
      0   5   10  15  20  25  30  35  40  45  50
    ```
    Points per Game

6. (MP) **Use Structure** Describe the box plot using the lowest value, the quartiles, median, and the greatest value. What does the width of the box say about the data?

    ```
    ←++++++++++++++++++++++++++++++++++++++++++++++++++→
    −40 −35 −30 −25 −20 −15 −10 −5   0   5  10  15  20  25  30  35  40
    ```
    Temperature (°F)

    _____

    _____

    _____

    _____

For Problems 7–8, find the median, lower quartile, and upper quartile of the data.

7. 27, 21, 24, 21, 26, 16, 24, 31, 0, 23

    _____

    _____

8. 4.9, 6.4, 3.6, 6.4, 4.6, 6.4, 4.2, 7.4

    _____

    _____

9. Andre likes to read a book in bed before he goes to sleep each night. For two weeks, he noted how many pages he read each night. He read 8, 12, 13, 6, 4, 19, 25, 7, 3, 18, 11, 15, 6, and 4 pages. Find the median, lower quartile and upper quartile of the data set. Then make a box plot for the data set.

_____

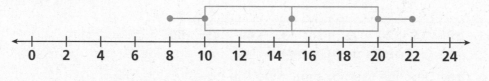

Number of Pages

10. (MP) **Attend to Precision** How can you find the median, lower quartile, and upper quartiles of a data set with 16 values? Explain.

_____

_____

_____

_____

11. **Open Ended** Describe a situation that could be represented by the box plot shown.

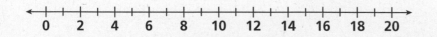

_____

_____

_____

12. Make a box plot for the data set.
11, 14, 13, 11, 13, 14, 9, 14, 20, 10, 5, 12, 17, 7, 9, 12

<----+----+----+----+----+----+----+----+----+----+---->
     0   2   4   6   8   10   12   14   16   18   20

⊟⊠
⊞⊡ **I'm in a Learning Mindset!**

What steps did I take to find the upper and lower quartiles in Problem 5?

_____

_____

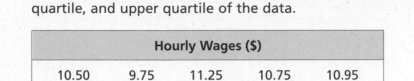
Display Data in Box Plots

1. Henry has taken a survey of the hourly wages of employees at a bakery. His results are shown. Find the median, lower quartile, and upper quartile of the data.

Hourly Wages ($)				
10.50	9.75	11.25	10.75	10.95
11.75	10.25	9.75	12.25	11.50

2. **STEM** A biologist is studying turkey vultures in Everglades National Park. Turkey vultures are one of the two vulture species native to the United States. The number of vultures the biologist spotted each day are 6, 9, 13, 8, 5, 12, 7, 18, 10, 14, 10 and 15. Make a box plot for the data set.

A turkey vulture has a wingspan of up to 6 feet long.

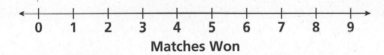

Number of Vultures Spotted Daily

3. **Math on the Spot** The number of matches won by a ping-pong team during each of the last 11 seasons are 7, 6, 8, 4, 0, 4, 8, 2, 3, 0, and 6. Use the data to make a box plot.

```
←—+——+——+——+——+——+——+——+——+——+——→
   0   1   2   3   4   5   6   7   8   9
              Matches Won
```

For Problems 4–5, find the median, lower quartile, and upper quartile of the data.

4. 5, 18, 7, 10, 14,
   9, 2, 11, 13, 25, 16

5. 35, 28, 17, 60, 41, 36,
   44, 55, 39, 50, 48, 19

_____

_____

_____

6. Make a box plot for the data set.
   25, 35, 5, 15, 85, 75, 65, 55, 45, 35, 25, 65, 75, 85

```
←—+——+——+——+——+——+——+——+——+——+——+→
   0  10  20  30  40  50  60  70  80  90 100
```

Test Prep

7. A softball team scored the following number of runs in the games they have played so far this year: 8, 5, 6, 9, 3, 1, 0, 4, 12, 14, 3, and 5. What are the lower and upper quartiles of this data?

(A) lower quartile = 1;
upper quartile = 8.5

(B) lower quartile = 1;
upper quartile = 12

(C) lower quartile = 3;
upper quartile = 8.5

(D) lower quartile = 3;
upper quartile = 12

8. Emile records the time he spends making dinner each night for 8 nights. What is the lower quartile of his data?

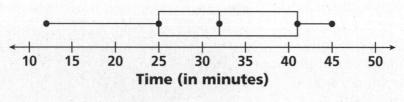

Time (in minutes)

---

9. What are the lowest and highest values on this box plot?

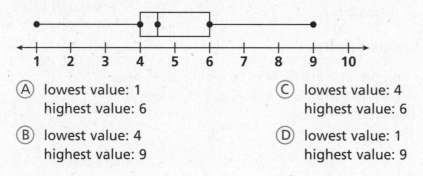

(A) lowest value: 1
highest value: 6

(B) lowest value: 4
highest value: 9

(C) lowest value: 4
highest value: 6

(D) lowest value: 1
highest value: 9

Spiral Review

10. Which of the following questions is a statistical question? Explain.
- How old is Mary's father?
- What time does school start at Lincoln Elementary?
- What color is the principal's desk at King Middle School?
- How did your classmates get to school today?

---

11. The number of hours Louisa worked each week over the summer were 19, 23, 18, 25, 16, 17, 21, 48, 20, and 13. Which measure of center best describes the data: mean, median, or mode?

© Houghton Mifflin Harcourt Publishing Company

Name _____

Find Mean Absolute Deviation

(I Can) find the mean absolute deviation of a data set.

Spark Your Learning

Gillian has taken 5 tests worth 100 points each. Her scores are shown. What score does she need on her next test to have an average of 90? Explain.

88   85   89   92   90

 Turn and Talk If the maximum score on any test is 100, is it possible for Gillian to raise her test average to 93 with her sixth test? Explain.

Build Understanding

1 Helen and Jeff record the time, in minutes, they spent practicing piano this week.

A. What is the mean for each set of data?

_____

_____

Piano Practice Chart (in minutes)

Helen	35	25	30	20	40
Jeff	45	55	5	15	30

B. The mean helps you to describe a set of data by identifying the center of the data. What do you notice about the means from Part A? Will they help you to distinguish between the two sets of data?

_____

_____

C. You can use another statistical measure to compare two data sets. The *mean absolute deviation*, or *MAD*, will help you to quantify how spread out each data set is and help you compare them. Begin by finding the distance from the mean to each data value for each data set. Use the means you found in Part A.

Connect to Vocabulary

Mean absolute deviation (MAD) is the mean of the distances between the data values and the mean of a data set.

Helen's times	35	25	30	20	40
Subtract lesser from greater	35 − ____	____ − 25	30 − ____	____ − 20	40 − ____
Distance from mean					

Jeff's times	45	55	5	15	30
Subtract lesser from greater	45 − ____	55 − ____	____ − 5	____ − 15	30 − ____
Distance from mean					

D. Find the mean absolute deviation for each data set by finding the mean of the distances in Part C.

E. Which data set has a greater mean absolute deviation? What does this tell you about the data?

_____

_____

502

Step It Out

2 ▸ Ana and Joe record their times running the 50-meter dash. Find the mean absolute deviation for each sprinter's times. Who is the more consistent sprinter?

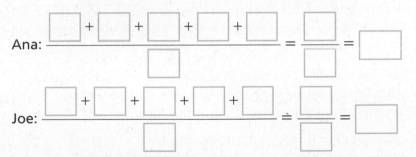

Joe's 50-meter times, in seconds: 7.3, 7.2, 7.0, 7.0, 7.0

Ana's 50-meter times, in seconds: 7.4, 7.2, 6.9, 7.3, 6.7

A. Find the mean time, in seconds, for each sprinter.

_____

_____

_____

B. Find the distance from the mean to each data value for each data set..

Ana's time	7.4	7.2	6.9	7.3	6.7
Subtract lesser from greater	7.4 − ___	7.2 − ___	___ − 6.9	7.3 − ___	___ − 6.7
Distance from mean					

Joe's time	7.3	7.2	7.0	7.0	7.0
Subtract lesser from greater	7.3 − ___	7.2 − ___	___ − 7.0	___ − 7.0	___ − 7.0
Distance from mean					

C. Find the mean absolute deviation for each data set.

Ana: $\dfrac{\boxed{} + \boxed{} + \boxed{} + \boxed{} + \boxed{}}{\boxed{}} = \dfrac{\boxed{}}{\boxed{}} = \boxed{}$

Joe: $\dfrac{\boxed{} + \boxed{} + \boxed{} + \boxed{} + \boxed{}}{\boxed{}} = \dfrac{\boxed{}}{\boxed{}} = \boxed{}$

D. Which data set has a greater mean absolute deviation? What does this tell you about the data? Who is the more consistent sprinter?

_____

_____

_____

> **Turn and Talk** In Part C, why was it necessary to find the mean of the distances? Explain.

The mean absolute deviation (MAD) tells you the average distance of data points from the mean. The data points whose distances to the mean are less than or equal to the MAD are *within the mean absolute deviation*.

3 Aaron surveyed the people in his apartment building to find out how many computers they owned. The mean of his data is 3 computers. The mean absolute deviation is 1.4. Find the values that fall within the MAD and the values that fall outside the MAD.

Number of Computers per Apartment									
Apt. A	Apt. B	Apt. C	Apt. D	Apt. E	Apt. F	Apt. G	Apt. H	Apt. I	Apt. J
1	5	3	2	7	3	2	1	2	4

A. Find the distance from the mean number of computers, 3, to each data value.

Value	1	5	3	2	7	3	2	1	2	4
Distance from mean										

B. If a data value's distance from the mean is less than or equal to the MAD of 1.4, then the value is *within the mean absolute deviation*. Which values from Aaron's survey fall within the mean absolute deviation?

_____

C. If a data value's distance from the mean is greater than the MAD of 1.4, then the value is *outside the mean absolute deviation*. Which values from Aaron's survey fall outside the mean absolute deviation?

_____

D. Another way to find the values that fall within the MAD is to add and subtract the MAD from the mean. This gives you the greatest and least values within the MAD. All values between the numbers will be within the MAD. For Aaron's data, find this range around the mean.

mean + MAD = 3 + ☐ = ☐   mean − MAD = 3 − ☐ = ☐

Values from _____ to _____ are within the MAD.

Check Understanding

For Problems 1–2, find the mean and the mean absolute deviation of each data set. Circle the data that falls within the mean absolute deviation.

1. 5 8 10 12 15 25 11 7 30 17   **2.** 9.5 10.5 11.25 10.75 9.25

Mean = _____   MAD = _____   Mean = _____   MAD = _____

On Your Own

3. The table shows the numbers of hours two friends spent swimming laps each week. Which data set is more spread out?

	Week 1	Week 2	Week 3	Week 4	Week 5
Serena	6	11	10	8	5
Lisa	2	9	12	6	11

A. Find the mean for each data set.

_____

_____

B. Find the distance from the mean for each data value.

Serena's hours	6	11	10	8	5
Subtract lesser from greater	____ − 6	11 − ____	10 − ____	8 − ____	____ − 5
Distance from mean					

Lisa's hours	2	9	12	6	11
Subtract lesser from greater	____ − 2	9 − ____	12 − ____	____ − 6	11 − ____
Distance from mean					

C. (MP) **Attend to Precision** Calculate the MAD for both sets of data.

_____

_____

D. The data set for _____ is more spread out, because the mean absolute deviation is _____.

4. Ramon is a pumpkin farmer. Each year he records the number of the pumpkins he sold for 5 weeks. The mean is 782 pumpkins and the mean absolute deviation is 52. List two possible values that are within the mean absolute deviation.

_____

5. A group of people is being trained to standardize the scoring of diving competitions. The same dive was judged by 10 different trainees at the beginning and at the end of their training. The results are shown.

Scores at Beginning of Training									
7.5	8	10	6	9.5	6.5	8	8.5	9	9.5

Scores at End of Training									
8	8.5	9	7.5	8.5	8	8	8.5	8.5	8.5

A. Calculate the mean absolute deviation for the scores at the beginning of training.

B. Calculate the mean absolute deviation for the scores at the end of training.

C. Did the trainees make progress in standardizing their scores? Explain.

6. (MP) **Reason** Two students had the following scores on five history tests. Which set of scores shows more variation? Use the MADs to justify your answer.

Student A: 82, 90, 87, 91, 97   Student B: 84, 91, 89, 95, 91

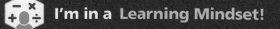 **I'm in a Learning Mindset!**

How did I apply prior knowledge to find the mean absolute value of a data set?

LESSON 16.3
**More Practice/
Homework**

ONLINE
😊Ed   **Video Tutorials and
Interactive Examples**

Find Mean Absolute Deviation

1. **STEM** A laboratory is studying brown anole lizards, which are native to Cuba and the Bahamas but are an invasive species in the southern U.S.A. from Florida to Texas. The length of 10 male lizards caught by researchers in Texas is shown in the table.

A brown anole lizard

Length of Brown Anole Lizards (cm)				
17.9	20.3	20.1	20.2	18
19.4	18	20.2	20	17.9

Calculate the mean of the lengths of the lizards. Then calculate the mean absolute deviation.

_____

2. **Math on the Spot** Professor Burger ran the 50-yard dash four times and recorded his times in seconds as 6.8, 5.9, 6.2, and 6.7. What is the mean absolute deviation of Professor Burger's times?

3. Several 2-pound bags of yellow onions at the supermarket are measured to see how much they actually weigh. Their weights are 2.1, 1.9, 2.3, 2.0, 2.4, 1.8, 2.1, and 2.2 pounds. What are the mean and the mean absolute deviation of the weights?

2.1 pounds

_____

_____

4. The mean of a data set is 9.4 and the mean absolute deviation is 1.2. List three data points that are within the MAD.

_____

5. The mean of a data set is 4.5 and the mean absolute deviation is 0.8. Find the range around the mean that describes the values which fall within the mean absolute deviation.

_____

Test Prep

6. The prices of muesli cereal at different stores are shown in the table.

Cost ($)					
5.09	3.79	4.80	4.39	3.88	4.99

   A. What is the mean price?

   _____

   B. What is the mean absolute deviation of the prices?

   _____

7. The mean of a set of data is 4.03 and the mean absolute deviation is 2.69. Which data points are within the mean absolute deviation? Select all that apply.

   Ⓐ 1.3   Ⓔ 5.8

   Ⓑ 2.3   Ⓕ 6.7

   Ⓒ 3.5   Ⓖ 7.5

   Ⓓ 4.6   Ⓗ 8.6

8. Which of the following is closest to the mean absolute deviation of the data set: 2.1, 3.5, 4.6, 5.8, 3.9, 4.2, 2.8?

   Ⓐ 0.89

   Ⓑ 1.6

   Ⓒ 3.84

   Ⓓ 3.9

Spiral Review

9. What is the volume of a rectangular prism that is $3\frac{1}{2}$ inches wide, $5\frac{1}{2}$ inches long, and 9 inches high?

   _____

10. Tyler collects data about how many animal companions (dogs, cats, birds, etc.) live at each house in his neighborhood. The number at each house is 1, 0, 2, 3, 2, 4, 12, 1, 2, and 6. Find the mean, median, and mode. What measure of center best describes the typical number of animal companions per household in his neighborhood? Explain.

   _____

   _____

   _____

Name _____

Explore Measures of Variability

(I Can) find and use range, IQR, and MAD to summarize a data set.

Step It Out

One measure of variability is the mean absolute deviation.

1 ▶ The ages, in years, of two teams of cyclists at the Tour de France are shown.

Team 1: 29, 32, 33, 26, 22, 32, 22, 23, 24

Team 2: 27, 33, 31, 29, 26, 30, 29, 33, 32

Connect to Vocabulary

A **measure of variability** is a single value used to describe how the values in a data set are spread out.

A. Remember that a measure of center of a data set summarizes its values with a single number. Find the mean age of each team.

Team 1 mean: ☐ years

Team 2 mean: ☐ years

B. Find the mean absolute deviation (MAD) for each team.

Team 1 MAD: ☐ years

Team 2 MAD: ☐ years

C. Compare the MAD of Team 1's ages to the MAD of Team 2's ages. What do the MADs tell you about the two teams' ages? Explain.

_____

_____

_____

_____

D. If the distance between a cyclist's age and the team's mean age is less than or equal to the MAD, that cyclist's age falls within the MAD. For Team 1, list the ages that fall within the MAD.

_____

 Turn and Talk What is the difference between a measure of center, such as the mean, and a measure of variability, such as the mean absolute deviation?

Other measures of variability are the *range* and *interquartile range*.

Connect to Vocabulary

Range is the difference between the greatest and least values in a data set.

The **interquartile range (IQR)** is the difference between the upper and lower quartiles in a data set.

 The prices for Wi-Fi routers at two stores are shown in the box plots. Find and compare the ranges and interquartile ranges of the prices at each store.

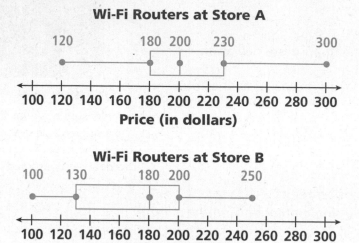

A Wi-Fi router

A. To find the range for each box plot, find the difference between the greatest and least values.

Store A

$300 - 120 =$ ☐

The range for store A is \$ ☐ .

Store B

$250 -$ ☐ $=$ ☐

The range for store B is \$ ☐ .

B. To find the IQR for each box plot, find the difference between the upper and lower quartiles.

Store A

$230 - 180 =$ ☐

The IQR for store A is \$ ☐ .

Store B

$200 -$ ☐ $=$ ☐

The IQR for store B is \$ ☐ .

C. Compare the range of the prices at each store and the interquartile range of the prices at each store.

Store A has a greater _____, but

Store B has a greater _____.

Turn and Talk Can you tell the exact price of any of the routers at the two stores? If so, explain how.

3 The number of visitors each day last week at a train exhibit hosted by a local museum were: 29, 3, 45, 33, 30, 38, and 25 visitors.

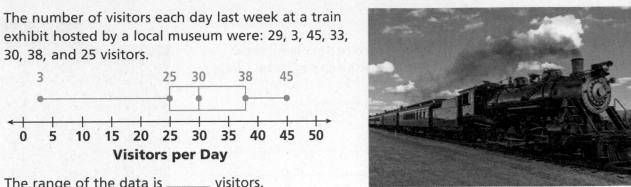

A. The range of the data is _____ visitors.

B. The interquartile range (IQR) of the data is _____ visitors.

C. Looking at the shape of the data, which measure of variability, range or IQR, best represents this data? Explain.

_____

_____

_____

Check Understanding

1. A new swimming club has just started. The ages, in years, of its members are 39, 27, 51, 42, 33, 73, 49, and 46. What is the mean absolute deviation of the ages of the club members? Which ages fall within the MAD?

_____

2. What are the range and interquartile range of the data set in the box plot? Why might the range be wide, but the IQR narrow?

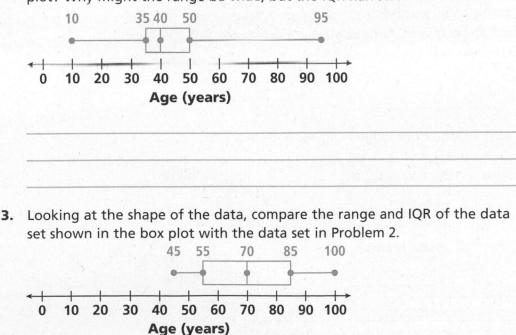

_____

_____

_____

3. Looking at the shape of the data, compare the range and IQR of the data set shown in the box plot with the data set in Problem 2.

45   55   70   85   100

0   10   20   30   40   50   60   70   80   90   100
Age (years)

_____

On Your Own

For Problems 4–7, use the box plot. It summarizes the number of goals per game for one team in a field hockey tournament.

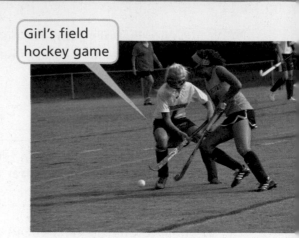

Girl's field hockey game

Field Hockey Scoring

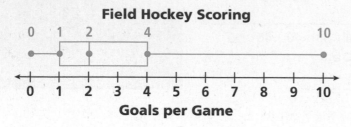

Goals per Game

4. The range of the data is _____ goals.

   The interquartile range of the data is _____ goals.

5. Looking at the shape of the data, which measure of variability, range or IQR, best represents this data? Explain.

   _____

   _____

   _____

6. Name one measure of variability for the data and give its value. What does this measure of variability tell you about the goals per game?

   _____

   _____

   _____

7. (MP) **Reason** Can you find the mean absolute deviation of the data set using the box plot? Explain.

   _____

   _____

Find the range and interquartile range (IQR) for each box plot.

8.

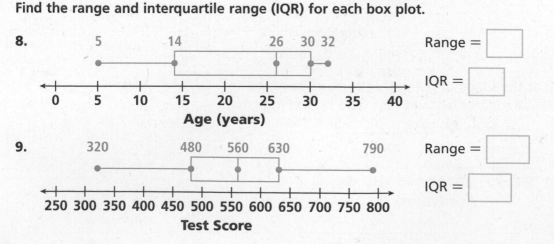

Range = ☐

IQR = ☐

9.

Range = ☐

IQR = ☐

10. The box plots summarize data about the ages of the people who live in two counties.

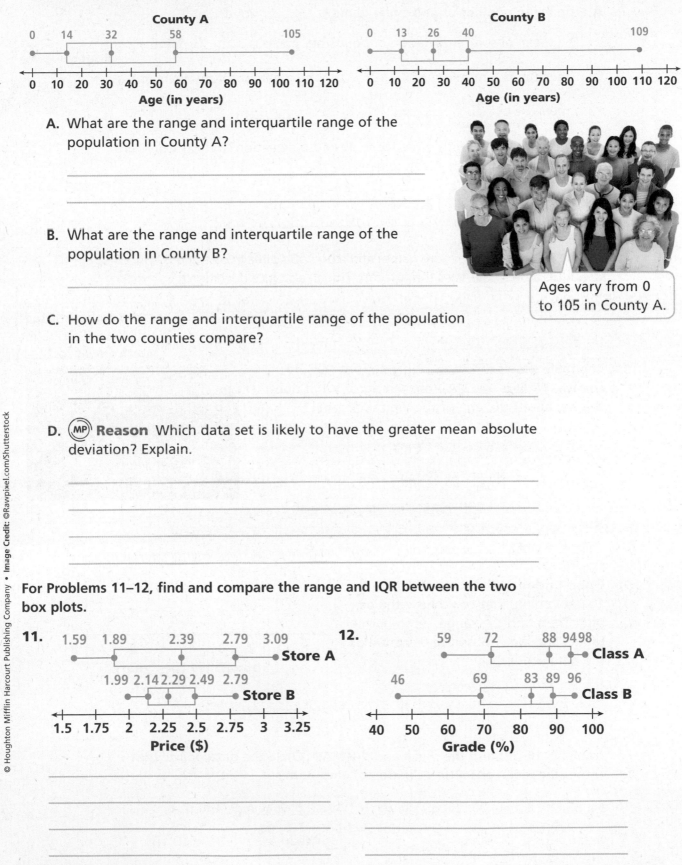

County A

0 14 32 58 105

0 10 20 30 40 50 60 70 80 90 100 110 120
Age (in years)

County B

0 13 26 40 109

0 10 20 30 40 50 60 70 80 90 100 110 120
Age (in years)

A. What are the range and interquartile range of the population in County A?

_____

_____

B. What are the range and interquartile range of the population in County B?

_____

Ages vary from 0 to 105 in County A.

C. How do the range and interquartile range of the population in the two counties compare?

_____

_____

D. (MP) **Reason** Which data set is likely to have the greater mean absolute deviation? Explain.

_____

_____

_____

_____

For Problems 11–12, find and compare the range and IQR between the two box plots.

11. 1.59 1.89 2.39 2.79 3.09
● **Store A**

1.99 2.14 2.29 2.49 2.79
● **Store B**

1.5 1.75 2 2.25 2.5 2.75 3 3.25
Price ($)

12. 59 72 88 94 98
● **Class A**

46 69 83 89 96
● **Class B**

40 50 60 70 80 90 100
Grade (%)

_____

_____

_____

13. The points scored by a youth basketball team in each of their games so far this season are 43, 30, 34, 26, 46, 47, 48, 37, 29, and 40.

A. The mean number of points per game is _____ points.

The mean absolute deviation of points per game is _____ points.

B. The mean is a measure of _____. The mean absolute deviation is

a measure of _____.

C. Which scores fall within the mean absolute deviation? Which scores are outside of the mean absolute deviation?

_____

_____

D. The team plays two more games and scores 15 points in one and 60 points in the other. How does this affect the mean absolute deviation?

_____

_____

> The members of the city council range in age from 34 to 72.

14. The table shows the ages of members of the city council. What is the MAD of their ages? What does this say about the age of the typical member?

Ages of Council Members (years)							
34	49	72	53	46	58	41	63

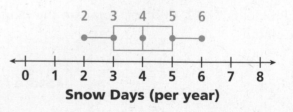

_____

_____

15. **Open Ended** Write a set of data with 10 data points that could have the box plot. Then find the range, interquartile range, and mean absolute deviation of the data set.

2 3 4 5 6

0 1 2 3 4 5 6 7 8
Snow Days (per year)

_____

_____

For Problems 16–17, find the mean and the MAD. Circle the data points that fall within the mean absolute deviation of each data set.

16. 45, 85, 70, 25, 80, 95, 75, 85, 90, 80   **17.** 3, 5, 2, 6, 4, 5, 4, 6, 2, 6

Mean = ☐   MAD = ☐   Mean = ☐   MAD = ☐

Explore Measures of Variability

1. Darren counts the number of devices that are plugged into
    the wall in each room of his house and records them in a list:
    1, 2, 0, 6, 5, 3, 4, 3. Which values fall outside the mean absolute
    deviation?

    _____

2. During a gray September, the amount of rainfall in
    millimeters per day over six days is 1.6, 1.3, 14.2, 11.7, 2.8,
    0.8. Find the range and interquartile range of the amount
    of rainfall. Which is the best measure of variability to
    describe this data? Explain.

    _____

    _____

    _____

    _____

PARK ELEMENTARY

14.2 millimeters rainfall today

3. The ages of people who competed in a road race last weekend are shown
    in the box plots. Interpret the differences in the range and the IQR for
    both groups to come to a conclusion about the runners.

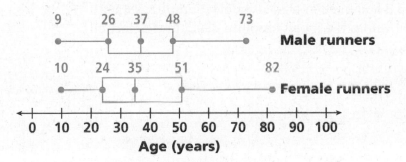

    _____

    _____

    _____

    _____

4. **Math on the Spot** Find the interquartile range for the data set. _____

    Data set: 11, 5, 16, 20, 31, 27, 9, 15, 26

5. Name a measure of variability and how it is calculated.

    _____

    _____

Test Prep

6. The box plot shows the numbers of grams of protein in several brands of protein bars. What are the range and interquartile range of the data?

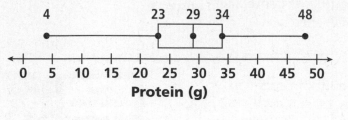

Range: _____ grams   Interquartile range: _____ grams

7. What are the range and interquartile range for the data set?

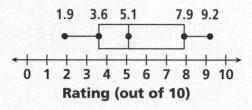

Range = _____   IQR = _____

8. A data set has a mean of 5.3 and a mean absolute deviation of 2. Which of the following points fall within the mean absolute deviation? Select all that apply.

Ⓐ 2   Ⓓ 6

Ⓑ 3   Ⓔ 7

Ⓒ 5   Ⓕ 9

Spiral Review

9. Juana and her friends have collected shells from the beach. The number of shells collected by each person is 4, 9, 7, 5, 12, 8, 6, 5. How many shells should each person get if they want to share them evenly?

_____

10. A college student made videos showing his dorm life each week for two months. The number of weekly videos he recorded were 3, 9, 5, 2, 14, 6, 7, 5, and 8. What is the median number of videos he recorded each week?

_____

Describe Distributions

(I Can) describe the shape, distribution, and range
of a data set, and use the shape, measures of center,
or variability to draw conclusions about the data.

Step It Out

1 ▸ A veterinarian monitored 18 pregnant cats. The
number of kittens per litter is summarized in the table.

Litter size	1	2	3	4	5	6	7	8	9
Frequency	1	3	4	3	3	2	1	0	1

A. What statistical question might these data have been collected to
answer?

_____

B. Since the table shows exact data values, a _____
is a good choice to display the data. Plot the data on
the dot plot.

C. Describe the shape, distribution, and range of the data.

_____

_____

Number of Kittens Born

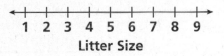

1 2 3 4 5 6 7 8 9
Litter Size

D. Find the mean, median, and mode of the data. Round to the tenths
place if necessary.

_____

_____

E. Looking at the shape of the data distribution in the dot plot, which of
these measures of center would best represent the data? Explain your
reasoning.

_____

_____

_____

 Turn and Talk Explain why the mode is the best measure of center for the data?

The table shows the distances some students at Valley Middle School live from a shopping mall.

Distance (miles)	0.01–2	2.01–4	4.01–6	6.01–8	8.01–10	10.01–12	12.01–14
Frequency (number of people)	2	4	6	9	8	5	1

A. What statistical question might these data have been collected to answer?

_____

_____

B. Complete the histogram.

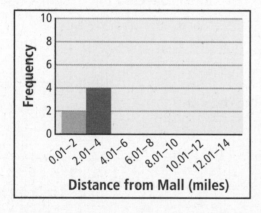

C. Describe the distribution of the data by identifying clusters, peaks, gaps, and symmetry.

_____

_____

_____

D. Draw one conclusion about the survey results based on a fact from Part C. Explain.

_____

_____

_____

 Turn and Talk Suppose there were 15 students missing from the sample. Seven students lived 2.01–4 miles from the mall, three students lived 4.01–5 miles from the mall, and five students lived 10.1–12 miles from the mall. How might your summary statement change? Explain.

3 ▶ The table shows the average daily temperature in degrees Fahrenheit during Maria's 8-day family vacation.

Day	1	2	3	4	5	6	7	8
Temperature (°F)	56	66	72	75	80	72	66	77

A. Since the table shows distinct data values that have a wide range of values and gaps between the data, a _____ is a good choice for the data display.

B. Complete the box plot.

C. The median of the data is _____.

The lower quartile is _____. The upper quartile is _____.

The interquartile range is _____ and the range is _____.

D. State one conclusion that can be drawn from the shape of the data and the range and one conclusion that can be drawn from the shape of the data and the interquartile range.

_____

_____

_____

_____

Check Understanding

Draw one conclusion from the data. State whether you used a measure of center or fact about the shape or spread of the data to draw your conclusion.

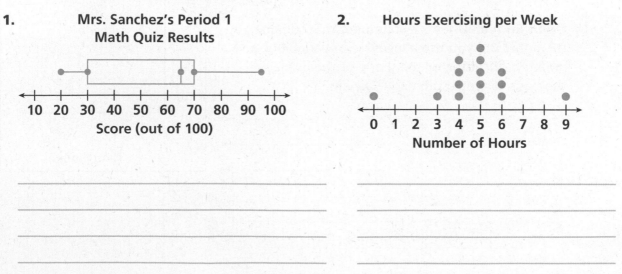

1.   Mrs. Sanchez's Period 1
        Math Quiz Results

Score (out of 100)

2.   Hours Exercising per Week

Number of Hours

_____   _____

_____   _____

_____   _____

_____   _____

On Your Own

3. The table shows the numbers of hours spent engaged in physical activity each week for 50 sixth-grade students.

Time (hours)	0–1.9	2–3.9	4–5.9	6–7.9	8–9.9	10–11.9
Frequency	3	6	8	10	13	10

A. What statistical question might these data have been collected to answer?

_____

_____

B. Why is a histogram a good way to show the data?

_____

_____

_____

C. Complete the histogram to display the data.

D. Describe the distribution of data based on your histogram.

_____

_____

_____

E. Open Ended What is a statement that summarizes the data? Did you use a measure of variability, a measure of center, or the shape of the display as the basis for your summary? Explain.

_____

_____

_____

_____

_____

_____

Time Spent in Physical Activity

Frequency (vertical axis): 0, 2, 4, 6, 8, 10, 12, 14

Time (hours) (horizontal axis): 0–1.9, 2–3.9, 4–5.9, 6–7.9, 8–9.9, 10–11.9

4. The table shown summarizes the numbers of computers and phones in the households of some families.

Number of devices	0	2	3	4	5	6	7	8	9	10	11	12
Frequency	2	1	3	5	4	7	5	5	6	5	4	3

A. What statistical question might these data have been collected to answer?

_____

_____

B. Why is a dot plot a good way to display the data?

_____

_____

_____

C. Draw a dot plot to display the data.

D. Describe the distribution of data based on your display in Part C.

_____

_____

_____

E. (MP) **Use Repeated Reasoning** Calculate the mean, median, and mode. Looking at the shape of the data distribution in the dot plot, which measure of center would best represent the data? Explain your reasoning. Round to the ones place if necessary.

_____

_____

_____

_____

5. The table summarizes the grade point averages (GPA's) for twelve students in the school band.

Student GPA's
4.0, 2.0, 2.33, 3.33, 3.67, 3.0, 2.67, 3.67, 3.0, 4.0, 2.67, 3.0

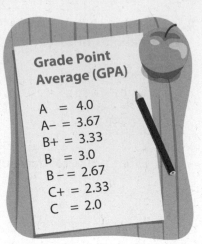

Grade Point Average (GPA)

A = 4.0
A– = 3.67
B+ = 3.33
B = 3.0
B– = 2.67
C+ = 2.33
C = 2.0

A. What statistical question might these data have been collected to answer?

_____

_____

B. Why might a box plot be a good way to display data about grade point averages?

_____

_____

_____

_____

C. (MP) **Attend to Precision** Draw a box plot to display the data.

D. Describe the distribution of data based on your dot plot.

_____

_____

_____

E. Write a statement using different measures of variability that could summarize the shape of the data. Explain.

_____

_____

_____

_____

_____

_____

LESSON 16.5
**More Practice/
Homework**

ONLINE
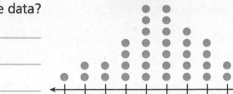
Video Tutorials and
Interactive Examples

Describe Distributions

1. The dot plot shows the results of 36 rolls of two number
cubes. Describe the distribution of the data. Which measure of
center—mean, median, and mode—best describes the data?

_____

_____

_____

_____

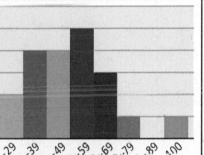

**Results from Rolling Two
Number Cubes**

2. The histogram shows the age distribution for members
in a small community band. Make a statement that
best summarizes the data. State the occurrence of
peaks or gaps.

_____

_____

_____

3. (MP) **Construct Arguments** The box plot shows the
annual snow depth for a ski resort over several winter
seasons. Make a statement that best summarizes the data.
Draw one conclusion from a measure of variability. Explain
how you reached your conclusion.

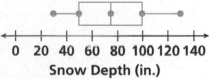

Snow Depth (in.)

_____

_____

_____

_____

_____

4. Find the mean, median, and mode of the data shown in
the dot plot. Which measure of center best describes the
distribution? Explain.

_____

_____

_____

Number of Books Read

Test Prep

5. The box plots show the distributions of wristbands sold at two stores for a local team. Which statement best describes the distributions for each store?

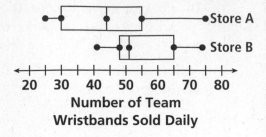

Number of Team Wristbands Sold Daily

   Ⓐ Store A has a greater IQR than store B.

   Ⓑ Store A has a greater median than store B.

   Ⓒ Store A has a greater mean than store B.

   Ⓓ Store A has a range that is less than that of store B.

6. The dot plot shows the results of rolling two number cubes 50 times. Select all the statements that are true.

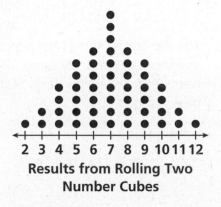

Results from Rolling Two Number Cubes

   Ⓐ Two is rolled fewer times than any other number.

   Ⓑ The median is 6.

   Ⓒ The mode is 7.

   Ⓓ The data are symmetric.

   Ⓔ The shape of the distribution suggests that most rolls are 8 or higher.

   Ⓕ 50% of the rolls are greater than 4 and less than 10.

   Ⓖ Most of the rolls are greater than 5 and less than 9.

Spiral Review

7. What is the opposite of −6?

_____

8. Write an equation that models the data in the table below.

x	1	2	3	4	5
y	5.5	11	16.5	22	27.5

_____

9. A parallelogram has a base length of 17 centimeters. The area is 85 square centimeters. What is the height of the parallelogram?

_____

Vocabulary

Choose the correct term from the Vocabulary box.

Vocabulary

box plot
lower quartile
upper quartile
mean absolute deviation (MAD)
measure of variability
range
interquartile range (IQR)

1. The mean distance of the data values from the mean of a data set is called the _____.

2. A _____ is a graph that shows the distribution of data using the median, quartiles, least value, and greatest value.

3. The median of the lower half of a data set is called the _____.

4. A single value used to describe how the values in a data set are spread out is a _____.

5. The _____ is the median of the upper half of a data set.

6. The difference between the greatest and least values in a data set is the _____.

7. The _____ is the difference between the upper and lower quartiles in a data set.

Concepts and Skills

8. **(MP) Use Tools** Eight chickens on a farm are weighed. Their weights are 5.8, 6.1, 5.5, 6.5, 7.1, 5.9, 6.2, and 5.7 pounds. What are the mean and the mean absolute deviation of the weights? State what strategy and tool you will use to answer the question, explain your choice, and then find the answer.

_____

_____

9. Look at the histogram. Which statement best describes the data shown in the graph?

   Ⓐ The data have a peak at 13 to 16.

   Ⓑ The data have an outlier at 0 and 10.

   Ⓒ The data have a cluster from 13 to 20.

   Ⓓ The data are approximately symmetric.

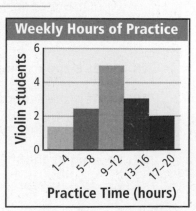

Weekly Hours of Practice

Violin students / Practice Time (hours)

For Problems 10–12, use the following information.

Eight stores at the mall sell the same style of pants. The prices of the pants are: $32, $35, $40, $38, $42, $37, $36, $44.

10. What is the median of the prices? _____

11. What is the lower quartile of the prices? _____

12. What is the upper quartile of the prices? _____

For Problems 13–16, use the dot plot. Round to the nearest tenth.

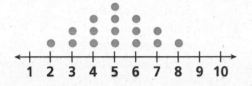

13. What is the mean of the data? _____

14. What is the mean absolute deviation of the data? _____

15. What is the median of the data? _____

16. Circle the data values that fall within the mean absolute deviation.

For Problems 17–21, use the box plot shown.

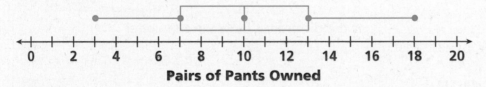

Pairs of Pants Owned

17. Which statements describe the distribution of the data in the box plot? Select all that apply.

Ⓐ Of the people surveyed, $\frac{1}{2}$ own 7 to 13 pairs of pants.

Ⓑ Of the people surveyed, $\frac{1}{4}$ own 3 to 10 pairs of pants.

Ⓒ Of the people surveyed, $\frac{1}{2}$ own 13 to 18 pairs of pants.

Ⓓ Of the people surveyed, $\frac{1}{4}$ own 3 to 7 pairs of pants.

Ⓔ Of the people surveyed, $\frac{3}{4}$ own 10 to 18 pairs of pants.

18. What is the median of the data? _____

19. What is the range of the data? _____

20. What is the interquartile range? _____

21. Looking at the shape of the data distribution, which measure of variability would best represent the data? _____

UNIT 1

MODULE 1, LESSON 1
On Your Own
7. −2 9. decreased by 1 minute; −1 11. −$15 and $15; They are the same distance from 0 but on different sides of 0 on a number line. 13. 4, −4 15.

2 °F is the opposite of −2 °F, −4 °F is the opposite of 4 °F, 7 °F is the opposite of 7 °F. 17. −1 19. 2
21.

More Practice/Homework
1A. 3 feet and −10 feet B. The opposite of 3 feet is −3 feet, which represents 3 feet below the surface of the water. The opposite of −10 feet is 10 feet, which represents 10 feet above the surface of the water.
3. −9 and 1 5. −2 7. 0 9. −8
11. D 13. 185 15. <

MODULE 1, LESSON 2
On Your Own
3B. −11 °F C. 0 °F D. −11 °F, −8 °F, −2 °F, 0 °F 5A. −30 feet
B. −30 < −25 or −25 > −30
C. The diver is at the surface of the water. 7. 6 > −1 or −1 < 6
9.

−4, −1, 0, 1

More Practice/Homework
1. Maria 3. Nathan 5. −2 < 1 or 1 > −2 7. D 9. > 11. 5 toys

MODULE 1, LESSON 3
On Your Own
3A. Andy B. 6 miles 5. −234 °F
7. 1 9. 0

More Practice/Homework
1. the change from Monday to Tuesday 3. the Wednesday night game 5. −2 7. −4 9. 3 11. |−8|
13. D 15. C 17. 228 19. 6.22

MODULE 2, LESSON 1
On Your Own
5A. −$10.40 represents a withdrawal; $8.50 represents a deposit. B. compare the absolute values to see which is larger 11. $\frac{6}{5}$ 13. $2\frac{3}{4}$

More Practice/Homework
3. 0; 5.5; 1.85; 2.2 7. 4.06, 4.06
9. −2.19, 2.19 11. −0.75, 0.75
13.

15. Point A: 3.25; Point B: 1.5; Point C: −1.5; Point D: 3.25
17. 11 > −9 or −9 < 11

MODULE 2, LESSON 2
On Your Own
3B. >; <; > 5B. The city park is to the left of the library; −0.52 < 0. C. The bookstore is to the right of the courthouse; |1.25| < |−1.5| D. The museum is to the left of the book store; 0.75 < 1.25. 7. > 9. < 11. <

More Practice/Homework
1A.

B. greater; right; less; left
3.

5. $-\frac{2}{5} > -0.5$; $-0.5 < -\frac{2}{5}$
7. A, B, D 9. −8 11. |−5| > |4| or |4| < |−5|

MODULE 2, LESSON 3
On Your Own
5A. 36 muffins B. 3; 2
7. Cameron 11. the seventh

graders 13. Springfield; Morristown 15. 8 17. 36
19. 45 21. 2 23. 13 25. 8 27. <
29. > 31. $-\frac{3}{8} > -\frac{5}{7}$ or $-\frac{5}{7} < -\frac{3}{8}$
33. $\frac{12}{16} > \frac{16}{24}$ or $\frac{16}{24} < \frac{12}{16}$
35. $-\frac{7}{10} < -\frac{5}{9}$ or $-\frac{5}{9} > -\frac{7}{10}$

More Practice/Homework
1. Martha; $\frac{5}{8} > \frac{6}{15}$ 3. after 30 minutes and after 60 minutes
5. 4 7. 6 9. $\frac{3}{21} < \frac{14}{21}$; $\frac{1}{7} < \frac{2}{3}$
11. $\frac{16}{24} > \frac{12}{24}$, $\frac{4}{6} > \frac{4}{8}$
13. $\frac{14}{21} < \frac{3}{9}$ 15. D
17. 91 minutes 19. −13 < −10 or −10 > −13 21. −18

MODULE 2, LESSON 4
On Your Own
3. $\frac{1}{3}$, 0.5, $\frac{4}{6}$, $\frac{4}{5}$ 5. $-\frac{4}{5}$, −0.5, $\frac{3}{10}$, 0.7
7. −2.1, $-\frac{9}{10}$, 0.7, $1\frac{2}{5}$

More Practice/Homework
1. −2.7°, −2.65°, −0.1°, 0.09°, 1.48°
3. 0.01, 0.07, 0.38, $\frac{5}{10}$, $\frac{12}{10}$
5. $-4\frac{1}{2}$, −4.22, 0.8, $\frac{4}{3}$, 8.4
7. $2\frac{17}{50}$, 2.19, −2.05, $-2\frac{8}{25}$
9. D 11. −9, 4, 7 13. 15, 7, and 3

MODULE 3, LESSON 1
On Your Own
3. 4 containers 5. 4 days
7. $\frac{11}{2}$ or $5\frac{1}{2}$ days 9. $\frac{4}{3}$ or $1\frac{1}{3}$ times
11. $12\frac{1}{3} \div \frac{1}{3}$; 37 birdhouses
13. 3 times

More Practice/Homework
1. 3 different exercises
3. $\frac{3}{4}$ of her walk 7. C 9. B
11. −5 > −6 or −6 < −5

MODULE 3, LESSON 2
On Your Own
7. 2 sections 9. 8 class periods
11. 5 whole batches

13. $\frac{3}{4}$ cup; $\frac{3}{16}$ cup 15. $\frac{16}{5}$
17. $\frac{1}{4}$ 19. $\frac{5}{4}$ or $1\frac{1}{4}$ 21. $\frac{8}{14}$ or $\frac{4}{7}$
23. $\frac{3}{12}$ or $\frac{1}{4}$ 25. $\frac{100}{120}$ or $\frac{5}{6}$
27. $\frac{112}{24}$ or $4\frac{2}{3}$

More Practice/Homework
1. 16 books 5. $\frac{8}{7}$ 7. $\frac{1}{12}$ 9. $\frac{9}{16}$
11. $\frac{18}{28}$ or $\frac{9}{14}$ 13. $\frac{120}{30}$ or 4
15. $\frac{300}{18}$ or $\frac{50}{3}$ 17. $\frac{176}{10}$ or $\frac{88}{5}$
19. C 21. B, D, E 23. $3\frac{1}{8}$

MODULE 3, LESSON 3
On Your Own
3. $1\frac{1}{4}$ hours 5. $6\frac{1}{5}$ feet
7. 7 pieces 9. $\frac{26}{15}$ or $1\frac{11}{15}$
11. $\frac{6}{19}$ 13. 26 tarts 15. 34 tiles
17. $\frac{37}{8} \times \frac{2}{5}$ 19. $\frac{27}{5} \times \frac{8}{15}$

More Practice/Homework
1. 4 pieces 3. $\frac{3}{10}$ pound
5. 18 days 7. $\frac{11}{12}$ 9. $\frac{20}{21}$
11. $\frac{7}{10}$ 13. A 15. C 17. $\frac{16}{15}$ or $1\frac{1}{15}$

MODULE 3, LESSON 4
On Your Own
9. 7 cans 11. $42\frac{1}{4}$ square inches
13. $5\frac{3}{5}$ feet 15. $6\frac{3}{4}$ pounds
17. 52 plants 19. $3\frac{1}{10}$ 21. 6
23. $3\frac{1}{11}$

More Practice/Homework
1. twenty-six $1\frac{1}{2}$-pound bags
3. $5\frac{2}{3}$ feet 5. $12\frac{1}{2}$ 7. $10\frac{1}{4}$ 9. $2\frac{2}{3}$
11. B, D 13. B 15. $\frac{1}{2}$ 17. $\frac{3}{10}$

MODULE 3, LESSON 5
On Your Own
7. $\frac{13}{24}$ 9. $31\frac{1}{2}$ miles per hour
11. $2\frac{3}{10}$ 13. $1\frac{23}{25}$ 15. 4 murals
17. $15\frac{1}{2}$ miles 19. 5 cones
21. $4\frac{21}{40}$ 23. $2\frac{3}{5}$ 27. $7\frac{3}{10}$ gallons
29. $17\frac{11}{14}$

More Practice/Homework
1. $5\frac{2}{5}$ hours 3. $\frac{19}{60}$

5. $1\frac{1}{2}$ pounds 7. $2\frac{13}{30}$ 9. $\frac{36}{37}$
11. $6\frac{1}{3}$ 13. C, E 15. A
17. 1.43

MODULE 4, LESSON 1
On Your Own
3. 1.21 miles 5. Add or subtract from right to left.
7B. 320 squares C. 3.2 or 3.20
9. 4.231 11. 0.429 13. Write a zero in the thousandths decimal place of the number with two decimal places to line up the decimal places. 15. no
17. 3.58 19. 0.908

More Practice/Homework
1. 9.05 hours 3. 1.49 5. 8.94 seconds 7. 0.014 9. 3.64
11. 0.423 13. 6.942 15. 4.71 seconds 17. $\frac{3}{10}$ 19. $-12 < -2$ or $-2 > -12$

MODULE 4, LESSON 2
On Your Own
3. 52.7 minutes 5A. 0.595 square mile B. 0.6 C. 0.357 square mile
7. 0.32

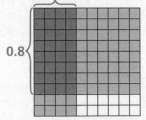

9. 40.29 11. If my product is a lot greater or a lot less than my estimate, I know I need to go back and check the total number of decimal places in the factors.
15. 95.12 17. 68.643

More Practice/Homework
1. 65.7 inches 3. no 5. $2.29
7. 0.1686 9. 9.398 11. 10.87294
13. 0.414 inch 15. C 17. 4 days

MODULE 4, LESSON 3
On Your Own
3A. 36 boxes B. 1 box with 80 shirts 5. 23 liters 7. no 9. 50; 44 11. 640; 581; 90 13. 34; 29; 251 15. 16 school buses
17. 14 offices 19. 15 21. 19
23. 96 R400

More Practice/Homework
1. 19 reams 3. about 7.6 American football fields tall
5. 58 teams 7. 25 R135 9. 17
11. 10 acres 13. $27 15. C
17. M and P

MODULE 4, LESSON 4
On Your Own
3. 9 members 5. 9 boxes 7. 5.8
9. 8.4 11. 32.6 13. 8.9 m
15. 57.8 miles per hour 17. $3.50 per pound 19. 15.4 gallons of gas 21. 5.6 23. 32.6

More Practice/Homework
1. 5 bookcases 3. 23.6-oz bottle
5. 7 miles per hour 7. 0.3 9. 12.6
11. 71 quarters 13. 3 bags
15. C, F 17. 238 boxes
19. 31.25 feet

MODULE 4, LESSON 5
On Your Own
5. $34.79 7. Gael did not line up the decimal points in the numbers. He actually harvested 84.75 pounds of potatoes.
9. 9 days 11. 0.525 centimeter
13. 0.5270 second 15. 47.4 ounces
17. 14.34 miles 19. 17.81
21. 7.15 23. 6.16

More Practice/Homework
1. $0.49 per ounce 3. 2 grams
5. 246.5 seconds 7. 7.6 cm
9. 9 homes 11. 26.1 hours 13. $\frac{8}{5}$
15. -86 meters

UNIT 2

MODULE 5, LESSON 1
On Your Own
3. 3:2, 3 to 2, or $\frac{3}{2}$ **5.** 36:12, 36 to 12, $\frac{36}{12}$ **7.** no

More Practice/Homework
1. For every 7 botia loaches, there are 20 African cichlids.
5. 2:50, 2 to 50, or $\frac{2}{50}$; yes **7.** C
9. 30:1, 30 to 1, or $\frac{30}{1}$
11. $221 **13.** 2

MODULE 5, LESSON 2
On Your Own
5A.

Bracelets	2	3	4
Beads	32	48	64

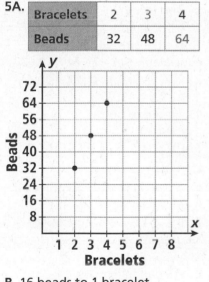

B. 16 beads to 1 bracelet
C. 160 beads
7. 45 minutes per practice; 135 min, or 2 h and 15 min
9A.

Time (s)	3	6	9
Spins	60	120	180

20 spins per second

B.
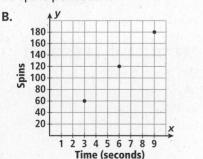

11. 9 grams per serving **13.** $80 per month

More Practice/Homework
1A. $30; $\frac{90}{3} = \frac{30}{1}$ or $\frac{120}{4} = \frac{30}{1}$ **B.** no
3.

Time (h)	Cost ($)
2	25
4	50
6	75
8	100

5. 28 oz per can **7A.** 30:1, or $\frac{30}{1}$, or 30 parts iron per part carbon
B. 9:1, or $\frac{9}{1}$, or 9 parts iron per part of all other elements
9. 311.55 **11.** 6 signs

MODULE 5, LESSON 3
On Your Own
3A.

Ratio for Each Runner	
Sprints	Laps
5	4
10	8
15	12
20	16

Ratio for Megan	
Sprints	Laps
11	8
22	16
33	24
44	32

B. Possible answer: The second row in table 1 and the first row in table 2 **C.** no **5.** Tim's paint mixture will be darker. **7.** no

More Practice/Homework
1A.
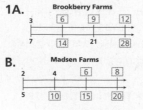

C. Brookberry Farms **3.** no
5. A, C, D **7.** yes **9.** $-10 < |-10|$ or $|-10| > -10$

MODULE 5, LESSON 4
On Your Own
3A. 14 inches of machine per inch of model **B.** 101.5 inches
5. It changes the rate of drainage to 8 gallons per minute. **7.** The movie pricing is less per person. **9.** 20 times
11. $4\frac{1}{2}$ inches wide **13.** 15 miles
15. 25 pumpkin bread loaves
17A. $\frac{1}{6}$ yard per minute
B. 3 yards **19A.** $7.25 per hour
B. $290.00 **21A.** $\frac{2}{5}$ inch per second **B.** 6 inches

More Practice/Homework
1. $7\frac{1}{2}$ hours **3.** 4-pack of light bulbs **5.** Franco's
7A. 86 heartbeats per min
B. 258 heartbeats **9A.** $0.07 per sq ft **B.** $105.00 **11.** 48-pack
13. $3\frac{1}{3}$ spools **15.** $22.23
17. the reef

MODULE 5, LESSON 5
On Your Own
5. 75 centimeters **7A.**

B. 44 **C.** $\frac{12}{21}$ **D.** $\frac{30}{70}$ **9A.** $\frac{5}{12}$ or 5 to 12 or 5:12 **B.** 72 hamburgers
11A. yes **B.** 35 free throws
13A. 1.5 centimeters
B. 36 centimeters

More Practice/Homework
1. $\frac{2}{3}$ or 2 to 3 or 2:3 **3.** $\frac{2}{2}$ or 2 to 2 or 2:2 **5.** yes **7.** 12 miles
9. D **11.** 49 questions **13.** 0.466 yard **15.** −4, 3

MODULE 6, LESSON 1
On Your Own
3. 120 residents; 40 residents; 80 residents

5.

Category	Angle Measure (degrees)	Time (minutes)
Music	210	35
News	60	10
Commercials	60	10
DJ talk	30	5

More Practice/Homework
1A. 1,800 calories;
B. carbohydrates: 180°; protein: 72°; fat: 108°
C.

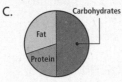

5A. $\frac{200}{500}$, or $\frac{2}{5}$ **B.** 144° **7.** $2\frac{1}{4}$ ounces

MODULE 6, LESSON 2
On Your Own
5. 5.6 kilometers **7.** yes
9. $\frac{63,360 \text{ inches}}{1 \text{ mile}}$ **11.** 36 **13.** 3,500
15. 6 **17.** Fiona **19.** 1.76 meters
21. 10 pints **23.** > **25.** >

More Practice/Homework
1. 12 quarts **3.** 20 quarts = 5 gallons **5.** 4 pounds **7.** 4,000 grams **9.** 64 oz > 60 oz **11.** 6 ft = 6 ft **13.** 1,200 mg > 950 mg
15. A, D, E **17.** B **19.** 15 songs for $15.00; $1 per song < $1.20 per song **21.** $4.25 per yard

MODULE 6, LESSON 3
On Your Own
3. Kathy does not have enough juice. **5.** 54.7 yards **7.** 5.5 pounds
9. 3.1 **11.** 80.5 **13.** 236.8
15. 500 kilometers is longer.
17. 68.3 miles per hour **19.** 5 feet 3 inches **21.** < **23.** > **25.** >

More Practice/Homework
1. yes **5.** 8.6 meters **7.** 254 centimeters > 250 centimeters; >
9. 3 miles < 3.1 miles; <
11. 5 liters > 4.7 liters; >
13. 10 feet, 4 meters, 200 inches, 600 centimeters **15.** $4.89 per kilogram **17.** Possible answer: 9 red marbles for every 6 blue marbles; 15 red marbles for every 10 blue marbles; 30 red marbles for every 20 blue marbles
19. 36.5 kilometers

MODULE 7, LESSON 1
On Your Own
9. more **13.** 95% **15.** 620%
17. 34% **19A.** 6.5 miles **B.** 25%
21. 14.29%

More Practice/Homework
1. 55% **3.** 36% **5.** 20% **7.** 33%
9A. $\frac{3}{4}$ **B.** 75% **11.** B **13.** 7
15. seven-twelfths, or $\frac{7}{12}$

MODULE 7, LESSON 2
On Your Own
7. 36 square feet **9.** $30
11. 11,388.8 **13.** 21 **15.** 603
17. $15 **19.** $24 **21.** 125
23. 10 **25.** 231

More Practice/Homework
1. 400 points **3.** 6.3 ounces **5.** 54
7. 9 **9.** 27 **11.** popcorn: 56 people; pretzels: 42 people; pizza: 14 people **13.** 56 marbles **15.** 20%
17. −12, −1, 0, 3 **19.** 0.019
21. 0.102 **23.** 325

MODULE 7, LESSON 3
On Your Own
5. 62.5% **7.** 20% giraffes; 80% zebras **9.** not reasonable
11. 12 **13.** 28.8 **15.** 100 **17.** 11
19. 90,000 gallons **21A.** 35 **B.** 196 students **C.** 0.35 **D.** 196

More Practice/Homework
1. 15 oysters **3.** $1.80

5. 96 points **7.** 40% **9.** 1,000
11. 20 **13.** B **15.** 48 people
17. 12 cats for every 16 dogs; 30 cats for every 40 dogs; 75 cats for every 100 dogs **19.** 5 feet

UNIT 3

MODULE 8, LESSON 1
On Your Own
5A. 9^5 **B.** $\left(\frac{1}{8}\right)^3$
7. $\frac{1}{3} \cdot \frac{1}{3} \cdot \frac{1}{3} \cdot \frac{1}{3} \cdot \frac{1}{3} \cdot \frac{1}{3} \cdot \frac{1}{3}$ **9A.** 3; 5
B. $3 \times 3 \times 3 \times 3 \times 3 = 3^5$

More Practice/Homework
1. 12; 12; 8 **3.** $3^8 = 3 \times 3 \times 3 \times 3 \times 3 \times 3 \times 3 \times 3$; $3^5 \times 3^3 = (3 \times 3 \times 3 \times 3 \times 3) \times (3 \times 3 \times 3)$; The two expressions are equivalent. **5.** $2 \cdot 2 \cdot 2 \cdot 2 \cdot 2 \cdot 2 \cdot 2 \cdot 2$ **7.** 8^5 **9.** B, C, D **11.** $4^5 = 4 \cdot 4 \cdot 4 \cdot 4$ **13.** 75%
15. 64-ounce bottle

MODULE 8, LESSON 2
On Your Own
5A. Possible answer: $2(2 + 1)$
B. Possible answer: $2(2 + 1 + 1)$
7. 9 **9.** 2 **11.** factors; product
13. $\frac{30}{5 + 7}$ **15.** $(12 \times 8) + 5$
17A. 2; 2^2; 11 · 2^3; 11 · 2^4
B. 176 dandelions **19.** 14 **21.** 15

More Practice/Homework
1A. Possible answer: $450 + 120$
B. Possible answer: $3(450 + 120)$
C. Possible answer: $3(450 + 120) + 380$ **D.** 2,090 inches
3. 50 hit targets **5.** 68 **7.** 9
9. 168 bandages; $5.04 **11.** 55; Square the 5. **13.** 216°

MODULE 8, LESSON 3
On Your Own
5A. above: x; below: $x − (21 + y)$
B. left: 25; right: $x − (25 + y)$
C. Larry **7.** $\frac{32}{b}$ or $32 \div b$ **9.** $\frac{1}{2}x$ or $x \cdot \frac{1}{2}$

More Practice/Homework
1. $75 + 10d$, or $10d + 75$
3. $\frac{5,000}{p}$ or $5,000 \div p$ 5. $\frac{10m}{7}$
7. variable: y; coefficient: 11; constant: 4.5 9. $20 + 0.25p$, or $0.25p + 20$ 11. $g - 8 - 9 - 4$, or $g - 21$ hours 13. 1.3 miles

MODULE 8, LESSON 4
On Your Own
7. 18 cubic inches 9. 150; 125
11. 3 13. 13.25 15. Bill is correct.
17. 14.3 pounds 19. 200 square centimeters 21. $8\frac{3}{4}$ 23. 16
25. 40 27. 138 29. 2 times
31. $\frac{1}{8}$ 33. 1,000 35. $\frac{1}{216}$

More Practice/Homework
1. 40 hours 3. 18 5. 24 7. 10.5
9. 37 11. 1 13. first row: $x = 3$; second row: $x = 5$; third row: $x = 4$ 15. 128 square feet
17. 3 neckties

MODULE 8, LESSON 5
On Your Own
3. Commutative; 2ℓ; $2w$; $2(\ell + w)$
5. Chris is correct. 7. Possible answer: $10(d + f)$ 9. $8x + 5$
11. $2x + 3$ 13. $3x^2 + 14$ 15. They are both equal to $24x + 18y$.
17. $2(5n + 9)$ 19. Commutative; Associative 21. not equivalent
23. Possible answer: $4(6 + x)$ and $24 + 4x$ 25. equivalent when $x = 3$, but not when $x = 0$ 27. $4x + xy$ 29. $8(3 + k)$ 31. $7g^3 + g^3h$
33. equivalent

More Practice/Homework
1. Possible answer: $2n - 1$
5. $2(\ell w + \ell h + wh)$
7. Commutative 9. not equivalent 11. 12; 12; do 13. B, D, E 15. Penny is taller. 17. 5^7

MODULE 9, LESSON 1
On Your Own
5. $3b = 27$; 9 blue marbles
7. $p + 20 = 85$; 65 pushups

9. Possible answer: An expression shows one value and an equation shows that two values are equal. 11. 5 13. 4 15. 3

More Practice/Homework
1. $23 = h - 12$; 35 members 7. is
9. is not 11. is not 13. $15p = 300$, or $\frac{300}{p} = 15$ 15. $67 - h = 5$, or $5 + h = 67$ 17. $9\ell = 72$; 8 inches
19. 75 square feet 21. 21 23. 3

MODULE 9, LESSON 2
On Your Own
5. $49 + b = 152.5$; 103.5 centimeters 7. $14.85 + c = 20$; \$5.15 9. 2 11. add; 75
13. subtract; 5.13 15. subtract; $\frac{3}{9}$
17. Possible answer: $56 + c = 200$; $c = 144$ 19. $1.27 + 3.74 = 5.01$; $q = 1.36$ 21. 3.35

More Practice/Homework
1. $s = 17$ 3. $x = 66$ 7. is 9. 55
11. 24 13. Add; 24 15. 23 miles
17. 4 pounds for \$1.40 is the lower rate. 19. 81 21. 1,000

MODULE 9, LESSON 3
On Your Own
3A. $2.4x = 33$ B. \$13.75
5B. 14 ounces 7. 2.5;

|---+---+---+---+---+---|
0   1   2   3   4   5

9. 15;

|---+---+---+---+---+---+---+---+---+---|
0 2 4 6 8 10 12 14 16 18 20
11. $\frac{x}{7} = 17.8$; 124.6 cm 13. $x = 19$
15. $x = 1\frac{1}{2}$

More Practice/Homework
1. $4p = 2.24$; $p = 0.56$;

|---+---+---+---+---+---|
0.3 0.4 0.5 0.6 0.7 0.8
3. $x = 14$ 5. 15 times 7. 48 9. 7
11. \$6.25 13. A 15. 18
17. $\frac{1}{4}, \frac{4}{12}, \frac{3}{8}, \frac{4}{9}, \frac{3}{6}$

MODULE 9, LESSON 4
On Your Own
3. 56 pretzel sticks 5A. $x + 300 + 280 = 990$ B. 410 ft 7A. $4\frac{2}{3}$ inches

B. $13\frac{5}{6}$ inches 11. $3.29 + x = 15.56$; $x = \$12.27$

More Practice/Homework
1. $x + 44 = 90$; $x = 46$
3. $x + 40 = 64$; 24 blue floor tiles
5. $\frac{x}{5} = 4$; 20 baseball cards
7. $120 = 15w$; 8 inches
9. 72.7 cm 11.

|---+---+---+---+---+---+---+---|
−8 −6 −4 −2 0 2 4 6

MODULE 9, LESSON 5
On Your Own
5. $s > 761$ 7A. $t > -9$ B. no
9. Possible answer: $4 \leq y$
11A. $h \leq 400$ B. yes 13. $x \geq 100$
15.

|---+---+---+---+---+---+---|
0 5 10 15 20 25 30

More Practice/Homework
1B. $d \geq 500$
C.

|---+---+---+---+---+---|
300 400 500 600 700 800

3.

|---+---+---+---+---+---+---|
−10 −8 −6 −4 −2 0 2 4

5A. 23, 41, 50, 25 B. $n \geq 23$ 7. C
9. $-5 > x$: third graph; $x < -3$: first graph; $x > 4$, fourth graph; $x > 2$: second graph 11. 20:43, or $\frac{20}{43}$ 13. 0.775 15. 0.775

MODULE 10, LESSON 1
On Your Own
3A. C; s
B.

Shirts	Cost
3	\$9.75
5	\$16.25
8	\$26.00
10	\$32.50

C.
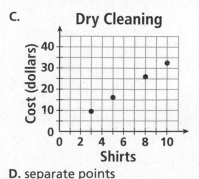
Dry Cleaning

D. separate points

Selected Answers

5A.

Tina	Gary
2.5	7
5.5	10
7	11.5
10	14.5

B. 2.5; 7; 5.5; 10; 7; 11.5; 10; 14.5

C.

Sibling Ages

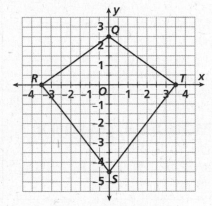

D. straight line **7.** $d = 57t$

More Practice/Homework
1. $C = 3p$ **3.** $m = 11n$
5. $y = x + 8$
7.

s	p
5	30
12	72
3.5	21
9	54

9. $m = 540h$ **11.** $y < 3$

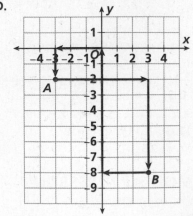

MODULE 10, LESSON 2
On Your Own
3A. $e = 12.25h$ **B.** $238.88
5. $y = \frac{5}{2}x$ **7.** $y = x + 4.5$
9. $c = 9.75t$ **13.** $w = s - 1,392$;
9,866 steps **15.** $d = 250 - f$

More Practice/Homework
1. $y = \frac{1}{9}f$ **3.** $3x = 126$
5. $F = H - 35$ **7.** $c = 2.49p$
9. $a = 135c$ **11A.** $s = m + 28.75$
B. $49.75 **13.** $t = 30 - s$; t is the
dependent variable **15.** 20%
17. the 5-pound bag

MODULE 10, LESSON 3
On Your Own
3. $d = 24g$ **5.** $C = 45.25n$
7A. $C = 25n + 35$ **B.**

n	1	2	3	4
C	60	85	110	135

C. after 5 months **9.** $y = x - 2$

More Practice/Homework
1A. $T = 4n$ **B.** $500 **3.** $y = 7.5x$
5. $y = x + 11.2$ **7B.** $y = 7x$ **9.** A
11. 3.5

UNIT 4

MODULE 11, LESSON 1
On Your Own
5. S: (0, −4.5); T: (3.5, 0)

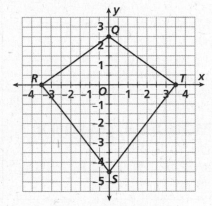

7. Quadrant II **9.** Quadrant III
11A. (−3, −2); Quadrant III
B. (3, −8); Quadrant IV **C.** Move
3 units left and 8 units up.
D.

More Practice/Homework
1. I; II; III; IV; rectangle

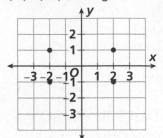

3. 4; 1; 0; 0; 0; −3 **5.** B, D, F
7. Point A: (1.5, −1.75); Point B:
(−1.75, 0.75); Point C: $\left(1\frac{1}{2}, 2\frac{1}{4}\right)$;
Point D: (0.75, −1); Point E: (2, 1);
Point F: (−2.25, 2), Point G: $\left(-1\frac{3}{4}, -2\right)$ **9.** $x \geq 42$

MODULE 11, LESSON 2
On Your Own
3. polygon; heptagon
5. Point (3, 2) or Point (1, 5)
7A.

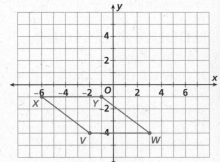

B. (−1, −1) **C.** 5 units; 5 units
D. Each side measures 5 units
9. polygon and octagon

More Practice/Homework
1. Not a polygon **3B.** Point (6, 3),
Point (0, 3),or Point (−12, −1)
5. Point (−2, 1) or Point (1, −1)
7. A, B, D, E **9.** 32 times

MODULE 11, LESSON 3
On Your Own
5. Possible answers: P and R, R
and T, P and T, U and Q, Q and
S, U and S **7.** 4 units; yes **9.** no
11A. 40 units **B.** 320 miles
13. 4 units; I subtract because the
points are in the same quadrant.

More Practice/Homework
1A. 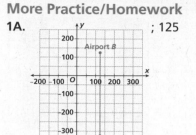 ; 125

B. 325 units, or 6,500 miles
C. 125 units, or 2,500 miles **D.**
9,000 miles **3.** 7 units **5.** 14 units;
I added the absolute values of
the x-coordinates of D and E.
7. 2.9 **9.** B
11.

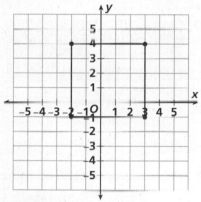

a square

MODULE 11, LESSON 4
On Your Own
3A. 10; 6; 60 **B.** 30 heads of
lettuce **C.** 2; 5; 10 **D.** 80 carrots
5. About 417 parallelograms
7A. 32 units **B.** 48 square units
C. yes; 12 equal-sized pieces
11. 48 square units

More Practice/Homework
1A. 9 square units **B.** 36 square
units **C.** 4 **3.** 18 units **5.** 4 units
7. 29 units **9.** C **11.** Quadrant III
13. $67 - c = 11$

MODULE 12, LESSON 1
On Your Own
5. 8,100 square feet **7.** 51 square
centimeters **9.** Possible answer:
$\ell = 5$ m, $w = 7$ m; or $\ell = 7$ m,

$w = 5$ m **11.** $8\frac{1}{8}$ in² **13.** 15.6 cm²
17. 12 cm

More Practice/Homework
1. $b = 8$ feet, $h = 4$ feet
3. 39.6 cm² **5.** 28.5 in² **7.** 54 cm²
9. 24 square meters **11.** $84\frac{1}{2}$ in²
13. $9.1 - 6.4 = 2.7$, $2.7 \neq 2.61$.
The correct solution is 9.01.

MODULE 12, LESSON 2
On Your Own
3. 20 in² **5.** 12 inches **7.** 256
square feet **9.** 39 m² **11.** 28 ft²
13. Prisha **15.** Possible answer:
$b = 7$ ft, $h = 2$ ft **17.** 8 ft
19. 9 in.

More Practice/Homework
1. about 15.6 square feet
3. 8 centimeters **5.** 9 ft²
7. 8.75 in² **9.** D **11.** 21 feet
13. $\frac{1}{8}$

MODULE 12, LESSON 3
On Your Own
5. 525 square feet **7.** 50 square
centimeters **9.** 10 meters **11.** 10 in²
13. 42 cm² **17.** 6 cm **19.** 7.5 m

More Practice/Homework
1. 1,575 square meters **3.** no
5. 12 feet **7.** 30 m² **9.** 13.5 cm²
11. 12.8 square meters **13.** A, B, C
15. $1.25 per song

MODULE 12, LESSON 4
On Your Own
3. 128 ft² **7.** 26 ft² **11.** 370 square
feet **13.** 26 m² **17.** 75 cm²
19. 64 cm²

More Practice/Homework
1. 2,112 square feet **3.** 6 cases of
flooring **5.** B, C, E **7.** $A = 8 \times 2 +$
$(8 \times 2) \div 2$, or $A = 8 \times 3$ **9.** 0.8

MODULE 13, LESSON 1
On Your Own
3A. no **B.** yes **C.** no
5. rectangular prism; 72 m²
7. square pyramid; 56 ft²

More Practice/Homework
1.

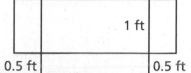

5 square feet **3.** cube; 24 cm²
5. first net: third figure; second
net: first figure; third net:
second figure **7.** 20 square
meters **9.** $t = 0.5m + 15$

m	t
5	$17.50
10	$20.00
15	$22.50
20	$25.00

MODULE 13, LESSON 2
On Your Own
3. $\frac{1}{2}$ yd³ **5.** 343 cm³ **7.** 1,710 ft³

More Practice/Homework
1. $4\frac{5}{36}$ ft³ **3.** $10,462\frac{1}{2}$ in³
5. $24,806\frac{1}{4}$ in³ **7.** 2.25 m³ **9.** $\frac{1}{30}$ ft³
11. $45.99

MODULE 13, LESSON 3
On Your Own
3. 27 in³ **5A.** $179\frac{13}{25}$ cubic inches
7A. Find the area of one face of
the cube, then multiply by the
number of faces, 6. **B.** 100 in²
C. 10 inches × 10 inches ×
10 inches **D.** 1,000 in³

More Practice/Homework
1. 512 in³ **3.** 6.5 meters
5. 8 inches **7.** A **9.** 743.75 in³
11. 6

UNIT 5

MODULE 14, LESSON 1
On Your Own
3. The second question is a statistical question, the first question is not. **5.** 2; meters and hundreds of years; 6

More Practice/Homework
1. How many days are there in March? **5.** number of players, average score per game, and average age; players, points, and years; 18 **7.** B **9.** 343 cm³

MODULE 14, LESSON 2
On Your Own
3A. 7.0 millimeters **B.** 8.0 millimeters **C.** 7.7 millimeters
5A. 11 games **B.** 4 games **C.** 6
D. $\frac{11}{16}$ = 68.75% **7A.** 20 students
B. 25% **C.** $\frac{9}{20}$ **D.** 104 pages

More Practice/Homework
1A.

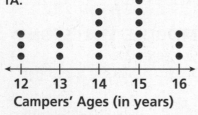

B. 15 years old **C.** 20 observations
D. 45% **3.** B **5.** 9 inches **7.** 304

MODULE 14, LESSON 3
On Your Own
3A.

Interval	Frequency
10–14	1
15–19	3
20–24	4
25–29	2

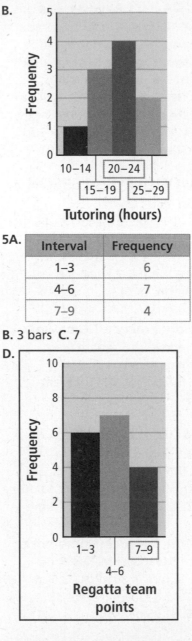

B.

Tutoring (hours)

5A.

Interval	Frequency
1–3	6
4–6	7
7–9	4

B. 3 bars **C.** 7

D.

Regatta team points

E. The frequencies, in order, are 8, 7, 5; no

7A.

Deliveries	Frequency
31–35	4
36–40	2
41–45	1
46–50	3
51–55	4

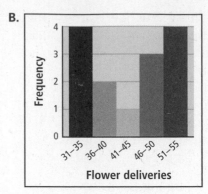

B.

Flower deliveries

C. The histogram bars will double in height.

More Practice/Homework
1A. 11, 12, 13, 15, 16, 17, 18, 18, 20, 21, 22, 23, 23, 24, 24, 25, 26, 28, 29

B.

Number of Loaves Sold (per hour)	Frequency
11–15	4
16–20	5
21–25	7
26–30	3

C.

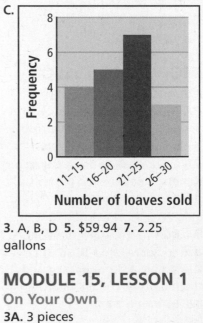

Number of loaves sold

3. A, B, D **5.** $59.94 **7.** 2.25 gallons

MODULE 15, LESSON 1
On Your Own
3A. 3 pieces

B. | ||| | ||| | ||| | ||| | ||| |

More Practice/Homework
1A. 7 crabs **B.** Possible answer: Move 2 crabs from the person with 9 crabs to the person with 5 crabs, and then move 1 crab from the person with 8 crabs to the person with 6 crabs so that all four people have 7 crabs.
3. Possible answers: 20 stacks of 1, 1 stack of 20, 10 stacks of 2, 2 stacks of 10, 5 stacks of 4, and 4 stacks of 5 **5.** B, C, D **7.** 4
9. 9 pounds

MODULE 15, LESSON 2
On Your Own
3B. 26.4 °F **C.** 23.5 °F **D.** 21 °F
5. the mean

More Practice/Homework
1A. 7 days **B.** 61 grams
C. 60 grams **D.** 60 grams
E. median and mode **3.** mean: 4; median: 2.5; mode: 2 **5.** 2.1; 1.4; 0.5 **7.** 68; 58; 0 **9.** D
11. 119.6 cm²

MODULE 15, LESSON 3
On Your Own
3A. Mean: 143 kg, Median: 156.5 kg, Mode: 160 kg **B.** 44 kg
C. Without the outlier, the mean increases to about 157 kg, the median increases to 157 kg, and the mode stays the same at 160 kg. **D.** Possible answer: the median; The mode is higher than every other weight. The mean is affected by the outlier.
5A. $45 **C.** The mean, median, and mode are all $40.
D. Possible answer: Since all of the measures are the same, they all represent the data well.

More Practice/Homework
1B. 70 feet; 72 feet; 80 feet
C. Without the outlier, the mean height increases to about 74 feet,

and the median height to 73.5 feet. The mode stays the same.
D. Possible answer: the median; Even though it changes without the outlier, it is right around most of the data values. Only one piece of data is around the mode.
3. The median best represents the data, because it is closest to the largest group of weekly telephone times. **5.** The median best represents the data. **7.** The mean is 56, the median is 55, and there is no mode. **9.** $y = 2x$

MODULE 16, LESSON 1
On Your Own
3. Possible answer: The majority of students study for at least 8 hours each week.
5. cluster from 10.2 to 10.4 seconds; gap between 10.7 and 11 seconds; peak at 10.4 seconds

More Practice/Homework
1. Possible answer: The distribution is not symmetric. There is a set of twin peaks at 15–19 mpg and 20–24 mpg, which suggests that the fuel efficiency for a typical automobile falls within the range of 15–24 miles per gallon. **3.** The data are symmetric around 79. **5.** 24 people **7.** 25 **9.** $2a + 7b + 4$

MODULE 16, LESSON 2
On Your Own
5A. median = 25; lower quartile = 19; upper quartile = 30
B.
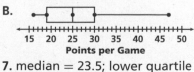
7. median = 23.5; lower quartile = 21; upper quartile = 26

9. median = 9.5; lower quartile = 6; upper quartile = 15
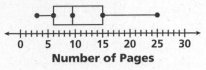

More Practice/Homework
1. median: $10.85; lower quartile: $10.25; upper quartile: $11.50
3.

```
 •———————————————•
    |——————|——————|
 +-+-+-+-+-+-+-+-+-+
 0 1 2 3 4 5 6 7 8 9
```

5. median = 40; lower quartile = 31.5; upper quartile = 49 **7.** C
9. D. **11.** median

MODULE 16, LESSON 3
On Your Own
3A. The mean for Serena's times is 8 hours. The mean for Lisa's times is 8 hours. **B.** Subtract (Serena): 8; 8; 8; 8; 8; Distance (Serena): 2; 3; 2; 0; 3; Subtract (Lisa): 8; 8; 8; 8; 8; Distance (Lisa): 6; 1; 4; 2; 3 **C.** Serena's MAD is 2 hours. Lisa's MAD is 3.2 hours.
D. Lisa; greater **5A.** 1.05
B. 0.34 **C.** yes

More Practice/Homework
1. Mean: 19.2 cm; MAD: 1 cm
3. mean = 2.1 pounds; MAD = 0.15 pounds **5.** 3.7 to 5.3 **7.** B, C, D, E, F **9.** 173.25 cubic inches

MODULE 16, LESSON 4
On Your Own
5. the IQR **7.** no **9.** 470, 150
11. Store A range is $1.50, IQR is $0.90; Store B range is $0.80, IQR is $0.35; The range and IQR are less at Store B. **13A.** 38; 6.8
B. center; variability **C.** Within: 43, 34, 37, and 40 points; Outside: 30, 26, 46, 47, 48, 29 points **17.** 4.3; 1.3

More Practice/Homework

1. 1, 0, 6, and 5 devices
3. The range of ages and the interquartile range in ages are greater for female runners than male runners in this road race, so there is more variability in the ages of the female runners. **5.** Possible answer: range; Subtract the least value from the greatest value in the data set. **7.** 7.3; 4.3
9. 7 shells

MODULE 16, LESSON 5

On Your Own

3A. How many hours do you participate in physical activity each week? **B.** Possible answer: The data are presented as frequencies of values in equal intervals.

C.

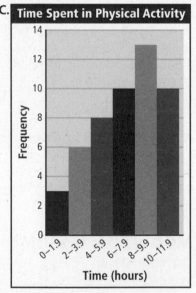

Time Spent in Physical Activity

D. Possible answer: The data are not symmetrical and there are no outliers. The data have a peak at 8–9.9 hours.

5A. What was your grade point average? **B.** Possible answer: It might be useful to break down data about grades into quarters and to see the median right away. This shows where the grades fall for each quarter of the students.

C.

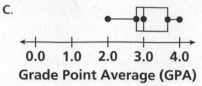

Grade Point Average (GPA)

D. Possible answer: The interquartile range is 1.0 and the range is 2.0. The median is 3.0. A quarter of the GPA's are 2.67 and less, a quarter are 3.67 or more.

E. Possible answer: Of the students sampled, 50% have a GPA 2.67–3.67 (which is a B–) and 75% of students are above 2.67 (which is a B–). The least and greatest grade point averages are 2.0 (C) and 4.0 (A).

More Practice/Homework

1. The distribution is approximately symmetric. The mean, median, and mode all describe the data well, as they are all close to one another (6–7). **3.** Possible answer: The snow depths over the course of many winters range from 30 inches to 130 inches. 50% of the time, the snow depth was 50–100 inches. **5.** A **7.** 6 **9.** 5 cm

Interactive Glossary

As you learn about each new term, add notes, drawings, or sentences in the space next to the definition. Doing so will help you remember what each term means.

Pronunciation Key

ă	add, map	g	go, log	n	nice, tin	p	pit, stop	û(r)	burn, term
ā	ace, rate	h	hope, hate	ng	ring, song	r	run, poor		
â(r)	care, air	hw	which	ŏ	odd, hot	s	see, pass	yoo	fuse, few
ä	palm, father	ĭ	it, give	ō	open, so	sh	sure, rush	v	vain, eve
b	bat, rub	ī	ice, write	ô	taught, jaw	t	talk, sit	w	win, away
ch	check, catch	îr	tier	ôr	order	th	thin, both	y	yet, yearn
d	dog, rod	j	joy, ledge	oi	oil, boy	th	this, bathe	z	zest, muse
ĕ	end, pet	k	cool, take	ou	pout, now	ŭ	up, done		
ē	equal, tree	l	look, rule	oo	took, full	oo	pull, book	zh	vision, pleasure
f	fit, half	m	move, seem	oo	pool, food	oor	cure		

ə the schwa, an unstressed vowel representing the sound spelled *a* in *above*, *e* in *sicken*, *i* in *possible*, *o* in *melon*, *u* in *circus*

Other symbols:
- separates words into syllables
′ indicates stress on a syllable

A

My Vocabulary Summary

absolute value [ăb′sə-loot′ văl′yoo] The distance of a number from zero on a number line; shown by | |

valor absoluto Distancia a la que está un número de 0 en una recta numérica. El símbolo del valor absoluto es | |

Addition Property of Equality [ə-dĭsh′ən prŏp′ər-tē ŭv ĭ-kwŏl′ĭ-tē] States that you can add the same number to both sides of an equation, and the expression remains equal

propiedad de igualdad de la suma Propiedad que establece que se puede sumar el mismo número a ambos lados de una ecuación y la expresión permanece igual

algebraic expression [ăl′jə-brā′ĭk ĭk-sprĕsh′ən] An expression that contains at least one variable

expresión algebraica Expresión que contiene al menos una variable

My Vocabulary Summary

angle [ăng′gəl] A figure formed by two rays with a common endpoint called the vertex

ángulo Figura formada por dos rayos con un extremo común llamado vértice

area [âr′e-ə] The number of square units needed to cover a given surface

área El número de unidades cuadradas que se necesitan para cubrir una superficie dada

Associative Property of Addition [ə-sō′shə-tĭv prŏp′ər-tē üv ə-dĭsh′ən] The property that states that for three or more numbers, their sum is always the same, regardless of their grouping

Propiedad asociativa de la suma Propiedad que establece que agrupar tres o más números en cualquier orden siempre da como resultado la misma suma

Associative Property of Multiplication [ə-sō′shə-tĭv prŏp′ər-tē üv mŭl′tə-plĭ-kā′shən] The property that states that for three or more numbers, their product is always the same, regardless of their grouping

Propiedad asociativa de la multiplicación Propiedad que establece que agrupar tres o más números en cualquier orden siempre da como resultado el mismo producto

average [ăv′ər-ĭj] The sum of the items in a set of data divided by the number of items in the set; also called *mean*

promedio La suma de los elementos de un conjunto de datos dividida entre el número de elementos del conjunto. También se le llama *media*

Interactive Glossary

axes [ăk′sēz′] The two perpendicular lines of a coordinate plane that intersect at the origin (singular: axis)

ejes Las dos rectas numéricas perpendiculares del plano cartesiano que se intersecan en el origen

B

bar graph [bär grăf] A graph that uses vertical or horizontal bars to display data

gráfica de barras Gráfica en la que se usan barras verticales u horizontales para presentar datos

base (in numeration) [bās] When a number is raised to a power, the number that is used as a factor is the base

base (en numeración) Cuando un número es elevado a una potencia, el número que se usa como factor es la base

base (of a three-dimensional figure) [bās] A face of a three-dimensional figure by which the figure is measured or classified

base (de un figura tridimensional) La cara de una figura tridimensional, a partir de la cual se mide o se clasifica la figura

base (of a trapezoid) [bās] Either of two parallel sides of a trapezoid.

base (de un trapecio) Cualquiera de los dos lados paralelos de un trapecio.

base (of a triangle) [bās] Any side of a triangle

base (de un triángulo) Cualquiera lado de un triángulo.

My Vocabulary Summary

box plot [bŏks plŏt] A graph that shows how data are distributed by using the median, quartiles, least value, and greatest value; also called a box-and-whisker plot

gráfica de caja Gráfica para demostrar la distribución de datos utilizando la mediana, los cuartiles y los valores menos y más grande; también llamado gráfica de mediana y rango

break (graph) [brāk (grăf)] A zigzag on a horizontal or vertical scale of a graph that indicates that some of the numbers on the scale have been omitted

discontinuidad (gráfica) Zig-zag en la escala horizontal o vertical de una gráfica que indica la omisión de algunos de los números de la escala

C

center (of a circle) [sĕn'tər] The point inside a circle that is the same distance from all the points on the circle

centro (de un círculo) Punto interior de un círculo que se encuentra a la misma distancia de todos los puntos de la circunferencia

circle [sûr'kəl] The set of all points in a plane that are the same distance from a given point called the center

círculo Conjunto de todos los puntos en un plano que se encuentran a la misma distancia de un punto dado llamado centro

circle graph [sûr'kəl grăf] A graph that uses sections of a circle to compare parts to the whole and parts to other parts

gráfica circular Gráfica que usa secciones de un círculo para comparar partes con el todo y con otras partes

Interactive Glossary

coefficient [kō′ə-físh′ənt] The number that is multiplied by the variable in an algebraic expression

coeficiente Número que se multiplica por la variable en una expresión algebraica

---

common denominator [kŏm′ən dĭ-nŏm′ə-nā′tər] A denominator that is the same in two or more fractions

denominador común Denominador que es común a dos o más fracciones

---

common factor [kŏm′ən făk′tər] A number that is a factor of two or more numbers

factor común Número que es factor de dos o más números

---

common multiple [kŏm′ən mŭl′tə-pəl] A number that is a multiple of each of two or more numbers

múltiplo común Un número que es múltiplo de dos o más números

---

Commutative Property of Addition [kŏm′yə-tā′tĭv prŏp′ər-tē ŭv ə-dĭsh′ən] The property that states that two or more numbers can be added in any order without changing the sum

Propiedad conmutativa de la suma Propiedad que establece que sumar dos o más números en cualquier orden no altera la suma

---

My Vocabulary Summary

Commutative Property of Multiplication [kŏm´yə-tā´tĭv prŏp´ər-tē ŭv mŭl´tə-plĭ-kā´shən] The property that states that two or more numbers can be multiplied in any order without changing the product

Propiedad conmutativa de la multiplicación Propiedad que establece que multiplicar dos o más números en cualquier orden no altera el producto

composite figure [kəm-pŏz´ĭt fĭg´yər] A figure made up of simple geometric shapes

figura compuesta Figura formada por otras figuras geométricas simples

constant [kŏn´stənt] A number whose value does not change

constante Valor que no cambia

constraint [kən-strănt´] A restriction of the value(s) of a quantity or variable

restricción Una restricción del valor de una cantidad o variable

conversion factor [kən-vûr´zhən făk´tər] A rate in which two quantities are equal but use different units

factor de conversión Tasa a la cual dos cantidades son iguales, pero que usan diferentes unidades

Interactive Glossary

coordinate grid [kō-ôr′dn-ĭt grĭd] A grid formed by the intersection of horizontal and vertical lines that is used to locate points

cuadrícula de coordenadas Cuadrícula formada por la intersección de líneas horizontales y líneas verticales que se usan por localizar puntos

coordinate plane [kō-ôr′dn-ĭt plān] A plane formed by the intersection of a horizontal number line called the *x*-axis and a vertical number line called the *y*-axis

plano cartesiano Plano formado por la intersección de una recta numérica horizontal llamada eje *x* y otra vertical llamada eje *y*

coordinates [kō-ôr′dn-ĭts] The numbers of an ordered pair that locate a point on a coordinate graph

coordenadas Los números de un par ordenado que ubican un punto en una gráfica de coordenadas

customary system [kŭs′tə-měr′ē sĭs′təm] The measurement system often used in the United States

sistema usual de medidas El sistema de medidas que se usa comúnmente en Estados Unidos

D

data [dā′tə] A set of information collected about people or things, often to draw conclusions about them

datos Conjunto de información recopilada sobre personas u objetos, generalmente con el objetivo de obtener conclusiones acerca de los mismos

© Houghton Mifflin Harcourt Publishing Company

My Vocabulary Summary

degree [dǐ-grē'] The unit of measure for angles or temperature

grado Unidad de medida para ángulos y temperaturas

denominator [dǐ-nǒm'ə-nā'tər] The bottom number of a fraction that tells how many equal parts are in the whole

denominador Número de abajo en una fracción que indica en cuántas partes iguales se divide el entero

dependent variable [dǐ-pěn'dənt vâr'ē-ə-bəl] The output of a function; a variable whose value depends on the value of the input, or independent variable

variable dependiente Salida de una función; variable cuyo valor depende del valor de la entrada, o variable independiente

diagonal [di-ag'ə-nəl] A line segment that connects two nonadjacent vertices of a polygon

diagonal Segmento de recta que une dos vértices no adyacentes de un polígono

diameter [di-am'i-tər] A line segment that passes through the center of a circle and has endpoints on the circle, or the length of that segment

diámetro Segmento de recta que pasa por el centro de un círculo y tiene sus extremos en la circunferencia, o bien la longitud de ese segmento

My Vocabulary Summary

dimension [dĭ-měn′shən] The length, width, or height of a figure

dimensión Longitud, ancho o altura de una figura

Distributive Property [dĭ-strĭb′yə-tĭv prŏp′ər-tē] The property that states if you multiply a sum by a number, you will get the same result if you multiply each addend by that number and then add the products

Propiedad distributiva Propiedad que establece que, si multiplicas una suma por un número, obtendrás el mismo resultado que si multiplicas cada sumando por ese número y luego sumas los productos

dividend [dĭv′ĭ-děnd′] The number to be divided in a division problem

dividendo Número que se divide en un problema de división

Division Property of Equality [dĭ-vĭzh′ən prŏp′ər-tē ŭv ĭ-kwŏl′ĭ-tē] States that you can divide both sides of an equation by the same number, excluding zero, and the expressions remain equal

propiedad de igualdad de la división Propiedad que establece que se pueden dividir ambos lados de una ecuación entre el mismo número, excluyendo al cero, y la expresión permanece igual

divisor [dĭ-vī′zər] The number you are dividing by in a division problem

divisor El número entre el que se divide en un problema de división

dot plot [dŏt plŏt] A visual display in which each piece of data is represented by a dot above a number line

diagrama de puntos Despliegue visual en que cada dato se representa con un punto sobre una recta numérica

E

equation [ĭ-kwā′zhən] A mathematical sentence that shows that two expressions are equivalent

ecuación Enunciado matemático que indica que dos expresiones son equivalentes

equivalent [ĭ-kwĭv′ə-lənt] Having the same value

equivalentes Que tienen el mismo valor

equivalent expression [ĭ-kwĭv′ə-lənt ĭk-sprĕsh′ən] Equivalent expressions have the same value for all values of the variables

expresión equivalente Las expresiones equivalentes tienen el mismo valor para todos los valores de las variables

equivalent fractions [ĭ-kwĭv′ə-lənt frăk′shəns] Fractions that name the same amount or part

fracciones equivalentes Fracciones que representan la misma cantidad o parte

Interactive Glossary

equivalent ratios [ĭ-kwĭv′ə-lənt rā′shōs] Ratios that name the same comparison

razones equivalentes Razones que representan la misma comparación

evaluate [ĭ-văl′yoo-āt′] To find the value of a numerical or algebraic expression

evaluar Hallar el valor de una expresión numérica o algebraica

exponent [ĭk-spō′nənt] The number that indicates how many times the base is used as a factor

exponente Número que indica cuántas veces se usa la base como factor

exponential form [ĕk′spə-nĕn′shəl fôrm] A number is in exponential form when it is written with a base and an exponent

forma exponencial Cuando se escribe un número con una base y un exponente, está en forma exponencial

expression [ĭk-sprĕsh′ən] A mathematical phrase that contains operations, numbers, and/or variables

expresión Enunciado matemático que contiene operaciones, números y/o variables

F

factor [făk′tər] A number that is multiplied by another number to get a product

factor Número que se multiplica por otro para hallar un producto

formula [fôr′myə-lə] A rule showing relationships among quantities

fórmula Regla que muestra relaciones entre cantidades

frequency [frē′kwən-sē] The number of times a data value occurs

frecuencia Cantidad de veces que aparece el valor en un conjunto de datos

frequency table [frē′kwən-sē tā′bəl] A table that lists items together according to the number of times, or frequency, that the items occur

tabla de frecuencia Una tabla en la que se organizan los datos de acuerdo con el número de veces que aparece cada valor (o la frecuencia)

G

greatest common factor (GCF) [grā′tĭst kŏm′ən făk′tər] The largest common factor of two or more given numbers

máximo común divisor (MCD) El mayor de los factores comunes compartidos por dos o más números dados

Interactive Glossary

H

height [hīt] In a triangle or trapezoid, the perpendicular distance from the base to the opposite vertex or side. In a prism, the perpendicular distance between the bases

altura En un triángulo o trapecio, la distancia perpendicular desde la base de la figura al vértice o lado opuesto. En un prisma, la distancia perpendicular entre las bases

hexagon [hĕk′sə-gŏn′] A six-sided polygon

hexágono Polígono de seis lados

histogram [hĭs′tə-grăm′] A bar graph whose bars represent the frequency of numeric data within equal intervals

histograma Gráfica de barras que muestra la frecuencia de los datos en intervalos iguales

I

independent variable [ĭn′dĭ-pĕn′dənt vâr′ē-ə-bəl] The input of a function; a variable whose value determines the value of the output, or dependent variable

variable independiente Entrada de una función; variable cuyo valor determina el valor de la salida, o variable dependiente

inequality [ĭn′ ĭ-kwŏl′ĭ-tē] A mathematical sentence that shows the relationship between quantities that are not equal

desigualdad Enunciado matemático que muestra una relación entre cantidades que no son iguales

integer [ĭn'tĭ-jər] An element of the set of whole numbers and their opposites

entero Un miembro del conjunto de los números cabales y sus opuestos

---

interquartile range (IQR) [ĭn'tûr-kwôr'tīl' rănj] The difference of the third (upper) and first (lower) quartiles in a data set, representing the middle half of the data

rango intercuartil (RIC) Diferencia entre el tercer cuartil (superior) y el primer cuartil (inferior) de un conjunto de datos, que representa la mitad central de los datos

---

interval [ĭn'tər-vəl] The space between marked values on a number line or the scale of a graph

intervalo El espacio entre los valores marcados en una recta numérica o en la escala de una gráfica

---

inverse operations [ĭn-vûrs' ŏp'ə-rā'shəns] Operations that undo each other: addition and subtraction, or multiplication and division

operaciones inversas Operaciones que se cancelan mutuamente: suma y resta, o multiplicación y división

---

isosceles triangle [ī-sŏs'ə-lēz' trī'ăng'gəl] A triangle with at least two congruent sides

triángulo isósceles Triángulo que tiene al menos dos lados congruentes

L

least common denominator (LCD) [lēst kŏm'ən dĭ-nŏm'ə-nā'tər] The least common multiple of two or more denominators

mínimo común denominador (m.c.d.) El mínimo común múltiplo de dos o más denominadores

least common multiple (LCM) [lēst kŏm'ən mŭl'tə-pəl] The smallest number, other than zero, that is a multiple of two or more given numbers

mínimo común múltiplo (m.c.m.) El menor de los múltiplos (distinto de cero) de dos o más números

like fractions [līk frăk'shəns] Fractions that have the same denominator

fracciones semejantes Fracciones que tienen el mismo denominador

like terms [līk tûrms] Terms with the same variables raised to the same exponents

términos semejantes Términos con las mismas variables elevadas a los mismos exponentes

line plot [līn plŏt] A number line with marks or dots that show frequency

diagrama de puntos Recta numérica con marcas o puntos que indican la frecuencia

lower quartile [ou′ər kwôr′tĭl′] The median of the lower half of the data

cuartil inferior Mediana de la mitad inferior de los datos

M

mean [mēn] The sum of the items in a set of data divided by the number of items in the set; also called *average*

media La suma de todos los elementos de un conjunto de datos dividida entre el número de elementos del conjunto

mean absolute deviation (MAD) [mēn ăb′sə-loot′ dē′vē-ā′shən] Mean of the distances between the data values and the mean of the data set

desviación absoluta media (DAM) Distancias medias entre los valores de datos y la media del conjunto de datos

measure of center [mĕzh′ər ŭv sĕn′tər] A measure used to describe the middle of a data set. Also called measure of central tendency

medida central Medida que se usa para describir el centro de un conjunto de datos; la media, la mediana y la moda son medidas centrales. También se conocen como medidas de tendencia central

measure of variability [mĕzh′ər ŭv vâr′ē-ə-bĭl′ĭ-tē] A single value used to describe how the values in a data set are spread out

medida de variabilidad Valor que se usa para describir cómo se dispersan los valores en un conjunto de datos

Interactive Glossary

median [mē′dē-ən] The middle number or the mean (average) of the two middle numbers in an ordered set of data

mediana El número intermedio o la media (el promedio) de los dos números intermedios en un conjunto ordenado de datos

metric system [mĕt′rĭk sĭs′təm] A decimal system of weights and measures that is used universally in science and commonly throughout the world

sistema métrico Sistema decimal de pesos y medidas empleado universalmente en las ciencias y por lo general en todo el mundo

mode [mōd] The number or numbers that occur most frequently in a set of data; when all numbers occur with the same frequency, we say there is no mode

moda Número o números más frecuentes en un conjunto de datos; si todos los números aparecen con la misma frecuencia, no hay moda

Multiplication Property of Equality [mŭl′tə-plĭ-kā′shən prŏp′ər-tē ŭv ĭ-kwŏl′ĭ-tē] States that you can multiply both sides of an equation by the same number, and the expressions remain equal

propiedad de igualdad de la multiplicación Propiedad que establece que se pueden multiplicar ambos lados de una ecuación por el mismo número y la expresión permanece igual

multiplicative inverse [mŭl′tə-plĭ-kā′tĭv ĭn-vûrs′] One of two numbers whose product is 1

inverso multiplicativo Uno de dos números cuyo producto es igual a 1

N

negative number [něg′ə-tĭv nŭm′bər] A number less than zero

número negativo Número menor que cero

---

net [nĕt] An arrangement of two-dimensional figures that can be folded to form a solid figure

plantilla Arreglo de figuras bidimensionales que se doblan para formar un cuerpo geométrico

---

numerator [noō′mə-rɑ′tər] The top number of a fraction that tells how many parts of a whole are being considered

numerador El número de arriba de una fracción; indica cuántas partes de un entero se consideran

---

numerical expression [noō-mĕr′ĭ-kəl ĭk-sprĕsh′ən] An expression that contains only numbers and operations

expresión numérica Expresión que incluye sólo números y operaciones

O

opposites [ŏp′ə-zĭt] Two numbers are opposites if, on a number line, they are the same distance from 0 but on different sides

opuestos Dos números que están a la misma distancia de cero en una recta numérica

Interactive Glossary

order of operations [ôr′dər ŭv ŏp′ə-rā′shəns] A rule for evaluating expressions: first perform the operations in parentheses, then compute powers and roots, then perform all multiplication and division from left to right, and then perform all addition and subtraction from left to right

orden de las operaciones Regla para evaluar expresiones: primero se resuelven las operaciones entre paréntesis, luego se hallan las potencias y raíces, después todas las multiplicaciones y divisiones de izquierda a derecha y, por último, todas las sumas y restas de izquierda a derecha

ordered pair [ôr′dərd pâr] A pair of numbers that can be used to locate a point on a coordinate plane

par ordenado Par de números que sirven para ubicar un punto en un plano cartesiano

origin [ôr′ə-jĭn] The point where the *x*-axis and *y*-axis intersect on the coordinate plane; (0, 0)

origen Punto de intersección entre el eje *x* y el eje *y* en un plano cartesiano: (0, 0)

outlier [out′lī′ər] A value much greater or much less than the others in a data set

valor atípico Un valor mucho mayor o menor que los demás valores de un conjunto de datos

P

parallelogram [păr′ə-lĕl′ə-grăm′] A quadrilateral with two pairs of parallel sides

paralelogramo Cuadrilátero con dos pares de lados paralelos

My Vocabulary Summary

pentagon [pĕn′tə-gŏn′] A five-sided polygon

pentágono Polígono de cinco lados

---

percent [pər-sĕnt′] A ratio comparing a number to 100

porcentaje Razón que compara un número con el número 100

---

perimeter [pə-rĭm′ĭ-tər] The distance around a polygon

perímetro Distancia alrededor de un polígono

---

point [point] An exact location that has no size

punto Ubicación exacta que no tiene ningún tamaño

---

polygon [pŏl′ē-gŏn′] A closed plane figure formed by three or more line segments that intersect only at their endpoints

polígono Figura plana cerrada, formada por tres o más segmentos de recta que se intersecan sólo en sus extremos

Interactive Glossary

positive number [pŏz′ĭ-tĭv nŭm′bər] A number greater than zero

número positivo Número mayor que cero

pyramid [pĭr′ə-mĭd] A three-dimensional figure with a polygon base and triangular sides that all meet at a common vertex

pirámide Figura tridimensional cuya base es un polígono; tiene caras triangulares que se juntan en un vértice común

Q

quadrant [kwŏd′rənt] The x- and y-axes divide the coordinate plane into four regions. Each region is called a quadrant

cuadrante El eje x y el eje y dividen el plano cartesiano en cuatro regiones. Cada región recibe el nombre de cuadrante

quadrilateral [kwŏd′rə-lăt′ər-əl] A polygon with four sides and four angles

cuadrilátero Polígono que tiene cuatro lados y cuatro ángulos

quartile [kwôr′tīl′] Three values, one of which is the median, that divide a data set into fourths

cuartil Cada uno de tres valores, uno de los cuales es la mediana, que dividen en cuartos un conjunto de datos

quotient [kwō′shənt] The result when one number is divided by another

cociente Resultado de dividir un número entre otro

R

radius [rā′dē-əs] A line segment with one endpoint at the center of a circle and the other endpoint on the circle, or the length of that segment

radio Segmento de recta con un extremo en el centro de un círculo y el otro en la circunferencia, o bien la longitud de ese segmento

range [rānj] In statistics, the difference between the greatest and least values in a data set

rango (en estadística) Diferencia entre los valores máximo y mínimo de un conjunto de datos

rate [rāt] A ratio that compares two quantities measured in different units

tasa Una razón que compara dos cantidades medidas en diferentes unidades

ratio [rā′shō] A comparison of two quantities by division

razón Comparación de dos cantidades mediante una división

Interactive Glossary

rational number [răsh′ə-nəl nŭm′bər] A number that can be written in the form $\frac{a}{b}$, where a and b are integers and $b \neq 0$

número racional Número que se puede expresar como $\frac{a}{b}$, donde a y b son números enteros y $b \neq 0$

reciprocal [rĭ-sĭp′rə-kəl] One of two numbers whose product is 1

recíproco Uno de dos números cuyo producto es igual a 1

rectangle [rĕk′tăng′gəl] A parallelogram with four right angles

rectángulo Paralelogramo con cuatro ángulos rectos

reflection [rĭ-flĕk′shən] A transformation of a figure that flips the figure across a line

reflexión Transformación que ocurre cuando se invierte una figura sobre una línea

remainder [ri·măn′dər] The amount left over when a number cannot be divided equally

residuo La cantidad restante cuando un número no se puede divider en partes iquales

rhombus [rŏm′bəs] A parallelogram with all sides congruent

rombo Paralelogramo en el que todos los lados son congruentes

right angle [rīt ăng′gəl] An angle that measures 90°

ángulo recto Ángulo que mide exactamente 90°

right triangle [rīt trī′ăng′gəl] A triangle containing a right angle

triángulo rectángulo Triángulo que tiene un ángulo recto

S

set [sĕt] A group of items

conjunto Un grupo de elementos

simplest form (of a fraction) [sĭm′pəl ĭst fôrm] When the numerator and denominator of a fraction have no common factors other than 1

mínima expresión (de una fracción) Una fracción está en su mínima expresión cuando el numerador y el denominador no tienen más factor común que 1

simplify [sĭm′plə-fī] To write a fraction or expression in simplest form

simplificar Escribir una fracción o expresión numérica en su mínima expresión

solid figure [sŏl′ĭd fĭg′yər] A three-dimensional figure

cuerpo geométrico Figura tridimensional

solution of an equation [sə-lōō′shən ŭv ən ĭ-kwā′zhən] A value or values that make an equation true

solución de una ecuación Valor o valores que hacen verdadera una ecuación

solution of an inequality [sə-lōō′shən ŭv ən ĭn′ĭ-kwŏl′ĭ-tē] A value or values that make an inequality true

solución de una desigualdad Valor o valores que hacen verdadera una desigualdad

statistical question [stə-tĭs′tĭ-kəl kwĕs′chən] A question that has many different, or variable, answers

pregunta estadística Pregunta con muchas respuestas o variables diferentes

Subtraction Property of Equality [səb-trăk′shən prŏp′ər-tē ŭv ĭ-kwŏl′ĭ-tē] States that you can subtract the same number from both sides of an equation, and the expressions remain equal

propiedad de igualdad de la resta Propiedad que establece que se puede restar el mismo número a ambos lados de una ecuación y la expresión permanece igual

My Vocabulary Summary

surface area [sûr′fəs âr′e-ə] The sum of the areas of the faces, or surfaces, of a three-dimensional figure

área total Suma de las áreas de las caras, o superficies, de una figura tridimensional

T

term (in an expression) [tûrm] The parts of an expression that are added or subtracted

término (en una expresión) Las partes de una expresión que se suman o se restan

transformation [trăns′fər-mā′shən] A change in the size or position of a figure

transformación Cambio en el tamaño o la posición de una figura

trapezoid [trăp′ĭ-zoid′] A quadrilateral with at least one pair of parallel sides

trapecio Cuadrilátero con al menos un par de lados paralelos

triangle [trī′ăng′gəl] A three-sided polygon

triángulo Polígono de tres lados

My Vocabulary Summary

U

unit rate [yo͞o′nĭt rāt] A rate in which the second quantity in the comparison is one unit

tasa unitaria Una tasa en la que la segunda cantidad de la comparación es una unidad

unlike fractions [ŭn-līk′ frăk′shəns] Fractions with different denominators

fracciones distintas Fracciones con distinto denominador

upper quartile [ŭp′ər kwôr′tĭl′] The median of the upper half of the data

cuartil superior Mediana de la mitad superior de los datos

V

variable [vâr′ē-ə-bəl] A letter or symbol used to represent a quantity that can change

variable Símbolo que representa una cantidad que puede cambiar

variation (variability) [vâr′ē-ā′shən] The spread of values in a set of data

variación (variabilidad) Amplitud de los valores de un conjunto de datos

My Vocabulary Summary

vertex (vertices) [vûr′tĕks′] On an angle or polygon, the point where two sides intersect

vértice (vértices) En un ángulo o polígono, el punto de intersección de dos lados

volume [vŏl′yōōm] The number of cubic units needed to fill a given space

volumen Número de unidades cúbicas que se necesitan para llenar un espacio

X

x-axis [ĕks ăk′sĭs] The horizontal axis on a coordinate plane

eje x El eje horizontal del plano cartesiano

x-coordinate [ĕks kō-ôr′dn-ĭt] The first number in an ordered pair; it represents the distance to move right or left from the origin, (0, 0)

coordenada x El primer número en un par ordenado; indica la distancia que debes avanzar hacia la izquierda o hacia la derecha desde el origen, (0, 0)

Interactive Glossary

Y

y-axis [wī ăk′sĭs] The vertical axis on a coordinate plane

eje y El eje vertical del plano cartesiano

y-coordinate [wī kō-ôr′dn-ĭt] The second number in an ordered pair; it represents the distance to move up or down from the origin, (0, 0)

coordenada y El segundo número en un par ordenado; indica la distancia que debes avanzar hacia arriba o hacia abajo desde el origen, (0, 0)

© Houghton Mifflin Harcourt Publishing Company

Index

with tangrams, 410
with tape diagram, 140, 141, 168, 171
with tree diagram, 233, 324
with verbal models, 327, 328

Review and Test
Are You Ready?, appears in every module. 4, 30, 60, 102, 138, 178, 204, 232, 272, 312, 340, 376, 412, 438, 464, 486
Module Review, appears in every module 27–28, 57–58, 99–100, 133–134, 175–176, 201–202, 227–228, 269–270, 309–310, 335–336, 373–374, 409–410, 433–434, 461–462, 483–484, 525–526

rhombus, 354, 381
vertices of, 354
rounding, 113
in finding estimate, 110, 112, 115, 127
RunWalk, 337

S

scale models, 169
signs. *See also* symbols
equal (=), 4, 12, 20, 30, 102
negative (−), 6
positive (+), 6
solid figures, 414, 418, 419
solution
of the inequality, 302, 309
square pyramids, 415, 418
base in, 415
faces in, 415
surface area of, 415
squares
area of, 382
classifying figures as, 340
perimeter of, 126, 296
sides in, 382
star
magnitude of a, 31
statistical data
exploring, 439–444
statistical questions, 440, 441, 442, 443, 444, 445, 461, 462, 500, 517, 518, 520, 521, 522, 526
STEM Task, 1, 19, 35, 41, 55, 73, 106, 107, 113, 119, 125, 131, 135, 149, 162, 165, 219, 223, 229, 236, 245, 257, 293, 304, 307, 319, 324, 333, 337, 347, 391, 397, 431, 435, 451, 481, 499, 507
subtraction
difference in, 25, 39, 41, 42, 51, 53, 54, 56, 60, 104, 105, 106, 107, 132, 133
with mean absolute deviation, 504
of multi-digit decimals, 103–108

in order of operations, 241
using equations in problem solving, 279–286
Subtraction Property of Equality, 282, 296
sum, 26, 44, 46, 49, 60, 103, 105, 106, 107, 109, 133. *See also* addition
surface area, 415, 433
exploring, 413–420
using nets in finding, 413–420
volume and, 411–434
symbols
absolute value (||), 22, 23
approximation (≈), 194
equal sign (=), 4, 12, 20, 30, 102
greater than (>), 4, 12, 16, 20, 28, 30, 48, 102, 190, 191, 198, 199, 301
greater than or equal to (≥), 301
less than (<), 4, 12, 16, 20, 28, 30, 48, 102, 190, 191, 198, 199, 301
less than or equal to (≤), 301
negative sign (−), 6
open circle (O), 302
percent (%), 206
positive sign (+), 6

T

Table of Measures, M1–M2
tables, *See also* represent
completing with a number line, 30
frequency, 453–460
patterns in, 43, 234, 312, 327, 328, 330, 334
relationships in, 6, 15, 23
representing equations in, 313–320
representing ratios and rates with, 145–152
writing equations from, 327–334
writing percents as, 207
tangrams, 410
tape diagrams, 140, 141,168, 171
technology and digital resources.
See Ed: Your Friend in Learning for interactive instruction, interactive practice, and videos.
temperature
absolute value of, 35
showing on a number line, 8, 10, 13, 17, 21, 41
terms
in numerical expressions, 240, 269
in ratios, 141
thermometer, 13. *See also* number line
tick marks, 7

transformations, 358
reflection as, 358
trapezoids, 394, 409
bases of, 394, 395, 396, 397, 398, 399, 400
developing and using area formula for, 393–400
height of, 394, 396, 397, 398, 399, 400
tree diagrams, 233, 234
triangles,
acute, 376
base of, 256, 366, 367, 389, 391, 392
developing and using formula for area of, 256, 366, 367, 385–392, 403, 412
height of, 256, 366, 367, 389, 391, 392
isosceles, 353, 388, 391
obtuse, 376
perimeter of, 263, 297, 300
right, 376
area of, 367, 386
hypotenuse in, 351
triangular pyramids, 417

U

unit fractions
division with whole numbers, 60
unit openers, 1–2, 135–136, 229–230, 337–338, 435–436
unit rates, 147, 149, 150, 151, 152, 175
finding and applying, 159–166
units
cubic, 226, 412, 427
square, 366, 367, 368, 370, 372, 374, 390, 406
upper quartile, 494, 495, 496, 497, 498, 499, 500, 519, 525

V

value
absolute, 21–26, 28, 30, 33, 34, 35, 36, 120, 357, 359, 360, 362, 363, 503
place, 102, 103, 109
variability. *See also* data
data distribution and, 485–526
explore measures of, 509–516
mean absolute deviation and, 501–508
measures of (*see* measures of variability)
variables, 248, 269
in algebraic expressions, 248, 253–260, 269, 272
dependent, 314, 315, 317, 321, 322, 335
independent, 314, 315, 317, 321, 322, 335
in inequalities, 301–308

Tables of Measures, Symbols, and Formulas

LENGTH

1 meter (m) = 1,000 millimeters (mm)

1 meter = 100 centimeters (cm)

1 meter ≈ 39.37 inches

1 kilometer (km) = 1,000 meters

1 kilometer ≈ 0.62 mile

1 inch = 2.54 centimeters

1 foot (ft) = 12 inches (in.)

1 yard (yd) = 3 feet

1 mile (mi) = 1,760 yards

1 mile = 5,280 feet

1 mile ≈ 1.609 kilometers

CAPACITY

1 liter (L) = 1,000 milliliters (mL)

1 liter = 1,000 cubic centimeters

1 liter ≈ 0.264 gallon

1 kiloliter (kL) = 1,000 liters

1 cup (c) = 8 fluid ounces (fl oz)

1 pint (pt) = 2 cups

1 quart (qt) = 2 pints

1 gallon (gal) = 4 quarts

1 gallon ≈ 3.785 liters

MASS/WEIGHT

1 gram (g) = 1,000 milligrams (mg)

1 kilogram (kg) = 1,000 grams

1 kilogram ≈ 2.2 pounds

1 pound (lb) = 16 ounces (oz)

1 pound ≈ 0.454 kilogram

1 ton = 2,000 pounds

TIME

1 minute (min) = 60 seconds (s)

1 hour (h) = 60 minutes

1 day = 24 hours

1 week = 7 days

1 year (yr) = about 52 weeks

1 year = 12 months (mo)

1 year = 365 days

1 decade = 10 years

Tables of Measures, Symbols, and Formulas

SYMBOLS

$=$	is equal to	10^2	ten squared
$\neq$	is not equal to	10^3	ten cubed
$\approx$	is approximately equal to	2^4	the fourth power of 2
$>$	is greater than	$\lvert -4 \rvert$	the absolute value of -4
$<$	is less than	$\%$	percent
$\geq$	is greater than or equal to	$(2, 3)$	ordered pair (x, y)
$\leq$	is less than or equal to	$^\circ$	degree

FORMULAS

Perimeter and Circumference

Polygon	$P =$ sum of the lengths of sides
Rectangle	$P = 2\ell + 2w$
Square	$P = 4s$

Area

Rectangle	$A = \ell w$
Parallelogram	$A = bh$
Triangle	$A = \frac{1}{2}bh$
Trapezoid	$A = \frac{1}{2}h(b_1 + b_2)$
Square	$A = s^2$

Volume

Right Prism	$V = \ell wh$ or $V = Bh$
Cube	$V = s^3$